"Given the rapid numerical expansion and dynamic intellectual growth of new Christian universities outside North America, this is an exciting moment for Christ-centered higher education worldwide. . . . The mosaic of international perspectives in this wide-ranging volume demonstrates how much all of us can learn as every part of the higher education body of Christ shares its gifts and opportunities."

— PHILIP G. RYKEN
Wheaton College

"This book shows what we at Handong Global University have long felt: God is at work renewing and inspiriting new institutions not only here in Korea but all over the world. Here we read of similar struggles and inspiring responses to God's call by our colleagues in Christian higher education. Praise to the Lord as he continuously works in each and every campus throughout the world!"

— YOUNG-GIL KIM
Handong Global University

"This is a welcome addition to an interesting but rarely studied segment of higher education globally."

— DANIEL C. LEVY
State University of New York at Albany

Christian Higher Education

A GLOBAL RECONNAISSANCE

Edited by

Joel Carpenter, Perry L. Glanzer, and Nicholas S. Lantinga

WILLIAM B. EERDMANS PUBLISHING COMPANY
GRAND RAPIDS, MICHIGAN / CAMBRIDGE, U.K.

Published 2014 by
Wm. B. Eerdmans Publishing Co.
2140 Oak Industrial Drive N.E., Grand Rapids, Michigan 49505 /
P.O. Box 163, Cambridge CB3 9PU U.K.

Printed in the United States of America

20 19 18 17 16 15 14   7 6 5 4 3 2 1

Library of Congress Cataloging-in-Publication Data

Christian higher education: a global reconnaissance /
edited by Joel Carpenter, Perry L. Glanzer, and Nicholas S. Lantinga.
    pages   cm
  Includes bibliographical references and index.
  ISBN 978-0-8028-7105-3 (pbk.: alk. paper)
    1. Christian universities and colleges. 2. Christian education. 3. Education
  and globalization.   I. Carpenter, Joel A., editor of compilation.

LC383.C495   2014
378'.071 — dc23

                                                    2013045760

www.eerdmans.com

Dedicated to

David Kasali
Young-gil Kim
and
Gerald Pillay

Their vision for great Christian universities
is "as rare a gift as Einstein's."

Sietze Buning, *Style and Class*

Contents

Acknowledgements   ix

Introduction: Christian Universities and the
Global Expansion of Higher Education   1
Joel Carpenter

1. Revolution in Higher Education in Nigeria:
   The Emergence of Private Universities   24
   Musa A. B. Gaiya

2. Development of Christian Higher Education in Kenya:
   An Overview   43
   Faith W. Nguru

3. Rise and Development of Christian Higher Education in China   68
   Peter Tze Ming Ng

4. Korean Christian Higher Education: History, Tasks, and Vision   90
   Kuk-Won Shin

5. Christian Higher Education in India: The Road We Tread   111
   J. Dinakarlal

6. Will the Parent Abandon the Child? The Birth, Secularization, and Survival of Christian Higher Education in Western Europe   134
Perry L. Glanzer

7. Resurrecting Universities with Soul: Christian Higher Education in Post-Communist Europe   163
Perry L. Glanzer

8. Christian Higher Education in Mexico   191
José Ramón Alcántara Mejía

9. Christian Higher Education in Brazil and Its Challenges   207
Alexandre Brasil Fonseca and Cristiane Candido Santos

10. Quest for Identity and Place: Christian University Education in Canada   230
Harry Fernhout

11. A Renaissance of Christian Higher Education in the United States   257
George Marsden

Conclusion: Evaluating the Health of Christian Higher Education around the Globe   277
Perry L. Glanzer and Joel Carpenter

Select Bibliography   306

Contributors   318

Index   321

Acknowledgements

This book represents the final phase of the Global Christian Higher Education Project, an initiative sponsored by the International Association for the Promotion of Christian Higher Education (IAPCHE). This research project, which was conducted in 2007-2009, performed a worldwide search for Christian universities, developed a database to offer a modicum of information on each institution it identified as a Christian university, and conducted a survey with these institutions' senior officers. We editors and our chapter writers referred to this database as we developed our narratives and formed our judgments. This study was underwritten by a major project grant from the Calvin Center for Christian Scholarship, so we owe a major debt of gratitude to its director, Susan Felch, her governing board, and her program coordinator, Dale Williams, for their generosity, encouragement, and, indeed, their patience.

Two of this book's co-editors, Perry Glanzer of Baylor University and Nick Lantinga of IAPCHE, led the research and database-building phase of the project. Anne Maatman, IAPCHE's Director of Operations, helped keep the research project organized and on track. IAPCHE's researchers, Helen Van Beek, Chris Kuiper, and Hani Yang, helped collect and organize the survey data at the IAPCHE offices; while at Baylor, Kellie Lewis, a former Baylor master's student, and Olivia Copeland, a Baylor undergraduate, did similar work. The research and design work at Baylor received generous support from the University Research Committee. Joel Carpenter at Calvin College's Nagel Institute for the Study of World Christianity worked with chapter authors and edited successive drafts. He was ably assisted in all aspects of the book project by Donna Romanowski of the Nagel Institute, a veteran of many such collaborative projects. We also thank David Den Boer, the book's creative and expert indexer.

The editors at Eerdmans, Jon Pott and David Bratt, heard about this project for several years, were unfailingly encouraging as they waited to see whether it would come to fruition, and were very swift in agreeing to publish it once they saw it. Christian higher education worldwide is a new and perhaps a strange realm for many people, but our friends at Eerdmans have excellent instincts, we think, in deciding that it is time to open up the conversation.

This book owes its existence to the chapter authors, an international cadre of remarkably talented and insightful scholars. Without their interest, diligence, and perspective, there would be no book. Their work is quite fresh and new. We editors, however, must acknowledge that we have borrowed a bit from earlier published versions of our thinking. A few sentences and quotes from chapter 7 have appeared in Perry L. Glanzer and Claudiu Cimpean, "The First Baptist University in Europe: An Explanation and Case Study," *Christian Higher Education* 8:5 (2009): 1-11; and Perry L. Glanzer, "The First Ukrainian Christian University: The Rewards and Challenges of Being an Eastern Anomaly," *Christian Higher Education* 11:5 (2012): 320-330. In addition, portions of the introduction and conclusion have been adapted from two articles by their authors: Perry Glanzer, "Dispersing the Light: The Status of Christian Higher Education around the Globe," *Christian Scholars Review* 42:4 (Summer 2013): 321-343; and Joel Carpenter, "New Christian Universities and the Conversion of Cultures," *Evangelical Review of Theology* 36.1 (2012): 14-30.

We dedicate this book to three educational visionaries and pioneers, each the founding leader of a new Christian university: David Kasali of the Bilingual Christian University of the Congo, Young-gil Kim of Handong Global University in South Korea, and Gerald Pillay of Liverpool Hope University in the United Kingdom. May the faith, hope, and love that animate their work continue to enliven the movement they represent.

Christian Universities and the Global Expansion of Higher Education

Joel Carpenter

During the decade that I served as provost of Calvin College, I received quite a few visitors, but none more interesting than the founders of new Christian universities. One of my guests was the Rev. Dr. Musiande Kasali, a Congolese theologian who was the leader of a prominent theological seminary in Nairobi, Kenya. He confided to me: "The Lord is calling me to found a Christian university," and he said that it would most likely be in Beni, in the eastern Congo. I was astonished. Beni was the epicenter of the brutal civil war in the Congo that claimed more than three million lives. The city was overcrowded with refugees from the surrounding countryside, and brigands out in the bush were still causing trouble. Why Beni? Kasali explained: "We must rebuild our nation. We need Christian leaders who will serve God's reign. Surely we have seen enough of Satan's hand in our land." One can hardly imagine a more impossible place to build a university, but Kasali and his countrymen had heard God's call. They founded the Christian Bilingual University of Congo in 2007 and graduated their first class in 2011.

I received another visit from Dr. Young-gil Kim, a dynamic Korean nuclear engineer who was educated at the Massachusetts Institute of Technology (MIT) and who worked on projects for the National Aeronautics and Space Administration. Kim led Handong Global University in South Korea, which had been founded in 1995. He shared with me his dream of Handong becoming an evangelical Christian MIT. Handong has assembled a strong Korean faculty and has recruited Western expatriates as well. It inhabits a gleaming new campus on a hill overlooking South Korea's eastern coast, and it enrolls about 3,500 high-achieving students. In a very short time, Handong has carved out a solid niche for itself within Korean higher education's sharply competitive ranking system. Not content to stop there, Handong has been lending its help to two new universities in North Korea and in northeastern China.[1] At Christian universities in the United States, we often worry about spreading ourselves too thin, so we tend to put some of our more ambitious dreams on hold. Yet I look at my African and Asian colleagues and marvel at their vision, risk-taking, and creative energy.

I realized that we had much to learn from these visionary agents and new developments in international Christian higher education, so I began to research this topic. I found that very little scholarship had addressed international Christian higher education, tried to measure its global scope, or engaged the challenges it faces. Yet these remarkable stories had to be told — and pondered. So I joined with colleagues from the International Association for the Promotion of Christian Higher Education (IAPCHE) in 2009 to launch a worldwide data-gathering and survey research project.[2]

This book builds on that research by featuring on-site, evaluative studies that offer reconnaissance on Christian higher education worldwide. Its eleven chapters assess the situation in Africa, Asia, Europe, North America, and South America. We found that around the world, Christians continue to create and sustain universities. Some are quite old, notably some Latin American Catholic universities, which, according to Alexandre Fonseca of Brazil and José Alcántara of Mexico, have maintained a Christian identity since colonial times. Others are being remade, such as some Eastern European Catholic and Protestant universities that, as Perry Glanzer makes clear, have been revived since the end of communist rule. Many more, in Africa, Asia, and Latin America, are quite new. In our worldwide study, we found 579 Christian universities outside the United States and Canada, a count that has since expanded to 595.[3] This is a story of growth as well as

---

1. Andrew Thompson, "Teaching the Dragon: Mission-minded Christian Educators Run Fast-Growing Universities in North Korea and Northeast China," *Christianity Today* 56:8 (September 2012): 19. As one might anticipate, given their situations, these new universities are not mandated to be Christian.

2. To learn more about IAPCHE and its seventy institutional members and more than nine hundred individual members worldwide, go to its website: http://www.iapche.org. To learn the results of the global research project, see Perry L. Glanzer, Joel A. Carpenter, and Nick Lantinga, "Looking for God in Higher Education: Examining Trends in Global Christian Higher Education," *Higher Education* 61:6 (2011): 721-755.

3. Perry Glanzer, "Dispersing the Light: The Status of Christian Higher Education around the Globe," *Christian Scholars Review* 42:4 (Summer 2013): 321-343.

persistence, since more than 30 percent of these institutions have started up since 1980.

Unfortunately, we have also heard another sort of story, and it represents a more sobering trend. At an academic conference where we had just presented our findings, a professor from a Latin American independent university rose to speak. He said that evangelicals founded his university forty years ago. "We wanted to honor the Lord in higher education," he said, "and we wanted to serve the needs of our people." But today, he went on, most of the professors are part-time, and not Christian. The university offers mostly business and technical topics, and the idea of a Christian worldview or a Christian perspective animating its courses is unknown. "Some of us wish that we could become a Christian university once again," he said. "What can we do?"

Indeed, one of the main themes in the history of higher education has been the secularization of religiously founded universities, and we have found that this process happens not only in Europe and North America, but in Africa, Asia, and Latin America as well. Some of the Christian-founded institutions in the global South and East have secularized very rapidly, in only a generation's time, as I found out firsthand when I spoke at the fiftieth anniversary of a private university in East Asia. So our story is not only about new Christian universities. We also want to look at the issues facing established Christian institutions. What tensions arise as they seek to sustain or regain their religious mission? To cite one common tension, can they serve the needs and goals of their Christian sponsors while also serving the interests of the government? Unique issues and situations arise in the various chapters we offer, but as you will see, there are some common themes as well, and secularization is one of the chief concerns.

Definitions

To many American readers, the idea of a Christian university or liberal arts college is not at all foreign. Church-founded colleges and universities exist in abundance in the United States, and they have earned a lasting place in the American higher education scene. In other places, however, universities have been seen as the unique responsibility of the state, and the higher education sector is assumed to be secular, whether or not the nation's universities had their origins in the educational work of churches. And in the United States, Canada, and around East Asia, many church-founded colleges and universities are now functionally secular. So what do we mean by "Christian university"? For the purposes of our study, we developed the following definitions.

University?

In a global setting, the terms "college" and "university" have a variety of nuances and meanings. "College" often means a sub-unit of a university, a sub-bachelor's degree tertiary training institute, or a secondary-level academy. So in this book we tend toward the more widely accepted generic use of "university" to denote degree-granting institutions. We also define "university" to mean a fairly comprehensive institution, not a specialty institution, such as a theological seminary, a teacher's college, or a free-standing engineering or medical college. Given churches' proclivity to found seminaries or Bible colleges first and the current trend for many of these to evolve into more comprehensive universities, it is especially important to mark a clear line between universities and seminaries. So we defined "university" to include at least two distinct areas of study beyond those related to church vocations.

We did not include colleges within universities that only refer to disciplinary units (e.g., colleges of arts and sciences) or residential colleges within universities that may or may not offer courses but largely provide room, board, and co-curricular activities. However, we did include more comprehensive colleges that operate in affiliation with larger universities and come under such a university's jurisdiction for offering degrees. This is standard practice, for example, in the very large network of Christian colleges in India, as we see in J. Dinakarlal's chapter.

Christian?

Deciding what constitutes a "Christian" university is, if anything, even more tricky and controversial than defining what "university" means. Institutions that were founded by churches but now appear to be secular often still recognize their heritage or may even still have some formal ties to their founding churches. Others wish to downplay these ties, even if Christianity still has special status on campus. Scholars in North America have tended to finesse the question by simply talking about "church-related" colleges and universities.[4] This approach avoids the issue of what it means for an institution to be substantially or functionally Christian. But for our purposes, it is important to make some judgments about the degree to which a particular church or

4. See, e.g., Merrimon Cunninggim, *Uneasy Partners: The College and the Church* (Nashville: Abingdon Press, 1994).

Christian beliefs and practices actually influence a college or university. This study addresses the issue of secularization throughout, so it is important for us to say that there are some features of a university's stated mission, policies, and practice that are definitive to its being classified as Christian. And "church-related" increasingly loses its relevance or comprehensiveness as a category because so much religiously inspired activity worldwide is no longer conducted by denominational agencies. Individuals or parachurch agencies frequently start Christian universities these days, such as Oral Roberts University in the United States or Baekseok University in South Korea.

So we decided to define as "Christian" those universities or colleges that currently acknowledge and embrace a Christian identity and purpose in their mission statements and shape aspects of their governance, curriculum, staffing, student body, and campus life in the light of their Christian identity. In general, we followed the thinking of the American theologian Robert Benne that Christian universities give a central, privileged place to Christian beliefs and practices. We realize that there are a variety of ways that Christian universities express and maintain this centrality, and we have exerted care to acknowledge and include them.[5]

This book is in many respects a pioneering study, but even fresh topics and ideas exist within contexts. One of these broader environments is the substantial and growing scholarly literature on Christian higher education — past, present, and future — in the United States,[6] where there are more than

---

5. Robert Benne, *Quality with Soul: How Six Premier Colleges and Universities Keep Faith with Their Religious Tradition* (Grand Rapids: Eerdmans, 2001), pp. 48-65, lays out a useful typology of the ways that American Christian universities express and maintain their religious character.

6. For some places to start on this literature, see James T. Burtchaell, *The Dying of the Light: The Disengagement of the Colleges and Universities from Their Christian Churches* (Grand Rapids: Eerdmans, 1998); Paul J. Dovre, ed., *The Future of Religious Colleges* (Grand Rapids: Eerdmans, 2002); Philip Gleason, *Contending with Modernity: Catholic Higher Education in the Twentieth Century* (New York: Oxford University Press, 1995); Richard T. Hughes and William B. Adrian, eds., *Models for Christian Higher Education: Strategies for Success in the Twenty-first Century* (Grand Rapids: Eerdmans, 1997); George M. Marsden, *The Soul of the American University: From Protestant Establishment to Established Nonbelief* (New York: Oxford University Press, 1994); Melanie Morey and John Piderit, *Catholic Higher Education: A Culture in Crisis* (New York: Oxford University Press, 2010); Mark Noll and James Turner, *The Future of Christian Learning: An Evangelical and Catholic Dialogue* (Grand Rapids: Brazos Press, 2008); William Ringenberg, *The Christian College: A History of Protestant Higher Education in America*, 2nd ed. (Grand Rapids: Baker Academic, 2006); and Samuel Schuman, *Seeing the Light: Religious Colleges in Twenty-first-Century America* (Baltimore: Johns Hopkins University Press, 2009).

six hundred Christian colleges and universities. There is very little, however, by way of studies on Christian higher education elsewhere in the world. That is not because of any lack of attention to the international scene. A tremendous amount of recent literature explores the international dimension of higher education, in both journals devoted to international and comparative themes in higher education and the more general publications of higher education studies. One scholar in particular, Philip Altbach of the Center for International Higher Education at Boston College, has built a substantial industry of investigation in this field in which he has networked higher education scholars worldwide.[7] And within the discussion of international higher education, one particular subfield has expanded with great vigor in recent years, matching the dynamism of its subject: private higher education.[8] In the many studies of this topic, Christian universities sometimes appear, for example, amidst studies of East African higher education, where they dominate the nongovernmental university scene.[9] But they are scarcely given more than incidental treatment. They do not neatly fit the commonly accepted profile or provenance of the new "private" universities.[10]

7. Philip G. Altbach, Liz Reisberg, and Laura Rumbley, eds., *Trends in Global Higher Education: Tracking an Academic Revolution* (Paris: UNESCO, 2009). See many more works by Altbach, an online bulletin titled *International Higher Education,* and other publications by Altbach's network of scholarly partners at the Center for International Higher Education's website: http://www.bc.edu/bc_org/avp/soe/cihe.html.

8. Philip G. Altbach and Daniel C. Levy, eds., *Private Higher Education: A Global Revolution* (Rotterdam: Sense Publishers, 2005); Daniel C. Levy, "The Unanticipated Explosion: Private Higher Education's Global Surge," *Comparative Education Review* 50:2 (2006): 217-240; and Daniel C. Levy, "An Introductory Global Overview: The Private Fit to Salient Higher Education Tendencies," Program for Research in Private Higher Education (PROPHE), PROPHE Working Paper no. 7, Albany, State University of New York, 2006. PROPHE is a prime spot for finding current and paradigmatic research on private higher education: http://www.albany.edu/dept/eaps/prophe/.

9. See, e.g., Okwach Abagi, Juliana Nzomo, and Wycliffe Otieno, *Private Higher Education in Kenya: New Trends in Higher Education* (Paris: International Institute for Educational Planning, 2005), p. 31; Wycliffe Otieno, "Private Provision and Its Changing Interface with Public Higher Education: The Case of Kenya," *Journal of Higher Education in Africa* 5:2-3 (2007): 173-196; Jane Osongo, "The Growth of Private Universities in Kenya: Implications for Gender Equity in Higher Education," *Journal of Higher Education in Africa* 5:2-3 (2007): 111-133; and Grace Karram, "The International Connections of Religious Higher Education in Sub-Saharan Africa: Rationales and Implications," *Journal of Studies in International Education* 15:5 (2011): 487-499.

10. Svava Bjarnason, Kai-Ming Cheng, John Fielden, Maria-Jose Lemaitre, Daniel Levy, and N. V. Varghese, *A New Dynamic: Private Higher Education* (Paris: UNESCO, 2009), pp. 16-17, offers a helpful typology of "private" educational institutions that includes religiously founded universities, but it claims, curiously, that the religious type is declining.

So in spite of the recent flurry of scholarship on international higher education and the rise of independent universities around the world, very little research has examined the scope and direction of Christian higher education. IAPCHE has collected and published the best papers from its conferences in order to provide some insights,[11] and a British educator, James Arthur, has a recent book that is more comprehensive. Arthur provides a helpful beginning, a general overview of religious colleges and universities around the globe.[12] He confirms that secularization of universities has occurred around the world, although it has developed unevenly and for different reasons. He also demonstrates that religious universities around the world struggle with some of the same problems, such as faithfulness to their religious mission, questions about how religious authorities and beliefs should relate to university governance, how to relate a religious tradition to new and current knowledge, and how to deal with matters of academic freedom. While Arthur's broad overview and comparison of these themes prove helpful, he does not provide extensive empirical insight into the current state of religious higher education. Overall, people who are interested in Christian higher education worldwide have until now lacked a clear idea of the numerical strength as well as basic data, such as enrollment, sources of funding, origins, programs of study, and institutional vision and direction.

So our research project was designed to provide more specific knowledge of this remarkable network of Christian universities.

Before you turn to the chapters of this book, which survey and analyze the situation in a number of countries, there are some things you need to know more generally about Christian higher education worldwide. We need to place it within three contexts:

1. the growth of higher education worldwide and what is driving it
2. the growth and emerging character of non-governmental, "private" higher education worldwide
3. the growth and maturation of Christian movements worldwide that are sponsoring Christian higher education

---

11. See, e.g., Nick Lantinga, ed., *Christian Higher Education in the Global Context: Implications for Curriculum, Pedagogy and Administration* (Sioux Center, Iowa: Dordt College Press, 2008); J. Dinakarlal, ed., *Christian Higher Education and Globalization in Asia/Oceania: Realities and Challenges* (Sioux Center, Iowa: Dordt College Press, 2010); and Bram de Muynck, Johan Hegeman, and Pieter Vos, eds., *Bridging the Gap: Connecting Christian Faith and Professional Practice in a Pluralistic Society* (Sioux City, Iowa: Dordt College Press, 2011).

12. James Arthur, *Faith and Secularisation in Religious Colleges and Universities* (New York: Routledge, 2006).

We will focus for the moment on the current scene, and the rise of new universities, although as the following chapters will clearly show, the persistence and renewal of older Christian universities is very much part of the story. So what of the current scene?

The Worldwide Growth of Higher Education

In North America, the byword in higher education is "crisis." We hear of the "crisis of ever-rising costs," the "crisis of educational purpose," the "crisis of the professoriate," or the "crisis of the for-profit, corporate invasion" of higher education. I do not want to belittle these concerns, which play into the very center of our story today, but outside North America and Western Europe, higher education is expanding at an astonishing rate, and the main crisis in higher education worldwide is how to meet the huge and growing demand for a university education with anything resembling university-quality teaching and learning. A second crisis follows closely on the first, and that is how to answer the "for what?" question: what are the proper aims and purposes of higher education? The forces driving the first global crisis in higher education and the second one are remarkably similar.

Massification: Expanding to Meet Huge Demand

Today we are witnessing a historic shift in higher education's social role. Here is how the authors of a sociological study put it:

> In 1900, roughly 500,000 students were enrolled in higher education institutions worldwide, representing a tiny fraction of 1 percent of college age people. . . . By 2000, the number of tertiary students had grown two-hundredfold to approximately 100 million people, which represents about 20 percent of the [university enrollment age] cohort worldwide.[13]

Those totals and percentages mask some huge disparities, however. In India, for example, there has been a very rapid growth in higher education, but India currently enrolls only about 13 percent of its relevant age group in higher education. The average across Africa is only about 2 percent. In South Korea,

---

13. Evan Schofer and John W. Meyer, "The Worldwide Expansion of Higher Education in the Twentieth Century," *American Sociological Review* 70:6 (December 2005): 898.

by contrast, more than 8 percent of traditional college-age young people are enrolled. In the United States, the number is about 34 percent. Whatever the relative reach of higher education in each country, the historic growth curves are remarkably similar in all parts of the world, rich and poor. Even in sub-Saharan Africa, the most educationally disenfranchised region of the world, the growth curve for higher education continues to bend upward, decade by decade.

It is not difficult to imagine why we are seeing this growth. Tertiary education is becoming a necessary basis for ordinary work in many realms today. The expansion of higher education thus reflects a radical change in the way the world is structured. We are seeing that a "world dominated by more traditional elites," such as "landowners, business owners, and [the heads of] political and military machines," is being replaced by one dominated by a new set of elites, and their status and authority come to a large extent from university-delivered knowledge. This historic change is occurring not only in rich and powerful countries like the United States, but also in poorer countries as well.[14] In this new form of society, both the learned professions and more ordinary office work require increasingly specialized knowledge. These opportunities are expanding rapidly, and because they address these basic social and economic needs, universities are becoming central social, cultural, and economic institutions, not just the enclaves of the elite.

Unstoppable Demand and Unbearable Systemic Strain

As societies and economies worldwide are changing in knowledge-driven ways, demand for access to higher education continues to grow. In much of the world, the traditional assumption regarding higher education was that it served broad public purposes. Therefore the government was obliged to provide it. It has become clear, however, that in most of the world governments cannot expand higher education fast enough to meet this demand.[15] National university systems across Africa, Asia, and Latin America have been strained and damaged as campuses are being forced to accommodate more and more students. Meanwhile the professoriate is experiencing parallel strains. In many

14. Schofer and Meyer, "Worldwide Expansion," p. 917.
15. Philip G. Altbach and Jane Knight, "The Internationalization of Higher Education: Motivations and Realities," *Journal of Studies in Higher Education* 11:3-4 (Fall-Winter 2007): 290-305.

countries, the percentage of teaching staff holding the relevant terminal post-graduate degrees has declined.[16] Even in rich countries with mature higher education systems, the percentage of government support for higher education is contracting even while enrollments continue to expand.

A Change in Values: Privatization

At the same time that higher education is under huge pressure to accommodate more students, it is experiencing a sea change in approaches and, ultimately, in values. Since ancient times, higher education has been like a craft, plied by highly skilled intellectual artisans and imparted from one generation to another in highly personal ways. It is a process of formation, not just the processing of information. It involves acquiring perspective and discernment and sound habits of mind and intellectual work. But now this traditional pattern of teaching and learning is under assault for being too inefficient.

Also since the early years of the university, there have been two basic sets of aims and values driving the enterprise. On the one hand have been the "liberal" or liberating values driving studies in the arts and sciences. They exist for the sake of making fresh discoveries and creations, for discerning what is true and worthy and what is not, and for inheriting and conserving humanity's store of wisdom and cultural achievement. On the other hand there are the more concretely "practical" values driving studies in the professions and technological fields: for attaining the knowledge and skill needed to start off as a competent practitioner, and for engaging in trustworthy practices that will make one's community flourish and prosper. Both of these sets of values were put into a larger frame, called the "public good." Universities equipped graduates to serve the community. In the West, these two basic aims are secular adaptations of the original vision of higher education in medieval Europe. The universities arising there were mandated to serve the glory of God and to help make a good and just society according to Christian norms. In East Asia, close parallels exist in Confucian thought about advanced learning.

In recent decades, however, we have seen these governing values become reduced and constricted. Contemporary policymakers around the world are constructing ever narrower understandings of the purpose and value of higher

16. Philip G. Altbach, "Center and Peripheries in the Academic Profession: The Special Challenges of Developing Countries," in *The Decline of the Guru: The Academic Profession in the Third World,* ed. Philip G. Altbach (New York: Palgrave Macmillan, 2003), pp. 1-22.

education. Studying the liberal arts and engaging in basic, new discovery research are fine, under this reasoning, if these endeavors can be related directly to efforts that boost the economy.[17] And what one needs to know to be competent in practice as a professional or a technician is being pushed more and more into a skills-based orientation, and away from broader perspectives and understanding. The belief that professionals and technicians might need critical thinking, or a broader sense of life's contexts and dimensions beyond the job, or wise judgment in order to do what is right and do no harm, is being downplayed while claims grow that the technical aspects of the job itself demand all of the educational time. Educational time and expense are increasingly under pressure from the cost-cutting metrics of the corporate world. There is something like an "industrial revolution" occurring, by which higher education is being thought of as a product, something capable of being rationalized and streamlined in production and traded like other commodities.[18]

The logic of this process also points to higher education as something that individuals acquire to enhance their own benefit. And if higher education is as much a private benefit as a public good, why should its support come so heavily from public coffers? In times when even wealthy Western nations have been facing increasing pressures to control public spending, this economistic approach has gained a great deal of support. In middle-income and lower-income nations, the natural desire to "build the nation" also has led to a narrowing of vision and value for higher education. All over Asia, observes Altbach, the humanities and social sciences are experiencing rapid declines. The traditional "public good" roles that these fields provided — including "cultural analysis and critique, the interrogation of science and culture, and the preservation of knowledge — have been largely pushed aside."[19] They are

17. I see this narrowing process in my home state of Michigan, where a blue-ribbon panel was commissioned to study the state's higher education system and make policy recommendations according to three mandates:

a. Double the percentage of residents who attain postsecondary degrees or other credentials that link them to success in Michigan's new economy.

b. Improve the alignment of Michigan's institutions of higher education with emerging employment opportunities in the state's economy.

c. Build a dynamic workforce of employees who have the talents and skills needed for success in the twenty-first century.

Final Report of The Lt. Governor's Commission on Higher Education & Economic Growth, Lansing, Michigan, December 2004, p. 2.

18. David Noble, "Technology and the Commodification of Higher Education," *Monthly Review* 53:10 (March 2002): 26-40.

19. Philip G. Altbach, "Globalization and Forces for Change in Higher Education," *Inter-*

pushed aside because at a time when the massive demand for higher education is pressuring higher education systems to provide the programs that students want, what they most want are courses that will directly lead to lucrative employment. All of the budgetary pressures run against keeping the humanities and social sciences programs that are less directly instrumental as training for particular jobs and have become less in demand.

So we see the values of higher education shifting from public good to private gain, from formation to information, from perspective and judgment to skills and techniques, all in a context of a seemingly insatiable demand for more access to higher education, and decreasing inability of governments, in rich nations as well as poor ones, to pay for it.

The Big Surprise: The Global Growth of "Private" Higher Education[20]

In response to these pressures and demands, we are also seeing all around the world, or at least outside Western Europe, the rapid growth of independently developed higher education. While in the United States there is a long tradition of independently founded colleges and universities, in many parts of the world, nongovernmental universities have been unheard of until recently.

New Nongovernmental Players

In China, for example, as the chapter by Peter Ng makes clear, there was no nongovernmental higher education at all from 1950 to the 1980s, but now about 14 percent of total enrollments are in the private sector. In Latin America, the regional average for private higher education is about 47 percent of total enroll-

---

national Higher Education, no. 50 (Winter 2008). *International Higher Education* is published online at http://www.bc.edu/bc_org/avp/soe/cihe/.

20. We are not satisfied that "private" is the proper category for nongovernmental higher education. We acknowledge, of course, that higher education is undergoing a privatization of its aims and purposes, and that nongovernmentally instituted colleges and universities are on the rise, but using "private" as a rubric for all independently governed colleges and universities seems to be saying that this field is wholly given over to the essentially self-regarding and narrowly instrumental aims and purposes that are at the heart of privatization. Therefore we prefer, unless we are speaking of proprietary or for-profit institutions, to use the terms "independent" and "nongovernmental" instead of "private." Yet we do not impose this preference on our chapter authors.

ment. Africa had a tiny percentage of nongovernmental higher education before 1990, mostly in schools for Christian ministry. But today, in a number of African nations, including Kenya, as our chapter by Faith Nguru shows, the enrollment percentage is about 20 percent. Across the world, an estimated 30 percent of all college and university students are enrolled in privately governed institutions.[21] In Ghana, for example, there were just two private universities in 1999, but only a decade later there were eleven, plus another nineteen private polytechnic institutes. Their students total 28 percent of national tertiary enrollments.[22]

Commercial Orientation, Including For-profit Universities

Nongovernmental colleges and universities are not news in the United States; today they make up nearly 60 percent of the institutions and 23 percent of the enrollments. Many of the nation's finest institutions, such as Princeton and Stanford, Harvard and Yale, are nongovernmental, independent institutions. The United States is the home to many Christian universities as well, the most well-known of which are the Catholic ones, such as Notre Dame, Loyola-Chicago, and the Catholic University of America. Protestant institutions tend to be smaller, but others are comparable such as Baylor University and Pepperdine University. The big news in the United States' independent educational sector, however, is the rise of for-profit universities, which now represent about 7 percent of all U.S. university enrollments, and nearly one-third of all private university enrollments. Many of these for-profit universities started as non-degree technical and business colleges, but now they are accredited bachelor's and master's degree–granting institutions. The largest of these is the University of Phoenix, which in 2010 enrolled 455,000 students online and in branch campuses nationwide, up from 25,100 15 years earlier.[23] This for-profit model is emerging all over the globe. Laureate Education, Inc., a publicly traded American corporation, now operates 69 institutions around the world, enrolling 740,000 students.[24]

21. Bjarnason et al., *A New Dynamic*, pp. 8-13.

22. Kajsa Hallberg Adu, "Ghana: Private Higher Education on the Rise," *University World News*, June 28, 2009. This publication is found online at http://www.universityworldnews.com.

23. Robin Wilson, "For-Profit Colleges Change Higher Education's Landscape," *Chronicle of Higher Education*, February 12, 2010, pp. A-1, A-16.

24. Information found on the Laureate website, http://www.laureate.net. See also Ann I. Morey, "Globalization and the Emergence of For-Profit Higher Education," *Higher Education* 48:1 (July 2004): 131-150.

Common Traits, according to PROPHE

Over the past decade, a study center at the State University of New York at Albany has been analyzing this remarkable worldwide trend. Its name is the Program of Research on Private Higher Education (PROPHE).[25] PROPHE engages an international network of dozens of scholars, and they have found eight prominent characteristics in the new private universities.[26]

1. Working the margins

The new surge in private higher education rarely comes as part of a nationwide effort to plan and develop higher education. It tends to arise more spontaneously to address needs and demands not met by governmental and traditional independent higher education. It has come as a surprise wherever it has arisen. Increasingly, after the fact, governments are hustling to impose quality standards and accountability mechanisms for private higher education.

2. Addressing access needs

The most commonly performed educational role of private higher education is to provide access to higher education that the state is unable to meet. The new private institutions are rarely students' first choices; they often are the fall-back options when students do not get into state institutions. The first private institutions to appear in China since 1980 were ones that enrolled students who did not have high enough scores on their qualification exams to enter the universities.

3. Offering little research or postgraduate study

Higher education is an integrated system that needs a supply of qualified scholars to discover new knowledge and to convert it into solid educational materials and teaching. The new private institutions worldwide tend to rely on scholars from other institutions to develop ideas; they hire some curriculum writers to provide classroom materials. The teaching is done largely by adjunct or part-time instructors. If the new private universities offer post-

---

25. Daniel C. Levy, "Analyzing a Private Revolution: The Work of PROPHE," *International Higher Education* (Spring 2005).

26. Levy, "An Introductory Global Overview."

baccalaureate programs, they tend to be for professional job fields, not for basic research. So these institutions feed off the larger system of creating knowledge, but do not feed back into it.

4. *Cutting costs and focusing on jobs*

The new private higher education tends to feature courses that are most in demand for immediate transfer into jobs. These schools offer various business majors, the information technology services end of computer science, and other commercial fields, such as hotel and tourism management. These programs are cheap to offer and they do not demand elaborate facilities like the sciences or engineering. Likewise, they do not feature arts and humanities courses, which need good studios and libraries, but offer fewer direct career tracks.

5. *Going light on cultural and social service*

The new private higher education tends not to feature programs such as social work, nursing, or teacher education, which requires internship sites and provides community service.[27] Likewise, the new privates tend not to make culture and share it with the community, via art galleries, orchestras, or drama programs.

6. *Part-timing professors*

Newer private institutions tend not to retain full-time professors. Part-timers are more likely. In Latin America, where they are called taxi-cab professors, quite a few are state university faculty members who are picking up extra work. In the United States, the new for-profits disaggregate professors' tasks and feature instructors who use pre-developed materials and have no responsibilities outside the classroom.

7. *Taking orders from the boss*

Whether they are legally not-for-profit entities, proprietary businesses, or multisite corporations, the governance structure in the new privates tends

27. A number of them, however, including the University of Phoenix in the United States, offer master's degrees or degree completion work in these fields. In this way they benefit from the undergraduate work their students completed in the laboratories, clinical studies, and externships that their prior education provided.

to be more authoritarian than is usually the case in state institutions or older church-founded institutions. The more localized institutions among the new privates are often run like a family business. Faculty co-governance and student input are much less likely.

8. Narrowing the mission

In sum, the new private universities tend to depart from the traditional higher educational aims, such as learning a cultural legacy, engaging in moral character formation, learning critical analysis and inquiry, or developing an ethic of service. The aims reduce down to this: equip the student with the knowledge and skills required to be certified into a particular line of work. Doing anything more, claim its advocates, costs too much and is irrelevant to the main mission.

New Christian Universities

A Worldwide Movement

Within the scholarly literature on private higher education, there is very little being said about a trend within the trend — the rise of new Christian universities.[28] Recently, this book's editors led a research project, Global Christian Higher Education, which has done a nation-by-nation global sweep to find Christian universities and a follow-up survey of the institutions we found. We now know that there is a movement afoot on several continents to found new universities, both Protestant and Catholic, and that it has resulted in the founding of 178 new universities outside North America since 1980, and 138 of these were founded since 1990. Here are some highlights of the research:

- Africa has been a hot spot, with forty-six new Christian universities founded between 1990 and 2010.
- In Europe, the main action has been in the formerly communist nations, where seventeen of the nineteen Christian universities formed in the

28. Bjarnason et al., *A New Dynamic,* pp. 16-17, do name a "religious/cultural" type of private higher education, alongside "elite/semi-elite" and "non-elite and demand-absorbing" types. But they insist that the elite/semi-elite type is relatively rare, the religious type is declining or secularizing, and the non-elite type predominates. The eight tendencies listed above in the text are predominantly those of the non-elite, demand-absorbing private institutions.

past twenty years have been planted. There are only two recently founded Christian universities in Western Europe: one is Liverpool Hope University, a Catholic and Anglican joint venture in England; and the other is the University of Ramon Llull, a Catholic institution in Spain.

- In Asia, we see a variety of trends, led by Indian Christian churches, which founded eighteen new Christian colleges during the 1980s and thirteen more since 1990.
- In South Korea, there are dozens of Christian universities, including some new ones now with several thousand students enrolled.
- Minority Christian movements in Indonesia, Taiwan, and Thailand also have new Christian universities.
- All told, we found twenty-five new Christian universities founded since 1990 in Asia and Australia.
- In Latin America, thirty-two new Christian universities have arisen since 1990, and fifteen of them are Protestant.

In sum, Christian higher education is a dynamic worldwide movement, enlisting Christian scholars and communities of support to do something fresh in higher education. Christian educators are building communities of learning that come out from under a pervasively secular academic shadow. It is an exciting time of fresh beginnings, under a worldwide variety of situations, each with unique opportunities and constraints.[29]

The most dramatic site for Christian university startups today is sub-Saharan Africa. The chapter by Musa Gaiya portrays a very dynamic situation in Nigeria, where government-chartered independent universities now number forty-one, twenty-one of them Christian.[30] Some have become substantially sized institutions in a very short period of time. Bowen University, which grew out of a small Baptist teacher training college in Iwo, southern Nigeria, officially opened its doors in 2002 with fewer than 500 students; today it enrolls 10,000.[31] Not all institutions have seen such dramatic growth, but of the twenty-seven African Christian universities for which we have recent student enrollment numbers, eighteen currently educate more than 1,000 students.[32]

29. Glanzer et al., "Looking for God in Higher Education."

30. Elizabeth Archibong, "Nigeria Gets Seven Additional Universities," *NEXT,* October 22, 2009, found at http://234next.com/csp/cms/sites/Next/Home/5472553-146/story.csp#.

31. For more information, see the Bowen University website: http://www.bowenuniversity-edu.org/home.php.

32. Glanzer et al., "Looking for God in Higher Education," p. 730.

The Christian Educational Impulse: After the Awakenings, Now What?

So what is prompting the rise of these new Christian universities? On every continent the story is somewhat different, but in very general terms, Christian university building is in part a response to the same trend that is prompting the rise of private universities of all sorts: the relentless growth of demand for higher education in the face of public constraints in higher education spending. In African contexts, we learn from this book's chapters on Nigeria and Kenya, the higher education crisis has been made even more critical by its extremity. Government education budgets were wracked first by falling commodities prices in the 1980s, then by International Monetary Fund (IMF) and World Bank directives to reallocate government spending in the 1990s, by ongoing serious leakages in revenues because of widespread corruption, and, in many nations, by civil disruptions and even civil wars. African public universities have been crowded far beyond their capacities while they starved for budget resources. They have frequently been focal points of civic unrest, with entire academic years lost to faculty or student strikes. And in eastern and southern Africa especially, universities were hotspots in the HIV/AIDS pandemic. So it is no wonder that educationally minded people, whether in religious communities or other networks, have taken the initiative.[33]

Christian universities thus are riding the wave of a largely secular privatization in higher education. They are able to receive university chartering at a time when governments worldwide accede to the demands for access to higher education by opening their chartering process to nongovernmental universities. But one has to ask why the Christians in particular are doing this: Might there be some dynamics internal to the Christian movements rising so dramatically in Africa, Asia, and Latin America that are prompting the startup of new universities?

More than one historian of modern Christianity has seen echoes in world Christianity to something that happened in the mid-nineteenth century, in the

33. On the multiple crises of African higher education, much has been written, but see Demtew Teferra and Philip G. Altbach, "African Higher Education: Challenges for the 21st Century," *Higher Education* 47:1 (January 2004): 21-50. On privatization as a response to the crisis of public higher education in Africa, see Wycliffe Otieno and Daniel Levy, "Public Disorder, Private Boons? Inter-sectoral Dynamics Illustrated by the Kenyan Case," Program for Research in Higher Education (PROPHE), PROPHE Working Paper no. 9, Albany, State University of New York, July 2007; and Mahlubi Mabizela, "Private Surge amid Public Dominance in Higher Education: The African Perspective," *Journal of Higher Education in Africa* 5:2-3 (2007): 15-38.

underdeveloped region that was then the American West.[34] This was a time of major cultural building and organization, when the young nation was moving, said the American historian John Higham, from a state of boundlessness to consolidation.[35] It was a time also when, in the wake of the Second Great Awakening, American evangelicals, led by the Methodists, were entering into a very dynamic phase of institution building. Out of this era of rapid western settlement and church growth came a wave of new institutions — missionary agencies, Bible and tract publishing firms, social reform movements and institutions, and academies and colleges. And this flurry of evangelical institutional organizing helped transform a frontier into a new society: the American Midwest.[36] According to the historian Timothy L. Smith, the new Christian colleges, whose mission was to shape and form new leaders, became "the anvil upon which the relationships between the people's religious traditions and the emerging political and social structures were hammered into shape."[37]

So once again, it seems, in many places around the world, new Christian movements and denominations in Africa, Asia, and Latin America are coming out of a season of awakenings and facing a "now what?" moment. People have experienced personal religious transformation, and they have shared that good news with many others. Churches have been planted and are growing. Many good works and the agencies to drive them have resulted. But now what? Might Christians just keep doing more of the same? But these Christian movements are not in the same social place that they once were. In many societies, such as South Korea, where they now number 30 percent of the nation, Christians have a new salience where they were once marginal and nearly invisible. With new status comes a new responsibility for the general welfare of society. So we see in a situation such as South Korea's, according to our chapter author Kuk-Won Shin, an energetic building out of Christian institutions. And Christian institution building invariably includes education, for the second half of the

34. See, e.g., Mark A. Noll, *The New Shape of World Christianity: How American Experience Reflects Global Faith* (Downers Grove, Ill.: IVP Academic, 2009).

35. John Higham, "From Boundlessness to Consolidation: The Transformation of American Culture, 1848-1860," in *Hanging Together: Unity and Diversity in American Culture*, ed. Carl Guarneri (New Haven, Conn.: Yale University Press, 2001), pp. 147-165.

36. Donald G. Mathews, "The Second Great Awakening as an Organizing Process," *American Quarterly* 21 (1969): 23-43. See also Daniel Walker Howe's magisterial history of the era, *What Hath God Wrought: The Transformation of America, 1815-1848* (New York: Oxford University Press, 2007), pp. 171, 175, 180-181, 192-194, and 201-202, which spotlights the organizing and institution-building dynamism of American evangelicalism, especially in education.

37. Timothy L. Smith, *Uncommon Schools: Christian Colleges and Social Idealism in Midwestern America, 1820-1950* (Bloomington: Indiana Historical Society, 1978), pp. 5-6.

missionary mandate that Jesus gave his disciples, after spreading the good news of personal salvation and baptizing those who accept it, was to "teach the nations." So in addition to founding community development agencies, publishing and media outlets, health clinics, women's associations, and youth groups, Catholics and Protestants alike are going into education. They are developing hundreds of primary and secondary schools, theological seminaries, and universities. These new Christian universities are a very small percentage of the major trends to expand higher education. Yet they are worth watching because they are rather distinctive.

Is Christian Higher Education "Private"?

How distinctive are Christian universities? Are these Christian groups resorting to higher education for Christian purposes, that is, to make good on churches' commitments to deepen Christian thinking and living and to extend a positive Christian presence across the culture? Or are the churches merely being opportunistic, not only riding the wave of privatization, but emulating its structure and values too? In some cases, the answer is strikingly positive. An annual report from Dr. Kasali, at the Christian Bilingual University of Congo, observed that "the government, the Church and the whole nation are now faced with enormous challenges to rebuild their nation after years of war, poverty and neglect. . . . The time has come for the people of God to rise up and be agents of a life giving transformation." So the university started its academic year, Kasali reported, by holding a public consultation on "the role of the Church in nation building."[38]

There is no comprehensive study available on the mission and vision of Christian universities in the global South or East, but it is remarkable how often that nation-building language appears. It is evidently a rather common aim for higher education in Africa and Asia, where building or rebuilding one's nation is very much on educators' minds, and often is a government-mandated university mission, as Kuk-Won Shin shows in his chapter on South Korea. But might Christians mean something deeper by this phrase? To what extent do new Christian universities apply their faith to a public role? Or do they simply

---

38. David Kasali, *Congo Initiative — Université Chrétienne Bilingue du Congo (CI — UCBC) Annual Report* (2007-2008), p. 3. Found at the website of the Congo Initiative, a U.S.-based support corporation for this university. http://www.congoinitiative.org/view.cfm?page_id=48.

follow the "privatization" of purpose and values that drives the new secular private universities? Are the new Christian universities structured like the more commercially and technically oriented private institutions springing up all over, or are they different? Current scholarship does not drill deep enough in any one place to give definitive answers, but this study provides some basic research along with firsthand impressions.

Some Differences

In some important ways, most of the new Christian universities look rather different than the secular, commercially oriented privates. Recall that the new secular privates tend to fashion their course offerings to match the job structures of the business world. They do not teach much basic science, music or philosophy. But in Chile, one researcher found, the five new Catholic institutions founded since 1980 had more comprehensive course offerings than the secular private universities, and they communicated a broader humanitarian purpose.[39] A researcher from Thailand found a similar pattern among Catholic and Protestant universities in her country.[40]

Another point of concern: the new private higher education relies on part-time instructors rather than developing professorial expertise of its own. In Kenya, however, the more mature Christian higher education institutions such as Daystar University and the Catholic University of Eastern Africa, both founded in 1984, have higher percentages of full-time professors than do the state universities.[41] As we shall see, however, in Faith Nguru's chapter on Kenya, some of the more recently founded Kenyan Christian universities rely heavily on part-timers.

How about course offerings in the new Christian universities — is their main idea of how to help "build the nation" confined, like the secular privates, to supplying more business workers and computer technicians? One of the partners in this study, Perry Glanzer, has taken this examination worldwide.

39. Andrés Bernasconi, "Does the Affiliation of Universities to External Organizations Foster Diversity in Private Higher Education? Chile in Comparative Perspective," *Higher Education* 52:2 (2006): 303-342.
40. Prachayani Praphamontripong, "Inside Thai Private Higher Education: Exploring Private Growth in International Context," Program for Research in Private Higher Education (PROPHE), PROPHE Working Paper no. 12, Albany, State University of New York, September 2008.
41. Otieno and Levy, "Public Disorder, Private Boons?" p. 4.

Of the sixty-eight Christian universities in our study that were founded since 1995, forty-four of them are in Africa. All but five of these African institutions provide a major in business, management, or commerce. More than half of them (twenty-five) also provide concentrations in information technology or computer science. So in these respects, they track closely with the trends in privatization. But many of these institutions also focus on what are tradition-ally known as "the helping professions." We found that twelve of them offer teacher education degrees, ten offer degree-level training in the health sciences or nursing, ten more offer degrees in agriculture, and nine offer law degrees. As one might anticipate, another twenty-one of these African Christian univer-sities provide majors in theology. More surprisingly, more than half of them (twenty-three) have some sort of science major, and seventeen have arts, social science, or humanities majors beyond theology.

The twenty-four other new universities in Asia, Latin America, and Eu-rope evidence a similar pattern. Sixteen offer business majors and ten offer some form of computer degree. Helping professions are scattered throughout (five offer nursing, three offer social work, and five offer education degrees). Only seven of them offer theology degrees, but sixteen offer some degree con-centration in the arts. The new secular private universities, as we have seen, tend to offer degree programs that are relatively cheap to teach and are in demand for jobs in business. But even though in most places the Christian universities also have to finance their work without government funding, an unusually high number of them are still committed to offering higher edu-cation in science, the service professions, and the liberal arts. In many places worldwide, as our chapters on India and Canada show, governments extend both inducements and pressure on Christian universities to serve narrower economistic ends. Even so, we feel confident that the broader and nobler aims of higher education are still alive in most of these new Christian universities.[42]

Some Similarities, Too

Even so, it appears that the most fully developed curricular areas, and presum-ably, those most heavily enrolled in many of the new Christian universities, are the commercial fields. Indeed, all of the new African Christian universities offer these fields but few offer a fully comprehensive array of programs across the arts, sciences, social sciences, and humanities. They show other signs of

42. Glanzer, "Dispersing the Light," pp. 336-337.

fairly shallow educational development as well, such as very little evidence of a research emphasis. As Faith Nguru's chapter on Kenya reveals, the new Christian universities, like the new secular privates, tend to be rather top-down and authoritarian in governance. Many of them rely quite heavily on part-time instruction. And frequently their libraries and laboratories are scantily equipped. To be fair, however, in many poorer countries, these relatively new facilities are superior to those in the crowded and stressed state universities. And these newly started universities may have begun by picking the "low-hanging fruit" in higher education, the popular commercial and low-end technical courses, while still planning to take on a broader traditional array of course offerings.

So while the idealism, courage, and energy of these new Christian communities are heartening, there are worrisome issues as well. As we have seen, there are tremendous pressures to reduce education to gaining knowledge and skills for a station in the workplace. In developing countries, where funds are scarce and the need for knowledgeable workers is great, governments relentlessly push for business and technology education over all else.[43] Moreover, Christian movements often arise out on the margins of society, and it is a fundamental matter of social justice for them to equip people to prosper. The Bible's vision of prospering, however, includes far more than commercial work and the creation of wealth. It is a whole-life vision that demands a holistic approach to higher education. How that is developed and sustained over time is one of the central questions lurking behind this book, which the concluding essay addresses and reflects on further.

But now it is time to turn to the main body of this study and look more intently at the texture of Christian higher education and its trends, on the ground in countries and regions around the world. We will hear from a distinguished team of ten Christian scholars, each a longtime "participant observer" of the higher education scene. They offer a fascinating survey of the landscape, and we are eager for you to take the tour.

---

43. In some ways, South Africa, with its relentless drive for economic growth, epitomizes this trend today. See, e.g., Christine Winburg, "Undisciplining Knowledge Production: Development Driven Higher Education in South Africa," *Higher Education* 51:2 (March 2006): 159-172.

CHAPTER 1

Revolution in Higher Education in Nigeria: The Emergence of Private Universities

Musa A. B. Gaiya

The year 1999 not only ushered in a new democratic regime in Nigeria but also a liberalization of university education. In that year, the government began to charter private-owned universities. From 1948 to 1999, university education in Nigeria was the sole responsibility of the federal and state governments of Nigeria. State governments began to open universities in 1979 with the founding of River State University of Science and Technology, Port-Harcourt; the last, at the time of writing, was Kwara State University. It is expected that more state governments will open their own universities. This is not only a response to the growing need for university education but it is also, as Joel Carpenter rightly argues, a growing desire, mainly in the non-Western world, to respond to the impact of globalization and change society through higher education.[1] An innovative move, however, was the establishment of privately owned universities, which has burgeoned since the first four were approved in 1999. At the time of writing, there were forty-one of them, while government universities numbered fifty-one, twenty-seven federal-owned and twenty-four owned by state governments. It has been suggested that Nigeria might need 500 private universities to cope with the demand for higher education.[2]

The rapid development of private universities raises a number of perti-

1. Joel Carpenter, "New Evangelical Universities: Cogs in the World System or Players in a New Game?" in *Interpreting Contemporary Christianity: Global Processes and Local Identities,* ed. Ogbu U. Kalu (Grand Rapids: Eerdmans, 2008), pp. 151-153.

2. Anthony U. Osagie, "Igbinedion University, Okada — The First Four Years," in *Change and Choice: The Development of Private Universities in Nigeria,* ed. Anthony U. Osagie (Benin City: Rawel Fortune Resources, 2009), p. 60.

nent questions: Why were private universities, especially Christian ones, established? What are these Christian universities in their nature and objectives? How different are the objectives of private Christian universities from those of secular private universities or public universities? What impact have Christian universities made on students and society? What challenges do Christian universities in Nigeria face? Before attempting to answer these questions, it might be helpful to sketch a history of university education in Nigeria.

University Education in Nigeria

University education started in Nigeria in 1948, when the Yaba Higher College was transformed into University College, Ibadan, and affiliated with the University of London for the award of degrees. This was meant to meet the growing need for high-level manpower. University College, Ibadan, was one of, as Henk J. van Rinsum puts it, "the first so-called Asquith colleges (i.e. colonial colleges meant to serve colonial purposes, especially preparing students to serve in colonial civil service)";[3] the others also established in Africa were Khartoum University College founded in 1947, the University College at Achimota (Gold Coast, now Ghana) established in 1948, and Makerere University College founded in 1949. At independence in 1960, the University College became autonomous and known as the University of Ibadan; in the same year another university was founded in Nsukka modeled after the American system. Other universities established two years later were those in Lagos, Ile-Ife, and Zaria, and the University of Benin that began in 1970. These are called "first-generation universities."

The "second-generation universities" were established between 1974 and 1977, including those located in Jos, Maiduguri, Kano, Sokoto, Ilorin, Calabar, and Port-Harcourt, and the Nigerian Defence Academy in Kaduna. These universities were to meet the demand for higher education through the Free and Compulsory Education project, a project embarked upon by the federal government of Nigeria at the height of the oil boom. Consequently, payment of fees in universities was abolished and higher education became a right for every Nigerian. There was, therefore, an increase in student enrollment that overstretched available facilities and infrastructure. To cope with high demand for higher education, the federal government of Nigeria created several universities

---

3. Henk J. van Rinsum, " 'Wipe the Blackboard Clean': Academization and Christianization — Siblings in Africa," *African Studies Review* 5:2 (special issue 2002): 34.

of technology between 1980 and 1992 in Bauchi, Makurdi, Owerri, Abeokuta, Yola, Minna, Akure, and three additional conventional ones at Uyo, Awka, and Abuja, which constituted what is known as the "third-generation universities."

Some state governments took advantage of the provision in the 1979 constitution, which placed the establishment of universities under the concurrent list of powers to establish their own universities. The first was Rivers State University of Science and Technology, Port-Harcourt, which began in 1979. As we have shown above other states followed suit. But still the absorption capacity of public universities was inadequate. In the 2007-2008 academic year, three million candidates sat for the Joint Admission and Matriculation Board (JAMB) examinations — a necessary requirement for admission into public and private universities in Nigeria. Only about 200,000 — fewer than 7 percent — were given places in various universities in Nigeria.[4]

These universities have had enormous problems. One of the major problems is funding. The collapse in the revenue accrued from oil in the 1980s affected university education greatly. And between 1999 and 2007, the percentage of budgetary allocation to education as a whole fluctuated wildly, ranging between 6 and 12 percent.[5]

Even so, these allocations were slight improvements on the allocations to this sector during the military regimes in Nigeria. None of the military leaders had attended university, and one of them, General Sani Abacha, considered university education a luxury. At his time, between 1993 and 1998, universities were shut for six months. Thus the 210 billion naira allocation to education in 2008 was at 13 percent the highest allocation to this sector since independence in 1960.[6] Perhaps this improvement came because both the president of Nigeria, Umaru Yar'adua, and his deputy had university degrees and were lecturers in higher institutions of learning in Nigeria. The attention given to education by the present regime was in recognition of the role of education in transforming the nation's economy into one of the twenty best economies of the world by the year 2020. It should be noted, however, that a 13 percent allocation is half of the 26 percent UNESCO minimum. Difficulties in funding higher education will continue to be a problem in the provision of higher

---

4. Anthony U. Osagie, "Doubts Remain about Private Universities," in *Change and Choice: The Development of Private Universities in Nigeria*, ed. Anthony U. Osagie (Benin City: Rawel Fortune Resources, 2009), p. 23.

5. Anthony U. Osagie, "Private Universities: Born out of Crises in Nigeria," in *Change and Choice: The Development of Private Universities in Nigeria*, ed. Anthony U. Osagie (Benin City: Rawel Fortune Resources, 2009), p. 3.

6. Osagie, "Private Universities," p. 3.

education in Africa. Dantew Teferra and Philip Altbach enumerate some of the ongoing problems on the continent:

- The pressures of expansion and "massification" that have added large numbers of students to most African academic institutions and systems
- The economic problems facing many African countries that make it difficult, if not impossible, to provide increased funding for higher education
- A changed fiscal climate induced by multilateral lending agencies such as the World Bank and the International Monetary Fund
- The inability of students to afford the tuition rates necessary for fiscal stability and in some cases an inability to impose tuition fees due to political or other pressures
- Misallocation and poor prioritization of available financial resources, such as the tradition of providing free or highly subsidized accommodation and food to students and maintaining a large and cumbersome non-academic personnel and infrastructure, among others[7]

In comparative terms, Teferra and Altbach report that "the budgets of individual universities in many industrialized countries exceed the entire national budgets for higher education in many African nations."[8] Thus the effect of this underfunding is "Serious shortages of published materials of books and journals, the lack of basic resources for teaching, the absence of simple laboratory equipment and supplies (such as chemicals) to do research and teaching, and, in some countries, delays of salary payments for months."[9] To ameliorate the situation "universities have either taken it upon themselves or have been pressured by governments to expand the financial and resource base as resources."[10] Many public universities in Nigeria have established an Advancement Office as a strategy to secure funds from donor agencies, foundations, and corporate bodies locally and abroad.[11]

Nigeria has fit rather typically into this larger context. While government funding was erratic, enrollments burgeoned. Between 1999 and 2006

7. Damtew Teferra and Philip G. Altbach, "African Higher Education: Challenges for the 21st Century," *Higher Education* 47:1 (2004): 26.

8. Teferra and Altbach, "African Higher Education," p. 27.

9. Teferra and Altbach, "African Higher Education," p. 27.

10. Teferra and Altbach, "African Higher Education," p. 28.

11. This advocacy for funding of higher education is being encouraged by the Council for Advancement and Support of Education (CASE), which is helping more than 3,400 universities in 61 countries around the world.

student population in public universities grew from 300,618 to 1,096,312.[12] Combined with the inadequate funding, this increase in student population in public universities has led to many problems. The most serious repercussion is the brain drain; many highly trained Nigerians have migrated abroad in search of greener pastures. The number is daunting, reportedly totalling "883 lecturers and professors [who] left the universities between 1992 and 1995"[13] alone. Replacement of these lecturers and professors is negligible. In addition, more than 18 million Nigerian professionals from different disciplines are either searching or working abroad. More strive to leave. This has led to a fall in standards, seen in "falling students' examination scores, reduced rigor in staff development and promotion criteria, diminished research output, and complaints by employers regarding the ability of University graduates to perform."[14] Add to these the frequency of examination malpractices, certificate racketing, and lecturers' absenteeism, all of which cast doubts on the quality of certificates being issued by Nigerian universities. Gone are the days when a graduate of a Nigerian university with a first- or second-class degree was admitted for postgraduate studies in any university abroad.

Public universities also have suffered disruptions as a result of strikes by university staff demanding improved funding and better conditions of service; or students' riots due to the poor conditions of hostels and classrooms. For instance, between 1999 and 2007 the Academic Staff of Nigerian Universities Union (ASUU) had gone on strike fifteen times.[15] As a way of coping with the deteriorating conditions students and staff of universities have formed pressure groups, generally called "cults." There are more than ten different cults on campuses of Nigerian universities unleashing terror on staff and students. Since the formation of the first campus cult in the 1950s to fight against social and academic injustice (called Pyrate Confraternity) by Wole Soyinka and Muyiwa Awe, cults have burgeoned on campuses of Nigerian universities. They operate as terrorist gangs. They have intimidated and killed many students and lecturers. Most members are armed with sophisticated weapons and are under the influence of drugs, especially cannabis. Cults have proved indestructible because politicians hire and use them as thugs. Public universities are part of the decaying Nigerian society characterized by corruption, sexual harassment, plagiarism, and ineptitude. To illustrate the level of mismanagement of public

12. Osagie, "Private Universities," p. 8.
13. Osagie, "Private Universities," p. 9.
14. Osagie, "Private Universities," p. 9.
15. Osagie, "Private Universities," p. 12.

funds in these universities, in 2009 one of the universities spent 30 million naira on its convocation ceremony alone.[16]

The World Bank policy on education in developing and underdeveloped countries in the 1970s and 1980s has compounded the problem. The policy, as Akilagpa Sawyerr puts it, was aimed at "privileging expenditure on basic education at the expense of higher education," which is based on the assumption that "the social rates of return on investments in basic education are higher than in higher education."[17] Kingsley Banya and Juliet Elu have further elaborated on this World Bank policy:

> The argument was made that developing countries needed basic education as that was the maximum level that the bulk of the population would ever achieve. As the largest lender of educational monies in the world, the World Bank's views of African universities are critical. Educational economists working for the Bank criticized the "over investing" in higher education and said that resources should be redirected to primary education. . . . The World Bank's (1971) Education Sector Policy Paper proposed more emphasis on primary and even non-formal education. The 1974 Education Working Paper criticized the disproportionate allocation of educational resources to secondary and higher education that served the modern sector, resulting in under-financing of basic education, which was the more efficient and more equitable investment. Donor and national investment strategies should place a high priority on achieving universal basic education while expenditure for secondary and higher education should be strictly related to critical manpower needs. . . . At a meeting with African vice-chancellors in Harare in 1986, the World Bank argued that higher education in Africa was a luxury and that most African countries were better off closing universities at home than training graduates overseas. . . . Universities were perceived no longer as the solution to the problem of development, but as a central part of the problem itself.[18]

World Bank policy on education in developing countries began to change in 2000, when higher education was "identified as a major agent of development and positive social change."[19] This new policy also added that "without more

16. *Daily Independent,* October 7, 2009.

17. Akilagpa Sawyerr, "Challenges Facing African Universities: Selected Issues," *African Studies Review* 47:1 (2004): 12.

18. Kingsley Banya and Juliet Elu, "The World Bank and Financing Higher Education in Sub-Saharan Africa," *Higher Education* 42:1 (2001): 23-25.

19. A. B. K. Kasozi, "The Role of the State in Addressing Challenges and Opportunities

and better higher education, developing countries will find it increasingly difficult to benefit from the global knowledge-based economy."[20] But the state of funding of public universities in Nigeria was dwindling, in spite of World Bank intervention, partly due to corruption and misplaced priority on the part of government. The solution, in the meantime, seemed to be the creation of private universities. This phenomenon, Carpenter says, is global.[21]

The constant closure, chaotic situation, moral decadence and falling standards of education in public universities forced parents who could afford it to send their children to schools overseas. This was happening in spite of the danger of separating children from their parents at such a tender age and also the difficulty in fitting into cultures other than that of their parents. Perhaps it was due to these problems that some churches challenged the government monopoly of higher education in Nigeria. One of these churches was the Nigerian Baptist Convention. "After all," the Baptist Convention argued, "Christian missions started Western education in Nigeria."[22] But the first to put such a challenge into action was a private individual, Nnanna Ukeagbu, who opened Imo Technical University in 1980. The government challenged the legality of the school in the Nigerian highest court, the Supreme Court, and the court ruled in favor of Ukeagbu. As a result of this ruling, twenty-five other private universities were established. Applications for approval of private universities continued to grow. The military government decided to ban all private universities with Decree No. 19 of 1984.[23] With the enactment of this decree, the hope of establishing a private university in Nigeria seemed to have been lost. This hampered development of private initiative in higher education, and Nigeria, the most populous country in Africa, fell behind other less endowed African countries in private initiative in higher education. Kenya developed nine private universities between 1980 and 1990 while Tanzania developed eleven private universities between 1980 and 2000. In the same period (1980-2000) private universities in Uganda and Democratic Republic of Congo numbered ten and four respectively.[24]

Posed by the Rapid Growth of Universities in Uganda Since 1988," *African Studies Review* 45:2 (special issue 2002): 125.

20. Kasozi, "The Role of the State," p. 133.

21. Carpenter, "New Evangelical Universities," pp. 175-176.

22. T. O. Olagbemiro, "Bowen University," in *Change and Choice: The Development of Private Universities in Nigeria,* ed. Anthony U. Osagie (Benin City: Rawel Fortune Resources, 2009), p. 92.

23. Osagie, "Private Universities," pp. 14-15.

24. Sawyerr, "Challenges Facing African Universities," p. 17.

Emergence of Private Universities

Private participation in the provision of education in Nigeria was undermined in 1972 when the military government took over all Christian mission schools; the only place that this did not happen was in what was then called Benue-Plateau State, where mission schools were not taken over. The churches were not happy with this development. Some of them engaged the government in a protracted battle in the courts to regain ownership of the schools. Most prominent was the Roman Catholic Church. Leading in the campaign in the 1980s was the archbishop of Lagos, Anthony Olubunmi Okogie (now a cardinal). The government was forced to return some of these schools to their owners because it realized that it alone could not provide education. Furthermore, government had poorly managed the schools; infrastructures were in shambles, and standards of discipline, morality, and learning had collapsed. Many well-meaning Nigerians bemoaned the condition of education and remembered with nostalgia their mission school experience. The leader of one of the fastest-growing Charismatic/Pentecostal churches, Enoch Adeboye, says the reason why he established a university was that he "longed for the return to the glorious days of mission schools, where students acquired high quality education with the fear of God and became useful citizens."[25] Today church schools (primary and secondary) have proliferated. Almost all church congregations, especially in cities, have a primary or secondary school or both. This development, therefore, anticipated the efforts for the establishment of Christian universities by Nigerian churches in the 1990s.

The story of private initiatives in higher education, which actually began in 1999, is checkered. The first event was the approval in 1993 given by the then governor of Anambra State in southeastern Nigeria for the founding of Madonna University. The governor gave the approval because, in that year, the federal government of Nigeria made a decree permitting private organizations to establish universities, provided they comply with government guidelines. Also the 1979 constitution placed education under the "concurrent" list — meaning both federal and state governments could provide education. But since Madonna was a purely private university, not a state one, the federal government issued a "stiff law saying that only Federal Government can legislate on Private Universities."[26] The event that indicated government might change its mind on the matter of private universities was the intro-

25. http://www.run.edu.ng.
26. Osagie, "Private Universities," p. 16.

duction of the deregulation of the Nigerian economy in 1999 under a civilian regime. The aim was to encourage private participation in Nigeria's economy and introduced private- and public-sector competition. It was felt that by allowing private hands in establishing and running universities it might stimulate government-owned universities to wake up from their slumber. Up until 1999 the establishment and running of universities in Nigeria was a monopoly of government. With this opportunity, forty-seven organizations applied to begin private universities in Nigeria, but only three were given licenses: Madonna University, Babcock University, and Igbinedion University. The first two universities were Christian, the last was owned by a Christian philanthropist living in Benin, southeast of Nigeria. At the time of writing, forty-one private universities have been approved by the federal government of Nigeria;[27] twenty-one of these are Christian, three are Islamic, and the rest secular. As of 2009 the total number of universities in Nigeria was 105. Thus private universities in Nigeria account for 39 percent of the institutions in this educational sector and if this trend continues, as we have noted above, the number is bound to increase. At time of writing there are forty-eight others described as "illegal universities" operating in different parts of the country; seven of these have been closed down, while nine others are being investigated and tried in the courts.[28] Some proprietors of many of these "illegal universities" were being prosecuted by the government's Economic and Financial Crimes Commission (EFCC) for "operating illegally and collecting money from innocent students and parents under false pretences."[29] Private participation in higher education, as can be seen, is late compared to countries like the United States, Japan, South Korea, India, and the Philippines or even African countries like Kenya and Uganda. This is a result of the government's deliberate policy to prevent private participation. Even so, Nigeria now would be one of the leading countries in Africa in private investment in higher education.

Government policy on private universities stipulates that these institutions would be given "provisional approval" for five years, in order "to create room for effective mentoring and qualitative growth. [During this period] the universities would be affiliated to older generation universities for academic and administrative mentoring to be moderated by the National Universities

27. *National Universities Commission (NUC) Monthly Bulletin,* November 16, 2009, pp. 11-15.

28. *NUC Bulletin,* p. 15.

29. *NUC Bulletin* 4:16 (April 2009): 1.

Commission (NUC)."[30] This policy brings private universities under the control of government agencies. These agencies include the NUC (a regulating body) and the Joint Admission and Matriculation Board (JAMB), the agency mandated to conduct admissions into all universities in Nigeria. In order to have more control over private universities, the NUC set up the Committee on Monitoring of Private Universities (COMPU) in 2003. The COMPU was set up to

- Conduct annual monitoring of all licensed private universities in Nigeria with a focus on such areas as academic-brief and master-plan implementation, management and governance of the institution, quality of students, staff and infrastructural input, and other issues pertinent to the delivery of quality university education
- Advise management, senate, council, and the proprietor(s) of the institution on areas needing immediate attention
- Prepare an annual report for the government through NUC management and board on the *State of Private Universities in Nigeria*[31]

In 2003 seven universities were visited: Covenant, Pan African, Babcock, Bowen, Madonna, Igbinedion, and Benson Idahosa Universities. The National Universities Commission gives private universities some amount of autonomy; however, all universities in Nigeria are meant to meet a certain minimum academic standard.

Emergence of Christian Universities

The reasons for the establishment of private universities in Nigeria as given by Isaac N. Obasi are the "public failure theory," "demand absorption," and the need for a different kind of service delivery.[32] But religious private universities also aimed at making a moral impact on society. Out of the twenty-four religious private universities, three are Islamic and twenty-one are Christian. Among the Christian universities, five are Roman Catholic, six are Charismatic/Pentecostal, and the rest were owned by individuals and other Protes-

30. *NUC Bulletin* 4:46 (November 2009): 1.

31. *State of Private Universities in Nigeria: Report of the 2003 Annual Monitoring and Quality Assurance of Private Universities in Nigeria* (Abuja: National Universities Commission, 2003), p. iii; emphasis in original.

32. Isaac N. Obasi, http://www.bc.edu/cihe/newsletter/Number45/p14_Obasi.htm.

tant churches (evangelical and mainline).[33] Islamic private universities seek "to embody the vision and aspiration of the Muslim Community of Nigeria [by] producing a balanced and well-rounded individual, sound in knowledge, high in discipline and morality."[34] Perhaps this idea is in line with the Islamic concept of knowledge. All knowledge comes from God and should be used for the cause of God. This principle characterized the history of the Islamic intellectual tradition and is reflected in the word of the Persian poet and scholar Abd al-Rahman Jami (d. 1492) in his *Lawacih* (Flashes of Light):

> O God, deliver us from the preoccupation with worldly vanities,
> and show us the nature of things as they really are.
> Remove from our eyes the veil of ignorance,
> and show us things as they really are. . . .
> Make this phenomenal world the mirror to reflect the manifestation of
> Thy beauty,
> not a veil to separate and repel us from Thee.[35]

This idea is being re-echoed in the "Islamization of knowledge" movement in contemporary discourse on Islam, science and learning.

The concern for religious or moral transformation is the goal of all Christian universities as well. Some of the mission goals of private Christian universities illustrate these. Renaissance University aims at bringing "a complete rebirth to the University education system in Nigeria . . . to produce the Total Man who is sound in learning, worthy in character, useful to himself, his community and the Nigerian State."[36] Madonna University prides itself as the first private university in Nigeria and the first Catholic university in Nigeria and "strives to revive in her community the age-long tradition of Catholic Education and the exacting demand of our contemporary society for sound education enrooted in salubrious life-promoting morality." The vision of Achievers University "is to be the best university in Africa and indeed one of the best in the world to produce a total person, morally sound, properly educated and entrepreneurially oriented, who would be useful to himself and to the society."[37] The exuberant leader of the Living Faith Church and founder

33. See the appendix at the end of this chapter.

34. http://katsinauniversityportal.ne.

35. Muzaffar Aqbal, "The Center for Islam and Science: A New Initiative," *International Institute for the Study of Islam in the Modern World (ISIM) Newsletter,* no. 6 (2000): 10.

36. www.rnu.edu.ng.

37. http://www.achieversuniversity.org.

of Covenant University also encapsulates his vision for the university in the concept of the "total man." He explains that the concept "centers on developing the man who will develop his world. It is designed to produce students who are intelligently conscious of their environment and who know how to maximize their potentials in life. The programs of the university are first directed at the person before addressing his profession."[38] The idea behind this vision is that, as the late Ogbu Kalu reasons, "it harps on a typical theme that the problem of the [country] is the lack of a leadership with a strong ethical orientation and adequate knowledge about the context of mission."[39] Due to this concern about morality and the transformation of Nigeria, the theological divisions of evangelical, liberal, and Pentecostal Christianity do not exist in Nigerian private universities as they do in other parts of the world such as North America. Denominational difference may exist, but they all share the same goal: the transformation of society through higher education.

Christian universities in Nigeria appear to lack a strong theological base. Private universities elsewhere that seem to have more successfully integrated a theological purpose and vision, such as African University in Zimbabwe, Daystar University in Kenya, and Chongshin University, a major Christian university in Seoul, South Korea, may have something to teach us in Nigeria.[40] Some of the Christian universities that grew out of Bible colleges do not seem to have made a distinction between ministerial training and training Christian professionals for the secular world. Typical is Benson Idahosa University, which evolved from Church of God Bible School. It aims at "raising an army of professionals and academics who would go in Christ's name to the ends of the world with the fire of the Holy Ghost to impact truth by precepts and example."[41] St. Paul's University, an Anglican institution, which emerged in similar circumstances, and Veritas University, Roman Catholic, separate the pastoral training from other fields with the department of religious and theological studies.[42] A more comprehensive perspective on Christian worldview in higher education is provided by Babcock University. The university emerged from the Adventist Seminary in 1999. It integrated theological/religious education with secular education in its attempts to harmonize the development of "the physical, the mental, [the] social and the spiritual powers." Thus, in

38. Ogbu Kalu, *African Pentecostalism: An Introduction* (Oxford: Oxford University Press, 2008), p. 129.

39. Kalu, *African Pentecostalism*, p. 130.

40. Carpenter, "New Evangelical Universities," pp. 181-182.

41. Kalu, *African Pentecostalism*, p. 130.

42. For similar cases, see Carpenter, "New Evangelical Universities," pp. 156-158.

addition to core subject areas, students of Babcock University are taught and encouraged to internalize "Christian doctrine and practice as believed and taught by Seventh-Day Adventists."[43] Graduates of the university are equipped to give a "spiritually inspired life of service to humanity."[44] This may sound evangelistic and sectarian, but as Adrian tells us, the Christian College Consortium in America had to make their faith position clear to avoid falling into the track many leading universities had fallen into when they separated faith from learning.[45] This means that Christian higher education should have a theological component. The problem, however, is that universities founded by Charismatic/Pentecostal groups may not have a strong theological base. What is important, however, is the fact that Christian universities in Nigeria seek to make a positive impact on the Nigerian society; perhaps this is what Carpenter means by the "second chapter in the story of revivalist Christianity's growth in the non-Western world."[46] It is hoped that Christian universities will transform Nigeria and its culture, which sadly is characterized by corruption, bad management of time, ineptitude, and violence. Furthermore, we may probably begin to see graduates of these universities going into the pastoral ministry, thereby making the pulpit intellectually stronger.

Most Christian universities in Nigeria are market-driven, influenced understandably by the collapse of the economy and the attendant high rate of unemployment in the country. The university that is essentially market-driven is Covenant University, founded in 2002 by Bishop David O. Oyedepo, who is also founder and president of Living Faith Church and the chancellor of the university. In its "comprehensive entrepreneurial education," Covenant University seeks to equip students to "become self-dependent, job and wealth creators."[47] This idea is encapsulated in the university's "Total Man Concept," by which it means "developing the man that will develop his world. . . . Specifically, it is charged with the responsibility for the empowerment of graduates,

43. Adekule A. Alalade and Ademola S. Tayo, "Management of Private Universities in Nigeria: Babcock University as a Case Study," in *Change and Choice: The Development of Private Universities in Nigeria,* ed. Anthony U. Osagie (Benin City: Rawel Fortune Resources, 2009), pp. 68, 72.

44. Alalade and Tayo, "Management of Private Universities," p. 69.

45. William Adrian, "Christian Universities in Historical Perspective," *Christian Higher Education* 4:3 (2005): 26.

46. Carpenter, "New Evangelical Universities," p. 164.

47. Famous Izedonmi, "Covenant University: Core Value, Total Man Concept and Entrepreneurship Development Studies," in *Change and Choice: The Development of Private Universities in Nigeria,* ed. Anthony U. Osagie (Benin City: Rawel Fortune Resources, 2009), p. 150.

and to produce creators of wealth and employment rather than job seekers."[48] The training is done through apprenticeship, internship, and project execution. Sawyyer says that similar training is happening at the Kwame Nkrumah University of Science and Technology (KNUST) in Ghana. He writes that the training at this university involves

> working with local mechanics at the nearby Suame Magazine, . . . also actively involved with the Cocoa Processing Company, which provides the university's chemistry department with both experience and income in return for the university's contributions to research and development.[49]

Kingsley Larbi, former vice chancellor of Central University, a Christian private university in Ghana, supports this idea; according to him Christian universities "must relate their programmes to the needs of tomorrow's labour market. The stakeholders of these emergent private institutions must be willing to adapt faster to changing technologies, else they will soon become irrelevant in the realisation of the African dream."[50] However, Carpenter cautions that Christian universities should beware of pursuing wealth alone, for "the Bible's vision of prospering includes far more than commercial work and the creation of wealth." Otherwise these universities could easily become "pensioners of global capitalism."[51]

Christian universities in Nigeria have performed creditably in many areas. The National Universities Commission's visitation panel rated private universities higher than public ones. During its accreditation visits to universities in 2005 and 2006, Covenant University topped the list of "twenty-four private universities and enjoyed as many credited courses/programs as the best among the old-generation of federal government-founded universities."[52] This is because private universities tend to maintain a good student-teacher ratio. At Covenant, the ratio is 26:1. Their acquisition of cutting-edge technology (such as computers, e-mail, internet connectivity and websites), a stable academic calendar (due to absence of secret cult activities on campuses, staff strikes, and student riots) and innovative courses and programs put private universities in

48. Izedonmi, "Covenant University," pp. 155, 162.

49. Sawyyer, "Challenges Facing African Universities," p. 22.

50. Larbi, "The Challenges of Leadership," quoted in Carpenter, "New Evangelical Universities," p. 179.

51. Joel Carpenter, "New Christian Universities and the Future of Christian Scholarship: Andrew Walls Lecture," Liverpool Hope University, March 17, 2010, p. 10.

52. Kalu, *African Pentecostalism*, p. 131.

the lead in higher education in Nigeria. On disruptive behavior by students, such as engaging in cult activities and rioting on campus, Edoba B. Omoregie, a lawyer, has argued that because private universities are not established by statute of parliament but by license, the relationship between students (and staff) and the university is contractual. As such, private universities could exercise discipline, as they deem fit, on student(s) or staff who breached the contract.[53] Other areas of improvement, as Obasi explains, include "more cost-effective, lean governance structures rather than the overly bureaucratized type of structures . . . also . . . the adoption of the cost-saving collegiate system in place of the conventional structures of faculties and departments."[54]

Nigeria has a growing number of Christian primary and secondary schools run by Christian churches and missions. Most of the teachers in these schools have been trained in secular public universities. Here academic freedom in teaching and learning is enshrined. To provide Christian teachers for these Christian schools there is the need for Christian universities to provide Christian teacher education curriculum. Babcock University, as an Adventist institution devoted to serving a denominational network of schools, has done this from the start. Another institution that is laying plans to do this is the University of Mkar, founded by Reformed Church educators. The university aims to produce Christian teachers to teach subjects like "religious studies, history, geography, economics, English language, biology, chemistry, physics, technology, agriculture, and primary education."[55] The university was clear in its goal, that is, to integrate "faith and learning." But it appears the school has yet to achieve such integration. Technical and commercial curricula came first and dominate the university currently. But plans are still on the boards to move into broader studies that will support teacher education and better reflect a Reformed theology of culture.[56]

Christian universities in Nigeria need to form a consortium to share ideas and create linkages. This will help in harmonizing their courses and programs

53. Edoba B. Omoregie, "Disciplinary Powers of Private Universities over Students in Nigeria: A Legal Perspective," in *Change and Choice: The Development of Private Universities in Nigeria,* ed. Anthony U. Osagie (Benin City: Rawel Fortune Resources, 2009), pp. 190-192.

54. Obasi, http://www.bc.edu/cihe/newsletter/Number45/p14_Obasi.htm.

55. T. Mkena, "The Institute of Christian Studies (Mkar, Nigeria)," in *Christian Education in the African Context, Proceedings of the African Regional Conference of International Association for the Promotion of Christian Higher Education,* Harare, Zimbabwe, March 4-9, 1992, pp. 120-121.

56. Joel Carpenter, interview with the vice chancellor of the University of Mkar, February 2010.

and avoid unnecessary duplications. Foundations and donor agencies, both local and international, would be pleased to fund collaborative research, which would involve many colleges, rather than research that has been carried out by one institution. Such grants are necessary, not only as a means of putting such schools on the global map of academic research but also for staff development locally and abroad.

The Challenges of Christian Universities in Nigeria

Christian universities have problems. A major challenge Christian universities face is funding. The main source of funding of private universities in Nigeria, whether Christian or Islamic or secular, is through school fees. In 2003 Babcock University had 95 percent of its funds coming from school fees and 5 percent from the parent church, the Seventh-Day Adventists.[57] This is why private universities would be under pressure to admit as many as can afford to pay the fees, sometimes even when candidates are not qualified, as a case at Tansian University shows. A local paper, the *Daily Champion,* reports that students in the university were being exploited but would not complain because "they lacked basic entry requirements including evidence of having sat for JAMB [exams], among others. Most students there allegedly have never written JAMB."[58] But in spite of the high school fees charged in private universities, they barely meet running costs, so that, as Osagie says, unless government comes to their aid by giving them grants from the Education Tax Fund, it may be difficult to maintain academic standards. Kasozi explains the specific areas in which the government can intervene to assist a private university: "key capital projects that enhance the creation, storage, and transmission of knowledge, including laboratories, classrooms, administrative structures, and training of academic faculty and administrators."[59] Private universities may also need to look elsewhere for sources of funding; an affiliation with the Council for Advancement and Support of Education (CASE) might help. In its last seminar on university funding in Accra, Ghana, private universities, like Redeemer's University, Babcock, Lagos Business School, and Pan African

---

57. *NUC: State of Private Universities in Nigeria: Report of the 2003 Annual Monitoring and Quality Assurance,* p. v.

58. Odogwu Emka Oogwu, "Tansian University: A Lingering Ownership Row: NUC, Ex-Minister's Link," *Daily Champion,* December 12, 2009.

59. Kasozi, "The Role of the State," p. 138.

University attended.[60] School fees charged by private university have courted criticism. John Okpako says the motive for establishing private universities "is profit maximization or entrepreneurial development."[61] Others say the high cost makes private universities elitist institutions.[62]

Most Christian universities in Nigeria have weak staff development programs,[63] partly due to financial difficulties. Thus they depend on part-time lecturers from public universities. This is helpful, but has its challenges, in that lecturers from public universities come from secular traditions where a sharp line is drawn between faith and learning. Many public university professors would resonate with the confession of the Korean professor of philosophy who was asked how he related his theology with his teaching. He retorted, "Young man, when I go into the classroom, I leave my religion in the hall."[64] I was told of this tension at the Bingham University, a Christian university founded by the Evangelical Church of West Africa — one of the largest conservative evangelical churches in West Africa.[65]

The critics are right to point out that some of the private universities in Nigeria are run as personal business enterprises. Igbinedion University, one of the first to have a government license and a secular university, is managed as one of the proprietor's companies. The proprietor, G. O. Igbinedion, is the chancellor and also performs the duties of the vice chancellor. But as Osagie says, Igbinedion does not know "management of a company is different in many ways from university management."[66] Hard hit by this mismanagement is the library. For instance in the 2001-2002 session, 5,744,877 naira were budgeted for the library at Igbinedion University, but only 477,500 naira, 8 percent, were released to the library budget by the proprietor. When compared with Babcock University, a Christian private university, the difference is phenom-

---

60. Sunday Saanu, "Training Fund Raisers for Varsity," *This Day,* October 15, 2009.

61. Okpako, quoted in Anthony U. Osagie, "Education, at What Cost?" in *Change and Choice: The Development of Private Universities in Nigeria,* ed. Anthony U. Osagie (Benin City: Rawel Fortune Resources, 2009), p. 37.

62. Osagie, "Education, at What Cost?" p. 43. For critiques of private universities globally, see Daniel C. Levy, "Latin America's Private Universities: How Successful Are They?" *Comparative Education Review* 29:4 (November 1985): 440-459; and Jandhyal B. G. Tilak, "The Privatization of Higher Education," *Prospects* 21:2 (1991): 227-239.

63. Almost all the private universities visited in 2003 and 2004 were advised to improve on staff development or recruit senior academics. See NUC's 2003 and 2004 *Annual Monitoring and Quality Assurance Reports.*

64. Carpenter, "New Evangelical Universities," p. 182.

65. Interview with Beatrice Kadangs, head of academics, October 6, 2009.

66. Osagie, "Igbinedion University," p. 54.

enal: in the same period 6,495,802.88 naira were budgeted and 9,238,263.58 naira were released.[67] Such tight grips on university management by proprietors were seen at Covenant University as well. The NUC monitoring team was surprised at this anomaly — "a peculiar administration/management structure distinct from what is obtained in regular universities and which was contrary to the provision of the university academic brief." This peculiar administrative structure had the proprietor, who was the chancellor, having "executive rather than ceremonial powers." The proprietor had explained that this "peculiar structure" came about as a result of "a vision coupled with a passion and determination to depart from the norm, innovate and effect change."[68] One might hope that Christian universities can develop structures that more closely follow Christian norms of accountability and subsidiarity as well as the visions of their founders.

Concluding Remarks

The evolution of private universities in Nigeria is indeed a revolution, not only in their number but also in the impact they are likely to play in a country that has been branded one of the most corrupt in the world. Although we are yet to see the impact these universities are having on the Nigerian society, they are a step forward in attempting to shape a better Nigeria. But these universities need help. I believe that the International Association for the Promotion of Christian Higher Education (IAPCHE) in collaboration with the Centre for the Promotion of Christian Higher Education in Africa (CPCHEA) can help Christian universities in Nigeria by organizing seminars and workshops focusing particularly on integrating faith and learning, university management (including funding), curriculum development, and student outreaches. With helpful resources such as these, we can hope that private Christian universities in Nigeria would be different from public ones in the areas of academic excellence, clear theological focus, and pursuance of Christian values. These improvements no doubt would encourage families to train their children here in Nigeria rather than send them to Christian colleges abroad.

67. R. Olorunsola and D. A. Idada, "Private University Libraries in Nigeria: A Comparative Study," *Middle Belt Journal of Library and Information Science* 3:2 (2003): 70-71.

68. NUC's 2003 *Annual Monitoring and Quality Assurance Reports*, pp. xi, 3, 7.

Appendix: Christian Universities in Nigeria 2009

University	Owner(s)
Babcock University, Ilishan, Remo	Seventh Day Adventist Church
Madonna University, Elele	Roman Catholic Church
Bowen University, Iwo	Nigerian Baptist Convention
Covenant University, Ota	Living Faith Church
Benson Idahosa Uni, Benin City	Church of God Mission
Redeemers University, Mowe, Ogun State	Redeemed Christian Church of God
Ajayi Crowther Uni, Oyo	Church of Nigeria (Anglican Communion)
Caritas University	Roman Catholic Church
Bingham University, Karu (Abuja)	Evangelical Church of West Africa
Crawford University, Igbesa, Ogun State	Apostolic Faith Church
University of Mkar	Church of Christ Among Tiv
Joseph Babalola Uni, Ikeji-Arakeji	Christ Apostolic Church
Caleb University, Lagos	Ola Adebogun
Obong University, Obong Ntak*	Ibibio Community
Salem University, Lokoja	Salem International Christian Centre
Veritas University, Abuja	Roman Catholic Church
Tansian University, Umunya	Partly Roman Catholic Church
Wesley University of Science and Tech	Methodist Church
St. Paul's University, Awka, Anambra State	Church of Nigeria (Anglican Communion)
Godfrey Okoye University, Ug-wuomu-Nike, Enugu St.	Roman Catholic Church
Wellspring University, Evboubanosa, Edo St	University of Benin, Benin City

*Its website states that "Obong University is built on Christian values and high standards of academic excellence" (http://www.obonguniversity.net/)

CHAPTER 2

Development of Christian Higher Education in Kenya: An Overview

Faith W. Nguru

Christian universities are springing up with surprising speed in Africa today. According to the Global Christian Higher Education Project and other informal sources, there are now at least seventy of them across the continent, where various counts and estimates of private universities total between eighty-five and one hundred. More than fifty of the Christian universities have been founded (or reorganized as universities) since 1990. Kenya has been in many respects the epicenter of this wave of new ventures in Christian learning. It has fifteen such institutions, including some of the earliest of the recent wave, which are now solidly established institutions such as the Catholic University of Eastern Africa and Daystar University, both founded in 1984 and chartered as universities in the early 1990s. More than half of these universities have their foundations in older church-sponsored theological and ministry training institutions.[1] In the past, higher education, with the exception of theology, was almost exclusively a government-sponsored enterprise in East Africa. However, the growing size and social responsibility of the Christian churches and the widespread recognition that the public universities are not able to serve the myriad developmental needs in the region have converged in the rapid development of Christian higher education (CHE) in East Africa. Each nation of the region has Catholic and Protestant universities, all founded since 1990, and

---

1. The Global Christian Higher Education institutions database for Africa is my main source. It can be accessed at http://www.iapche.org/. Reliable information about newly chartered institutions in Kenya and beyond, however, shows that this list of institutions is incomplete. Christian higher education is a dynamic, growing field.

the general patterns of their development are quite similar. The case of Kenya is more easily documented, however, so it will be the focus of this chapter.

The Kenyan institutions discussed in this essay are grappling with difficult questions in an effort to establish their own identity and place in Africa's higher education landscape. They are developing within the context of the sociocultural, economic and political struggles that characterize African higher education more generally. I shall make this broader context the stage on which to play out the challenges of the CHE movement. The two major needs that this context lays at the feet of CHE are the urgent need to increase access to higher education for the ever increasing number of high school graduates, and the relative lack of Christian-formed servant leaders in all sectors of society.[2]

A brief description of the history and practices of selected institutions from the survey data provided by the Global Christian Higher Education Project[3] and additional data from the universities' websites and a variety of publications will be used to situate the struggles and achievements that Christian higher education faces in its attempts to meet national, global, and kingdom mandates. This essay traces how Kenyan Christian universities were founded and their efforts to come to terms with the challenges of private higher education more generally in the region, and more particularly their quest to establish authentically Christian approaches to university structures and practices.

Educational Tradition from the Pre-Colonial Period

Higher education has a long history on the African continent, but it is evident that the early developments were all in the North of Africa. According to Paul Zeleza, a renowned historian, the origins of higher education in Africa, including universities as communities of scholars and learning, can be traced to three institutional traditions: first, the Alexandria Museum and Library,

2. More than 80 percent of Kenyans claim to be Christians, but Christian ethical principles and sociopolitical thought play a very weak role in Kenyan public life. This judgment is confirmed by John Karanja, "Evangelical Attitudes toward Democracy in Kenya," in *Evangelical Christianity and Democracy in Africa*, ed. Terence O. Ranger (New York: Oxford University Press, 2008), pp. 67-93, and is documented quite dramatically in Paul Gifford, *Christianity, Politics, and Public Life in Kenya* (New York: Columbia University Press, 2009).

3. IAPCHE, the Nagel Institute for the Study of World Christianity, and Baylor University collaborated on the Global Christian Higher Education Project, a research reconnaissance and survey of international Christian higher education. Its database, listing African institutions, can be found at http://www.iapche.org/.

sustained in Ptolemaic Egypt; second, the early Christian monasteries; and third, the Islamic communities of learning, culminating in Al-Azhar (f. 972) in Cairo, the great seat of Islamic learning yet today. Evidently the generation and conservation of knowledge — archetypal university activities — were seminal to Africa's ancient heritage of scholarship. As far as Christianity and academic development are concerned, Zeleza notes that

> It was also in Egypt, one of the earliest centers of Christianity in the world, that monasteries first developed in the third century A.D. Tens of thousands of Christians gathered in the monasteries in the desert not only to escape the executions of Roman rule, but also for a life devoted to spiritual contemplation . . . reflection, writing and learning. [Another] country where monastic education developed early was Ethiopia where Christianity was introduced in the fourth century A.D. and became the state religion. From the period of the Zagwe dynasty in the twelfth century this system included higher education, which was largely restricted to the clergy and nobility.[4]

It appears that for many centuries after this growth in the North of Africa not much was happening in the development of higher education in the continent farther to the South. An important exception was the Islamic center of learning in Timbuktu, West Africa, on the southern edge of the Sahara. By the twelfth century A.D., when the earliest European universities were only just beginning, Timbuktu was attracting a huge community of scholars, ranging from primary school age through the highest circles of advanced learning.[5]

The modern university era in Africa began as a feature of European overseas expansion. The first "Western"-style universities first took root in countries adjacent to the sea routes from Europe: at Freetown, Sierra Leone (Fourah Bay College, 1827 — now part of the University of Sierra Leone), at Monrovia, Liberia (Liberia College, 1863 — now the University of Liberia), and at Cape

---

4. Paul T. Zeleza, "Beyond Afropessimism: Historical Accounting of African Universities," *Pambazuka News* 263:30 (August 2008). Retrieved from http://www.pambazuka.org. More comprehensive surveys include J. F. Ade Ajayi, Lameck K. H. Goma, and G. Ampah Johnson, *The African Experience of Higher Education* (Athens: Ohio University Press, 1996), and Y. G.-M. Lulat, *A History of African Higher Education from Antiquity to the Present: A Critical Synthesis* (Westport, Conn.: Praeger Publishers, 2005).

5. Most of what we know about Timbuktu's academics today resides in the large collection of manuscript texts, some 16,000 in number, now being conserved and studied by a team led by Malian and South African scholars. See Souleymane Bashir Diagne, "Toward the Intellectual History of West Africa: The Meaning of Timbuktu," in *The Meanings of Timbuktu,* ed. Shamil Jeppe and Souleymane Bashir Diagne (Cape Town: HSRC Press, 2008), pp. 19-30.

Town, South Africa (South African College, 1829 — now the University of Cape Town). These early institutions were established by European settlers and by European, African, and African American Christian missionaries.[6]

In East Africa, the era of the state-sponsored university system had its beginning quite recently, with the formation in 1963 of the University of East Africa, consolidating university colleges in Kampala, Nairobi, and Dar es Salaam. These institutions had histories that included the formation of technical training colleges (Kampala in 1922; Nairobi in 1956), and university colleges affiliated with the University of London (Kampala in 1949, Dar-es-Salaam in 1961, and Nairobi in 1961). After a very brief career under one university rubric, the three campuses became three separate national institutions in 1970: Makerere University in Kampala, the University of Nairobi, and the University of Dar-es-Salaam. These universities were to be the national standard-bearers in higher education, tasked with equipping cadres of professional, intellectual, and political leaders to build the new nations. The main assumption about responsibility for higher education in these systems was very similar to those of Great Britain: higher education was the domain of the national government, to be funded publicly and offered free of charge or at very minimal cost to those who qualified. The only major exception to this pattern would be the education of clergy, which was to be borne by the various religious communities.[7]

Since those heady early days, East African universities have encountered enormous challenges. Despite the rapid development of additional universities and technical colleges, and the rapid enrollment increases of existing institutions, higher education enrollments have not kept up with the enormous increase of secondary school leavers who meet university acceptance standards on their qualifying examinations. In 2009, Kenya had seven traditional universities and twelve university colleges under state control, and twenty-two private colleges and universities of various kinds and accreditation status. All institutions enrolled about 123,000 students, with 80 percent of them in the public institutions. The demand for university enrollments, however, has been overwhelming. In 2007, 82,000 Kenyan secondary school graduates qualified for a university education on their examinations, but the government could fund the enrollment of only 10,000 of these, while offering admission to another 10,000 on a tuition-paying basis. Another 5,000 entered private, tuition-

---

6. Lulat, *A History of African Higher Education,* pp. 261-330.

7. Philip G. Altbach and Damtew Teferra, eds., *African Higher Education: An International Reference Handbook* (Bloomington: Indiana University Press, 2003): C. Ngome, "Kenya," pp. 359-371; N. B. Musisi, "Uganda," pp. 611-623; and D. Mkude and B. Cooksey, "Tanzania," pp. 583-594.

charging institutions. Out of the national age cohort, however, only 3 percent of university-aged Kenyans are enrolled.[8] Years of austerity budgets, and in the 1980s and 1990s, World Bank pressures to reallocate government education funding toward primary and secondary schooling, have eroded early government support for higher education. Higher education budgets have done better in recent years, but austerity funding and overwhelming enrollment pressures have taken their toll on public institutions. The faculty strikes, students strike, dormitory life degenerates, more able faculty depart for better pay and work in more affluent nations, and libraries and laboratories crumble. In response to these multidimensional crises in higher education, governments have decided to charge students for some educational programs and services, allow for selective development and differential fees and salaries in some technical and commercial fields, and open university chartering to private institutions.[9]

Christian higher education in Kenya arises out of this context, offering an alternative to a struggling state-run system. Christian universities offer an attractive option to many families, yet they too have issues and challenges to address.

Kenyan Christian Higher Education Institutions

The last two decades have seen a period of phenomenal expansion of public and private higher education in Kenya and the East African region. In response to this rapid growth, the Kenyan government has established a number of legal bodies, notably the Commission for Higher Education in Kenya, to oversee the

---

8. Wycliffe Otieno and Mary Ngolovi, "Country Profile: Kenya," prepared for the Program in International Higher Education Finance at the Graduate School of Education, University of Buffalo, 2002; rev. eds. 2006, 2009. Accessed August 22, 2012. www.gse.buffalo.edu/org/intheredfinance/files/Country_Profiles/Africa/Kenya.pdf.

9. For the case of Kenya in particular, where faculty and student strikes were particularly devastating in 2003 and 2004, see Wycliffe Otieno and Daniel Levy, "Public Disorder, Private Boons? Inter-sectoral Dynamics Illustrated in the Kenyan Case," Program for Research on Private Higher Education (PROPHE), PROPHE Working Paper no. 9, Albany, State University of New York, July 2007. Accessed at the website of PROPHE, http://www.albany.edu/dept/eaps/prophe.

This critical state of affairs in African higher education is frequently recounted, but see especially Akilagpa Sawyerr, "Challenges Facing African Universities: Selected Issues," *African Studies Review* 47:1 (April 2004): 1-59; Damtew Teferra and Philip G. Altbach, "African Higher Education: Challenges for the 21st Century," *Higher Education* 47:1 (January 2004): 21-50; and Kingsley Banya and Juliet Elu, "The World Bank and Financing Higher Education in Sub-Saharan Africa," *Higher Education* 42:1 (January 2001): 1-34.

establishment and maintenance of standards of private universities. Kenya was the first country in East Africa to establish private universities. Today, there are more than eighty-five private universities in sub-Saharan Africa. More than half of these have arisen since 1990, and as we have seen, the great majority of them, at least seventy now, are Christian.[10] However, private universities remain small. In Kenya, where they outnumber the roster of state universities seventeen to seven, private colleges and universities account for about 18 percent of the total number of students in university education.[11] There is a growing scholarly literature on the role of private higher education from Kenya, as one might infer from the reference notes herein.[12] These studies address important structural and contextual questions such as the reasons for the rise of private education, its issues of quality, finance, curriculum, and professoriate, and this chapter reflects on several of these matters as well. But the current literature does not raise some of the questions that are especially compelling for those who inhabit these institutions. So this chapter emphasizes the internal character of these institutions, how well they embody their aims and purposes in offering an education that is distinctive because of its Christian foundations, and how they sustain those foundations in a competitive religious, political, and ideological climate.

10. "Sub-Saharan Africa's Private and Public Higher Education Shares (2002-2009)," PROPHE Table 117, accessed at the website of the PROPHE, http://www.albany.edu/dept/eaps/prophe.

11. Okwach Abagi, Juliana Nzomo, and Wycliffe Otieno, *Private Higher Education in Kenya: New Trends in Higher Education* (Paris: International Institute for Educational Planning, 2005), p. 31. See also Otieno, "Private Provision and Its Changing Interface with Public Higher Education: The Case of Kenya," *Journal of Higher Education in Africa* 5:2-3 (2007): 173-196. See also Faith Nguru, "What Can Christian Higher Education Do to Promote Educational Well-Being in Africa?" in *Christian Higher Education in the Global Context*, ed. Nicholas Lantinga (Sioux Center, Iowa: Dordt College Press, 2006), pp. 135-150.

12. Professor Wycliffe Otieno of Kenyatta University has led in this fresh outpouring. See, e.g., Abagi, Nzomo, and Otieno, *Private Higher Education in Kenya;* Otieno, "Private Provision"; and Otieno and Levy, "Public Disorder, Private Boons?" See also Jane Osongo, "The Growth of Private Universities in Kenya: Implications for Gender Equity in Higher Education," *Journal of Higher Education in Africa* 5:2-3 (2007): 111-133. Three broader studies that use Kenyan examples are Semeon Mulatu, "Transitioning from a Theological College to a Christian University in East African Context: A Multi-Case Study" (Ph.D. dissertation, Southern Baptist Theological Seminary, 2012); Bev Thayer, "Private Higher Education in Africa: Six Country Case Studies," in *African Higher Education: An International Reference Handbook*, ed. Damtew Teferra and Philip G. Altbach (Bloomington: Indiana University Press, 2003), pp. 53-60; and Grace Karram, "The International Connections of Religious Higher Education in Sub-Saharan Africa: Rationales and Implications," *Journal of Studies in International Education* 15:5 (2011): 487-499.

The seventeen Christian universities in Kenya have strong historic and in several cases ongoing ties to Western churches and mission-sending agencies. Whether originally founded as Bible colleges or seminaries, or training institutes in practical trades, or in some recent cases as more comprehensive universities, they have enjoyed external funding support and the services of expatriate, "missionary" teachers and administrators. One notable exception is Kabarak University, which has an explicitly religious mandate but was founded by the second president of Kenya, H. E. Daniel Arap Moi. As the table below suggests, they are a diverse group, some denominational, some ecumenical and interdenominational, and some nondenominational. Their enrollments are not large in comparison to state-sponsored institution, but they are several times larger than the traditional Bible college or theological seminary, from which base most have developed. Their approximated enrollment figures, noted below, range from 220 to 11,500 in the diploma, undergraduate, master's, and doctoral programs.

Table 1. Kenyan Christian Universities and Colleges

University	Charter	Original Name	Established	Enrollment*
Catholic University of Eastern Africa (CUEA)	1992	Catholic Higher Institute of Eastern Africa	1984	7,000
University of Eastern Africa, Baraton	1992	Baraton Animal Husbandry Research Station	1980	2,400
Daystar University	1994	Daystar University College	1984	4,500
Africa Nazarene University	1994	African Nazarene University	1994	3,000
Scott Christian University	1997	Scott Theological College	1962	500
Kabarak University	2001	Kabarak University	2001	5,000
Strathmore University	2002	Strathmore College	1961	6,000
Pan Africa Christian University	2006	Pan Africa Christian College	1978	2,400

University	Charter	Original Name	Established	Enrollment*
Kenya Methodist University	2006	Kenya Methodist University	1997	11,500
Adventist University of Africa	2006	Adventist University of Africa	2005	350
Presbyterian University of East Africa	2007	Presbyterian College	1994	3,000
St. Paul's University	2007	Divinity School, St. Paul's United Theological College	1903	3,000
Africa International University	2011	Nairobi Evangelical Graduate School of Theology	1983	600
International Leadership University	N/A	Nairobi International School of Theology	1981	250
The East Africa School of Theology	N/A	The East Africa School of Theology	1979	500
Kenya Highlands Evangelical University	2011	Kenya Highlands Bible School	1932	220
Kenya Anglican University	N/A	Kenya Anglican University	2011	N/A

*Approximate figures for 2012— excluding affiliate colleges — gathered from key administrators

As the table makes clear, most of the institutions began as Bible colleges and/or theological institutions and achieved university status sometime in the last twenty years upon the award of a university charter. Of necessity, many of them had to change their names. However, a change of name does not necessarily mean a change in the image of the institution. In an environment where publicly funded higher education has been the norm, people identify with the more well-known public universities in terms of what is perceived to be solid academic training. Unfortunately, whether true or not, the small theological seminaries and Bible colleges had the reputation of being places where students enrolled who could not get into a university. In that context, these institutions' desire to create a new brand or image and to shed their earlier identities is understandable. But this re-branding effort creates concern amongst the traditional constituents that their institutions are becoming more secular in the process, and it has not brought an immediate change to the larger public's perception about quality.

Several of these institutions will be used as case studies to illustrate the bumpy road that most of the Christian Higher Education (CHE) institutions are taking as they play their role in the African Christian educational enterprise.

Daystar University was co-founded in 1964 in Bulawayo, Zimbabwe, by Dr. S. E. Mutsoko Pheko, a political refugee from South Africa, and Dr. Donald and Mrs. Faye K. Smith, an American missionary couple. They established a Christian publishing and media research ministry under the name Daystar Publications and Daystar Communications. As early as 1971, this agency began to offer training in communications, a five-week intensive course. Daystar eventually moved to Nairobi in 1973 and established a small campus in downtown Nairobi. In 1976 it offered a two-year tertiary diploma in Christian communications. Two years later, in collaboration with Wheaton College, in Illinois, Daystar began a two-year master's degree program in communications and Christian ministries. In 1984, with the collaboration of Messiah College in Pennsylvania, Daystar began a four-year bachelor's degree program with a small variety of major concentrations. Prior to 1985 when the Commission for Higher Education was created with the mandate to accredit private universities, and until Daystar received its charter, it offered the bachelor's degrees of Messiah College, Grantham, Pennsylvania, and the master's degrees of Wheaton College, Wheaton, Illinois.[13] These two American Christian liberal arts colleges extended their human resources and curriculum development expertise to the budding institution in a manner that laid strong foundations as well as opened up opportunities for student and staff exchange programs. The sharing of God's resources globally appears a good biblical principle to apply even in the educational sector. In 1994 Daystar was granted a Kenyan university charter, which enabled it to offer a wide array of diploma and degree programs.

A variety of questions emerge as these institutions rise up as (or are transformed into) universities, especially in a context where the state was once the sole founder of universities. What is the meaning of a "Christian university"? Is this identity dependent on the founding vision and mission? Is it dependent on its articulation in its university charter? Does the policy on admitting Christian students or its faculty and staff hiring practices matter? Is it dependent on the teaching-learning environment being Christ-centered? And how should

---

13. *Operations Report: All the Important Facts about Daystar University: Situation as of March 31, 1997,* a document co-prepared by Daystar University staff and the SF Foundation, p. 5.

such an institution be sustained? Should Christian institutions accept funding from all types of foundations, or should supporting and collaborating bodies be subject to scrutiny to ascertain their commitment to the cause of Christ? Kenya Highlands Evangelical University, which existed for many years as a Bible college, addresses some of these questions up front. On its public web pages, it explains:

> The distinction between a Christian University and a non-Christian University is found in the life styles and the approach to academics. KHEU, as a Christian University, endeavours to educate the head, the heart and the hands, while a non Christian University focuses on human reason as the sole power for doing and deciding on issues. A Christian University depends on God as the guide to reason and its activities.[14]

Even when they have clear founding principles, Kenyan Christian universities have struggled over how these principles should be manifested in operations. The matter of student admission is one controverted issue among them. In the prior lives of many of these universities as seminaries for educating clergy, it virtually went without saying that the students should all be Christians. But when the educational purposes broaden, what does that have to do with the personal Christian faith and character of the students? Should Christian universities admit only Christians into their programs? Should they allow a given proportion of the student population to be people of other faiths, or should they not restrict their admission procedures according to student religiosity, but make it a point to evangelize as they educate? It is not clear whether all African Christian institutions of higher learning have formal admission policies that address the question of who should be the recipient of CHE, but in practice three basic approaches appear: (1) admitting professing Christians only, (2) allowing a proportion of non-Christians to enroll, or (3) offering admissions with no religious criteria. These positions follow analogies, implicit if not explicit, drawn from other Christian ministries.

Churches and Christian hospitals, to cite two examples, do not restrict admittance to Christians only. They are open to all, they welcome all, and they hope to serve all in Christ's name. Yet they also encourage their guests to make faith commitments. Might not a church-founded university have the same approach to student admissions? We find that Christian universities with

14. http://www.khbc.ac.ke/.

these more open admissions policies hope to influence and structure campus life in Christian directions by requiring that students sign codes of conduct, and requiring attendance at chapel sessions regardless of religious affiliation. These conditions apply, for example, at both the University of Eastern Africa Baraton (Adventist) and African Nazarene University.

Daystar University, which is a nondenominational evangelical institution, has a "Christians only" admissions policy. In its charter, awarded by the government in 1994, it clearly states its position: "A member of the University shall profess personal faith in Jesus Christ as Lord and Saviour, accept the University's Christian philosophy as provided for under Section 5 (1) of the Charter and satisfy the Council of his soundness in faith and practice of the Christian doctrine demonstrated through acts of justice, mercy and love in the Church and society."[15]

This policy of "membership" holds for students, professors, and administrative staff alike. Students too are members, not merely guests, so the standards of upholding the university's deepest beliefs and purposes apply to them as well. Potential students in particular are required to complete a form in which they respond to the question "do you acknowledge Jesus Christ as your personal Saviour?" Further, they are expected to explain in a paragraph what their relationship with Christ means. An endorsement from a Christian leader or church pastor is also expected. Where the admission committee believes that the responses provided do not conform to the vision and mission of the university, students are not admitted. To confirm this commitment, students are made to sign a statement of assent. This selection process does not always yield the desired results, as there are some students who join the university and come later to a personal faith in Jesus Christ, or graduate without ever coming to that point in their life.

Two analogies seem to be at work in Daystar's policy here. The first and most obvious is "membership." Instead of saying that students are like visitors who are welcomed at a church or patients admitted to a Christian hospital, Daystar is saying that they are more like church members, who are full and responsible enlistees in the community. The second analogy is more implicit. Daystar started as a training institute for parachurch workers in communications. The training being offered was for Christian activists to accomplish Christian purposes. Even though Daystar now educates students for a wide variety of professions in society and not only for church and parachurch work,

---

15. Government of Kenya, Charter for Daystar University: The Universities Act Cap 2108, Nairobi, Kenya.

it is saying, in effect, that its main purpose still is to prepare its graduates for Christian service, albeit in non-church professions. Hence it has a policy of a Christian education, for Christians, equipping them to serve Christ and humanity, out in society.

So how do these policies play out in practice? First, Daystar's policy is not foolproof. Daystar University has experienced instances when church leaders give a "false testimony" regarding potential students' spiritual standing. They often do so to please the students' parents, who may happen to be prominent church supporters. On the other hand, they may not wish to be blamed for denying a young person an opportunity for an education. Such is the strong sense of community and high value of education at all costs in a nation where university education is at a premium. Daystar intends that its graduates will engage in transforming society by applying a biblical worldview to all of life. Students tend to come to the university when their basic worldview is already formed and they do not necessarily go through experiences that can reform their worldview. If they come as Christians under false pretenses, they may well bring disrepute to the whole concept of Christian higher education by displaying values and engaging in practices that make a mockery of the ideals of evangelical Christianity.

Daystar University's categorical position has been challenged in some quarters by those who believe that it discriminates against people of other faiths. Such people believe that qualified students have a constitutional right to access education in any institution. Yet it seems clear that the government acknowledges that privately founded universities may establish special standards and purposes. The university charter, which mandates the university to "train Christian servant leaders," was carefully reviewed and awarded by the government and therefore Daystar can confidently proceed with its mandate.

Even so, the specifically Christian mandates and stipulations of Kenyan Christian universities raise a variety of issues. Institutions that define CHE as providing education to Christians by Christians not only have to deal with issues of student admissions or the hiring of faculty (at Daystar, all faculty must profess Christian faith and subscribe to university values and philosophy). They also have to deal with the tension relating to research and funding agencies that do not understand or appreciate this position. In recent years, Kenya's political climate has become increasingly tense in religious terms. A vocal and politically adept Muslim minority has won major concessions in the recently approved constitution, and most Kenyan CHE leaders expect increasing pressure to admit Muslim students. The advice that the leaders of the more established institutions give to those who are just starting out is to make sure that specifically Christian aims and operating principles are written into the university charters.[16]

In Kenya and probably most of the African nations today, a legal provision to admit Christians only or to boldly state and pursue Christian purposes in other ways is still possible. The integration of Christian faith and scholarship in very direct ways can go forward freely. In many parts of Africa today Christian educational entrepreneurs and sponsoring churches can and should take this golden opportunity to establish strong Christian institutions before the window of opportunity is closed by public sentiment and policies that are not sympathetic to the idea of Christian higher education.

St. Paul's University illustrates another issue in Kenyan CHE: the "identity crisis" that haunts many former theological schools that are now more comprehensive universities. St. Paul's was begun as an Anglican divinity school that was established in 1903 by the Church Missionary Society in Frere Town, Mombasa, on Kenya's coast, to train church leaders for the church in Africa. It moved to its current main campus in Limuru, nineteen miles (thirty kilometers) outside Nairobi, in 1930. In 1955 the school changed its focus to become St. Paul's United Theological College, adding to its Anglican heritage the Methodist, Presbyterian, and Reformed Churches. In 1993 the National Council of Churches in Kenya became the fifth sponsoring partner, and St. Paul's also began to bring in leaders from African Instituted Churches to access higher education. The aim was to train African men and women to face the challenges of the church and society in a post-colonial age. Some of the notable graduates, like Archbishop David Gitari, Bishop Alexander Muge, Bishop Henry Okullu, and Dr. Timothy Njoya, became great national champions — and in some cases martyrs — for social justice and political integrity.[17]

For one hundred years St. Paul's trained church ministers, but in the last ten years it has expanded from offering degrees and diplomas in theology to other degrees in business, communication, information technology, and development studies. It has gone further to affiliate private secular business and computer diploma awarding institutions. St. Paul's growth is evident since taking this direction; it has opened up campuses in the Nairobi Central Business District, Machakos, and Nakuru. St. Paul's once enrolled about 150 seminarians, on a small and close-knit campus. Now it enrolls some 3,000

16. Leah Marangu, "Challenges with Government and Accreditation," presentation at the conference "Challenges for Emerging Christian Universities," Athi River, Kenya, May 8-11, 2012.

17. Karanja, "Evangelical Attitudes toward Democracy in Kenya," pp. 79-84.

students, including 1,500 in the predominantly commuter campus in Nairobi. It has twenty different degree concentrations on offer for students.

A very natural question for leaders of institutions that have been transformed so radically in purpose and patterns of instruction is "what makes all of this Christian?" When St. Paul's was a small seminary, the answers were rather obvious. The students were all, presumably, devoted Christians with a definite call to Christian ministry, being supported by their respective churches to take courses in Christian theology and related topics. They were also a largely residential community with common worship. Under the new university structure, the "faculty of Theology" has more professors and twice as many students, but they are but one part of a transformed institution. The ages and vocations of the students have changed, the subject matter has changed, and the campuses are dispersed. So what makes St. Paul's Christian? Do non-theological topics make the institution more secular? The leaders of St. Paul's — Vice Chancellor Joseph Galgalo and Deputy Vice Chancellor Academic Esther Mombo — are Christian theologians. They say that even though their programs lean heavily toward business and other "practical" fields, such as agriculture, computer science, social work, and teacher education, they are trying to incorporate theological and Christian "boundaries" into all that they teach. All programs have common "core" courses, one in Christian worldview, one in Christianity and health (with HIV/AIDS emphasis), and one on Christianity and the environment. Yet the leaders admit that most of the courses are staffed with part-time teachers and these instructors do not receive much guidance in teaching from a Christian perspective.[18]

The patterns of development at St. Paul's are now being replicated at a number of other schools of ministry. Nairobi International School of Theology (NIST) is seeking a charter to become International Leadership University, and the Nairobi Evangelical Graduate School of Theology (NEGST) recently was chartered as Africa International University (AIU). These two nondenominational theological seminaries have taken on names that mute the "Christian" label; "international" and "leadership" labels appear to be more saleable. Pan Africa Christian College, a Pentecostal Bible and ministry training school founded by missionaries from the Pentecostal Assemblies of Canada (PAOC), has been chartered as Pan Africa Christian University. It is currently co-sponsored by Christ Is the Answer Ministries, now the major stakeholder, plus the Pentecostal Assemblies of God and PAOC. The change

18. Joel Carpenter, notes from a conversation with Joseph Galgalo and Esther Mombo, St. Paul's University, Limuru, May 5, 2012; shared with the author.

of ownership to a local church was required by the Commission for Higher Education before the award of the charter. This regulatory body insists that local ownership of private universities is critical for their sustainability. Scott Theological College in Kenya was chartered as a university several years ago but retained its name and to a great extent its traditional course offerings and ethos. Interestingly, along with an expanded curriculum will come a name change, to Scott Christian University. Scott, evidently, seeks to retain something of its longstanding reputation in the transition. This business of labeling has some ambiguity to it. Reverend Tom Obengo, who has served as a registrar in two such institutions, notes that

> The name of an institution can hamper its growth. Marketing of its non-theological courses becomes difficult and so does the way the job market interprets its qualifications. Change of name to a neutral one helps some people become more comfortable. Many potential students [however] do not mind a name that has a Christian tag, e.g. Uganda Christian University, provided they get professional training.[19]

Beyond the matter of naming, leaders from Scott, NIST, and AIU/NEGST joined with other seminary and university leaders from around Africa recently at a conference, "Challenges for Emerging Christian Universities," held at Athi River, Kenya, May 8-11, 2012, to address the greater challenges they face as they transition toward university status and structure. They reviewed a recent study of the outlook and concerns of five East African institutional leaders who were engaging in the transition. For leaders embarking on what appeared to many outsiders as bold new ventures, there were some remarkable signals of hesitation and misgivings. It was clear from this survey that while the leaders of these new universities expressed positive hopes for a more comprehensive educational ministry to their societies, most of them felt that they had been pressured in this new direction. Their church constituencies and sometimes their national accreditors had pushed them to broaden their curricula to university status. They also felt compelled by the chronic problems of sustainability experienced by small theological schools continent-wide. It would be too cynical to say that the leaders wanted simply to cash in on the great demand for more undergraduate education, but these "push" factors seemed at least as powerful as motives for becoming universities, as did the more positive calls to broader service. It was clear from this study, and from the conversation

19. Reverend Tom Obengo, interviewed by the author in Nairobi, March 3, 2010.

at the meeting, that these leaders were quite anxious about how they would withstand the various pressures to secularize: from the government, from the student body, and from the curriculum itself. How could they remain a Christian community of learning while teaching predominantly nonreligious topics to students whose own faith commitments were less certain, and in a political environment that was less favorable to sustaining Christian purpose in institutions? That was the greatest question of the hour for these leaders.[20]

Identity

The developments noted above illustrate the fact that African institutions of higher learning cannot pretend to be intellectual sanctuaries engaging in academics for knowledge' s sake. They are also dynamic social institutions struggling to survive financially as they prepare graduates to meet market needs in an East African context. It appears that most people's perception of what Christian higher education is or should be in Kenya is thoroughly framed by this secular vision of their purpose. The expectation from the society is that universities exist to be engines for economic and social progress, including the provision of essential training for the continent's future leaders in the public and private sectors. Universities' religious affiliations seem to many to be slightly irrelevant. They have in effect segmented and segregated life into a variety of realms, with the spiritual realm not having any influence in the academic, intellectual, and professional realms. Christian scholars and administrators wrestle against this dominant perspective since they feel called to bring wholeness and authenticity into all realms by asserting Christ's lordship over all, including issues of identity and justice.

The story of Christian higher education in South Africa provides an example of what Kenyan Christian university educators hope to avoid. Guided by a misuse of Reformed theology, South African higher education took the notion of separate spheres of life to include segregation by race and ethnicity, even in higher education. Paul Zeleza reports that very early on, some institutions were set up for the English settlers (South African College, later University of Cape Town, 1829); for Afrikaner settlers (Stellenbosch Gymnasium, later Stellenbosch University, 1918); and the Lovedale Missionary Institute for

20. Mulatu, "Transitioning from a Theological College to a Christian University in East African Context: A Multi Case Study," presented at the conference "Challenges for Emerging African Christian Universities," Athi River, Kenya, May 8-11, 2012.

Africans was created in 1841.[21] Racial segregation is certainly inimical to the development of the hope and unity that Christianity stands for. The universities in Kenya have seen riots and violence in recent years that reflected ethnic rivalries and conflict. They should provide us with a sobering reminder of the deep problems resulting from any policy that segregates some people from others and some values from others as well. Negative ethnicity is not confined to public institutions. The governance structures of Christian higher education institutions are staffed by individuals from polarized ethnic communities. Some have not yet overcome the demons of ethnicity and this colors their leadership practices in such institutions. For example, some Christian leaders may be driven by their ethnic communities to appoint some of their own to positions of authority regardless of their competencies in performing given tasks. This definitely does not contribute to a productive environment for Christian scholarship and service. Christian universities are not immune from such conflicts; those founded by denominations with certain ethnic ties need especially to be on their guard in Kenya.

Governance

Human resource experts say that succession management is critical to any organization. In their view the best systems are developmentally oriented rather than simply replacement oriented given that succession planning does the job of monitoring the succession process. Most of the Christian universities are very young and are still being run by the founders or appointees of the sponsoring agencies. As the vision bearers retire, there is a likelihood of a derailed vision if the appointing authorities do not ensure that new leaders are being developed.

A major characteristic of the succession management process is planning and staff development for leadership transitions. Having someone to step into an important vacancy is a critical measure of the effectiveness of succession management. A recent example in Kenya serves to show the importance of smooth transitions and proper succession management that CHE institutions ought to consider seriously if they are to achieve sustainability, credibility, and good will in society.

The Business Daily, April 7, 2010, ran a banner headline, "Wrangles Shock Hits Methodist University." The story that was featured on all the television

21. Zeleza, "Beyond Afropessimism."

and radio stations highlighted difficulties that plague institutions of higher learning — that of student unrest, abrupt closures, and subsequent uncertainty regarding degree completion.[22] In the case of the Kenya Methodist University several pertinent areas in the succession management were highlighted by an educational researcher and the top leaders of the regulatory body — the Commission for Higher Education. The researcher noted that conflicts over who does what between the divisions of the university are rampant in Kenyan institutions of higher learning. The commissioners reported in similar fashion: "Leadership and succession battles are common in our universities . . . they are likely to hurt the quality of governance and learning in affected institutions."[23] In this particular scenario, teaching and administrative staff were locked up in a management feud, pitting the sponsors against the senate. The university management accused the sponsors of acting in breach of the charter through active participation in important decisions such as introduction of new courses, physical expansion, and staff movement. This was not an isolated case. For careful planning Kenyan Christian universities need clear and detailed structuring of duties, powers, and procedures, and prayerful selection of leaders.

Finance

Partnership for higher education in Africa has been provided by several international and governmental agencies. The World Bank and the International Monetary Fund (IMF) have shaped the sector by periodic provision and withdrawal of funds. Organizations such as the Japanese International Co-operation Agency (JICA), the German Academic Exchange Service (Deutscher Akademischer Austausch Dienst, or DAAD), the Ford Foundation, the Rockefeller Foundation, and the Carnegie Foundation, among others, have contributed financial and technical resources for initiating reforms in the universities. It is apparent that the dependency they have created provides a false impression of exactly how much scholarly activities actually cost. Christian institutions of higher learning that do not normally benefit directly from these development partners may benchmark their activities and outputs against their public university counterparts to their detriment. The global ranking of universities, for example, is more often than not based on their research

22. http://www.businessdailyafrica.com. Accessed April 7, 2010.
23. Everest Standa, former secretary of the Commission of Higher Education, Kenya. Cited in http://www.marsgroupkenya.org/multimedia/cache/cache. Accessed March 14, 2012.

web presence and may serve to unnecessarily discourage faculty and staff on Christian campuses. Probably a different ranking criterion specifically created for such institutions that depend on fee tuition and little other support should be created for Christian-based colleges. These could include assessment of teaching effectiveness, quality of campus life, student engagement, and corporate social responsibilities, among others.

Resources mobilization functions and structures of most CHE institutions are poorly developed apart from the periodic fundraising efforts made by the heads of these institutions when they travel abroad. Few personnel are recruited or trained for such functions. The Council for Advancement and Support of Education (CASE), a U.S.-based organization that focuses on fundraising, outlined several constraints and causes of resistance to fundraising in particular and advancement activities in African universities:

- The presence of council members from yester years
- The belief that the government can fund education (including the universities) if the economy is managed better and corruption eliminated
- The belief that funds not spent on academic activities and university services are a waste
- The suspicions of university communities about the motives behind promotion of advancement activities
- The belief that governments are trying to divest universities of their responsibilities
- Suspicion about motives of funding agencies, especially IMF and World Bank
- The conservatism of university communities and the prominence of Ivory Tower mentality[24]

Christian higher education institutions, being privately funded, need to interrogate the values of their council members. Probably most of them graduated from the public universities in the days of heavy government funding and therefore do not support advancement efforts. To a very large extent, Christian universities have not yet embraced the idea of engaging in income generation activities (IGAs). They have not aggressively sought to commercialize their intellectual property rights and this has left them more impoverished. The

24. Roger Makanjuola, paper presented at the Council for Advancement and Support of Education's Educational Advancement Workshop, Kampala, Uganda, October 21-23, 2008, pp. 23-28.

fundraising and development functions are in their infancy and much more needs to be done to assure their sustainability. Daystar University is in the process of incorporating a company whose proceeds are expected to support the academic and spiritual nurture programs of the university. Uganda Christian University is doing something quite similar. These early efforts, however, are yet to be documented. If successful, they may point a way to address issues of pervasive poverty among learners and institutions. Public universities have been more successful in IGAs. Both the University of Nairobi and Makerere University (in Kampala) have successful private companies.

Teaching and Learning

The majority of East African higher education institutions employ the traditional mode of teaching. Students attend lectures, take notes, and sit for examinations. The large numbers of students for each unit often make it impossible for lecturers to engage in better teaching-learning methods. These are methods geared toward a shift from the importance of acquiring a particular body of knowledge to that of developing the skills for acquiring new knowledge and the capacity for using knowledge as a resource in addressing societal needs.

Christian higher education should provide teachers with skills for deepening students' learning, including research-based curricula that push students to inquire and investigate. In turn these graduates will be prepared to move on to postgraduate levels and thus become suitable candidates for professors in the CHE sector. Molding young Christians to embrace "the outrageous idea of Christian Scholarship"[25] will probably not be as difficult as attempting to mold mature professionals, such as those who populate the evening or parallel programs of some Christian universities in Africa.

Many private universities in Africa rely heavily on part-time teachers. There is a shortage of qualified and experienced academics in both public and private universities. According to N. V. Varghese of the International Institute for Educational Planning, relying on the teaching staff from public universities is a good mechanism to ensure quality in teaching and savings in expenditure.[26] However, the question on the impact of such a practice on Christian

25. George M. Marsden, *The Outrageous Idea of Christian Scholarship* (New York: Oxford University Press, 1997).

26. N. V. Varghese, *Private Higher Education in Africa* (Paris: International Institute for Educational Planning, 2004), p. 18.

universities needs to be analyzed further. How easily can a professor coming over from the state-sponsored university switch from operating in a "faith-excluding mode" to an "integration of faith and knowledge mode"? Unless the Christian lecturer has been firmly grounded in the vision and values of integrally Christian learning, the transition in the classroom may be quite difficult to execute. Indeed, one study of early teaching at a Christian university in Uganda suggested that students' development as Christian thinkers and actors had been changed very little by the teaching there. Professors, many of them part-time, had very little idea of what a Christian perspective on their discipline might be.[27]

Fortunately, some organizations are beginning to take up this concern in Africa's rapidly growing Christian university sector. The Christian Higher Education Faculty Development Network (CHEFDN)[28] is one such organization that is seeking to address the issues of building capacity for lecturers in Christian universities. It has several objectives among which are to

- enhance professional teaching skills of faculty members
- provide a communication structure for sharing professional development resources
- offer faculty development consultancy services

According to Charles Kingsbury, CHEFDN has conducted several workshops, mostly in Anglophone African institutions, with very positive results. The thrust in the training is to encourage critical transformative teaching methodologies as opposed to the "banking" style of teaching, whereby students are supposed to receive and store "knowledge deposits" from lecturers.[29] In addition, the International Association for the Promotion of Christian Higher Education (IAPCHE) recently opened its Africa regional office in Kenya and has been sponsoring faculty enrichment programs in East Africa. We expect that it will play an important role in developing and retraining

27. Joseph J. Owor, "Faith and Learning: The Impact of Uganda Christian University Programmes on the Spiritual Development of Its Students: The Case of Business Faculty Students," presentation at the 20th Annual Conference of the Christian Business Faculty Association, San Antonio, Texas, October 28-30, 2004.

28. Author's interview with Charles Kingsbury, coordinator of the Centre for Excellence in Teaching and Learning, Daystar University, Nairobi, March 2010.

29. Charles Edward Kingsbury, "Barriers and Facilitators to Teaching for Critical Reflective Thought in Christian Higher Education in Anglophone Africa" (Ph.D. dissertation, Florida State University College of Education, 2002).

faculty who are more intellectually attuned to Christian perspectives for the Christian universities.

If Christian higher education is to improve in its grasp and delivery of learning in a Christian mode and from a Christian worldview, it should not separate itself from the efforts of Christian schooling at the primary and secondary levels. There is a burgeoning movement among the churches across Africa to develop new Christian schools, and there is a strategic need to invest resources, including human resources, toward the development of Christian primary and secondary education.[30] Graduates from such schools would populate African Christian universities, which in turn would train educators for the schools. Christian universities would see improvements in the quality of academic preparation and character formation in their enrollees, and Christian schools would see an improvement in the academic quality and Christian vision and character of their teachers. Unfortunately, not many of the institutions have made teacher education a priority. To do so in many places runs against the popular prejudice regarding the teaching profession and in some places against the structured in institutional separation of teacher education from the mainstream universities. Christian universities could do something countercultural here, by elevating teachers' professional development to a place of high energy and honor among their programs.

Information and Communication Technology

There is a great possibility that information and communication technology (ICT) can be used to address some of the issues of access and quality that face African CHE. In different parts of the continent, several ICT entities are spearheading development on this front. The Kenya Education Network (KENET),[31] for example, recently conducted a survey of fifty East African universities on the use of ICT for teaching, learning, research, and management. The survey contained seventeen indicators grouped into five categories: network access, networked campus, networked learning, networked society, and institutional ICT strategy. Among the universities surveyed were eight CHE institutions. The study selection criteria were a student population greater

30. Nguru, "What Can Christian Higher Education Do to Promote Educational Well-being in Africa?"

31. KENET, "E-readiness Survey of East African Universities," http://eready.kenet.or.ke. Accessed October 28, 2009.

than 1,000, more than five degree programs, at least more than one science-technology degree program, and more than two PCs for every 100 students with internet bandwidth of > = 128 Kps.

The main conclusion of the survey was that the higher education community, especially the university community in Kenya, is ready to use increased ICT for learning, teaching, research, and management. However, the institutional leadership (drawn mainly from the older generations that have little exposure to ICT) does not seem to recognize ICT as a strategic priority for transforming teaching, learning, and research. Consequently, the institutions are allocating some operational budget toward ICT, but are not investing adequately in campus networks. They lack strategies for building the capacity of faculty to use ICT effectively to support their teaching and research activities. In addition, most of the universities have not automated their operational systems and processes, including library operations.

The results showed that it was the very large and well-established universities that were effectively transforming learning via ICT. These were mainly in the public university category. CHE institutions could then be said to be lagging behind in the use of ICT, a serious need that the sponsoring churches or individuals should take note of. This lack of ICT facilitation leads to weak scholarly output at the regional and global levels. ICT needs and opportunities exist in a radically globalized field, and it would seem to be a natural area for Kenyan Christian universities' partners in the global North to do more as supportive partners. Few things would do more to revolutionize scholarship and teaching in Kenyan Christian higher education than more robust access and use of ICT.

Conclusion and Way Forward

Looking back to the past five decades, one can perceive that higher education in general, and public universities in particular, have gone through several critical phases in their development. These phases are closely intertwined with the socioeconomic and political developments in the various countries. They have obviously had an impact on the manner in which CHE institutions have been established and run. Initially the institutions of higher learning were founded to produce bureaucrats to serve the colonial governments — at the expense of educating science-driven technologists to serve in agricultural and industrial sectors or creative professionals to serve in other fields. To date most countries have not achieved food security and are still dependent on imported technologies.

The majority of Christian universities in Kenya, being privately funded, have begun academic programs that are not capital intensive enough to produce graduates who can address all of these needs. They have produced individuals with skills to serve as teachers, pastors, youth workers, attorneys, journalists, and business entrepreneurs in various fields, however. This trend is likely to continue for some years. The hope is that in the future there will be a better critical alignment between the type of curricula and skill endowments of graduates from universities and the needs of the nations of Africa. Curricula in Kenya and across Africa should address African realities — such as chronic problems in health, income, employment, leadership, urbanization, international exploitation, basic education and literacy, war and violence, ethnicity, gender, and family integrity. Moreover, the creative arts and recreational opportunities should also not be ignored, as the biblical vision of human flourishing clearly shows.

When the great German poet and intellectual prophet Johann Wolfgang von Goethe visited the University of Tübingen in 1797, he wrote to the Duke of Weimar:

> The academy is very weak, even though there are many meritorious professors and an enormous sum of money is spent on the various faculties; yet the old form contradicts the progress of life, their efforts do not fit together and they are dominated by the concern of how to keep the institutions in the same old rut.[32]

Kenyan Christian universities are not suffering the problems of old and traditional institutions, but when it comes to necessary reforms, such as establishing a Christian foundation and outlook, these relatively new institutions still need to overcome the inertia that pulls at higher education more generally. The fact is that African Christian universities currently function in very difficult circumstances in terms of both the social, economic, and political problems facing the continent and in the context of globalization, where ideas, people, institutional forms, and funding fly about so rapidly and can so easily pass by those who are isolated.

So the road to future success will not be an easy one. Christian educational leaders Samson Makhado of South Africa and Dean Spalding of Australia noted that networking existing institutions, training leaders, and developing

---

32. Quoted in Cay Etzold, "Quality Assurance through Curriculum Design: A Case Study of Higher Education Management in East Africa," paper presented at the International Conference on Higher Education Management, Nairobi, Kenya, March 22-24, 2003.

teachers and context-based Christian curriculum are huge challenges in Africa. In some respects the even more basic challenges, they said, are the needs to reconcile unhelpful dichotomies between theory and practice, real-world and laboratory/classroom experiences, and reason and faith.[33] The goal of Christian higher education is not merely spirituality. Neither is the goal to exclude different types of knowledge beyond theology. The goal is a form of education that gives authoritative place to Jesus Christ and to the Bible in its understanding of the world and the human condition. The commitment then is to glorify God and accomplish his purposes in the universe. Such education also recognizes and seeks to embrace the view that human knowledge, culture, and experience all live, move, and have their being in God.[34] It is within the context of these African challenges that seventeen Kenyan Christian universities are seeking to serve and flourish. The relationship between such organizations as the Council of Christian Colleges and Universities (CCCU), the International Association for the Promotion of Christian Higher Education (IAPCHE), the Association of Christian Schools International (ACSI), and local associations will play a significant role in the future of higher education in Kenya and beyond. Engaging with these global stakeholders will lead us to greater accountability and to all the resources in the Christian scholarly community worldwide.

Today we see before us in Kenya a growing, critical mass of educated Christians who can pay tuition fees for themselves, their children, and, we hope, for others. It is this rising potential constituency that Christian universities must serve if they will be able to progressively expand their niche and contribute to national development. May we have God's grace and power, then, to develop the institutional strength and integrity and the intellectual and spiritual depth to do our part.

33. Samson Makhado and Dean Spalding, "Challenges to Christian Educators in Southern Africa," www.transformingteachers.org. Accessed October 24, 2009.

34. James Kombo, "Christian Higher Education for Africa: Need, Relevance, and Value," http://www.iapche.org. Accessed October 28, 2009.

CHAPTER 3

Rise and Development of Christian Higher Education in China

Peter Tze Ming Ng

Introduction: To What Does "Christian Higher Education in China" Refer?

Robert Morrison, the first Protestant missionary from the London Missionary Society, arrived in Canton, China, in 1807. Morrison soon realized that the Chinese Qing government had prohibited all kinds of missionary activities within the country. He spent ten years exploring ways to launch long-term missionary work in China, and in 1817 he came up with a formal proposal known as the "Ultra-Ganges Mission Plan" in which one of the suggestions was to start an Anglo-Chinese college in Malacca, an outlying island south of China, while waiting for the opening of the country.[1] Defeats at the hands of Western powers forced the Qing government to sign the Treaty of Nanking in 1842, which, among other concessions, opened China to Western mission-

---

1. See William Milne, *A Retrospect of the First Ten Years of the Protestant Mission to China* (Malacca: Anglo-Chinese Press, 1820). Robert Morrison hoped that through the establishment of this Anglo-Chinese College, he could not only preach the gospel, but also promote Sino-Western cultural exchange, hence the name "Anglo-Chinese College" was given to this new school. See also Wu Yixiong, *Zai Zongjiao Yu Shisu Zhijian — Jidu Xinjiao Chuanjiaoshi Zai Huanan Yanhaide Zaoqi Huodong Yanjiu* (Guangzhou: Guangdong Educational Press, 2000), pp. 42-57. In the middle of the nineteenth century, Anglo-Chinese College became the first research center in Southeast Asia that had a clear consciousness of "glocalization." Indeed, Christian education in China is an excellent example for scholars to reflect on and to explore the subject of "glocalization" today. See also Peter Tze Ming Ng, *Quanqiu diyuhua shijiaoxia de Zhongguo Jidujiao Daxue* (Christian Higher Education in China — From the Perspective of Glocalization) (Taiwan: Cosmic Light Press, 2006).

aries. Hence, Christian missionaries began to realize Morrison's vision by establishing educational institutions in the China mainland, starting with the primary and secondary levels. This work was not without tensions, as some early missionaries were still hesitant to launch educational work in China. Missionaries like John Fryer, W. A. Martin, Young J. Allen, Timothy Richard, and Calvin Mateer all made much effort in convincing other missionaries and their missionary societies to establish an educational policy and invest in higher education in China.[2] It was only after the Boxer movement, however, that the missionary societies were willing to join hands together for the development of Christian higher education in China in the first two decades of the twentieth century.[3] So higher education institutions arose, built mainly for the purpose of providing a Western education within a heavily religious context. The twin goals of mission schools at primary and secondary levels were applied to higher education as well: the evangelization of the Chinese people, including the intellectuals, and the training of Christian leaders for the churches in China. These institutions were mostly situated in the major cities of the country; by the early 1940s, they were consolidated into thirteen Protestant universities that are well known in the missionary history of China. They are:

1. Yenching University in Peking (Beijing)
2. Shangtung Christian University (Cheeloo) in Jinan
3. University of Nanking (Jinling) in Nanking (Nanjing)
4. Ginling Women's College in Nanking (Nanjing)
5. University of Shanghai (Kujiang University) in Shanghai
6. St. John's University in Shanghai
7. Hangchow University in Hangchow (Hangzhou)
8. Soochow University (Dungwu) in Soochow (Suzhou)
9. Central China University (Huazhong) in Wuhan

2. See, e.g., the arguments for educational work in China, in *Records of the General Conference of the Protestant Missionaries of China held at Shanghai, 1877 & 1890*, 2 vols. (Shanghai: American Presbyterian Mission Press, 1878 and 1890). It was against this context that the idea of "education as a means for evangelization" evolved among the missionaries in late-nineteenth-century China. See, e.g., discussions in Peter Tze Ming Ng, *Changing Paradigms of Christian Higher Education in China, 1888-1950* (Lewiston: Edwin Mellen Press, 2002), pp. 2-5.

3. See the discussion in Peter Tze Ming Ng, "Some Scenarios of the Impact of Boxer Movement on the Work of Christian Education in China," in *The Boxer Movement and Christianity in China*, ed. Angelo S. Lazzarotto et al. (Taiwan: Fu Jen Catholic University Press, 2004), pp. 201-224.

10. West China Union University (Huaxi) in Chengdu
11. Fukien Christian University in Foochow (Fuzhou)
12. South China Women's University (Huanan) in Foochow (Fuzhou)
13. Lingnan University in Canton (Guangzhou)[4]

Challenges and End of Missionary Schools in the Twentieth Century

There is no doubt that early missionaries built schools as a means of reaching the Chinese people for evangelization. In order to strengthen religious education in their schools, they made religious courses compulsory for all students. Many missionaries were soon shocked, however, to realize that they were running schools in a context totally different from those in their home countries. The status of religion was obvious and significantly important in most of the contemporary Western societies from where the missionaries came. But China was a "non-Western," "non-Christian," and, in the Western sense, "nonreligious" country. The Chinese culture was such that religion had never been allowed a central or significant place in human and social life. For the Chinese, religion was both nonaggressive and nonexclusive. But the Christianity brought by the missionaries, argues the historian Jacques Gernet, was "a religion that changed customs, called into question accepted ideas and, above all, threatened to undermine existing situations."[5] Most missionaries believed that there was only one true religion and that Christianity was it. Christianity, they taught, demanded that its followers abandon their former beliefs and practices as proof of their conversion. This was what the Chinese people generally could not accept; their national culture accommodated several faiths. Chinese officials and intellectuals could not favor any form of religious curriculum in any schools in China, and most Chinese students were not interested in any religious courses offered by the missionary schools. Hence, Christian missionaries in China encountered cultural shock and great challenges to their educational assumptions. As a result, missionary educators had to rethink seriously their understanding of religion and religious education in a context such as the one they found in China.

The situation was even worse when the high tide of nationalism began with the May Fourth movement in China in 1919 and was followed in the

---

4. For a comprehensive study of these Christian colleges and universities, see Jessie Lutz, *China and Christian Colleges, 1850-1950* (Ithaca, N.Y.: Cornell University Press, 1971).

5. See Jacques Gernet, *China and the Christian Impact* (Cambridge: Cambridge University Press, 1985), p. 1.

mid-1920s with the strong opposition from Chinese intellectuals and gentry who launched the nationwide anti-Christian movements and the Restore Educational Rights Campaign throughout China. These movements targeted especially Christian higher education, which was widely criticized as a manifestation of Western imperialism. Such opposition consequently led to the issuance of government regulations for missionary schools in 1925 as follows:

a. Any institution of whatever grade established by funds contributed from foreigners . . . will be allowed to make application for recognition at the office of the proper educational authorities of the Government according to the regulations as promulgated by the Ministry of Education;

b. Such an institution should prefix to its official name the term *sze lik* [meaning "privately established"];

c. The president or principal of such an institution should be a Chinese. If such president or principal has hitherto been a foreigner, then there must be a Chinese vice president, who shall represent the institution in applying for recognition;

d. If the institution has a board of managers [directors], more than half of the board must be Chinese;

e. The institution shall not have as its purpose the propagation of religion;

f. The curriculum of such an institution should conform to the standards set by the Ministry of Education. It shall not include religious courses among the required subjects.[6]

In short, the Chinese government was demanding that all schools, including the missionary schools, should no longer have among their aims the propagation of any religious faith, even Christianity, which was thought in the West to be "the Queen of all knowledge" (whereas religion had no place at all among the intellectuals in China). The government also mandated that religious courses should no longer be compulsory. Many Christian missionaries of the time could not accept such government regulations because these demands symbolized an external authority which all missionaries, regardless of their denominational or national origins, had to obey. The Chinese government wanted to supersede whatever authority the missionaries claimed to have. Yet these were fairly sensible demands, and most of the educational leaders eventually came to that conclusion. In his report to the board of trustees, John

6. See Edward Wallace, "Report on Christian Education in China," in *China Christian Yearbook, 1926*, ed. Frank Rawlinson (Shanghai: Christian Literature Society, 1926), pp. 227-228.

Leighton Stuart, then president of Yenching University, explained that "'the nationalist movement is thoroughly reasonable and its demands are only those which any self-respecting people have a right to make."[7] Looking back, we see one rather amazing precedent also emerging from these regulations. The Chinese government was suggesting a new category for Christian universities. The term in point (b) above, *sze lik* (literally, "private") pointed precisely to the possible privatization of Christian higher education in China. The Christian universities were allowed greater autonomy if they were registered as private universities in China. The privatization of Christian higher education in China was started in the 1920s.

The Chinese government's assertion of control over Christian higher education in these and in subsequent regulations might have easily been seen as "a process of secularization" encountered by Christian colleges. This is indeed a picture one could draw for the development of Christian higher education in China.[8] However, the thesis of secularization focuses so much on the decline of Christian influences that it has overlooked the great accomplishments being made by the Christian educators of the time. As a matter of fact, Christian colleges like Yenching and others responded rather positively by revising and modifying their religious curricula so as to serve better the changing Chinese society.[9] So the "modernization of Christian education," more than its secularization, more aptly describes what was happening.[10]

Thus a "a process of modernization" took place in the ensuing years, implementing a revised understanding of Christian higher education and its place in the Chinese educational system. Three significant changes were seen in the late 1920s and in the early 1930s: more emphasis on the study of national culture; a broader conception of religious education; patriotism in Christian colleges.

7. See "Minutes of the Board of Trustees of Peking University," December 9, 1927, p. 299. To this, Professor Timothy T. Lew echoed: "What is meant (by the government regulations) is that a school should have an educational purpose, expressed in educational terms." See Wallace, "Report on Christian Education in China," p. 229.

8. See, e.g., Lutz, *China and the Christian Colleges*, ch. 8.

9. See, e.g., the report in Peter Tze Ming Ng, "From Theological Education to Religious Studies — An Enquiry into the Development of Religious Education at Yenching University, China" (Chinese), *Journal of the History of Christianity in Modern China* 2 (October 1999): 49-66.

10. See Peter Tze Ming Ng, "Secularization or Modernization: Teaching Christianity in China Since 1920s," *Studies in World Christianity* 5:1 (January 1999): 1-17; and also discussions in Peter Tze Ming Ng, *Changing Paradigms of Christian Higher Education in China, 1888-1950* (Lewiston: Edwin Mellen Press, 2002), ch. 2.

More Emphasis on the Study of National Culture

The existence of the study of national (Chinese) learning and research programs of Chinese studies *(Guoxue yanjiu)* in Western-founded Christian colleges could be regarded as a paradoxical phenomenon. Yet these courses were so crucial in responding to the issue of cultural imperialism and in nurturing the Chinese cultural identity that they became a unique and significant aspect of Christian colleges in China. John Leighton Stuart recalled in his memoirs, "I believe that imperialism and missions could be and should be divorced."[11] "My original aim had been . . . that it [Yenching] would ultimately become essentially a Chinese university retaining its Western origin largely as a historical memory."[12] The setting up of Harvard Yenching Institute in 1928 was to enhance and foster more research, teaching, and publication in the field of Chinese studies. And with financial support from the institute, Christian colleges in China were able to establish a number of Chinese studies research centers *(Guoxue yanjiu suo)*, employ well-known scholars, and launch serious teaching and research programs. Among the reputed research centers were those at Cheeloo University in Jinan, Shandong Province; at the University of Nanking (Jinling) in Nanking; at West China Union University (Huaxi) in Chengdu; at Central China University (Huazhong) in Wuhan; and at Lingnan University in Canton (Guangzhou).[13]

Indeed, because of their interests in Chinese language and cultural studies, many missionaries became sinologists and great scholars of Chinese studies in their later years, such as James Legge of Ying Wa College, John Leighton Stuart of Yenching University, and John Ferguson of the University of Nanking. And the *Guoxue yanjiu suo* of the Christian colleges have produced a generation of scholars in Chinese literature, Chinese philosophy, Chinese history, Chinese geography and archeology, and the like. Among them were William Hung and Geng Rong of Yenching University, Yuguang Chen of the University of Nanking, and Jiqing Lin of Cheeloo University.[14] The emphasis on teaching and research in Chinese cultural studies did not bring any harm to the aims of Christian colleges in China; rather, it created a new platform for more educational dialogue and exchange between Christianity and Chinese culture, and

11. J. L. Stuart, *Fifty Years in China* (New York: Haddon Craftsmen, Inc., 1954), p. 71.
12. Stuart, *Fifty Years in China*, p. 72.
13. For a comprehensive study of these research centers, see Tao Feiya and Peter Tze Ming Ng, *Jidujiao daxue yu Guoxue yanjiu* (Chinese Studies Research and Christian Colleges in China) (Fujian: Fujian Educational Press, 1998).
14. See *Jidujiao daxue yu Guoxue yanjiu*.

subsequently pushed Christian colleges, such as Yenching University and Ling-nan University, to become centers for intercultural dialogue and exchange.[15]

A Broader Conception of Religious Education

Regarding the teaching of religious education, Chinese and Westerners had fundamentally different perceptions of its place in the curriculum. And in order to accommodate the Chinese context, theological education had to be shifted from the core to the periphery of the college curriculum. Also, religious courses in the Christian colleges were transformed from their traditional dogmatic, evangelistic orientation to a more academic, educational orientation that was more appropriate to a secular setting. Religious instruction moved beyond the mere teaching of the Christian Bible and more attention was paid to its relevance to the Chinese cultural and social environments.[16] In addition, Christianity was not the only religious tradition taught in Christian colleges. There were also courses on other religious and cultural traditions found in the Chinese context such as Buddhism, "Mohammedanism" (Islam), Confucianism, and Taoism (Daoism). There were also courses such as primitive religions, comparative religions, psychology of religion, science and religion, and philosophy of religion, which suggested that religions were studied not for confessional or evangelistic purposes, but for academic as well as interdisciplinary study purposes.[17] To cite one example, Yenching University developed a comprehensive curriculum for the academic study of religion in the late 1920s. The announcement of courses offered at the interdenominational Yenching University in 1929-1930 provides one good illustration:[18]

Area I History of Religion
   Primitive religions
   Comparative religions

15. It is interesting to note that because of such academic exchange between Harvard University and these Chinese universities, Harvard soon became one of the leading centers of East Asian studies in the world, and its East Asian Library was the first of its kind in the United States.

16. See also the discussion in Ng, "Secularization or Modernization."

17. See Ng, "From Theological Education to Religious Studies."

18. See, e.g., *Yenching University Bulletin — College of Arts and Letters Announcement of Courses 1929-1930*, from United Board for Christian Higher Education in Asia Archives, New Haven, Yale Divinity School Library Special Collections, Box 314:4807, p. 103.

Mohammedanism

Confucianism and Taoism

History of Christianity

Studies in the history of Christianity in China

Area II Psychology of Religion

Introduction to the psychology of religion

Problems of character training in homes

Problems of character training in schools

Area III Philosophy of Religion

Problems of religion

Philosophy of religion

Science and religion

Religion and life

Religious implications of contemporary philosophy

Area IV Religious Literatures

Buddhist literature

Elementary Greek

Poetic and wisdom literature of the Hebrews

Area V Religious Arts

Religious music of the world

History of religious arts in the West

Religious music — singing

Religious music — harmony

Indeed, curriculum changes like this evinced a rather modern reconstruction of the Christian understanding of religion in Christian colleges in China. It was remarkable that such a broad conception of religion and a comprehensive curriculum on religious studies could be found in the 1920s in China.[19]

Patriotism in Christian Colleges

Was patriotism suppressed in Christian colleges? This issue existed long before the communist government took over China after 1949, indeed, ever since the beginning of Christian colleges in China. There had been harsh criticism against Christian colleges as "foreign and unpatriotic agencies" during the high tide of anti-foreignism in China during the 1920s and 1930s.

19. See also the discussion in Ng, "Secularization or Modernization."

Christian colleges were tested for their patriotism in the Sino-Japanese War (1937-1945). During the war, all Christian colleges were challenged to decide whether they would work seriously to promote "nationalism" against the Japanese invasion; if they did not, they would be accused of being imperialistic and unpatriotic. Chinese professors and students had to ask themselves whether they would "love their country more than loving their religion." This was the most difficult time for all Christian colleges in China. Yet it turned out to be another great time to test and testify their Christian faith. Take Lingnan University as an example. The motto of "For God, for China and for Lingnan"[20] was reformulated during the wartime and it was put in a different order — "For China, for God, and for Lingnan," or more precisely was represented by a new formulation, namely: "Love Country, Love Religion."[21] Nevertheless, Christian colleges in China had demonstrated significantly their faith and service to the country and they received much acclaim for their "patriotism" during the war.[22] For instance, on April 6, 1938, Madame Chiang (Song Mei Ling, the president's wife) addressed a group of Christian missionaries in Wuhan:

> The most influential and valuable contribution you have done to our nation was not merely the work itself, but the Christian spirit you have shown in your humble work. . . . I am so glad to tell you that those who had been criticizing Christian missionaries in the past have now turned to praising you for you have eventually gained their full confidence and trust in you.[23]

20. The motto was borrowed from Yale University where it was expressed as "For God, For Country, For Yale." An alumnus of Lingnan, Kan Yau Man brought it back and converted it to be "For God, For China, and For Lingnan" in one of their school songs.

21. As it was later reported by one of the alumni, recalling that "The Spirit of Lingnan was comprised of various good wills derived from four different traditions, namely: the spirit of service and brotherhood from Christianity; the spirit of freedom and equality from democracy; the spirit of patriotism from nationalism; and the spirit of good health from sportsmanship." The statement suggested that "patriotism from nationalism" was placed more significantly than "cosmopolitanism or internationalism." See Qi Tian, "On the Spirit of Lingnan," in *Lingnan Tung Hsun* (Newsletter), vol. 6, July 20, 1955, p. 9. Kan Yau Man even attempted an account of the history of Lingnan University by demonstrating her spirit of patriotism in concrete words. See, e.g., Kan Yau Man, "Lingnan My Lingnan (Part III)," in *Lingnan Tung Hsun* (Newsletter), vol. 17, September 9, 1958, pp. 6-27.

22. See the discussion in Liu Jia-feng and Liu Tianlu, *Christian Universities During the Sino-Japanese War Time* (Fuzhou: Fujian Educational Press, 2003).

23. As quoted from Tao Fei Ya, "A Textual Study of Cultural Aggression," *Journal of Literature, History and Philosophy* 5 (2003): 35.

Hu Shih, the Chinese ambassador to the United States, commenting on the work of Christian colleges in China during the Sino-Japanese War, said that they had already become "the universities of China." Even Mao Zedong, the communist leader who became chairman of the new government in 1949, had once given such high regard to the work of Yenching University in Beijing that he had written *Yanjing Daxue* at the western gate of the university.[24] Dr. Edward Hume, the former president of Yale-in-China, also remarked on Lingnan University in 1941, saying, "[it] is blazing an educational trail in South China. It is doing an educational job thoroughly in each field it has entered, and it is rapidly becoming so thoroughly naturalized that all Chinese, whether government officials, educational leaders, or private citizens, have come to think of it as their own. These two achievements entitle it to the most loyal support."[25]

In short, the historical development of Christian higher education in China signified an obvious trend that it was serving the country and the people in China. It was during the Sino-Japanese War that Christian colleges had identified themselves with the nation and the people, so much so that Christian colleges in China had become "100 percent Chinese universities."

China was invaded and occupied by Japan during the Sino-Japanese War, from 1937 to 1945. Most of the Christian colleges and universities had to leave their campuses and move to the interior, as far as Chengdu in Sichuan Province in western China. Most of the teaching and research programs in these colleges were stopped or could only be kept at a minimum. After the war, they were able to move back and gradually recovered their life and work in their original cities. But then came the Civil War of 1946-1949, between the Nationalist Party (Kuomintang) and the Communist Party in China, which ended with the emergence of the People's Republic of China in 1949. And while the Christian colleges and universities were about to adapt to the new era as China became a communist country, another great war broke out in 1950. It was the outburst of the Korean War in 1950 and the subsequent breakdown of the Sino-American relationship that finally led to the closing down of all Christian colleges and universities in China.[26] The communist government

24. As recalled from He Di, "Yenching University and the Modernization of Chinese Education," paper presented at the First International Symposium on the History of Pre-1949 Christian Universities in China, Huazhong Normal University, Wuhan, June 1989.

25. See Charles H. Corbett, *Lingnan University* (New York: Trustees of Lingnan University, 1963), p. 175.

26. As Christian universities had to break any connections with the outside world, especially European and American countries, and most of the Christian missionaries had to leave China immediately after the onset of the Korean War, the Chinese government seized

took over all Christian colleges and dissolved them in the national reorganization of higher educational institutions, by eliminating from them all Christian elements, especially Christian names, and breaking down their departments and programs and reallocating them into the national system.

Remnants of CHE in Hong Kong and Taiwan After 1951

There were thirteen Protestant and three Roman Catholic universities in China at the time of the closing down of all Christian colleges. Although Christian schools did not continue on the China mainland after 1952, the faculty and students of some of the Christian schools moved to Taiwan, Hong Kong, and Southeast Asia, and continued the work of providing a Christian education to the Chinese people there. In the area of university education, Taiwan's Fu Jen Catholic University and Soochow (Dong Wu) University had both moved from the China mainland and continued their educational work in Taiwan.[27] Today there are nine Christian colleges in Taiwan and three in Hong Kong.[28]

Of the three Christian colleges in Hong Kong, Chung Chi College was the first. It was founded in October 1951 by the representatives of Protestant churches in Hong Kong together with the missionaries who had retreated from China. The name "Chung Chi" means "Honoring Christ" and the college was established with the aim to continue, on the periphery of China, the Christian cultural and academic activities and the Christian ideals that had been pursued by the former thirteen Protestant Christian universities in China.[29] In 1956 the

---

the opportunity to take over all Christian universities and reallocated them into the national system. See, e.g., the discussions in He Di, "Yenching University and the Modernization of Chinese Education."

27. Later, Chinese Christians established Tung Hai University and Chung Yuan Christian University, as well as other universities. In 1999 when Taiwan's Fu Jen Catholic University celebrated the seventieth anniversary of its founding (1929-1999), their dates were based on the establishment of the Fu Jen Catholic University in Peking.

28. The nine Christian colleges in Taiwan include Soochow (Tung Wu) University, Tung Hai University, Chung Yuan Christian University, Providence University, Chang Jung Christian University, Christ College, St. John's University, Adventist University, and Fu Jen Catholic University; the three in Hong Kong are Chung Chi College, Hong Kong Baptist University, and Lingnan University.

29. See *Report of the Ad Hoc Committee on the Establishment of Chung Chi College,* kept at Yale Divinity School Library, Record Group No. 11A, Box 110A, File 1518. Readers may also consult "Dangdai Jidujiao Daxuede Yige Xinshiming" (A New Mission for Christian Higher Education in Asia Today), in Peter Tze Ming Ng, *Jidu Zongjiao Yu Zhongguo Daxue Jiaoyu*

college was moved to its permanent site at Ma Liu Shui, the New Territories of Hong Kong, which is just thirty miles from the border of the China mainland. The college badge was engraved with a Nestorian cross and the lotus, symbolizing the attempt to integrate Christianity and Chinese culture, which is the central mission of the college. The building of a college chapel demonstrated this Christian presence in the campus. It was stated explicitly in the college constitution that Chung Chi sought "to promote Christian faith, learning and research" and it continued to strive for Christian scholarship even when it was incorporated as one of the three foundational colleges of the Chinese University of Hong Kong in 1963.[30] Later Hong Kong Baptist University and Lingnan University were established.[31] Hong Kong Baptist University began as the Hong Kong Baptist College in 1956 and was upgraded to university status in 1995, whereas Lingnan University begun as Lingnan College in 1967 and was renamed Lingnan University in 1999. By the middle of the 1970s, the three colleges — Chung Chi College, Hong Kong Baptist College, and Lingnan College — joined as members of the Association of Christian Universities and Colleges in Asia (ACUCA).[32]

The Christian colleges and universities in Taiwan and Hong Kong were working out different ways to maintain a Christian presence in higher education in the Chinese contexts. Besides attaching themselves as private institutions to the public education system, some colleges and universities like Hong Kong Baptist University were seeking to develop Christian studies as one of the subjects within an academic discipline, such as religion and philosophy.[33] Some were seeking to integrate Christian values and beliefs in their general education programs, such as those developed in Hong Kong Lingnan University and Chung Yuan Christian University in Taiwan.[34] When Chung Chi College was incorpo-

---

(Christianity and University Education in China) (Beijing: Chinese Academy of Social Sciences Publishing House, 2003), pp. 304-316.

30. See *Chung Chi College Handbook 1993-94* (Shatin, Hong Kong: The Chinese University of Hong Kong Chung Chi College, 1994), p. 11. Since the Chinese University of Hong Kong is a government-subsidized secular university, Chung Chi College becomes a uniquely Christian college within the secular university setting.

31. In 1963 Chung Chi College became one of the colleges at the newly founded Chinese University of Hong Kong. Baptist College and Lingnan College became Baptist University and Lingnan University in 1995 and 1999 respectively.

32. The Association of Christian Universities and Colleges in Asia was established in 1975, and Chung Chi College was one of its active founding members.

33. See, e.g., the curriculum set up in the Department of Religion and Philosophy, in *Hong Kong Baptist University Bulletin, 1999-2000*, pp. 128-131.

34. For instance, a chaplaincy office was set up at Hong Kong Lingnan University in 1995

rated as one of the three foundational colleges at the Chinese University of Hong Kong, it was seeking to demonstrate the possibility of integrating Christian faith into a secular university. Over the past sixty years, it has done a very successful job and has become an integral part of the university system in Hong Kong. For instance, Chung Chi College has developed a strong Department of Religion (now the Department of Cultural and Religious Studies) and committed itself to the promotion of quality teaching and research in religious studies, including the study of Christianity. There is also a Chung Chi Divinity School set up within the campus to offer courses on theology and provide programs leading to the degrees of bachelor of arts (in theology), bachelor of divinity (B.D.), master of divinity (M.Div.), master of theology (M.Th.), and doctor of theology (D.Th.).[35] Besides, Chung Chi was also aware of a new mission in mainland China arising after the return of Hong Kong to China, when greater opportunities arose to link up with universities in mainland China. Hence, Chung Chi set up a new Centre for the Study of Religion and Chinese Society in 1996, with the aim of fostering the development of academic research on religion and Chinese society, focusing on the contribution of religious phenomena to Chinese society.[36] When a new Department of Religion was established at Peking University in 1996, a joint venture was started for scholarly conferences and exchange between the two academic units.[37] The Centre became a useful serving tool to train young scholars from mainland China.

In short, after the return of Hong Kong to China in 1997, Hong Kong's Christian schools, including Chung Chi College of the Chinese University of Hong Kong, Hong Kong Baptist University, and Lingnan University, legally

---

to provide Christian counseling and support within the university while it was moving into a new campus. Edward K. Y. Chen, the president, restated its mission "to become a world-class liberal arts institution producing all-round, quality students who will be able to ride with the tide of the world and accept challenges in the next century." See "Message from the President," *Lingnan University Chronicle* 8 (Fall 1999): 1-2.

35. It should be noted that some degrees are granted by the Southeast Asia School of Theology, through Chung Chi College as an area center, whereas some degrees are granted directly by CUHK, such as the bachelor of arts (in theology) and the master of divinity (M.Div.); hence they are fully recognized by the government of the People's Republic of China. See Peter Tze Ming Ng, *Chung Chi College and Her Christian Education in the Past Fifty Years* (Chinese), Occasional Paper no. 4 (Hong Kong: Centre for the Study of Religion and Chinese Society, Chung Chi College, Chinese University of Hong Kong, 2001).

36. See *Special Issue for the 10th Anniversary of Centre for the Study of Religion and Chinese Society, 1996-2006* (Hong Kong: Chung Chi College, Chinese University of Hong Kong, 2006).

37. See, e.g., the report in *Newsletter of the Centre for the Study of Religion and Chinese Society* 2 (February 1998): 2.

became the only Christian institutions within the public educational system of the People's Republic of China. These three Christian universities are witnessing not only to the possibility of providing Christian higher education in the People's Republic of China, but also to the significance of Christian higher education in Asia today.

Resurgence of Christian Studies in Mainland China since the 1980s

Ever since the communists took over mainland China in 1949, Chinese scholars have generally adopted an exclusively Marxist view of Christian higher education in China. Marxist-Leninists in the People's Republic of China have labeled Christianity as superstitious, unscientific, and contrary to the progressive, materialist, and scientific doctrines of Marxism and communism. All endeavors of the Christian missionaries, including Christian colleges, were seen as evidence of "Western cultural imperialism." Hence, Christian colleges were not considered as having any positive role in the history of modern education in China.[38] It was only in the early 1980s when Deng Xiaoping began his "reform and open door" *(gai ge kai fang)* policy in China that many intellectuals were released and started inquiring into different schools of thought: Western liberalism, Neo-Marxism, Christianity, postmodernism, and other ideas and theories. Such yearning for new ideas and philosophies as a substitute for orthodox Marxism reached a high point in the late 1980s and this was referred to in China as "culture fever" *(wenhuare)* and "Christianity fever" *(jidujiaore)*. At this time, many scholars turned to Christianity or Christian faith for intellectual enlightenment and psychological solace. Some felt that Christianity could fill the void of a post-Marxist vacuum in faith, while others thought Christianity was the foundation of Western culture, including the ideas of liberty, freedom, capitalistic spirit, and democratic traditions. At any rate, there was a substantial growth of interest in Christianity, not only attracting more people to the churches but also getting more young intellectuals into the new and emergent areas of Christian studies, including the studies of the history of Christian higher education and Christian missions in China.

Zhang Kai Yuan was the pioneer and most influential leader in this emerg-

38. Two examples of the traditional view that could still be found in the 1980s were Gu Zhangsheng, *Chuanjiaoshi yu jindai zhongguo* (Missionaries and the Modern China) (Shanghai: The People's Press, 1981), and Li Chucai, ed., *Diguo zhuyi qinhua jiaoyu shiliao-jiaohui jiaoyu* (Church Education — Historical Resources of Western Imperialistic Education in China) (Beijing: Science of Education Press, 1987).

ing field. Zhang was a former student of Miner S. Bates at the University of Nanking in the early 1940s. He recalled that his research in this area began in 1985, following a conversation with James T. C. Liu from Princeton University, who said to him: "This is perhaps a good time to re-examine the history of China's Christian colleges and universities. . . . And you are the most suitable person for this job."[39] Zhang accepted the calling and began by retrieving the archives of Central China University (Huazhong University) from Hubei Provincial Archives in 1988. He then mobilized alumni and scholars from those formerly Christian colleges. The First International Symposium on the History of Pre-1949 Christian Universities in China was held on June 1-3, 1989, at Huazhong Normal University, Wuhan, China, where Zhang was the president.[40] At the opening address of the conference, Zhang urged that Chinese scholars should be able to break through the ideological constraints that associated Christian colleges with Western imperialism. He said that the traditional view had been biased "because there was no clear distinction drawn between the educational role of Christian colleges and their religious role which later became less significant; and there was no distinction drawn between the normal educational activities in Christian colleges and the imperialistic policies of the Western powers."[41] At the conference, Zhang also called for a new direction for the study of Christian colleges in China, namely, seeing them as a product of Sino-Western cultural exchange.

Since then, a new approach has evolved that emphasizes the study of Christian colleges as an avenue to explore the development of East-West cultural exchanges in modern Chinese history. Chinese scholars began to work on more positive approaches to the study of Christian colleges. Examples are Shi Jinghuan, *Dixiaoren yu Situ leideng zai hua jiaoyu huodong* (The Educational Activities of Calvin Mateer and John Leighton Stuart in China);[42] Xu

39. Zhang retold his story in "Zhang's Preface," in *Zhongguo jiaohui Daxue wenxian mulu* (China Christian Colleges Catalogues series), ed. Peter Tze Ming Ng et al., vol. 1, p. xiii. Liu was a graduate from Yenching University and Zhang from Nanking University, both in the 1940s. See Peter Tze Ming Ng et al., *Changing Paradigms of Christian Higher Education in China, 1888-1950* (Lewiston: Edwin Mellen Press, 2002), pp. 13f.

40. See Zhang Kaiyuan and Arthur Waldron, eds., *Zhongxi wenhua yu Jiaohui Daxue* (Christian Universities and Chinese-Western Cultures) (Wuhan: Hubei Educational Press, 1991).

41. See Zhang, "Zhang's Preface," p. 3.

42. Shi Jinghuan, *Dixiaoren yu Situ leideng zai hua jiaoyu huodong* (The Educational Activities of Calvin Mateer and John Leighton Stuart in China) (Taiwan: Men Wei Publishing Co., 1991).

Yihua, *Religion and Education: St. John's University as an Evangelizing Agency*;[43] He Xiaoxia and Shi Jinghuan, *Jiaohui xuexiao yu zhongguo jiaoyu jindaihua* (Church Schools and the Modernization of Chinese Education);[44] and Wang Lixin, *Meiguo chuanjiaoshi yu wanqing zhongguo jindaihua* (American Missionaries and the Modernization of China in the Late Qing Period).[45] The substantial growth of interest in Christianity could be verified by the fact that there was a vacuum of research or publication in Christian studies throughout three decades (1950-1980) in mainland China; but there have been more than one hundred doctoral and master's research theses on Christian studies, more than five hundred scholarly books, and more than one thousand journal articles and papers written on Christianity in the past three decades (1980-2010).

Another significant mark was the establishment in May 1998 of the Research Centre for the Study of Christianity in the Institute of World Religions of the Chinese Academy of Social Sciences (CASS), Beijing. Zhuo Xinping, who was then the associate director of the CASS, a leading think-tank of the Chinese government, was the founding director.[46] Since 1998, the Centre has organized twelve annual national conferences and published twelve volumes of proceedings and papers for professors and scholars who are interested in Christian studies, many of whom are from leading academic institutions in the country. The attendance has reached 150 in recent years and it forms a substantial group of expertise in the field. The Centre has been doing a great job in drawing the Chinese scholars' attention to a wide range of topics about Christianity in the past years.[47] Notably, He Guang Fu, a professor from the

---

43. This was Xu's doctoral thesis at Princeton University in 1994.

44. He Xiaoxia and Shi Jinghuan, *Jiaohui xuexiao yu zhongguo jiaoyu jindaihua* (Church Schools and the Modernization of Chinese Education) (Guangzhou: Guangdong Educational Publishing House, 1996).

45. See Wang Lixin, *Meiguo chuanjiaoshi yu wanqing zhongguo jindaihua* (American Missionaries and the Modernization of China in the Late Qing Period) (Tianjin: The People's Press, 1997).

46. See, e.g., Zhuo Xinping et al., eds., *Ji Du Zong Jiao Yan Jiu* (The Study of Christianity), vol. 1 (Beijing: Religious Culture Press, 1999), a valuable index of historical works published between 1949 and 1997.

47. These were the topics chosen for the annual conferences: Contemporary Study of Christianity in China (1998); Contemporary Study of Religions in China (1999); Christianity and the Twenty-first Century (2000); Contemporary Scholars in the Study of Christianity (2001); Christianity and the Study of Humanity (2002); Christianity in the Context of Secularization (2003); Glocalization and Chinese Christianity (2004); Christianity and Civil Society (2005); Christianity and Cross-cultural Dialogues (2006); Christianity and Harmonious Society (2007); Christianity and Public Values (2008); Christianity and Social Transformation

People's University of China, Beijing, admitted that the movement of Christian studies has enriched Chinese academia in three particular areas: (1) in encouraging critical thinking; (2) in distinguishing the transcendental from the mundane; and (3) in providing a holistic and three-dimensional approach as well as a sense of the "holy" to the study of humanities.[48]

The growth of interest in Christian studies took place mostly among the professors and scholars who were from those universities that were related in some ways to the thirteen pre-1949 Christian universities. The present Peking University (Beida) is situated on the ground of the former Yenching University; and Shandong University is now on the campus of the former Shantung Christian (Cheeloo) University; University of Nanjing is on the campus of Nanjing (Jinling) University; Nanjing Normal University is on the campus of the former Ginling Women's College; Huazhong Normal University is on the campus of Central China (Huazhong) University; Sichuan University is on the campus of the former West China Union (Huaxi) University; Fujian Normal University is on the campus of the former Fukien Christian University; Hangzhou University (now part of Zhijiang University) is on the campus of Hangchow University; and Zhongshan University is on the campus of the former Lingnan University. Historical monuments and old buildings might reveal to the living generation some facets of the forbidden past and arouse in young minds a sense of curiosity, perhaps a challenging subject for serious research.

There were some attempts to restore the Christian universities as privatized higher education in China in the late 1980s and early 1990s, but they did not succeed due to the restrictive government policy. Christian universities had been registered in China as private higher education in the 1920s, but since the communist government took over all Christian universities in the early 1950s, Christian names are not allowed for any higher educational institutions. There has been a demand for privatization of higher education in China in recent years, and many privately founded, tuition-driven business and technical colleges have arisen.[49] Yet the matter of a religious basis for higher education is still very sensitive. The Chinese government welcomes

---

(2009). Interested readers may consult the twelve volumes of *Ji Du Zong Jiao Yan Jiu* published by the Religious Culture Press, Beijing, from 1998 to 2009.

48. See He Guang Hu, "Christian Studies and Its Significance for Chinese Academia," in *The Christian Religion and Contemporary Religion*, ed. Xin Ping Zhuo and Josef Sayer (Beijing: Religious Culture Press, 2001), pp. 150-152.

49. See, e.g., Fengqiao Yan and Daniel C. Levy, "China's New Private Education Law," *International Higher Education* 31 (Spring 2003): 9-10, and Yingxia Cao and Daniel C. Levy, "China's Private Higher Education: The Impact of Public Sector Privatization," *International*

educational and scholarly contributions by individual Christians and cultural and academic exchanges from foreign institutions, including Christian ones. Yet it is still not yet ready to accept any direct mission work from distinctively Christian groups or organizations, especially those with explicitly evangelistic purposes. There are some informal reports circulating of Chinese and foreign Christians participating in new private university startups, but their status as "Christian universities" is not at all clear.

Even though the history of Christian higher education was still a "sensitive" if not a "taboo" subject in China for decades from the early 1950s to 1990s, the mere existence of the formerly Christian university campuses and the emerging growth of interest in Christian studies have indeed opened up a new venue for the younger generation to recover their historical traditions. The re-establishment of the Department of Religion at Peking University in 1996 was indeed a good example of such an attempt to revive religious studies since the pre-1950 efforts of T. C. Chao (Zhao Zi-chen) in the Yenching School of Religion.[50]

Being situated close to mainland China, Chung Chi College has seized the opportunity to contribute some effort to promote and support such scholarly activities in the mainland. Chung Chi professors not only attended most of the conferences in China, but they also helped to organize an international symposium on historical archives of pre-1949 Christian higher education in China in December 1993. Besides publishing the conference proceedings, they have also launched the publication of five volumes of the China Christian Colleges Catalogues series as guidebooks for Chinese scholars.[51] In 1994 Huazhong Normal University set up a Centre for Historical Research on China Christian Colleges, under the directorship of Zhang Kaiyuan. Chung Chi College helped Zhang make requests for financial support from the Henry Luce Foundation, Inc. and also helped the new Centre print its first issue of the Centre's newsletter.[52] And in 1996 Chung Chi College established the Centre for the Study

---

Higher Education 41 (Fall 2005), available at http//www.bc.edu/bc_org/avp/soe/cihe/newslet ter/Number41/p14_Cao_Levy.htm.

50. See "Introduction to the Formation of Department of Religion at Peking University," a pamphlet issued by Peking University, 1996, pp. 1-2.

51. See the conference proceedings, Peter Tze Ming Ng, ed., *Zhongguo jiaohui Daxue lishi wenxian yantaohui lunwenji* (Essays on Historical Archives of Christian Higher Education in China) (Hong Kong: Chinese University Press, 1995); and the five volumes, published as *Zhongguo jiaohui Daxue wenxian mulu* (China Christian Colleges Catalogues series), ed. Peter Tze Ming Ng and Philip Leung Yuen Sang (Hong Kong: Chinese University Press, 1996-1998).

52. The Centre is now renamed Research Centre for East-West Culture Exchange, located at Central China (Huazhong) Normal University in Wuhan, China.

of Religion and Chinese Society to further encourage and support Chinese scholars to attempt more in-depth research on Christianity and especially on Christian colleges. After about ten years of academic conferences, scholarly exchanges, and publications, Christian studies has now become a relatively popular academic discipline in China and cross-disciplinary research is quite impressive. There are in mainland China more than fifteen university-established independent Departments of Religion as well as special courses of religious studies, including Christian studies in relevant departments. Examples are Peking University, Qinghua University, The Peoples' University of China, Fudan University, Shanghai University, Nanjing University, Sichuan University, Huazhong Normal University, Zhejiang University, Fujian Normal University, and Guangzhou's Zhongshan University. The Centre at Chung Chi College has played a very significant role in this regard.[53]

In 2002 the Centre organized the First International Young Scholars' Symposium on Christianity and Chinese Society, which provided a platform for young scholars who were doing their doctoral or master's research on Christianity and Chinese society. There was also the launching of the Ph.D. Dissertation Award Scheme in 2003. The response from mainland China was overwhelming, so much so that the award scheme and the symposium continued every other year, with about fifty scholars attending the symposium each time. Over the years, hundreds of scholars and young professors attended Young Scholars Symposia and other conferences run by the Centre and as a result, more than thirty young scholars have joined and completed the Ph.D. program in religious studies at the Chinese University of Hong Kong in the past ten years.[54] Most of them returned to the mainland after their graduation and they will indeed be professors of high caliber in China in the years to come. Hence, Chung Chi College has now found a new mission as a Christian college in China.

Being constituted as part of a secular university, Chung Chi College is now positioned somewhere between the church and the world. Yet, it is precisely this distinctive position that creates for the college a new platform on which to work for the nation and the kingdom of God, by helping to develop greater interests in the study of Christianity among professors and students in all universities in China. These professors and students are potential leaders of

---

53. See also the report in *Special Issue for the 10th Anniversary of Centre for the Study of Religion and Chinese Society, 1996-2006* (Hong Kong: Chung Chi College, Chinese University of Hong Kong, 2006).

54. *Special Issue for the 10th Anniversary*, pp. 26-34.

their own universities and of the churches in China especially if they become church members. On the one hand, though the theses of secularization and privatization of Christian higher education have seemed to be pessimistic and restrictive to any significant impact of Christian higher education in the modern world,[55] there are indeed some other ways Christian colleges like Chung Chi College can experiment and explore ways of serving God and the nation, even within an atheistic, communist state. On the other hand, the role of a Christian college should no longer be confined to one university or one campus, but instead be extended to networks among professors and scholars throughout China, whether they are Christians or are attached to universities that were formerly related to Christian colleges or universities. Chung Chi is now committed to promoting and helping foster interdisciplinary research on the study of Christianity or religious studies and its interaction with Chinese traditions and modern Chinese society.[56] It is in this way that Chung Chi College is serving both God and China, by building an academic bridge between them.

Concluding Remarks

Studies have shown that Christianity has been a leading force in the development of higher education in Asian countries in the past century.[57] There are even greater challenges for Christian higher education in China in the twenty-first century. In the past, Christian educators have been seeking ways to define the mark of "a Christian college," whether it should be a college with a strong Christian administrator, a college that upholds strong Christian scholarship, a college with a Christian worldview across the curriculum, or a college with 100 percent Christian faculty, or other marks. The most significant mark of a Christian college besides the above criteria, as the Chinese experiences reveal, is whether the college can realize for itself a workable Christian mission. Especially in the case of Chung Chi College, rather than focusing on what it has from within, the college is striving hard to look outwardly, seeking for a Christian mission in which it can serve not only the local Christian churches,

55. See, e.g., George Marsden and Bradley J. Longfield, eds., *The Secularization of the Academy* (New York: Oxford University Press, 1992).

56. *Special Issue for the 10th Anniversary,* p. 21.

57. See, e.g., the discussion in Carver Yu's "Christian Higher Education in the Contexts of Rapid Economic Growth and Educational Expansion in Asia," *ACUCA Exchange* 1:1 (May 1991): 29-58.

but also the Chinese society and the wider academic community in China today. The college is seeking a mission and a role as that of a bridge, namely: a bridge between the East and the West, and a bridge between Hong Kong and mainland China. More still, the college is serving as a bridge between Christianity and other cultures, especially Chinese culture, and a bridge between Christianity and other religions, especially Chinese religions. Chung Chi College knows that it can be used as an effective instrument, if the Lord so wills. And the results have been both fruitful and stimulating. It is indeed our vision that besides the integration of faith and learning, Christian higher education in Hong Kong can work hard to promote the study of religion and cultures, including Chinese culture and Western Christianity, which can contribute toward the betterment of human civilizations.

It is clear that we all share one common Christian mission in Christian higher education today, that is, to glorify God in the countries where we are situated. Yet, we understand also that there may be different ways to fulfill our mission in different countries, and God will grant us his great wisdom so that we can glorify him in our distinctive ways. Noting that the Chinese experiences are one possible state of global Christian higher education, we are especially reminded of the following three scriptural passages.

1. When Philip was on his way to Gaza, he was led by an angel to meet an Ethiopian eunuch who was reading the Book of Isaiah in his chariot. Being moved by the Spirit, Philip ran up and asked, "Do you understand what you are reading?" The eunuch said, "How can I, unless some one guides me?" (Acts 8:26-31). Then, Philip began to explain the scriptures and told him the good news of Jesus (Acts 8:35). After Philip had completed his job, he baptized the eunuch but did not require him to join any particular church. Then the Spirit of the Lord took Philip away and the eunuch went on his way, rejoicing (Acts 8:39). Like Philip, Christian colleges and universities in China, especially Chung Chi College in recent years, have learned to be humble and asked, "Do you (China) need any help?" before they realized the mission that was set before them. And we could hear the Chinese professors crying for help: "How can I, unless some one guides me?" Our job is precisely what the Lord wanted Philip to do. Are we ready to respond as Isaiah did: "Here I am. Send me, O Lord" (Isa. 6:8).

2. Jesus once said to his disciples, "You know that those who are supposed to rule over the Gentiles lord it over them. . . . But it shall not be so among you. . . . For the Son of man came not to be served but to serve, and to give his life as a ransom for many" (Mark 10:45). In serving China, Christian colleges and universities have learned to broaden their understanding of religious ed-

ucation, not to impose Western culture or theology, but to pay due respect to Chinese culture and Chinese religions, as well as to pay more attention to the educational aspect of religious education in their teaching curricula. This was what Yenching University and the other Christian universities in China did in the 1920s and 1930s. And Chung Chi College has indeed also learned to serve Chinese professors and young scholars by helping them to develop more scholarly research in methodology and contents in their religious studies, including the study of Christianity or other related subjects. Can we follow the way of Jesus, who "came not to be served, but to serve"? And perhaps, we should pray for the Lord's guidance, so that we are working in the name of Christian higher education in China, not merely for the accomplishment of our own agenda, but to serve the Chinese people and provide what they need.

3. Jesus also said, "Truly, truly, I say to you, unless a grain of wheat falls into the earth and dies, it remains alone; but if it dies, it bears much fruit" (John 12:24). The thirteen Christian colleges and universities in China were forced to close down or "die" in the early 1950s, yet the seeds the missionaries had sown in China never "die" and their work could blossom and "bear fruit" even after several decades, as we are now witnessing the revival and blossoming of Christian work in China again in recent years. This was precisely what we can learn from the experiences of Christian higher education in China. Hence, it is hoped that the Chinese story would help us to foster a better understanding of the state of global Christian higher education and the work of God today.

CHAPTER 4

Korean Christian Higher Education: History, Tasks, and Vision

Kuk-Won Shin

Higher education is extremely popular in Korea today. National statistics show that 83.8 percent of high school graduates move on to colleges and universities, rising from 22.9 percent in 1990. Christian institutions were the pioneering leaders of Korea's modern higher education since it began 115 years ago, and have contributed to its more recent growth as well. Currently there are 185 four-year colleges and universities in Korea, of which only twenty-six are public. Christian institutions of higher education occupy 38.3 percent (61 out of 159) of the four-year private colleges and universities.[1] Despite their celebrated past, however, Korean Christian universities are facing serious challenges from secularization and are thus in danger of losing their distinctive identity and vision. This chapter's objective is to review the legacy, current challenges, and vision of Korean Christian higher education.

---

1. This information is based on "Educational Statistics" in the "Social Index of Korea 2009" prepared by Statistics Korea. Korean Educational Development Institute (KEDI), http:// eng.kedi.re.kr/khome/eng/webhome/Home.do. Cf. Center for Education Statistics, http://cesi .kedi.re.kr/index.jsp. The rate steadily rose from 33.2 percent in 1990, to 45.3 percent in 1994, 51.4 percent in 1995, 60.1 percent in 1997, 70.5 percent in 2001, and 81.3 percent in 2004. Although the rate dropped 1.9 percent in 2009 for the first time, perhaps due to the worldwide economic crisis, it does not indicate a serious turnaround of the trend. The rate of enrollment in higher education among young people of college-going age in the same year rather rose 0.4 percent in comparison to the previous year (67.2 percent).

A Short History of Korean Christian Higher Education

Modern higher education in Korea[2] started in 1885 when Gwanghyewon (Widespread Relief House), the country's first Western hospital, began to train students.[3] The hospital was established in Seoul by an American Presbyterian doctor, Horace Newton Allen. This happened two months before two American ordained Presbyterian and Methodist missionaries arrived.[4] While Taehak (Great School, established in A.D. 372) of the ancient Koguryo kingdom is considered to be the first higher education institution, colleges established by missionaries, such as Ewha Hakdang for girls (1886), Soongsil Hakdang (1897 in Pyongyang, changed its name to Union Christian College in 1906), and Severance Union Medical College (1905) are regarded as Korea's first modern colleges.[5] These "mission schools" (a collective term for colleges that were established as a branch of missions) pioneered modern higher education in Korea far earlier than the public sector. The first public institution of higher education, Lawyer's School (becoming Seoul Junior College of Law in 1911), appeared in 1895. The first public university, Seoul Imperial University, was founded in 1924 as one of the six national universities established by Japan during colonization.[6] The development of Korean Christian higher education (hereinafter, CHE) reflects the turbulent history of Korea throughout its struggle for independence against Japanese colonization, civil war, ideological conflicts with communism, industrialization, and democratization. Thus, the history of Korean CHE can be divided into three main periods: mid-1880s to 1945; mid-1940s to 1970s; 1980s to present.

Mission schools dominated Korea's education at all levels in the first pe-

---

2. There are many "mission (founded) schools" and Christian educational institutions from kindergarten to graduate school in Korea. All "higher education institutions" in this chapter refer to accredited undergraduate, graduate, and professional schools with at least the authority of granting a junior bachelor's degree.

3. Gwanghyewon changed its name to Jejungwon (House of Universal Helpfulness) and to Severance Hospital (named after a large contributor). Another missionary, Dr. Oliver R. Avison from Canada, is responsible for making the hospital the first medical school of Korea.

4. Although the first Protestant missionary K. F. A. Gutzlaff (1803-1851) came in 1832 and stayed for a month, the foundations of Korean Christianity were laid in 1887 by Koreans who read the Bible on their own. Eventually these people started two churches in Seoul, according to the early missionary John Ross's report in 1887. Missionaries came to Korea in 1885, but their activities were largely limited to hospitals and schools for years.

5. Horace H. Underwood, *Modern Education in Korea* (New York: International Press, 1926), pp. 120-148.

6. Jong-Chul Kim, *A Study of Korean Higher Education* (Seoul: Pakyoungsa, 1979), p. 35.

riod, which lasted until the end of Japanese occupation in 1945. The goal of these schools was not only to evangelize but also to raise Christian leaders.[7] They were successful in both objectives. The mission leaders had a broad vision and did not limit their efforts in education to training indigenous pastors in seminaries. They perceived higher education as an important strategic basis for evangelization. Despite the fact that Christian schools were suppressed to the level of junior colleges, so that they were subsidiary to Seoul Imperial University, they led higher education in both numbers and quality. They also became the center of the nationalist spirit and independence movement. Unlike in countries that were colonized by Western nations, in Korea missionaries and their schools sided with the oppressed people during the Japanese occupation. This is reckoned as one of the reasons for the success of Christian missions in Korea.[8]

Mission schools were also the centers of modernization. They were windows through which the young people of this "hermit nation" could see the world. Many prominent leaders in various fields were raised through these schools. "The students in Soongsil College . . . were not a bit shameful [ashamed] to be called as leaders of Chosun [land of morning calm, Korea] in their character and learning."[9] Mission schools not only introduced Western education, but also contributed to the dismantling of feudalism and laid the foundation for modern Korea. For example, Ewha, the first higher education institution for women, was revolutionary for this nation where women were seldom offered a formal education. Prior to this time, Confucianism had dominated since the turn of the fifteenth century, when the Yi dynasty adopted it as the ruling ideology. CHE broke the long hegemony of Confucian ideology. By opening up a new world of modern education, CHE left a splendid legacy in these years. All of the early CHE institutions were able to develop into prominent universities. Widespread church growth and a positive image earned through CHE's earlier contributions to liberation and modernization helped it earn a good standing in Korean education.

The second period falls between the mid-1940s and the 1970s, during which

7. *Catalogue of the Union Christian College for the Year Ending June, 1913* (Pyongyang, 1913), p. 2. The primary purpose of a "mission school" was "to train up candidates for the ministry and missionary work of the Korean church and to produce trained teachers for our church schools."

8. Kyu-Won Han, *A Study of Nationalism Education of Korean Christian Schools* (Seoul: Gukhakjaryowon, 2003).

9. Yong-Ryul Yoo, "The First Modern College: Soongsil College," in *What Are Universities in the Transition Period?* (Seoul: Hangilsa Publishing, 2000), p. 78.

mission schools began to gradually lose their distinctive Christian identity. Two notable changes occurred to Korean higher education during this stage: an expansion of size and a shift toward "practical training." Both public and private universities began to grow rapidly after being liberated from colonialism (1945) and more so after the Korean War (1950-1953). Many new colleges and universities opened in order to meet the increasing demand for higher education, triggered by a desire for reconstruction and by population growth. But a more significant change occurred in the direction of education. Rebuilding a nation from the ruins of war demanded an emphasis on science, technology, and economics. Government educational policy and support focused on these areas. Public universities began to lead the change and the large private universities followed the lead. The emphasis on "practical disciplines" made the concept of distinctive Christian education appear irrelevant and difficult to implement into the curriculum.[10] Challenges were real, though not insurmountable, had CHE institutions been fully committed and equipped to integrate faith with learning. Unfortunately, they were unable to cope with these changes well. Government education policy and regulation under military dictatorship in the 1960s and 1970s also suppressed the free development of CHE.[11]

The third period encompasses the 1980s to the present. Many more CHE institutions have been established in recent times as the baby-boomers, who were born after the war, began attending college, and as the Christian churches in the nation experienced rapid growth and institutional maturation. As mentioned in the beginning of this chapter, higher education now has become virtually a minimum requirement for success in Korea. New CHE institutions vigorously expanded in the past few decades, and continue to do so today. For example, Baekseok University, which was established in 1996, has reached 15,000 students with 360 faculty members in only fifteen years. These schools pursued expansion through aggressive student recruitment and promotion tactics. These universities soon faced critical compromises with the secular values of capitalism.

---

10. The struggle to maintain a uniquely Christian educational institution at the secondary level is even more difficult since the government controls its curriculum, and the general focus in Korean high school education is geared to preparing for the university entrance examination.

11. For example, the Korean government required military disciplines to be part of a compulsory curriculum, and restructured student councils after the military format. There were other regulations on how to conduct admissions, academic years, and degree-granting, and so on. Recently, the Ministry of Education introduced a nationwide evaluation of all universities and colleges in Korea.

Another major development during the 1980s was Korea's struggle for democratization. Protests against dictatorship swept through the nation until the late 1980s. Universities and colleges were preoccupied with politics based on liberal and revolutionary ideals. The Christian community was divided. Liberals participated in the democratic movement and developed *Minjung* (people's) theology, a version of liberation theology. On the other hand, the evangelicals insisted on separation of religion and politics and renounced liberation theology for mixing up Christianity with Marxist ideology. This created uneasiness in conscience, a sense of alienation, and frustration among socially engaged scholars and students in evangelical churches. They did not agree with the liberals and their way of coping with the injustices of the dictatorial government. Yet they felt an urge to engage the situation in a biblically responsible way. Searching for an alternative to the socialist revolutionary vision led them to a Christian worldview developed in the Reformed tradition. A worldview study movement began to take root among students with the help of a few pioneers who were trained in the traditions of Dutch and North American universities and seminaries.[12]

As a result, a vision for an integral CHE grew. Those who were involved with the movement realized that one's worldview matters greatly in how one deals with cultural issues. From this experience they also realized the importance of Christian education and became aware that "mission schools" did not provide a sufficient form of Christian education. Higher education especially needed to be founded on a clear biblical worldview and pursued with a conscious effort to integrate Christian faith with scholarly activities. CHE institutions should serve as strategic centers for developing and promoting Christian culture. Above all they should serve as a place where the foundation of Christian education, curriculum, and programs for lower-level education are created and evaluated. Although the movement is still very limited and its achievement is meager, it has inspired a growing sense that distinctively Christian education is necessary and worthwhile to pursue. It also helped clarify the basic idea of Christian education.

Government policy insisting on specialization in higher education could make the problem worse, however, by pushing Christian colleges to limit their focus to "Christian" subjects.[13] Specializing and being limited are two different

12. Joshua Young-gi Hong, "Evangelicals and the Democratization of South Korea since 1987," in *Evangelical Christianity and Democracy in Asia*, ed. David H. Lumsdaine (New York: Oxford University Press, 2009), pp. 185-233.

13. The Korean government made special provision for "graduate colleges," which are small institutions of graduate schools that focus on specific areas: mostly seminaries, arts,

issues. These colleges need to be allowed to broaden their perspective while strategically focusing on liberal arts programs. Reductionism in educational aims and purposes, however, will cause difficulty in coping with today's postmodern environment, which promotes cultivating a multi-perspective and interdisciplinary approach in scholarship and education. The mainstream intellectual emphasis has been changing from uniformity to plurality. Most Korean Christian universities, however, are not well informed of this change. A conservative spirit hinders them from progressing, so they are still busy conforming to the unified standard prescribed by established secular academia. They are shunning efforts to establish a stronger and more distinctive Christian identity. Yet it is time to take advantage of the pluralistic spirit of our time and be creative in developing genuine Christian education and scholarship.[14]

Current Issues and Challenges

The proportion of Christian institutions among four-year private colleges and universities is high (38.3 percent), given the fact that Protestant Christians are less than 20 percent of the population.[15] Along with the primal Shamanist Korean spirituality, Buddhism and Confucianism have been the dominant religions of Korea since the fourth century. Yet there are only one Confucian and two Buddhist universities. Some of the former mission schools, however, have developed to become the most prestigious universities of Korea, notably Yonsei and Ewha Women's universities. These universities are known for their academic excellence, high-achieving faculties, fine facilities, research capabilities, and financial resources. They boast a network of alumni who constitute a significant portion of highly regarded leaders in every field. They are also especially proud of patriotic alumni who were liberation fighters in the colonial years. Yet the Christian iden-

---

Korean studies, engineering, economics, and the like. Many seminaries became officially accredited graduate schools through this provision.

14. George M. Marsden discusses the openings for Christian perspective made possible by postmodern critiques of modernist uniformity in Marsden, *The Outrageous Idea of Christian Scholarship* (New York: Oxford University Press, 1997), pp. 44-45.

15. Korea's religious soil is complex, mixing the oldest tradition of Shamanism and two major world religions, Buddhism and Confucianism, which arrived in the fourth century from China. Buddhism was the dominant religion for one thousand years until the Yi dynasty suppressed it in favor of Confucianism, which became the ruling ideology at the turn of the fifteenth century. Within its varied sub-communities, Christianity interacts more or less consciously with each of these traditions.

tity of these institutions has been seriously compromised with secularization. It is a process similar to that of Harvard and Yale Universities in the United States.[16]

This problem is not confined to the institutions that become prestigious. As early as 1973, a team report from three other major Christian universities — Soong Jun, Seoul Woman's, and Keimyung Christian — addressed concerns about losing their Christian identity.[17] Major Christian universities went with the general trend of prioritizing academic excellence and "practicality" as the most important pursuits of education. Secularization resulted from this uncritical following of the shift away from education for the sake of gaining perspective and discernment toward gaining practical skills and technical knowledge that swept through Korean education. Christian universities felt a need to catch up with the trend in order to maintain their status and competitive edge. The emphasis on "practical disciplines" made a distinctive Christian education seem irrelevant. Consequently, according to one critic, Korean university curriculum was "based on practicality, efficiency, and market value."[18] In this respect, the majority of Christian colleges and universities in Korea began to be the "Christ of culture" type, to use H. Richard Niebuhr's terminology, simply assuming that Christian values were well embedded in their work while losing their ability to interrogate mainstream cultural trends and values.[19]

This change in Korean Christian universities was not all voluntary nor was it easily avoidable. Korean colleges and universities are required to submit to the regulations of the Ministry of Education for accreditation. Some requirements even descend to the level of micro-management. For example, the Education Law stipulates that "all education in Korea is done in the benevolent spirit for all human beings" must appear in the first line of their statement of purpose. No school can avoid putting this sentence into its statement of purpose, even though its ideology may conflict with the sentence's humanistic sentiments. Admission policy and entrance examinations are under strict gov-

16. George M. Marsden, *The Soul of the American University from Protestant Establishment to Established Nonbelief* (New York: Oxford University Press, 1994), pp. 90-93, 123-131, 181-193. Marsden argues that an Enlightenment-derived secular rationalism replaced a more particularly Christian vision in higher education as universities felt the need to find an umbrella of common beliefs broad enough to serve their widening constituencies. They became dominated by professors who were not devoted to Christianity.

17. Joint Research Project Team, *A Comprehensive Study on the Functions and Characteristics of Educational Programs of Christian Higher Education in Korea,* unpublished conference proceedings, 1973.

18. Hee-Chun Kang, "The Future of the Christian University," *Yonsei Journal of Theology* 7 (2002): 213.

19. H. Richard Niebuhr, *Christ and Culture* (New York: Harper & Row, 1951), ch. 3.

ernment control. Curriculum is also regulated. These regulations were initially intended to secure equal opportunity in education, but they have hindered the unique development of CHE.

In having to comply with government control, Christian institutions became undistinguishable from other universities except they continue to offer chapel services and a few courses on Christianity. Admission is almost entirely decided on the basis of scholarly merits. Although students are required to attend chapel once in a week, services have been transformed into "cultural events" with edifying lectures rather than sermons, in order to alleviate complaints. Celebrating a university's Christian vision is rarely done, even in convocations such as anniversaries and commencement. Hardly any effort is put into proselytizing nonbelieving students. Students are seldom given Christian counseling in academic and personal matters. Courses on Christianity are usually elementary moral or spiritual studies, and would not be attractive to students had they not been required. Some of these schools have been compelled to introduce several varieties of chapel to fit the varying levels of faith. These institutions have not totally abandoned their faith and mission school ideals; their vision remains to influence students to turn to the faith, at least in later stages of their life. Or at the least, perhaps they can prevent students from becoming anti-Christian. These goals, however, are dismal in comparison to what mission schools' original purpose was in the past.[20]

Government regulations have loosened since the 1990s as the nation enjoys more democratic trends. Yet now a more subtle and sophisticated control has been laid on government-supported evaluation agencies. The standards and requirements of these agencies are not always in accordance with Christian ideals. Schools are chiefly measured in quantitative terms, such as size, facilities, quality of professors and students, academic productivity of faculties, and the number of graduates who are able to secure jobs. In order to maintain good standing and to compete with other schools, Christian institutions have worked hard to comply with these standards. The only exception has been a major opposition against recent revisions of the Private Educational Institution Law. Christian schools, regardless of theological orientations, are united against the government on this matter. One of the main issues is the mandate that 25 percent of the school's board members must be from outside the school community.[21] Schools are insisting that the mandate will bring

---

20. Joint Research Project Team, *A Comprehensive Study*, pp. 105, 160-163.

21. *Private Educational Institution Law*, Chapter 3, "Organization," article 3. It was revised on July 27, 2007.

structural changes that seriously infringe a Christian identity. The government argues that the changes are merely meant to secure the "public" nature of private education. The fight for revising the article is still ongoing.

In this struggle for maintaining Christian identity, "theological colleges" that stemmed out of a seminary are in better position. They expanded "pre-seminary" programs by adding departments of education, music, social welfare, and so on, while remaining as small humanities colleges. They are affiliated with denominations that closely hold on to doctrinal traditions. Chongshin and Kosin Universities are examples of such universities. They neither started as mission schools nor ever considered themselves as such. Instead they aimed to train Christian leaders. As a result, they have been able to retain as universities some of the features they enjoyed as theological schools. Chongshin, for example, requires a certificate of baptism for all applicants. Kosin recently lifted the requirement, but still requires church membership. These requirements cause conflicts with the government policy for equal opportunity in education. However, these schools believe that these requirements are necessary to maintain their distinct Christian identity. These institutions require faculty members not only to profess the Christian faith but also to attend the denominational church. Campus culture is embedded with the Christian tradition. Chongshin has chapel every morning. Students are required to attend a certain percentage, depending on their year in school. Faculty and staff are also required to attend. All ceremonies, celebrations, meetings, and even some classes begin with a service or devotional prayer. Some schools have interdisciplinary foundational courses on Christian worldview required for all incoming freshmen.

There are perils, however, for these "theological colleges," and they are opposite to those of secularized Christian universities. What Niebuhr calls the "Christ against culture" tendency prevails at these institutions. They are at risk of cultural indifference and isolation from mainline academics. As a result, they are ineffective in their cultural engagement. They become "special" schools in Korean educational parlance, a separate category from colleges and universities. Their vision is limited to the church and does not reach beyond theology, ministry, mission, church education, and music. In these colleges, a different kind of dualism reigns — the theology department assumes superiority over other disciplines as the supervisor of faith and academics. In this respect, to borrow Niebuhr's term again, the danger of becoming the "Christ above culture" type is also present.[22] Also, while maintaining close ties with a denomination is an asset, these ties may cause the relationship between schools

22. Niebuhr, *Christ and Culture,* chs. 4 and 5.

and their supporting communities to be in tension. The church and specific denominations do not support universities in a substantial way, but they send a board of trustees to oversee the content and thrust of a school's education and administration. Students and faculty may not share all of the denomination's particular interests and concerns and at times will come into conflict with the board concerning doctrinal, political, and cultural issues. These conflicts raise issues of academic freedom. Ecclesiastical politics and policies can also bleed over into aspects of education and the institution's existence. For example, doctrinal disputes in the supporting community that have little to do with higher education can affect the educational institution directly and can even cause it to split. An example of such a split occurred between the Hapdong and Tonghap Presbyterian churches with their colleges and seminaries in 1959.

Another worrisome development comes from rapid expansion, which often erodes quality control. Some of these new Christian colleges have quickly expanded into large universities such as Hansin, Anyang, Baeksoek, Hansae, Pyongtaek, and Sungkyul Universities. Expansion is often motivated by financial considerations as more students bring higher revenue. Yet the number of high school students is diminishing. Korea's birth rate of 1.22 per family in 2010 was the lowest among developed countries.[23] Universities that are focused on local cities are already experiencing difficulty in recruiting students. A vicious cycle starts when these schools begin to relax Christian elements and academic standards in order to secure enrollment numbers, which eventually damages the Christian identity of the school.

Two new CHE institutions made notable breakthroughs with unique tactics for this struggle. Handong Global University in Pohong was not founded by a Christian board, but the vision of its president has been the main force driving the university to become seriously Christian. Handong has successfully grown in both size and reputation in the last fifteen years. That Handong, in spite of its location in a rather remote local village outside a regional industrial city, currently enjoys a high rate of applications from highly ranked students is evidence of its successful establishment in a very short period of time. The success of Handong is complex but it certainly has to do with its tactic in filling a gap in the education market. There are many Christian parents who feel that there is a lack of excellent Christian universities in which to enroll their children. Prestigious private universities are not only difficult to enter, but have also been secularized to an extent that they cannot be regarded as true

---

23. http://www.index.go.kr/egams/stts/jsp/potal/stts/PO_STTS_IdxMain.jsp?idx_cd= 1428.

Christian education. Theological colleges, on the other hand, are too narrow and their academic standing and reputation are not very high. This gap is what Handong filled with its unique vision of creating a school reputable not only in academics but also in holistic Christian virtues.

Anglican University is another school that filled a gap left behind by most liberal Christian universities. Liberal schools like Hansin University used to be at an ideologically radical front with *Minjung* theology during the democratization struggle of the 1970s. Hansin seemed to have given up its previous theological edge as it expanded in size in recent years. Anglican, by hiring professors known for progressive sociopolitical thinking, took Hansin's place, and is becoming known for special programs such as its course on leadership in nongovernmental organizations.

The success of these schools depends heavily on their ability to meet the current demands of students and being able to adjust to changing circumstances. Their history is too short to make any definite judgment, however. They also do not present a clear solution to the failures of the prestige universities and theological colleges. Furthermore, enthusiastic vision can lead to false optimism and pride. A high success rate of graduates getting good jobs and the level of faculty members' activism in society and politics are not proper measures of Christian education. Radicalism and too close relations with a particular ideology are other dangers for these schools. While it is difficult to maintain distance from influential ideology, Christians should not uncritically adopt fashionable ideologies as the foundation for their education. To be perceptive about a particular situation is one challenge. But knowing how to cope with longer-term sociocultural realities in a distinctively Christian way is perhaps the greater challenge. CHE cannot afford to lose one either. It cannot emphasize one at the cost of the other.

Task and Vision

The history and description of Korean CHE may give the reader the impression that its outlook is not very bright. The situation is not irremediable.[24] Most Christian colleges and universities appear to be aiming in the right di-

24. There are multiple assessments of the same issue in the United States. For example, James M. Penning and Corwin E. Smidt criticize James D. Hunter's pessimism on the trend of the American Christian colleges and university and project a different picture. Cf. Hunter, *Evangelicalism: The Coming Generation* (Chicago: University of Chicago Press, 1987); Penning and Smidt, *Evangelicalism: The Next Generation* (Grand Rapids: Baker Academic, 2002).

rection. Their official statements of purposes declare that their schools are built on Christian principles and values. They acknowledge that education limited to the spirit of humanistic and philanthropic values is not sufficient. In addition to requiring Christian studies, they declare the importance of a Christian worldview as their foundation. They also stress developing Christian virtues, visions, and missions. They even mention the importance of integral studies or integration of faith and learning.[25] Although the reality of campus life and classroom discourse may not fully achieve a school's statements of purpose, setting one's aims in the right direction is still a positive factor. If only we would live up to our statements of purpose!

In fact, this task of making higher education genuinely Christian has begun to be undertaken in fresh ways by a few institutions. Interest in conducting scholarship from Christian perspectives has grown in Korea recently. Christian universities and colleges have sponsored conferences and lectures, and even established a center for furthering the cause.[26] It is encouraging to see institutions moving beyond preliminary discussions on worldview foundations toward concrete programs. But the progress is hardly sufficient. One great disadvantage is that professors who are practicing genuinely integrated Christian scholarship are scattered in different universities. It is true that Christian education does not need to be confined to Christian institutions. If professors working in secular universities were to teach according to their Christian convictions, Christian education could be accomplished. On the other hand, if Christian institutions are not based on authentically Christian academic approaches backed by the academic and personal authority of their professors, all the special lectures and even sermons will be ineffective.[27] Unfortunately, there are many Christians in the academic world who do not view their scholarly activities through the eyes of faith. Many believe that merely trying to be able and better teachers and giving Christian witness in sincerity and humility is enough. Another disadvantage is that even many of those who speak of integrating faith and life often do not truly understand this

25. Joint Research Project Team, *A Comprehensive Study*, pp. 23-25, 101.

26. Many theological colleges, for example, have initiated research projects, symposia, lectures, conferences, and programs for teachers from various school levels. Seoul Woman's University (SWU) also hosted a number of conferences on alternative education on the basis of Christian worldview. Scholars from Dordt College in Sioux Center, Iowa, and Bob Jones University in Greenville, South Carolina, cooperated with SWU in these conferences.

27. Bong-Ho Son, "Christian Higher Education in Korea: Problems and Prospects," *Proceedings at International Symposium on Christian Higher Education* (Pusan: Kosin University Press, 1996), p. 19.

notion. For these reasons, practices of true integral scholarship are definitely rarer than existing conversations about it. There is a great need for Christian scholars who can exemplify how such integration can be done with concrete examples.[28] There is also a need for the development of domestic and international collaboration since cooperative networking provides ways to utilize resources effectively. It goes without saying that these needs can be best met in a Christian university setting.

It is important to remember that the success of early CHE in Korea depended on these universities' ability to raise Christian leaders. Today the more prestigious schools of Christian heritage fail in this task because of secularization. Other Christian universities are unsuccessful in this mission because of their difficulties in attracting good Christian students. Even many Christian families do not prefer these new Christian universities. Successful CHE depends on scholars and schools being able to work effectively with a supporting community. Raising public support is vital for education because teaching the next generation is always the work of community, not the school alone. This is particularly so in Christian education. The Korean church is well known for its missionary zeal. Its eyes are constantly concentrating on the end of the world. This vision does not reach very deep or wide. There are already warnings that the next generation will be a different generation, young adults "who know neither the Lord nor what he has done" for the nation and the church. The Korean Christian community must realize the importance of CHE for its survival and welfare. It needs to open its eyes to the central role that higher education plays in our time. The Korean church has not been perceptive about the relevance of Christian scholarship for evangelism and expansion of God's kingdom. This is because of the church's narrow understanding of salvation and mission. Thus far, the church has been very much preoccupied with its own growth and not so much with the evangelical responsibility of transforming society and culture. It therefore needs to rebuild a broader vision for the Christian calling in all aspects of life.

In order to do so, it is essential to broaden the concept of CHE. This is necessary because the fundamental difficulties of Korean CHE stem from the dualistic worldview that is prevalent in the church. The church's concern for higher education often does not reach far enough beyond seminary and religious education. And parents tend to reduce university education to narrowly

---

28. I have in mind what scholars like Herman Dooyeweerd in jurisprudence, Nicholas Wolterstorff and Alvin Plantinga in philosophy, George Marsden in history, Jacques Ellul in sociology, and Clifford Christians in communication ethics have done in their fields.

pragmatic and instrumental terms. Christian scholars and institutions need to demonstrate that the church can prosper and function rightly in today's world. One way to do so is by working out Christian worldview foundations for all of life, especially for education. Christian universities must develop concrete programs to equip students with knowledge, skill, and virtues that are grounded on this worldview. These activities may be able to show that it is indeed feasible to recover a holistic life, where one is both competent to serve in a profession and equipped to serve God's reign in its fullness. Such a holistic view of Christian education must replace reductionism.

It is also important to enhance Christians' sensitivity toward cultural changes. Globalization is rapidly transforming Korean society and culture, which has remained highly monolithic throughout its five thousand–year history. Korea is well known for its one blood, one language, and one culture. This is why unification talks between North and South Korea are easily swamped with sentimentalism despite their huge differences in ideologies and politico-economic structures. Talk of multiculturalism is becoming popular, however, and it seems increasingly necessary because of the fast-growing numbers of migrant workers and international marriages. Korea is also being deeply affected by a postmodern cultural spirit that is moving from uniformity to plurality and diversity. Rationalistic and theological reductionism will cause difficulty in coping with the current trends, which require multidimensional and interdisciplinary approaches to scholarship and education. Unfortunately, Korean CHE institutions are slow to respond to this change. Most of them do not realize the opportunity that could open for them to develop and strengthen a distinctively Christian identity. Not many of them are aware that they should be taking advantage of the pluralistic spirit of the current society for the sake of establishing a unique set of options: Christian education and scholarship.[29]

These are two reasons why developing a unique vision for Christian education is strategically crucial in the current Korean situation. First, it is an effective way to combat secularization. In Korea today as in other countries, the biggest challenge for CHE institutions is secularization. A firm foundation in a Christian worldview can keep Christian institutions on their proper footing, which in turn will help them maintain a distinctive Christian identity. Second, Christian education suggests a way out of the nation's educational crisis. Today, Korean education up to secondary school level is exclusively focused on the university entrance examination. Extreme competition involving this examination has distorted much of the structure and purpose of secondary educa-

29. Marsden, *The Outrageous Idea of Christian Scholarship,* pp. 109-111.

tion. Egoism, individualism, reductionism, abnormal and unethical activities within schools, and an incredible funneling of money toward private education are caused by this faulty system. All of these flaws require fundamental healing as the students enter university. An educational vision based on a biblical worldview has many things to offer toward healing these problems such as a holistic view of life and learning, a communitarian and cooperative ideal, the idea of calling, and the use of gifts in service. This vision can also show how to enhance the integration of learning and living, while teaching young people how to become responsible citizens.

Korean CHE institutions must also revive the vision of integral education. Simply reinforcing moral education by reforming curriculum and encouraging social service is not enough.[30] Not many schools have developed a systematic curriculum that reflects seriousness for CHE. Resurrecting "authentic liberal education" to revive the "ethical and religious perspective" of students is not sufficient.[31] Strengthening the "atmosphere of the Christian university, the relationship between professors and students, students to students, the system of administration, non-credit programs," and the "hidden curriculum" may only exert implicit influence.[32] There is a strong need for truly integral and therefore transformational programs. Korean Christian universities need to invest serious effort to develop the theological and philosophical foundations.

There is some encouraging development in integrating faith and learning at several institutions. For instance, Chongshin and Kosin Universities have integrated interdisciplinary courses such as "Spiritual Leadership Training," which all freshmen are required to attend. They are training and encouraging both old and new faculty to develop integrated Christian learning. New faculty members must also attend doctrinal and Christian worldview seminars to learn how to integrate their discipline with faith. In the past several years, Baeksoek, Handong, and Kosin sponsored Christian faculty training seminars in conjunction with faculty members from Calvin College in Grand Rapids, Michigan, to share their experiences in forms of lectures and intense discussions for three days. The steering committee of this seminar is trying to extend its invitation to other interested institutions and individual professors. Besides

---

30. Some emphasize this factor. Referring to R. M. Hare's *Moral Thinking* (Oxford: Clarendon Press, 1981), Hee-Chun Kang argues that this is a way to recover the identity of Christian universities. Kang, "The Future of the Christian University," pp. 213, 217-218.

31. Douglas J. Elwood, ed., *The Humanities in Christian Higher Education in Asia: Ethical and Religious Perspective* (Quezon City: New Day Publishers, 1978), pp. iii-vi.

32. Hee-Chun Kang argues that this too is a way to recover the identity of Christian universities: "The Future of the Christian University," p. 214.

these international and inter-university conferences, some institutions have been developing their own worldview and Bible/theological curriculum and textbooks. Most CHE institutions have committees for developing Christian education. Many of these institutions have taken on a systematic approach to revive chapel attendance. They realize that chapel can be a time for the community to meet together and share its vision, and can play a central role in the life of the institution and its education.

Korean CHE is standing at a critical juncture as competition for students and resources is becoming fierce with the dwindling numbers of students.[33] Only by equipping themselves with a genuine Christian vision, academic excellence, and quality educational service will they secure survival and prosperity. This is not going to be an easy task. Not many of the Christian universities

33. It has been predicted that the number of students entering college will be below the capacity of existing universities and colleges after 2004. This means that some schools will eventually have difficulty maintaining their operations because of the lack of students. In fact, the total quota of freshmen was reduced in 2004 for the first time in the history of Korean higher education. This reduction was due to voluntary cutbacks of several universities to cope with an expected decline of numbers of high school graduates as the chart below shows. Cf. Korean Education Development Institute (Education Policy Network Research Laboratory), "Current Evaluation of Rate of Possible Admission to Universities and Colleges and National Scholastic Achievement Level" (2012, pp. 2, 10): http://edpolicy.kedi.re.kr/EpnicForum/Epnic/EpnicForum02Viw.php?PageNum=1&S_Key=&S_Menu=&Ac_Code=D0010203&Ac_Num0=13888.

A = High School Graduates
B = Students Taking Korean SAT
C = Universities and Colleges Freshman Quotas
D = Possible Admission to Universities and Colleges/High School Graduates (%)
E = Possible Admission to Universities and Colleges/SAT-Taking Students (%)

	A	B	C	D	E
1995	649,653	809,804	495,300	76.2	61.2
2000	764,712	868,366	646,275	84.5	74.4
2005	569,272	574,218	625,541	109.9	108.9
2006	568,055	570,583	596,313	105.0	104.5
2007	571,357	551,884	584,789	102.4	106.0
2008	581,921	550,588	581,991	100.0	105.7
2009	576,298	559,475	580,635	100.8	103.8
2010	633,539	638,216	571,842	90.3	89.6
2011	648,468	668,991	569,121	87.8	85.1

in Korea today are in the academic forefront. They act more like huge liberal arts colleges. They are not advanced research universities. Thus they need to work hard to improve in both academic excellence and quality of education in order to maintain good standing among higher education institutions.

Community and Resources

The biggest asset of Korean CHE is the church, but as we have seen, the relationships between the various Christian communities and their universities are rather ambivalent. Let us explore this matter further. First, there is a deep set of cultural values to reckon with that predate Christianity in Korea. Koreans are enthusiastic about education due to their Confucian heritage. Confucian ideals of filial piety are still deeply embedded in Korean education, namely honoring parents and the ancestors by "achieving a great success in the world and making one's name famous." Entering the good schools is considered to be the best means for this purpose.[34] CHE can be helped by this cultural tradition. Yet Christian education should transform the ideal into bringing up a more holistic person with a sense of responsibility that is broader than filial piety and personal excellence, including matters of justice, freedom, sincerity, human equality, responsibility, love, service, and stewardship. CHE institutions need to promote these virtues among their students and faculty. Such Christian service and transformational spirit have to be cultivated with a humble spirit.

Despite the high enthusiasm for education in Korea, support for Christian education is meager even among Christians. The Christian community is slowly awakening to the importance of Christian scholarship for the church and Christian culture, however. The number of scholarship funds and research grants provided by Christian foundations and individuals for high-level studies is increasing, though they are still mostly for students in theology. Churches and a few foundations have also begun to support students studying Christian subjects in universities and seminaries in the United States or various European countries.

Presbyterian denominations comprise a large part of CHE in Korea. But the Methodist, Lutheran, Baptist, Pentecostal, Nazarene, Anglican, and Catholic churches have their own institutions of higher education as well. Christian universities and colleges are also affiliated with faith communities to different

---

34. Unknown author, trans. Min-Jae Do, *HyoKyung (Book of Filial Piety)* (Seoul: Zmanz, 2008), 68 (14/11a-b).

degrees. Some are still under direct supervision by denominational governing boards. A few universities are sponsored by local churches or individuals. For example, there are two mega-churches that support universities: Yoido Full Gospel Church established Hansae University, while Onnuri Church is the major financial contributor to Handong University. But in most cases, financial contributions from supporting communities are seldom substantial. Since churches contribute little to operating expenses, institutions are largely dependent on tuition for their operating revenue. Where church members send their students matters more to these institutions than where they send their gifts.

Christian higher educational institutions can also be grouped according to their theological orientation. Institutions affiliated with liberal denominations constitute the mainline. They surpass conservative evangelical institutions in number and size. They tend to be academically stronger and better organized as institutions. Yet they also tend to be less distinctively Christian and more secularized. Evangelical institutions place a stronger emphasis on maintaining a Christian identity, and are better at doing so. Unfortunately, they are often less successful in achieving academic excellence and keeping up with competitive scholarship. Consequently, they have no well-established and highly respected institutions of higher education apart from seminaries and theological colleges. Because of this, their influence is very limited, even within Christian circles.

Resources for CHE are not confined to Christian institutions. There are also the Christian scholars, who are scattered over various universities. They often gather, formally or informally, into Christian professors' fellowships. Working in the secular academic environment does not allow them many opportunities to integrate their academic efforts with faith. Those who were involved with the early Christian worldview movement in the 1970s and went on to study in various fields are different. They have been able to spread the idea of integration of faith and learning. Groups interested in the Christian worldview began to form on many campuses. Although those who have been able to demonstrate an integral approach to their academic discipline with concrete examples are rare, the number of them is continuing to grow.

In the last two decades, a number of research centers for integration of faith and academic learning have been established. Those who were involved with the Christian worldview movement formed Christian Worldview Studies Association of Korea in 1984.[35] This association has more than 150 scholars in different fields who occasionally gather in subdivision meetings of philosophy,

---

35. Website for the association: http://www.dew21.org/subpage/csak/info_03.asp.

literature, cultural studies, education, science, engineering, films, arts, and more. It also offers worldview classes to the public as well through Christian Worldview Academy, which is the educational service agency of the association. Economists and management scholars from the association also established a separate institute, the Korea Christian Academy of Management, for those in their field of study. Other scholars actively endeavoring for integrating faith and scholarship have organized the Society for Integration Studies, Annual Conferences on Christian Learning, Biannual Christian School Teachers' Conference, Christian Educators Association, several Christian culture study institutes, Christian Lawyers Fellowship, and the Christian Medical Doctors' Association.

These organizations helped CHE in both direct and indirect ways by producing text materials and practical results from their experiences of integral practices. For example, several Christian professors and teachers' associations believed that CHE institutions should play a key role in extending Christian education to all age levels. They tried to support Christian education at lower levels through research, curriculum development, and continuing education for teachers. Attempts are being made to establish a center to support alternative and home schooling.[36] Such projects in turn are providing further topics for research and study in Christian universities and colleges.

Many Christian publishers are providing opportunities for scholars and writers to put out their research and findings. The Korean Christian Philosophy Society, several Christian education societies, and some theological societies are active in this way. Many Christian academic journals, published either by academic societies or Christian universities and colleges, come out regularly. There are also plenty of newsletters, Christian newspapers, and magazines being printed. These publications, along with many conferences and academic society meetings, provide a forum for academic exchange in Christian scholarship and public services. While Korea is quickly moving to become a cyber communication society, the numbers of the Internet websites related to Christian subjects are developing fast as well.

There are also Christian student groups on all campuses that can act as the "hidden curriculum." There are Bible study groups that are particular to each campus, and local branches of Inter Varsity Christian Fellowship, Campus Crusade for Christ, Navigators, Youth with Mission, L'Abri, University Bible Fellowship, and Joy Mission that are working actively on almost every

36. Korean Christian education under the secondary level lately is experiencing important developments with increasing interests in Christian alternative and home schooling.

college and university campus in Korea. Although these groups are mainly interested in evangelism and discipleship, they have some interest in learning basic scholarly responsibility and worldview. In America and other countries, annual conferences of Korean Students in All Nations have been bringing Christian graduate and undergraduate students studying abroad together. Since especially many of the graduate students eventually become professors and scholars in their fields, the conferences provide an opportunity for networking and fellowship among the students, and they feature speakers who are often university faculty members.

Networking with the international community of CHE has been done primarily with various American institutions. This is natural because of early missionary connections. It also has to do with the fact that the majority of university faculty members were trained in American institutions. Most universities, colleges, and seminaries try to broaden their international relationships and seek affiliation with foreign institutions. Broadening relationships beyond North America to include Asian, Oceanian, African, and European institutions is also considered desirable. This is important since today many Korean missionaries are working in different parts of the world and have established seminaries and colleges as part of their mission work.[37] There are also many foreign students in Korean seminaries and theological colleges. In this way the Korean Christian community is becoming increasingly aware of its international responsibility as a richly blessed church.

Church education can prepare students in the fundamental elements of faith. This way the higher education institutions will not have to begin from the basics. A strong church can provide an abundance of human resources for developing CHE. There are many devoted Christian scholars in most fields of study. Admittedly, as mentioned, many of them are not well informed about integral Christian scholarship. Neither are they very enthusiastic about integrating faith and scholarship in other than "spiritual" or church activities. Not many Christian universities and colleges have developed a systematic and effective curriculum that reflects seriousness for CHE. When such an effort is carried out by individuals or institutions, it is often difficult to gain support from the community. The church's lack of understanding of the importance of higher academic enterprise is also disheartening. It is important to remem-

37. This has occurred in countries like the Philippines, Mongolia, Cambodia, Nigeria, Uganda, and China. For example, Korean missionaries established the Reformed Theological College in Uganda, which now grants B.A. degrees in cooperation with the University of Potchefstroom in South Africa. The Vancouver Institutes for Evangelical Worldview in Canada offers a Korean Christian Worldview program in affiliation with Trinity Western University.

ber, however, that Christian education is more of a task to pursue rather than an achievement about which to boast.[38] Working toward the development of Christian scholarship is a difficult but exciting task. Awaking and promoting the integral vision of CHE in Korea is a challenge but certainly not an impossible dream.

Conclusion

Just as Korea has developed fast in the last century, CHE also grew rapidly. CHE occupies a significant portion of the nation's private higher education. Successful growth, however, brought challenges of secularization. Christian universities and colleges, especially prestigious ones, have lost much of their Christian identity in the process of adjusting to the changes of context, government education policy, and competition in the education market. They have mainly tried to cope with the difficulties by struggling to maintain exterior elements of Christian identity, namely, chapel and Bible classes. It is now clear that such a dualistic approach to academics and faith will not provide a sufficient solution. Without securing both excellence in educational performance and uniqueness of Christian identity, CHE's future in Korea may not be as bright as its earlier history. As several cases indicate, an integral approach to faith and scholarship and education is the way to overcome the challenge for Korean CHE at the crossroads.

38. C. Stephen Evans, "The Calling of the Christian Scholar-Teacher," in *Faithful Learning and the Christian Scholarly Vocation,* ed. Douglas V. Henry and Bob R. Agee (Grand Rapids: Eerdmans, 2003), p. 28.

CHAPTER 5

Christian Higher Education in India:
The Road We Tread

J. Dinakarlal

Introduction

The history of Christian higher education in India is so tightly and inseparably intertwined with the history of Christian missions that one cannot understand the contributions of either unless looked at as one entity. Education was introduced in India by the early missionaries, who believed that they were commissioned to spread knowledge and justice in a country with many social evils. The missionaries offered school and higher education as part of their attempt at humanization of a society that suffered from casteism and practices like black magic and even human sacrifice. Missionary zeal was noticeable in every component of education offered by early visionaries, and higher education was no exception. CMS College, founded in Kottayam, Kerala State, in 1817 by British missionaries of the Church Missionary Society (now managed by the Church of South India) was the first of a long line of Christian colleges, soon followed by Serampore College, famously founded by the British Baptist missionaries William Carey, Joshua Marshman, and William Ward in 1818. All told, this remarkable movement for Christian higher education in India has resulted in several hundred Christian colleges being established across the subcontinent.[1]

---

1. Rudolf C. Heredia, "Education and Mission: School as Agent of Evangelisation," *Economic and Political Weekly,* September 16, 1995, pp. 2232-2340, offers a very helpful survey, albeit in the context of a fairly harsh analysis of this endeavor. For more historical background, see Commission on Christian Higher Education in India, *The Christian College in India: The Report of the Commission on Higher Education in India* (London: Oxford University Press, 1931),

It is important to understand this original impulse, so this chapter looks at Christian higher education in India right from its start before analyzing its current state of affairs in a globalized and commercialized world. It then asks what Indian Christian higher education should be and become in its multi-religious, socially pluralistic Indian context.

Beginning of CHE in India: A Challenge to the Way Things Were

To understand why the early missionaries to India from the West took special interest in spreading education, one should look at the sociopolitical and socioeconomic condition of the people of India in that period. India was a country where people practiced a social caste system that had religious endorsement. Caste structure and practices had given rise to several social evils and inhumane practices, and the missionaries believed that without education it was not possible to open the eyes of the Indian masses to these harmful social realities and customs. As Premalatha Dinakarlal points out, the best way to achieve a broad recognition of these issues was by "offering an education that was affordable to the poor masses." Education, she reveals, was considered to be "the prerogative of the people of the upper caste," but the missionaries "took special interest in education as they believed that education in the Western model should go side by side with any attempt to spread the Gospel and education should be offered not only to Christians but also to people of all faiths."[2]

It was with this agenda that the missionaries embarked on giving formal education to the masses in a country where only the chosen few of the upper castes were expected to be lettered. The introduction to the *Directory of Church Related Colleges in India,* published in 1995 by the All India Association for the Promotion of Christian Higher Education (AIAPCHE), makes clear the vision of the early missionaries and founders of Christian institutions in India: they encompassed "a wide spectrum of religious, spiritual, moral, national, secular and academic concerns including the integrated development of the human person, stress on character formation, women's development, emphasis on the

---

and Richard Dickinson and S. P. Appasamy, *The Christian College and National Development* (Madras: Christian Literature Society, 1967). For a sense of the full scope of this movement today, see Reny Jacob and Carolyne John, eds., *Directory of Church-related Colleges in India* (New Delhi: All India Association for the Promotion of Christian Higher Education, 2001).

2. Premalatha Dinakarlal, "Religious Diversity and Christian Higher Education in India: Prospects and Problems," in *Christian Higher Education and Globalization in Asia/Oceania: Realities and Challenges,* ed. J. Dinakarlal (Sioux Center, Iowa: Dordt College Press, 2010), p. 22.

spirit for service and an openness to people of all faiths." To the missionaries, education was at the same time God's work and an inevitable instrument of social change. The missionaries' higher education movement produced

> an educated leadership in the church, society and the government. It opened new vistas of knowledge to all. Notwithstanding their religious motives, [the missionaries] served the cause of education as none else did. The methods they used, the values they cherished, the commitments they made, the convictions they maintained, the humiliations and hardships they willingly suffered, and above all their love and passion for the people remain a source of inspiration even today.[3]

The services rendered to the cause of higher education by the missionaries cannot be ignored; the Christian missionaries were responsible to a very large extent for sowing the seed of systematic higher education in India on the Western model. The sufferings and challenges they boldly faced speak volumes about their commitment and also their love and passion for the people of the country to which they came. Speaking to the politically charged situation in contemporary India prompted by Hindu nationalism, Premalatha Dinakarlal insists that Indians must

> acknowledge the selfless service of early Christians in this land of Hindus, as most of these colleges were built not with brick and mortar but with prayers, tears, blood and sacrifice. Christian educational institutions never restricted themselves to serving Christians, for their noble aim was to transform humanity, and hence they opened their doors for Christians and non-Christians alike, though some political forces in India today underplay the contribution of such institutions and aspire to curtail their right.[4]

There were 25 colleges managed by the Christian churches at the end of the nineteenth century. According to the data published by All India Association for the Promotion of Christian Higher Education, there are thirty-six Christian colleges that have completed 100 years or more, nineteen colleges that have completed seventy-five to one hundred years, and sixty-eight colleges that have completed fifty to seventy-five years. When India achieved indepen-

3. "Developing a Christian Academic Community: Opportunities and Challenges in India," a communal paper presented by the Indian delegation to the Manila Leadership Conference of International Association for the Promotion of Christian Higher Education, Manila, Philippines, October 2002.

4. Dinakarlal, "Religious Diversity and Christian Higher Education in India," p. 23.

dence in 1947, out of the 516 colleges and universities in the country, sixty-six were Christian colleges. By 2005, after massive development and growth in higher education, there were 17,973 colleges and universities in India, out of which 7,720 were privately founded. Only about 500 of these are Christian colleges, but it is evident that this particular group in higher education has been expanding too.[5]

Challenges to Early Christian Institutions

In the nineteenth century, there were many forces working against offering education to the common men and women. Indian traditions made education the sole prerogative of people belonging to the so-called upper castes. Needless to say, leading people across Indian society to realize the importance of education and starting educational institutions to serve them were no easy tasks. The early Christian educators realized that it was their responsibility to give a socially relevant education to the Indian masses and for this it was imperative that education addressed itself to many of the burning social issues. Fighting social evils was a prerequisite for bringing about any meaningful change and establishing an educated and cultured society. "As we look at the history of Indian CHE," says Premalatha Dinakarlal, "we understand that apart from imparting education, these institutions have taken a very bold stance in eradiating social evils: Sati [immolation of widows], child marriage, gender and caste discrimination, social exploitations and oppressions, illiteracy," widespread occult practices, and economic underdevelopment.[6] Behind every Christian institution of higher learning, this was the reforming vision. Dr. Mani Jacob, the general secretary of AIAPCHE, in his introduction to the 1995 edition of the *Directory of Church-related Colleges in India* says that it was a shared vision, solidly backed by local initiative and sacrifice, Christian and otherwise:

> The superstructure of Christian higher education was constructed on strong missionary foundations, by the Christian community of India using indigenous resources — human, intellectual, material and financial — [and] with the support and cooperation of people of different faiths living together in the pluralistic environment of India.[7]

5. Pawan Agarwal, "Higher Education in India: The Need for a Change," Working Paper no. 180, Indian Council for Research on International Economic Relations, 2006.

6. Dinakarlal, "Religious Diversity and Christian Higher Education in India," p. 23.

7. Mani Jacob, "Introduction," in *Directory of Church-related Colleges in India*, ed. Mani

Of particular concern to the early missionaries were the potentialities of women. Indian traditional society did not attach much importance to the education of women. A note of Reverend James Fleming Kearns, Society for the Propagation of the Gospel (SPG) missionary to South India in the mid-nineteenth century, shows how difficult it was to impress on the male-dominated society the need to educate women:

> Noticing the almost total absence of the women I enquired of the Catechist the cause. He told me that they never came and that they never would! I called the men together and showed them how wrong it was to keep their wives from church. To my great grief they told me in reply that it was an unheard of thing to teach women and that consequently they could not consent to such conduct without being highly reproached![8]

Women throughout India were leading a life of insult, humiliation, and subhuman status. The belief was widespread that women were meant only for taking care of domestic chores. That being the case, education for women was not thought to be necessary. Women of the lower castes had to bear the torment of an oppressive social structure and they were doubly discriminated against — for their caste and also for being women. Women of India of that time were yet to see the ray of enlightenment; they were confined to their houses and education was not their cup of tea. The Indian historian Joy Gnanadason observes that there was a common belief "in some parts of India that girls who were taught the three R's (reading, writing and arithmetic) would become widows soon and widowhood was the bitterest experience for a woman."[9] The early missionaries who founded Christian education in India had enormous responsibility and had to face many challenges and oppositions, especially when they attempted to offer education to women.

Educating women has remained an uphill task for educators. In spite of the brave struggles of the government and the Christian colleges and universities, women's education has not yet reached a respectable level. The literacy rates in British India were very low. In 1911 the rate was only 6 percent overall,

Jacob (New Delhi: All India Association for the Promotion of Christian Higher Education, 1995), p. xiii.

8. Quoted in David Gore, "Faith and Family in South India: Robert Caldwell and His Missionary Dynasty," accessed May 22, 2012, http://www.britishempire.co.uk.

9. Joy Gnanadason, *A Forgotten History: The Story of Missionary Movement and the Liberation of People in South Travancore* (Chennai: Gurukul Lutheran Theological College and Research Institute, 1994), p. 34.

and women's rates were estimated to be much lower. By 1931 the overall rate was just 8 percent, and by 1947 it had moved only to 11 percent. The number of literate women among the female population of India was perhaps 2 to 6 percent during these same years.[10] The new nation has made literacy a major priority, but female literacy rates continue to lag. By 2001 the overall rate was 65 percent, but female literacy was 54 percent. In 2011 the overall rate reached 74 percent but the female rate still ran behind, at 65.5 percent.[11]

When studying the education of women and also the service it has rendered to women's emancipation, one cannot be blind to the contributions of India's Christian colleges and universities. The *Directory of Church-related Colleges in India* (2001), published by AIAPCHE, states that, out of its 274 member colleges, five colleges are for men, 196 are co-educational, and seventy-three are exclusively for women.[12] Clearly Indian Christian higher education has made women's education a priority. The first women's college, Isabella Thoburn College, was established in Uttar Pradesh State in 1886 with the noble goal of sharing with women the love of the Lord through higher education. The ultimate aim was to prepare them to serve others, especially other women. Quite aptly the motto of the college is "We Receive to Give." This was followed by the establishment of the second college exclusively for women, Sarah Tucker College (1895), in Palayamkottai, Tamilnadu, a highly conservative and underdeveloped area. The missionary zeal behind this college once again is revealed by the motto: "So Run That Ye May Obtain the Incorruptible Crown" (1 Cor. 9:25). In 1947, the year of independence, out of the seventy-two Christian colleges in India, sixteen were exclusively for women. Most of the other Christian institutions were admitting women too. Since then, the number of Christian women's colleges has increased more than fourfold. Quite interestingly, all four Christian colleges started in 1948, the first year of independence, were for women. Indian Christian higher education was devoted to the idea that real social transformation takes place when women too are enlightened and educated.

Another important issue the early missionaries had to handle was health. In an epidemic-prone country, where scientific medical treatment and prevention were largely unknown, it was not an easy task for the missionaries to attend to the health needs of the people. The missionaries, besides training

10. "Education during the British Raj," accessed May 23, 2012, http://www.xtimeline.com.

11. "Literates and Literacy Rates — 2001 Census (Provisional)," accessed May 23, 2012, http://www.nlm.nic.in; "Literacy Rate in India," accessed May 23, 2012, http://www.indiaonlinepages.com.

12. Jacob and John, eds., *Directory of Church-related Colleges in India*, p. 363.

the Indians in allopathic medicine, attached importance to nursing schools and training midwives. Their aim was to serve all who were in need. Samson Nessiah, who heads a Christian medical college, notes that medical missions were "targeted at people of all faiths. This of course was the best Christian witnessing in a pluralistic society, as people understood the love of the Lord who went about healing people wherever he went for preaching."[13]

When one imagines the huge "burden" or agenda of the missionaries — dissuading people from harmful traditional practices, bringing medical healing and teaching healthy living, educating women and affording them respect in society, preparing people for leadership roles in the church and society, and above all taking the Good News to the unlettered — it is no wonder they believed in education. Their holistic approach to human development demanded much learning, so higher education was a strategic part of their vision.

Early Christian Colleges

Early Christian colleges in India had the direct patronage of the church. In some cases, denominations came together to form a Christian educational society, which then founded colleges. Service to the Indian masses was the main motive of these colleges. They were started as part of the founders' attempts at humanization, and where possible, Christianization. These pervasive institutional commitments encouraged Christians and non-Christians alike who entered these colleges to be sensitive to the needs of the society and aware of social evils. The history of these colleges speaks of how education motivated graduates to work for the eradication of evils like caste-ism, untouchability, and even sati, the heinous practice of burning a widow on her husband's funeral pyre.

As was stated briefly at the start of this chapter, Christian higher education in India has deeply Christian and missionary origins. CMS College in Kottayam, Kerala State (f. 1817 by the Church Missionary Society), came first and established the trend: Its motto, "Thy Word Is Truth," speaks of the vision of the founders. Only a year later Serampore College near Calcutta (Kolkatta) was founded by the great Baptist missionary trio, William Carey, Joshua Marshman, and William Ward. The motto of the college is "Gloriam Sapientes Possidebunt" (The Wise Shall Possess Glory). The early Protestant colleges were as widely

13. Samson Nessiah, "Christian Witnessing through Medical Education in Indian Pluralistic Society," in *Christian Higher Education and Globalization in Asia/Oceania*, pp. 66-67.

dispersed as the missions themselves, which gave the movement a pan-Indian outlook: Scottish Church College (Kolkatta, 1830), Wilson College (Mumbai, 1832), Madras Christian College (Chennai, 1837), Noble College (Machilipattinam, 1843), St. John's College (Agra, 1850), Christ Church College (Kanpur, 1866), Baring Union Christian College (Batala, 1874), St. John's College (Palayamkottai, 1878), St. Stephen's College (New Delhi, 1881), and The American College (Madurai, 1881). Some of the early colleges were started in big cities — Calcutta, Madras, Delhi, and Bombay — but many early founders tended to prefer rural areas. Colleges were started in small towns like Agra, Kanpur, and Madurai, and in remote places like Palayamkottai, Machilipattinam, Batala, Guntur, Indore, and Nagercoil. They reflected the missionaries' determination to reach out to the ordinary people of India and not simply favor the urban high-caste elites.

Roman Catholics commenced a robust and sustained interest in higher education with the founding of St. Joseph's College in 1844 in Tiruchirappalli by the Fathers of Society of Jesus, followed by St. Xavier's College, Kolkatta, in 1860; St. Xavier's College, Mumbai, in 1869; St. Aloysius College, Mangalore, in 1880; and St. Joseph's College, Bangalore, in 1882 — all by the Society of Jesus. No women's college was started by the Catholic Church or one of its orders until the twentieth century.

Expansion and Privatization of Higher Education in India

By the time of Indian independence, the nation's higher education enterprise was already growing rapidly, to a total of 516 colleges and universities. Since then the government has worked feverishly to build out its tertiary educational system, so that colleges and universities now number more than 18,000, with a total of about 10 million students enrolled. Even at that explosive rate of growth, Indian higher education manages to enroll only as many as 11 percent of its college-age cohort, with a goal of serving 15 percent by 2012. In this context, there was huge pressure on the Indian governments, state and national, to accommodate the educational needs of their citizens. In response, Indian governments have been busy chartering private educational institutions. Of the more than 18,000 colleges and universities in India today, 7,870 are private — some 43 percent of all the institutions. And they enroll more than 3 million students, more than 30 percent of the national total. No country in the world has more colleges and universities than India, and no country has more privately founded institutions. Church-founded colleges and universities have grown in number too, to more than 500. But they are a small part of a very large and volatile higher education sector.[14] Clearly, the Indian government has felt overwhelmed by the demand for higher education, and has given over a large share of the build-out of its system to privately chartered institutions. Critics charge the government with wanting to shake off its responsibilities in higher education, and many of the state governments have announced an end to government-aided courses. At the national level, spending for higher education in the mid-2000s shrank from 1.24 percent of the budget to 0.035 percent.[15]

These actions sent different signals to the various stakeholders of higher education. Educators in public and partially supported public institutions feel undercut in their work. Parents and students are responding variously, according to their means, with many of the wealthier families moving to tuition-based institutions. And privately held educational firms, small-time entrepreneurs, and even corporate bodies sensed that it was the right time for them to jump into the fray of higher education whether for direct profit or competitive advantage in recruiting trained workers. These educational entrepreneurs, with ample financial backing and readiness to invest in infrastructure, have started many new institutions of higher learning. Since education was found to be a high-growth, profitable business, there was no hesitation on the part of these entrepreneurs to invest huge sums.[16]

Globalization has had its impact on every sphere of Indian life, and it has not spared higher education. The enrollments and credentialing race is on, as Indian young people desire to become equipped for service in high-tech international firms, and many private entrepreneurs and corporations enter the fray of higher education, quite understandably, driven not by a motive to serve, but rather by the profit that educational institutions seem to offer. Even public national universities have become interested in foreign expansion and the offshore marketing of their educational wares. Australians, for example,

14. Daniel C. Levy, "Indian Higher Education in Comparative Perspective," PROPHE Working Paper no. 13, October 2008, pp. 1-4, accessed May 23, 2012, http://www.albany.edu/dept/eaps/prophe; and Asha Gupta, "International Trends and Private Higher Education in India," *International Journal of Educational Management* 22:6 (2008): 576-577. See also Santosh Mehrotra, "Indian Higher Education: Time for a Serious Rethink," *International Higher Education*, no. 56 (Summer 2009): n.p., accessed January 29, 2010. http://www.bc.edu_org/avp/soe/cihe; and Philip G. Altbach, "Tiny at the Top," *Wilson Quarterly* 30:4 (Autumn 2006): 49-51.

15. Dinesh Abrol, "Commercialisation of Higher Education: Implications of the GATS 2000 Negotiations," *Social Scientist* 33:9-10 (September-October 2005): 85-86; Jandhyala B. G. Tilak, "Fees, Autonomy and Equity," *Economic and Political Weekly*, February 28-March 5, 2004, pp. 870-873.

16. Gupta, "International Trends and Private Higher Education in India," pp. 580-582.

are both eagerly recruiting Indians to come and study with them, and bringing campus extensions to India.[17] Under these conditions, the noble traditional aims of higher education — to seek truth, form character, make culture, and serve society — seem overwhelmed in the rush for private gain. What the Korean philosopher Bong Ho Son observes in his own country could well be said about India:

> Universities themselves also begin to be interested in material profits. Running a university is becoming a good business. Top or national universities still emphasize prestige. But some private universities of intermediate standings are tempted to operate their institutions more for profits than for fame. If they still value good reputation it is not the end in itself, but means to get more profits.[18]

The Indian theologian and educator Ken Gnanakan also observes that higher education "has been taken over by people with restricted agendas and commodified. Francis Bacon said 'knowledge is power,' and as with all forms of power, few people take it over and exploit it for their own ends. This power today is measured in terms of wealth."[19]

But can private institutions be squarely blamed when the people of India are willingly sending their children to for-profit private schools and colleges, preferring them over publicly aided church and government institutions? Ishpreet Bindra notes that private unaided institutions have seen a rise in enrollment shares, from 10.5 percent to 18.8 percent. In urban areas, he says, "more than 50 percent of students are going to private schools at the primary, middle, secondary and higher education levels."[20]

The Indian government is now permitting the already existing aided colleges to have self-financed streams (e.g., in popular and cheaply offered fields such as commerce and computer technology) along with the aided courses. Many such colleges saw this change as not merely the right opportunity for

17. Michael Gillan, Bill Damachis, and John McGuire, "Australia in India: Commodification and Internationalisation of Higher Education," *Economic and Political Weekly*, April 5-11, 2003, pp. 1395-1403.

18. Bong Ho Son, "The Challenges of Globalization for Christian Higher Education," in *Christian Higher Education and Globalization in Asia/Oceania*, p. 7.

19. Ken Gnanakan, "Response to Bong Ho Son," in *Christian Higher Education and Globalization in Asia/Oceania*, pp. 16-17.

20. Ishpreet Bindra, "As Expenditure on Education Increases, Private Institutions Turn Major Gainers: Survey," *Education Master*, May 2010, accessed March 20, 2011, http://www.educationmaster.org/news/.

developing new courses but also as an ideal situation in which to make money. This prompted these institutions to develop courses as quickly and as cheaply as possible, resulting in an increasing commercialization of higher education. These decisions exacerbated the already chronic problem in India's rapid collegiate growth — of underpaid and unqualified staff, high fees, intellectually shallow and socially less relevant courses, and, above all, waning student interest in aided institutions and aided courses. Education thus is becoming the prerogative of those who can afford the fees and is moving away from the reach of ordinary Indians. Sadly, the self-financed stream means that underpaid teachers work on the same campus with another set of teachers drawing very comfortable salaries with all perks and privileges. Administrations of such institutions take profits off the work of underqualified persons who never question their lean pay packets.

This profit-driven atmosphere gave rise to the mushrooming growth of hundreds of arts and science, engineering, medical, teacher education, business, and para-medical institutions of higher learning. Many of these institutions were started in remote areas, not so much with the intention of educating the rural masses, but because land was cheap.[21] It is a sorry sight to see many of the self-financed engineering colleges in the state of Tamilnadu, situated in far-off, god-forsaken dry places. Students in these colleges are cut off totally from the rest of the world, and little positive student development work is being done for them. One has to answer in the negative to the question whether the students who study in such colleges acquire the required skills to be employable. High-tech jobs still go begging for workers, not because of a shortage of graduates, but because of a shortage of degree-holders who are truly qualified.[22]

Many of these institutions are run using all the modern management principles of corporate life. These institutions levy very heavy fees, sometimes above the amount permitted by the government, and the students bear the brunt. Not infrequently, "compulsory donations" are collected from the students, adding to their burden. To add fuel to the fire, students report heavy fines, for opaque reasons. Managers also collect money from students for uniforms, at canteens and stores, for buses, and additional fees for unspecified services, all under monopolistic situations. Hostels at some of these institutions are in awful condition.[23]

21. Gupta, "International Trends and Private Higher Education in India," pp. 581-583.
22. Altbach, "Tiny at the Top," p. 49.
23. Gupta, "International Trends and Private Higher Education in India," pp. 584-586, discusses some of the litigation that has led to increasing regulation of these institutions.

The newly sprouted education-for-profit institutions take advantage of the realization of the importance of education and the urge of the common man and the ignorant but enthusiastic first-generation learners to take up higher education. The government of India, through its nationalized banking system, is offering huge sums as educational loans to students to take up higher education and the nationalized banks cannot deny a loan to an aspiring student. The government has noble aims, no doubt, as it tries to make higher education available to the masses. There has been a steep hike in educational loans by the public-sector banks since these loans come under the priority sector lending category, for which banks are instructed to lend a minimum of 40 percent of their total loans.[24]

In a country like India, where many educated youth remain unemployed after graduation, the desire to take up education, availability of bank loans, extraction of high fees by privatized higher education, and subsequent unemployment form a vicious circle; some students are caught in this devastating whirlpool, never to escape.

Such are the results of a major shift of values, as higher education moves from being a public good to being a commercial commodity. The logic of higher education is running, says Joel Carpenter, "from public good to private gain, from formation to information, from perspective and judgment to skills and techniques. This shift is driven by a seemingly insatiable demand for more access to higher education, and a decreasing ability of governments, in rich nations as well as poor ones, to pay for it."[25]

Ken Gnanakan warns that higher education is becoming yet one more instance of the global reach of materialistic values:

> All forms of social life have been placed within the context of the market and profit making potential. Parents in India force their children into money-making professions and with this even the noble profession of teaching changes its face. Fierce competition drives people to develop self-centered, empire-building plans while Biblical Christian values of love, compassion, sharing etc. are relegated to the rear.[26]

Do educational loans help financially underprivileged students? The educational economist Jandhyala Tilak warns that educational loans "can create

---

24. Neelima Shankar, "PSU Banks: Education Loan Portfolio to Rise in Current Fiscal," *Rupee Times,* March 4, 2009, accessed March 18, 2011, http://www.rupeetimes.com/news/.

25. Joel A. Carpenter, "New Christian Universities and the Conversion of Cultures," *Evangelical Review of Theology* 36:1 (January 2012): 18.

26. Gnanakan, "Response," pp. 18-19.

more problems than they solve." Loans shift "the responsibility of funding higher education from the society to the families," and even to the individual student. Some are able to bear the burden as they find professional or technical employment, but others, in an economy with high unemployment rates, enter a debt trap. Thus the shift of values from education as social good to personal benefit can very well lead to a serious social ill.[27]

Privatization and CHE in India

So, the natural question is, what has been the attitude of India's Christian colleges and universities in an era of privatization? While some college leaders marched forward, eschewing profit by strictly adhering to their institutions' original missionary aims and purposes, most have fallen prey to the temptation of making higher education a profiteering market. Some churches have very boldly adhered to their vision and have started new colleges in remote tribal areas and rural districts, thus taking higher education to the unreached. Some even took policy decisions not to mix aided curricular streams with self-financed streams and preferred not to start self-financed courses in government-aided colleges. But with experts warning that they will fall to the competition, many of the Christian institutions fell victim to the temptation of making education a marketable commodity. In a multi-religious context where the Christian colleges were once change agents and centers that radiated the love of the Lord through education, we see today an increasingly commercialized spirit within Christian higher education.

While an old and prestigious Christian college, such as St. Stephen's College, New Delhi, adheres to its Christian principles and suffers poverty and debt, newly started self-financed Christian colleges show the way to earn unimaginably high income, establish prolific infrastructure, and present an opulent lifestyle. But impressed church officials may be ignoring the fact that underneath this lavish exterior lurk the sweated labor of underpaid teachers and the scarce funds extracted from students. Behind what appears to be a college with an enviable lifestyle is too often a campus that flouts the norms of qualification prescribed by the University Grants Commission. The faculty in many of the new colleges do not have reasonable service conditions and security, pushing them into a suffocating position where they are not able to question any injustice meted out to them. What Joel Carpenter describes as the

27. Tilak, "Fees, Autonomy and Equity," p. 872.

common worldwide pattern of the new private, commercially oriented colleges is true of such colleges in India also: "Private institutions tend not to retain full-time professors. Part-timers are more likely. . . . quite a few are state university profs picking up extra work."[28] These part-time and guest lecturers, who are picked up to suit the convenience of the administration, quite naturally lack commitment to the college and dedication to the vocation and eventually fail to make any contribution to the vision and mission of the college. These "taxi cab professors" are proud that they are needed by several colleges, and colleges in turn use the names of such professors for the purpose of advertisement. Some of these professors in Indian colleges make their appearance only on a day when there is an inspection. Many of these colleges offer "scholarships" and speak of their social service activities, but, quite ironically, scholarships and social activities are used only as shields to protect them from the ire of the public and to camouflage their money-making activities. Claims of these institutions that they are undertaking the service of education like the old missionaries can be easily seen through, looking at the wealth they have amassed.[29] Christian higher education has not fully succumbed to these temptations, and one sees evidence of Christian values in their broader course offerings and continued devotion to service.[30] Yet the temptation toward commercialization is very strong. Many Christian college officers, both in India and elsewhere, have not fully considered the implications of making commercially oriented changes.

Autonomy, University Status, and Indian Christian Higher Education

The government of India has sanctioned as autonomous and even deemed university status to some of the Christian colleges in India.[31] When auton-

28. Carpenter, "New Christian Universities," pp. 20-21.

29. A helpful guide to these traits, found in the new private higher education worldwide, is Daniel C. Levy, "The Unanticipated Explosion: Private Higher Education's Global Surge," *Comparative Education Review* 50:2 (2006): 217-240. See also Ann I. Morey, "Globalization and the Emergence of For-Profit Higher Education," *Higher Education* 48:1 (July 2004): 131-150.

30. See, e.g., Andrés Bernasconi, "Does the Affiliation of Universities to External Organizations Foster Diversity in Private Higher Education? Chile in Comparative Perspective," *Higher Education* 52:2 (2006): 303-342; and Prachayani Praphamontripong, "Inside Thai Private Higher Education: Exploring Private Growth in International Context," PROPHE Working Paper no. 12, September 2008, pp. 5-6, 11-13, accessed May 25, 2012, http://www.albany.edu/dept/eaps/prophe.

31. An autonomous college is affiliated with a university and it is the university that awards the degree. Yet an autonomous college has the privilege of designing the curriculum,

omy was introduced for the first time in India in 1978, four Christian colleges took up autonomy. A variety of factors, notably record of achievement, competency of the faculty, and quality of campus facilities, were the criteria for the conferment of autonomous status. Many Christian colleges were offering quality education and eventually opted for autonomy. In 1994, out of the 107 autonomous colleges in India there were twenty-one Christian colleges with autonomous status. Today there are at least forty-two Christian colleges that are autonomous.[32]

Later some of these institutions opted for deemed university status, as Christian autonomous colleges became trendsetters in asking for university status. It is sad to note, however, that a Christian autonomous institution that became the first Christian deemed university later came under criticism and the government had to initiate legal action. This institution was supposed to promote postgraduate education and research, but like the prodigal son, lost its way and went after money making, forsaking research and development. Flouting all norms, it illegally introduced distance education. What is there to boast of Christian witnessing, if Christian institutions themselves lose track and go with the rest of the market world? What Geoffrey Chaucer said long ago quite sadly still applies:

If gold rust, what then will iron do?
For if a priest be foul in whom we trust,
No wonder that a common man should rust.[33]

Conferring the status of autonomy or university on colleges should be taken as a rare privilege to work for furthering the aim of higher education. It should motivate institutions to experiment with innovations in curriculum, teaching-learning methodology, and even administration. But very often the opportunity given is misused to further the selfish interests of colleges that have an eye on profiteering. These "universities," instead of promoting research, misuse many of the privileges offered to them. To cite an example, these "universities" clamor for twinning programs with foreign universities

---

conducting the examination, and publishing the result. A deemed university (the name is no longer used) is one that has all the powers and qualities of a university, but cannot have affiliated colleges.

32. These findings were compiled from Jacob, ed., *Directory of Church-related Colleges in India* (1995); Jacob and John, eds. *Directory of Church-related Colleges in India* (2001).

33. Geoffrey Chaucer, *Canterbury Tales,* prologue, part one, accessed May 23, 2012, http://chaucer.classicauthors.net/CanterburyTales/CanterburyTales1.html.

in courses like the M.B.A. degree, for which they levy very high fees. Indian students who have dreams of education in foreign universities easily fall prey to such temptations. Out of the forty-four universities disqualified by the human resource development ministry recently, one happens to be a Christian institution. This does not mean that all is well with the other institutions. In a country where Christian higher education is called on to take up education as a means of witnessing, it is quite sad that some Christian institutions have become the butt of laughter and ridicule.

CHE and Quality Consciousness

In spite of the rough weather Christian higher education in India has steered through the challenges and political antagonism it has faced from time to time. Many of the colleges have not lost sight of their mission and have always striven to offer quality education combined with values. They have not, by and large, sacrificed quality, and many of the Christian colleges have been accredited with very respectable scores by the National Assessment and Accreditation Council. Four Christian colleges confidently came forward to take up autonomy when it was introduced for the first time in India in 1978. Out of the forty-seven colleges chosen by the University Grants Commission as "Colleges with Potentials for Excellence," offering major funding for developmental activity, thirteen are Christian institutions. The leading Indian magazine, *India Today,* conducted a survey among the institutions of higher learning in 1997. It looked at caliber of students, caliber of faculty, mean percentage marks scored, kind of research output by faculty, infrastructure, extracurricular activities, quality of course materials, lab time available to students, and recognition of the college by other universities. Out of the ten colleges surveyed, five were Christian institutions: St. Stephen's, New Delhi (first rank, managed by the Church of North India); St. Xavier's College, Bombay (fourth rank, managed by the Society of Jesus); Loyola College, Chennai (fifth rank, managed by the Society of Jesus); St. Xavier's College, Calcutta (seventh rank, managed by the Society of Jesus); and Stella Maris College, Chennai (eighth rank, managed by the Franciscan Missionaries of Mary Society). Out of the five top medical colleges chosen by the magazine, the Christian Medical College, Vellore, managed by an interdenominational council of Protestant churches, got the second rank, and St. John's Medical College, Bangalore, managed by the Catholic Bishops' Conference of India Society of Medical Education, got the fifth rank. These studies illustrate the importance Indian Christian colleges attach to quality.

Three Damoclean Swords

Christian colleges in India have been torch bearers of quality and pioneers in experimenting with new methods in imparting education. Christian institutions in general maintain high academic standards and discipline. The older ones in particular have attracted the cream of the crop in the student community and have given shape to many leaders, administrators, and professionals who serve the country and the world at large. But in spite of this great contribution, Christian higher educational institutions in India feel the presence of a perpetually threatening Damocles' sword hanging over them on three counts: the passing of an anti-conversion bill by several state legislatures, the scant respect shown to the minority rights, and conflicts between the church and some college administrations or fights within a given administration.

The anti-conversion bill states that no person will convert or attempt to convert, either directly or otherwise, any person from one religion to another by use of force or by inducement or by any fraudulent means, nor shall any person abet any such conversion. Proponents of the bill argued that coerced conversions would not be reported or prosecuted without legal sanction. Opponents tended to belong to religious minority communities, and they argued that the bill was aimed to restrict their freedom to propagate their faith, as guaranteed by the Indian Constitution.[34] As a correspondent put it on the web pages of the Indian Christian Council, "India's Anti-conversion laws are loaded in favor of the majority Hindu religion. These laws, however, actually serve to infringe upon religious freedom and contradict rights protected within international agreements and the Indian Constitution. Such laws are motivated by a religious ideology driven by an irrational and insecure Hindu xenophobia that is antagonistic to religious minorities."[35] By 2011, the courts in India had admitted a petition by the Catholic Bishops Conference of India and another by the Evangelical Fellowship, each challenging the anti-conversion laws of a different Indian state.[36]

The seven Indian states with anti-conversion legislation, known as Freedom of Religion Acts, are Madhya Pradesh, Chhattisgarh, Orissa, Arunachal

34. Arpita Anant, "Anti-conversion Laws," *The Hindu*, online edition, December 17, 2002, accessed February 10, 2011; www.thehindu.com.

35. "India's Anti-conversion laws loaded in favour of majority Hindu religion," Indian Christian Council, January 16, 2007, accessed May 25, 2012, http://indianchristians.in/news/content/view/896/43/.

36. "Court Admits Petition against Anti-Conversion Law in India," All India Christian Council, February 22, 2011, accessed May 25, 2012, http://indianchristians.in/news.

Pradesh, Rajasthan, Gujarat, and Himachal Pradesh. In each location, the issue is linked to the conversion of tribal peoples. The natural question is how this legislation affects Christian educational institutions. In the state of Madhya Pradesh the government received a number of complaints that there was large-scale conversion of tribals to Christianity by threat, inducement and other fraudulent means by foreign missionaries. There was a plea that the government should put an end to this unhealthy practice. The government then formed an inquiry commission that toured 14 districts and visited 77 places. It examined 11,300 persons coming from 770 villages and sent questionnaires and received reports from 375 institutions, which included 55 Christian institutions. The commission submitted a comprehensive report to the government in 1956 stating that Christian missionaries were converting innocent and ignorant people to Christianity by offering various inducements such as free education, free medical facilities, and employment opportunities. The report also said that Christian institutions were receiving funds and other contributions from foreign countries and these Christian institutions were controlled by the churches of foreign countries and these acts were the reason for the government to enact anti-conversion legislation. Whatever the source of the laws, they clearly involve the self-determination of minority peoples and the constitutional provisions for religious freedom.[37]

This decades-long debate has put a cloud over the reputation of India's Christian colleges and universities. The majority of the students are not Christians, and because of these public debates over Christian agencies and "forced conversions," the general public suspects that Christian institutions seek to materially induce or psychologically pressure their students to convert. This controversy has fanned the ire of Hindu fundamentalists and intensified attacks, both rhetorical and actual, on churches, monasteries, missionaries, and Christian institutions, including educational institutions. Bearing this cross for the sake of educational uplift and the welfare of neglected peoples has not deterred Christian colleges and universities from their work, but it has frequently put them under the cloud of suspicion.

Another perennial problem that Indian Christian colleges and universities face is the interference of the government or the state university with

37. Christophe Jaffrelot, *The Hindu Nationalist Movement and Indian Politics: 1925 to the 1990s* (London: Hurst, 1993); Abraham V. Thomas, *Christians in Secular India* (Madison, N.J.: Fairleigh Dickinson University Press, 1974), pp. 133-136; and James Andrew Huff, "Religious Freedom in India and Analysis of the Constitutionality of Anti-Conversion Laws," *Rutgers Journal of Law and Religion* 10:2 (Spring 2009), accessed May 25, 2012, http://org.law.rutgers.edu/publications/law-religion/vol10.shtml.

their internal affairs, including the formation of the colleges' governing bodies, appointments, and admissions. The constitution of India guarantees certain rights to the institutions run by minority communities, including Christian institutions. Article 26 of the Indian Constitution gives the right to all religious minorities to establish and maintain institutions for religious and charitable purposes, and to manage their own affairs, in any manner they wish in accordance with the laws. Article 29 protects the cultural rights of minorities and Article 30 (1) gives them the right to establish and administer educational institutions of their choice. But in the last two decades many laws passed by the government infringe on these rights assured by the constitution. The government not only discriminates against minority institutions in granting aid, but also imposes many rules and restrictions to prevent minority institutions from appointing their own candidates as faculty. When vacancies come up in institutions the administrations are forced to accept the state's choice to fill them and on many occasions Christian educational institutions had to go to court to get justice.

Christian colleges in India are smothered by unsympathetic and antagonistic directives issued by the government from time to time on admission and appointment. This compels many of the institutions to spend much of their energy on court cases. Needless to say, this serves as a heavy obstruction to the development of Christian institutions. One wonders how a society can so easily forget the great contributions of these colleges to nation building and social transformation and thanklessly obstruct them by interfering in their rights. One is reminded of the sufferings of St. Stephen's College and the Allahabad Agricultural Institute when they were dragged to court to decide whether they were entitled to have their admission policies that facilitate admission of Christian students. Recently, in 2008 St. Stephen's College once again had to knock at the doors of the court and put up a bitter legal battle with the University of Delhi when its right to appoint its principal was challenged.

One also has to acknowledge, with heavy heart, that because of infighting in administrations, many Christian colleges cannot be good witnesses to the Christian spirit that has to be displayed in a pluralistic society like India. Litigations served as a bottleneck to the development of many institutions, and much energy, time, and money were wasted on inconsequential legal battles. Still worse is the fight between the church and institutions managed by church-related bodies. The American College, Madurai, and Madras Christian College, Chennai, can be cited as examples of casualties of such an unfortunate situation. Many Christian institutions of higher learning are embroiled in self-destructive litigation and shamelessly unchristian infighting as people with no knowledge of or no interest in higher education and with scant respect for the vision of the early founders take up positions of power in administration. Christian higher education has to keep its house in order before embarking on ambitious plans of service to humanity through education.

CHE in India and Its Contributions: An Evaluation

When we look at the contribution of Christian higher education to Indian society, it is amazing. It is heartening to note that the influence of Christian higher education has permeated every walk of life. Christian higher education has catered to the educational needs of people of all religious and socioeconomic groups. It can proudly speak of being the alma mater of many of the great leaders of India. To cite examples, the former president of India, Dr. S. Radhakrishnan, the master teacher, whose birthday is celebrated in India as Teachers' Day, had his education in Voorhees College, Vellore, and later at Madras Christian College, where he graduated with a master's degree in philosophy in 1906. Another former president, K. R. Narayanan, had his education in CMS College, the first Christian college of India. Before joining CMS College, he had studied in Christian schools. It is a matter of pride that CMS College extended its helping hands to this future president of India belonging to the Dalit community by offering a merit scholarship that helped him complete his intermediate schooling. Yet another president of India, Dr. A. P. J. Abdul Kalam, popularly known as the "Missile Man of India" for his work on the development of ballistic missile and space rocket technology, had his schooling in a Christian school and later his higher education in St. Joseph's College, Tiruchirappally, the first Catholic college in India. This great nuclear scientist and a role model for present-day Indian youth very vociferously acknowledges the contributions of Christian educational institutions in shaping him. R. Venkataraman, another president of India, obtained his masters degree in economics from Loyola College, Madras (Chennai). The great freedom fighter of India, Subash Chandra Bose, obtained his B.A. in 1918 in philosophy from the renowned Scottish Church College of the University of Calcutta. The most respected soldier of India, Field Marshal Sam Manekshaw, received his education in Sherwood College, Nainital. Morarji Desai, the former prime minister of India, graduated from Wilson College, Mumbai. This list is not exhaustive and all-inclusive, but it does include national leaders from several faith traditions.

Even today, it is really inspiring to note that Indian Christian colleges do not restrict their contribution to a narrow religious minority in the nation. The majority of students in Christian colleges in India are non-Christians. Although we do not have current data, the *Directory of Christian Colleges in India* has the following information for 2000-2001. Out of the 353,683 students studying in Christian colleges with membership in AIAPCHE, only 123,245 are Christians and the rest, 230,437, belong to other faiths. Out of the 16,776 teachers in these colleges 10,089 are Christians and the rest, 6,687, belong to other faiths. Only 2.9 percent of colleges in India are run by Christians and only 37.2 percent of students and 60.7 percent of teachers in the Christian colleges are Christians. Service to humanity is still the priority of Christian higher education in India. Many of the Christian colleges in India, especially the recently started colleges in the self-financed stream, have an urban bias, but credit goes to Christian higher education for taking its learning to far-off, underdeveloped tribal and Dalit belts. In the year 2000-2001, Christian colleges in India had 18,478 tribal students and 27,603 Dalit students. This is a great service rendered to the marginalized. But the major challenge before Indian Christian higher education is whether it can rise above all monetary considerations and the craze for "overnight development" and remember its great mission in this country, where Christians form less than 3 percent of the population.

Christian Higher Education in India: *Quo Vadis?*

India, with all its developments in information and communications technology, transportation, space research, and industry, is moving toward becoming a developed country. To equip itself to face the demands of the fast-developing world, the country has realized the inevitability of paying greater attention to education. Alya Mishra writes that for 2011-2012, India increased its higher education budget by 34 percent, but "most of the allocation is for projects already in the pipeline rather than for ambitious plans to expand the number of higher education institutions in the coming years." At the same time, the nation is planning for universal access to secondary education, so the higher education sector still needs to keep growing.[38]

So this great field of endeavor, which the missionaries started a little more than two centuries ago, remains incomplete as far as higher education is concerned. In the words of Robert Frost, we have "miles to go" in search of "fresh

---

38. Alya Mishra, "INDIA: Budget Hikes Spending on Higher Education," *University World News*, March 13, 2011, accessed February 7, 2011, http://www.universityworldnews.com/.

woods and pastures new" as there is still a generation of people thirsting for higher education. The challenges for education in India are stiff indeed. More than a quarter of the population is still illiterate, including more than one-third of the women. As of 2009, 23 percent of the age cohort was enrolling in upper secondary school, and only about one-third of the college and university instructors hold Ph.D. degrees.[39]

Christian higher education should take up this challenge and keep pace with the needs and expectations of the world. The blemishes, imperfections, and shortfalls pointed out in the earlier parts of this chapter are not to belittle and demean the contributions of Christian higher education in India. They are pointed out as an incentive for introspection and to check whether the road traveled by the institutions is right. It only shows that there are serious problems in the affairs of at least some institutions of Christian higher learning. The revelations made during this self-analysis should not deter and dissuade us from the road map prepared by early missionaries, but should rather give us the determination to carry on our service to humanity.

Christian higher education in India has many opportunities before it. More than any other institutions, Christian colleges have ample openings to serve humanity by making the best use of the opportunities before them. In our globalized context, networking of Christian institutions worldwide is sure to bring about many changes. Instead of misusing and commercializing the opportunities of twinning programs, and exploiting the ambition of the Indian youth to be educated, there can be very meaningful partnerships among Christian institutions worldwide that will result in highly productive and beneficial relationships. It is indeed a matter of pride that Christian higher education in India can very boldly negotiate with the Christian universities in other parts of the world as it caters not only to the poor through its institutions in remote areas, but also has some top institutions comparable to any Western institution in academic standards, staff quality, and campus facilities.

We see the ugly and at times the gory face of communal rivalries and religious fundamentalism around us and even face the wrath of narrow-minded religious fanaticism. Christian institutions are run by different denominations — Reformed, Orthodox, and Catholic — and also by Christian educational societies and different religious orders of the Catholic Church. First of all we have to come together for mutual support resulting in an enriching relationship. Establishing contacts with Christian universities and colleges of the developed and developing world will aid easy mobility of teachers and students among

---

39. Altbach, "Tiny at the Top," p. 50; Mehrotra, "Indian Higher Education."

the universities. Indian Christian educational institutions are called to identify the special educational needs of the country and the world and be trendsetters.

In India, primary education is compulsory and a state obligation; it became a fundamental right of every Indian citizen when a bill was passed in the Indian parliament in 2002, resulting in an amendment of the Indian Constitution. And what does this suggest for Christian higher education in India? This fundamental right to education guarantees education only up to the age of fourteen. Is it not our responsibility to ensure that we offer quality education to children above this age who are not guaranteed education? Now that would be a mission worthy of our founders.

CHAPTER 6

Will the Parent Abandon the Child?
The Birth, Secularization, and Survival of
Christian Higher Education in Western Europe

Perry L. Glanzer

Western Europe gave birth to the Christian university more than eight hundred years ago. As one scholar noted in a recent three-volume history of European universities: "No one today would dispute the fact that universities, in the sense in which the term is now generally understood, were a creation of the Middle Ages, appearing for the first time between the twelfth and thirteenth centuries."[1] Or as another scholar of Islamic higher education observed, "The university is a twelfth century product of the Christian West."[2] In fact, the only institution in Europe that is older than European universities is the Catholic Church.[3] Not surprisingly, the church and the Christian worldview it sustained proved instrumental to the creation of Western European universities. Rodney Stark claims more baldly: "The university was a Chris-

1. See Jacques Verger, "Patterns," in *A History of the University in Europe,* vol. 1, *Universities in the Middle Ages,* ed. Hilde de Ridder-Symoens (Cambridge: Cambridge University Press, 1992), p. 35. Verger affirms, "It is no doubt true that other civilizations, prior to, or wholly alien to, the medieval West, such as the Roman Empire, Byzantium, Islam, or China, were familiar with forms of higher education which a number of historians, for the sake of convenience, have sometimes described as universities. Yet a closer look makes it plain that the institutional reality was altogether different and, no matter what has been said on the subject, there is no real link such as would justify us in associating them with medieval universities in the West" (p. 35).

2. George Makdisi, *The Rise of Colleges, Institutions of Learning in Islam and the West* (Edinburgh: Edinburgh University Press, 1982), p. 287.

3. Notker Hammerstein, "Relations with Authority," in *A History of the University in Europe,* vol. 2, *Universities in Early Modern Europe (1500-1800),* ed. Walter Rüegg (series ed.) and Hilde de Ridder-Symoens (vol. ed.) (Cambridge: Cambridge University Press, 1996), p. 113.

tian invention."[4] Certainly, as this essay will reveal, the influence of Christianity contributed to why universities as we know them today originated in Western Europe[5] and not in other parts of the world.

Today, however, few of the oldest Western European universities identify themselves as "Christian," although some of these universities' theology faculties still have a relationship to a particular Christian tradition. Over the past three centuries the vast majority of Western European universities that were established with the support of the Catholic Church, or with the help of Protestant churches after the Reformation, abandoned their Christian identities. The first part of this chapter outlines the original role of the church in the development of European universities and the factors contributing to the marginalization of the church and Christian theology from most of Europe's universities. While this story may appear to support Philip Jenkins's observation, "At least in its institutional form . . . European Christianity seems to be terminally ill,"[6] I would suggest that a more tragic metaphor in line with more active understandings of secularization may be appropriate.[7] Western Europe, the parent of Christian higher education, is now abandoning and in some cases actively rejecting the child it created, the Christian university.

This secularization narrative, however, does not comprise the entire story. Some Christian universities, particularly from the Catholic tradition, maintained their church connections and new Christian universities have continued to emerge while older universities secularized. Despite the lack of cultural support, the church continues to nurture the life of the mind to some degree. The second part of the chapter shows the extent and degree to which Christian higher education continues to survive in Western Europe despite the hostile climate. It also describes the challenges these now unusual institutions face in light of larger trends in European higher education.

4. Rodney Stark, *For the Glory of God: How Monotheism Led to Reformations, Science, Witch-hunts and the End of Slavery* (Princeton, N.J.: Princeton University Press, 2003), p. 62.

5. For purposes of convenience, I divide Western and Eastern Europe using the old iron curtain of communism. The two countries that do not fit easily into this division, Germany and Greece, I divide into the West (Germany) and the East (Greece).

6. Philip Jenkins, *God's Continent: Christianity, Islam, and Europe's Religious Crisis* (Oxford: Oxford University Press, 2007), p. 26.

7. Christian Smith, ed., *The Secular Revolution: Power, Interests, and Conflict in the Secularization of American Public Life* (Berkeley: University of California Press, 2003).

Christianity and the Birth of Higher Education

While a variety of political, social, economic, and ideological factors[8] led to the creation of the first Western European universities, the particular role of the church and Christianity proved an indispensable one. Marcia Colish argues that the universities emerged out of a unique integration of theology, the liberal arts, and the professions in the great cathedral schools found in places such as Paris. This brand of integration helps explain why universities emerged in Western Europe:

> In striking contrast with Byzantium and Islam, all of these subjects flourished and were supported in the same schools. Basic education in the trivium and quadrivium ensured that scholars in law, medicine, and theology had a command of logic and the other verbal disciplines as well as mathematics and science. The fact that scientists and philosophers studied in faculties adjacent to theologians trained to raise questions about ultimate values, and that theologians interacted with colleagues in fields not informed by religious criteria, forced all involved to take account of the perspectives and ground rules of other disciplines as well as the disagreements within their own. The scholastics who created this heady educational environment rapidly outpaced monastic scholars as speculative thinkers.[9]

These scholars also began to desire new institutional arrangements. Eventually, well-known teachers and clerics started teaching independently of the cathedral schools and monasteries. They became known for innovation and soon formed themselves into guilds of scholars that grew into what would eventually be called *universitas,* or universities. The University of Bologna (est. end of twelfth century) and the University of Paris (est. beginning of the thirteenth century) are commonly considered the two earliest universities that eventually became models for other famous European universities such as Oxford, Cambridge, and Padua.[10]

With regard to Christianity, these universities were nurtured by both particular theological ideas carried by teachers who advanced this unique form

8. Walter Rüegg, "Themes," in *A History of the University in Europe,* vol. 1, *Universities in the Middle Ages,* ed. Hilde de Ridder-Symoens (Cambridge: Cambridge University Press, 1992), pp. 9-14.

9. Marcia Colish, *Medieval Foundations of the Western Intellectual Tradition, 400-1400* (New Haven, Conn.: Yale University Press, 1997), p. 266.

10. Rüegg, "Themes," pp. 6-8.

of higher education and the Catholic Church, which gave these teachers and their students vital support, legal legitimacy, and protection. Identifying the ways that the Christian worldview shaped the thought produced in universities would require more space, but Walter Rüegg provides a helpful list of seven values legitimated by Christian thought that nourished the desire to learn and know *(amor sciendi)* that found institutional expression in the first European universities:

1. The belief in a world order, created by God, rational, accessible to human reason, to be explained by human reason and to be mastered by it; this belief underlies scientific and scholarly research as the attempt to understand this rational order of God's creation.
2. The ancient understanding of man as an imperfect being and the Judeo-Christian idea of a creature fallen into sin, and the proposition deriving from these ideas about the limitation of the human intellect operated in the Middle Ages as driving forces impelling intellectual criticism and collegial cooperation. . . .
3. Respect for the individual as a reflection of the macrocosm or as having been formed in the image of God laid the foundation for the gradually realized freedom of scientific and scholarly research and teaching.
4. The absolute imperative of scientific truth, which already had led in scholasticism to the basic norms of scientific and scholarly research and teaching such as the prohibition of the rejection of demonstrated knowledge, the subjection of one's own assertions to the generally valid rules of evidence, openness to all possible objections to one's argument, and the public character of argument and discussion.
5. The recognition of scientific and scholarly knowledge as a public good which is ultimately a gift of God.
6. *Reformatio,* the principle which regarded one's scientific efforts as the renewal and further development of previously established knowledge "in the cause of improvement," and
7. The equality of human beings, which is part of natural law, first found an institutional arrangement for scientific and scholarly study in the setting provided by the university.[11]

The Catholic Church also helped provide important institutional support that cultivated these ideas in return for the support provided by the universi-

11. Rüegg, "Themes," pp. 32-33.

ties in advancing rationally intelligible doctrine against heresies, strengthening the institutional church, and providing educated staff.[12] The church placed a high priority on teachers and scholars and labeled them the "mirror of the church," since the church's leadership came from the academic world.[13] It also granted students and teachers certain "universal" rights and privileges in the sense that they transcended all local divisions (such as towns, dioceses, principalities, and states).[14] Teachers and students were placed under the protection of papal authority, given legal protection by the church against local and regional political authorities, and the degrees conferred allowed graduates to teach not only in a local area but across Christendom. In this way, the church provided a limited version of communal academic freedom for the faculty and students over and against the interests and control of the political authorities.[15]

The Reformation's Contribution to Christian Higher Education

Ironically, the academic freedom fostered in the universities resulted in calls for theological reformation within the church that ultimately further undermined the church's unity. Three of the most well-known protesters against particular Roman Catholic Church doctrines and practices — John Wycliffe, John Hus, and Martin Luther — originally taught in universities. In fact, what many consider the start of the Reformation began at what eventually became one of the first Protestant universities, Martin Luther's young Wittenberg University (est. 1502).[16] The religious cleavages produced by the Reformation transformed the identity of old universities and produced a whole array of new confessional Protestant universities. Oxford and Cambridge in England became Anglican universities. German universities such as Leipzig and Tübingen became Lutheran. The Scottish universities, St. Andrews, Glasgow, Aberdeen, and eventually Edinburgh, became Presbyterian. Some universities caught in

12. Rüegg, "Themes," pp. 15-16.
13. Rüegg, "Themes," pp. 14-18; Paolo Nardi, "Relations with Authority," in *A History of the University in Europe,* vol. 1, *Universities in the Middle Ages,* ed. Hilde de Ridder-Symoens (Cambridge: Cambridge University Press, 1992), pp. 81-82.
14. Verger, "Patterns"; Nardi, "Relations with Authority."
15. Nardi, "Relations with Authority." See also W. J. Hoye, "The Religious Roots of Academic Freedom," *Theological Studies* 58 (1997): 409-428.
16. Willem Frijhoff, "Patterns," in *A History of the University in Europe,* vol. 2, *Universities in Early Modern Europe (1500-1800),* ed. Walter Rüegg (series ed.) and Hilde de Ridder-Symoens (vol. ed.) (Cambridge: Cambridge University Press, 1996), pp. 43-110.

the middle, such as Heidelberg and Frankfurt, would switch identities from Catholic to Lutheran to Calvinist.

Despite the upheaval produced by the Reformation, and in fact because of it, this time period actually saw the creation of numerous new Catholic and Protestant universities. Religious competition spurred creativity. Thus, between 1501 and 1600 Catholics started fifty-three new universities while between 1551 and 1650 Protestants started twenty-six.[17] The new confessional organization of political territories helped spur this creativity. The Jesuits, who proved to be the most successful, started or took over twenty-five universities in their efforts to counter the influence of the Protestant Reformation.[18] Altogether by 1750, Europe would boast eighty-two Catholic and thirty-nine Protestant universities with all but six of these being in Western Europe.[19]

The Nationalization of the Western European Universities

In ways similar to the church, universities attempted to be exactly what their original name suggests — universal institutions that attempted to transcend the division of knowledge and the divisions caused by ethnic or national boundaries and distinctions. Writing in 1775, Jean-Jacques Rousseau lamented the uniformity of European higher education: "Today there are no longer any French, Germans, Spanish or even Europeans. They all have the same tastes, the same passions, the same morals, because none of them received a national moulding from a particular institution."[20] Nonetheless, this universalizing trend was replaced in the late eighteenth and early nineteenth centuries by what I will call nationalization. By nationalization, I mean changes within universities' leadership, purposes, curriculum, and culture that made the interests and ideology of the state and its leaders more important than the interests of the church. As Hans Kohn, the well-known scholar of nationalism, observed, "Nationalism is a state of mind in which the supreme loyalty of the individual is felt to be due the nation-state."[21] This "state of mind" could also apply to the culture of an institution. National universities were supposed to serve primarily political leaders, as well as a whole nation and its interests. In Western

17. Frijhoff, "Patterns."
18. Frijhoff, "Patterns."
19. Frijhoff, "Patterns," p. 71.
20. Cited in Rüegg, "Themes," p. 4.
21. Hans Kohn, *Nationalism: Its Meaning and History* (Princeton, N.J.: D. Van Nostrand, 1955), p. 9.

Europe, nationalization was the first step to secularization, and it took place for a variety of reasons.

First, the major new Protestant churches (Anglican, Lutheran, and Reformed) existed in symbiosis with political rulers to obtain both protection and legitimacy. Although most European rulers espoused some confession, as they gained primary control over older universities at the expense of weakened churches or orders and started new ones, their interest and the interest of the faculty in using universities to strengthen the empire or nation-state, or particular professions the state needed, often resulted in the marginalization of the church and Christianity from the life of universities in favor of the interests of the political order. For example, old and new German universities began to be seen as German first and Christian second.[22] Similarly, English political leaders observed that student and faculty admission to Oxford and Cambridge should not be limited to members of the Church of England. As one critic noted at the time, "Oxford ought to be a national institution but is bound hand and feet by the clergy of one sect."[23]

Second, while the Catholic Church had a different relationship with ruling leaders, political leaders in Catholic countries also began to direct university life so that it would support the particular ends of their countries. Internal church events also indirectly supported this transformation. When Pope Clement XIV disbanded the Jesuit Order in 1773, national leaders stepped into the void left by the Jesuits and transformed Jesuit universities into national universities.[24] In the Hapsburg Empire, Spanish and Italian reformers sought to use universities to create a strong national state that reformed the Catholicism taught in the universities to be more subordinate to the state.[25]

Third, the above developments were reinforced by the Enlightenment-fueled growth of secular thinkers who rejected religious thought and argued that the state should control universities to promote liberty. Christian universities, they contended, restricted free thought, caused divisions, and did not always produce the professional, scientifically trained graduates that met the needs of the nation. These late-eighteenth- and early-nineteenth-century Enlightenment thinkers began to perpetuate the view that "Universities were a state concern because they maintained the scientific level of the professions on which a modern state depended, embodied the principles of free thought and

22. Robert Anderson, *European Universities from the Enlightenment to 1914* (New York: Oxford University Press, 2004), pp. 51-65.

23. V. H. H. Green, *Religion at Oxford and Cambridge* (London: SCM Press, 1964), p. 153.

24. See Anderson, *European Universities,* pp. 26-34.

25. Anderson, *European Universities,* p. 29.

progress, and created unity and common values among the elite of the nation-state."[26] While the churches once nurtured the universities, these critics claimed they now blocked educational progress. Thus, they believed the state needed to secularize the universities and become the defender of intellectual freedom. For example, the French Revolution, which championed both reason over revelation and a militant form of secular nationalism, provides an extreme example of the influence of this movement. The confiscation of church property and endowments in 1789 weakened the universities, as did imposition of an oath of loyalty to the constitution that resulted in large-scale resignations and emigration of the clergy. Between 1791 and 1793, the French revolutionaries abolished Catholic universities and created new institutions meant to serve the state.[27]

Ironically, the Enlightenment-inspired French Revolution and the Napoleonic conquests that followed devastated Europe's university system. Between 1789 and 1815, sixty of Europe's 143 universities ceased to exist, leaving only eighty-three universities.[28] The majority disappeared in Western Europe. Germany lost eighteen, Spain lost fifteen, and France lost all twenty-four universities.[29] Europe would not reach the same number of universities again until the late nineteenth century. Later, Napoleon, while restoring some rights to the Catholic Church, did not restore its role in university education, and the French state continued to control education in order to "give direction to the 'public mind' and 'have a means of directing political and moral opinions.'"[30] Perhaps the most obvious sign of increasing state control over higher education was the establishment of national Ministries of Education throughout the 1800s.[31]

The changes entailed by the nationalization of universities did not necessarily mean that universities completely dechristianized in all cases. As Anderson observes of Europe, "Although by the early nineteenth century universities were essentially secular institutions in the sense that the state rather than the church was the directing authority, religion had by no means lost its importance."[32] In this respect, it is important to distinguish between nationalization and secularization as well as different types of secularization.

26. Anderson, *European Universities*, p. 89.

27. Anderson, *European Universities*, pp. 39-50.

28. Rüegg, "Themes," p. 3.

29. Rüegg, "Themes," p. 3.

30. Anderson, *European Universities*, p. 45.

31. Paul Gerbod, "Relations with Authority," in *A History of the University in Europe*, vol. 3, *Universities in the Nineteenth and Early Twentieth Centuries (1800-1945)*, ed. Walter Rüegg (Cambridge: Cambridge University Press, 2004), pp. 83-100.

32. Anderson, *European Universities*, p. 88.

Nationalization created a situation in which political ends and interests became primary within the university, which led to one type of secularization, the secularization of the European mind.[33] The secularization of mentalities, as C. John Sommerville observes, is different than other understandings of secularization employed by scholars: the secularization of society, institutions, activities, or populations.[34] In other words, most European countries still supported a particular established church. Therefore, the institution of the university still identified itself as Christian and sponsored theology departments in which the church played some controlling role in hiring. With regard to activities, chapel requirements and a religious ethos also still existed at many schools.[35] Likewise, confessional hiring requirements continued to exist among the university faculty, and those with controversial religious views continued to face various types of repercussions, leaving the university population nominally Christian.[36] Consequently, while nationalization occurred in certain areas, most Western Europeans still considered their universities Christian.[37] Nonetheless, European leaders and faculty increasingly exhibited a growing propensity "to do without religion."[38]

Moreover, the elevated role of the state now influenced every aspect of university life and even extended to the creation of new universities.[39] Instead of being partnerships between churches and states, the new universities became primarily state-funded and controlled endeavors in which the state church or churches participated at the state's discretion and control. This situation especially influenced Protestant participation in universities. The Catholic Church, however, would succeed in establishing a different path.

33. Owen Chadwick, *The Secularization of the European Mind in the Nineteenth Century* (New York: Cambridge University Press, 1975).

34. C. John Sommerville, "Secular Society/Religious Population: Our Tacit Rules for Using the Term 'Secularization,'" *Journal for the Scientific Study of Religion* 37 (1998): 249-253.

35. James Arthur, *Faith and Secularisation in Religious Colleges and Universities* (London: Routledge, 2006), p. 18.

36. Arthur, *Faith and Secularisation*, pp. 90-91.

37. One scholar identifies one hundred universities with a Christian ethos in 1850. The denominations included: Catholic, 67; Lutheran, 17; Reformed, 10; Orthodox, 4; Anglican, 2. It should be noted, however, that the churches did not necessarily control these universities or even sponsor theology departments within them. See Walter Rüegg, "Theology and the Arts," in *A History of the University in Europe*, vol. 3, p. 405.

38. Chadwick, *The Secularization of the European Mind*, p. 16.

39. Perry Glanzer, "The Role of the State in the Secularization of Christian Higher Education: A Case Study of Eastern Europe," *Journal of Church and State* 53 (Spring 2011).

Protestant Universities

By 1850, only thirty Protestant universities had survived the French Revolution and the conflicts that followed. Ten Reformed universities existed in Scotland, Holland, and Switzerland, three Anglican universities existed in England, and seventeen Lutheran universities existed in Germany and Scandinavia.[40] At a number of these universities, particularly in Germany, theology still played a major role in the university and between 10 and 20 percent studied it (in Halle more than 30 percent of students did).[41] Moreover, Protestant theology was still seen as a respectable discipline. The theologians gained this respectability, however, by developing and nurturing both theological liberalism and the rising tide of nationalism. In many respects the two went together. Since Protestant pastors were state employees, they were trained in theology at state universities. Of course, this created problems with regard to theological orthodoxy since the state now retained control over hiring, theological orthodoxy, and moral discipline instead of the church.[42] While this did result in greater room for theological innovation for the Theology faculty, it also nurtured the rise of theological liberalism.

Theological liberals in turn nurtured the political aspirations of the state through the university. For instance, Friedrich Schleiermacher in Germany, considered the father of theological liberalism, served as a key leader in the development of the premier example of the modern national university, the University of Berlin.[43] Not surprisingly, due to the fact that many church hierarchies functioned as appendages of the state and not as transnational organizations, they demonstrated little interest in fighting the increasing marginalization of Christianity in state universities. This lack of initiative also extended to starting and administering new universities. For instance, after creating Durham University in 1834, the Anglican Church played little role in the formation of additional English universities and the state would begin the funding of Oxford and Cambridge at the turn of the century.[44] Most new universities in Lutheran countries or Reformed areas would first and foremost be state institutions with Lutheran or Reformed theology departments. Even when the state disestablished a church, such as the case of the Netherlands

---

40. Rüegg, "Theology and the Arts," p. 405. For some reason Rüegg omits Durham from his list of Anglican universities.

41. Rüegg, "Theology and the Arts."

42. Anderson, *European Universities*, pp. 88-102.

43. Rüegg, "Theology and the Arts," pp. 406-414.

44. Christophe Charle, "Patterns," in *A History of the University in Europe*, vol. 3, p. 62.

in 1821, liberalized confessional theology departments at state universities continued to exist.[45] The neutering of the creative impulse among Protestant churches meant that they ceased to create new institutions in Europe and only created new institutions on other continents. As the rest of the essays in this volume reveal, there are now more Anglican, Lutheran, and Reformed universities outside Europe than within it.

The Netherlands would be the only place where a new Protestant model of higher education developed in Europe after 1850, perhaps because the state had already disestablished the Reformed tradition. Abraham Kuyper, the well-known Dutch theologian, pastor, politician, and journalist, helped found the Reformed Free University of Amsterdam in 1880. The "Free" referred to the fact that neither the state nor the church controlled the university. Kuyper envisioned the university offering an education in all faculties (and not just theology) that would be grounded in the Reformed *Weltanschauung,* or world-view.[46] Funded by the Reformed churches and other private contributions, the university was open only to Reformed Christians. Against proponents of more nationalized and secularized universities, Kuyper and his associates succeeded in establishing what became one of the last vibrant Protestant universities in Europe.

Catholic Universities

The Catholic Church also did not give in easily to the nationalization of its universities. Some complained that the Catholic Church defended itself with guns, bows, and arrows, and certainly some of the Vatican's heavy-handed efforts to resist modernism proved unproductive and resulted in the sequestering of Catholic theology into seminaries.[47] Nonetheless, the Catholic Church also succeeded in sustaining old institutions and building new ones. After Belgium achieved its independence in 1830, the Catholic Church opened its own university, which eventually moved to Louvain and thus became the successor to the old medieval Catholic university started in 1425. Today, the Dutch Katholieke Universiteit Leuven and the French Université Catholique de Louvain claim to be the oldest universities that

45. Arie Theodorus Van Deursen, *The Distinctive Character of the Free University in Amsterdam, 1880-2005: A Commemorative History* (Grand Rapids: Eerdmans, 2005).

46. Van Deursen, *The Distinctive Character of the Free University in Amsterdam.*

47. Rüegg, "Theology and the Arts," pp. 395-97.

still identify and embrace their Christian identity and heritage. Two other Catholic Belgium universities that still proclaim their Catholic identity, the University of Fribourg (1889) and the Catholic University of Mons (1896), also began during this time.

The Catholic Church also succeeded in starting other new universities that today still profess a Catholic identity. In 1875 France passed a law allowing for "free" or Catholic universities, but these universities faced severe restrictions. For instance, an 1880 act stipulated that private higher educational institutions could not actually use the term "university" in France since only the state institutions can be called universities (however, most English publications granted them this title). By 1900, the three new Catholic institutions — Catholic University of the West (1875), Lille Catholic University (1875), and the Catholic University of Lyon (1875) — still educated only 1,200 students compared to 27,000 in state universities.[48] Other Catholic universities still claiming their Catholic identity today were started in Spain (University of Deusto, 1886) and Switzerland (University of Fribourg, 1889) during the late 1800s.

From the 1790s to the 1930s

Overall, while the number of universities in Western Europe remained basically stagnant between 1790 and the 1930s, the Christian church still played an active role in starting new institutions.[49] Despite these new institutions, however, Christianity and Christian theology faculties continually moved to the margins of universities as other disciplines outside theology became secularized and the ethos of institutions dechristianized. The growth of a student body that was less interested in theology contributed to this movement. For example, while the number of university students increased by fivefold in German lands between 1830 and 1914, the number of students registering in theology faculties dropped by half.[50] European institutions also did not develop a core liberal arts curriculum that would require non-theology majors to gain some academic training in this area. Moreover, states such as Prussia, France, and Great Britain also started professional technical schools that met national needs but that excluded theological education. In fact, these specialized schools accounted for most of the growth in higher education between

48. Charles Phillips, *The Church in France, 1848-1907* (London: SPCK, 1936).
49. Charle, "Patterns," p. 73.
50. Charle, "Patterns," p. 58.

1800 and the 1930s, which saw an increase in the number of students from 80,000 to 800,000.[51] The practical needs of the economy and the concern with training professionals now drove educational innovation.

The Secularization of Western European Universities: From World War I to 1980

The disestablishment of various European state churches after World War I would only further reduce state promotion of theology or other Christian studies at universities and lessen their influence.[52] Even in countries with state churches, institutional secularization at the university level increasingly gained strength. For instance, the secularization of Oxford and Cambridge in the fifty years after World War I "proceeded steadily"; today Oxford and Cambridge can no longer be described as Christian in a broad institutional sense.[53] The same thing is true of Durham and King's College. In light of such developments, one might easily question whether such a thing as a Christian university even existed in England by 1980.

The same pattern occurred in other European countries. The private nature of the Free University of Amsterdam did not prevent it from proceeding down the path of secularization, but it may have been aided because it shed this distinction. In the 1960s it began receiving government funds and opened up admissions to all citizens. Furthermore, due to its inability to fund qualified professors within the Calvinist tradition, it began to broaden its hiring practices and its outlook to become more ecumenical. Consequently, "the number of teachers who seldom if ever any longer posed the question concerning the relationship between belief and science increased."[54] These new faculty began placing more emphasis on the social implications of Christianity in ways that

51. Charle, "Patterns," p. 73.

52. Portugal had already disestablished Catholicism in 1910. Various German principalities disestablished their state churches in 1918, Austria in 1918, Czechoslovakia in 1920, Finland in 1919, Wales in 1920, and Scotland in 1921.

53. Vivian Hubert Howard Green, *Religion at Oxford and Cambridge* (London: SCM Press, 1964), 338. Some colleges or halls affiliated with the two institutions are still sponsored by particular Christian orders or churches. Thus, the colleges have denominational chaplains and activities, but the universities as a whole no longer identify themselves as Christian or Anglican. See Gavin D'Costa, *Theology in the Public Square: Church, Academy, and Nation* (Malden, Mass.: Blackwell Publishing, 2005).

54. Van Deursen, *The Distinctive Character of the Free University in Amsterdam*, p. 303.

neglected or downplayed theological distinctives. By the 1980s, the Free University had already gone through a rather quick secularization process.[55] At its one hundredth anniversary in 1980, Rector H. Verheul proclaimed, "to develop Christian science as one used to think of it is no longer the pretense of the Free University."[56] Soon afterward, an administrator would straightforwardly admit, "The Free University is not a Christian university."[57] Today, it primarily sees "its tradition of Christian standards and values" as being found "in the emphasis placed upon social involvement in the university's teaching and research programmes" (Mission 2009). With the Free University's secularization, by 1980 it would be difficult to describe any formerly Protestant university in Western Europe as "Christian" in the sense that we are using the word in this volume.

Catholic institutions proved slightly more resilient due to a number of factors. The countries where they existed also experienced a slower process of national secularization (Spain did not disestablish the Catholic Church until 1978 and Italy did not disestablish it until 1984). The centralized nature of the church also meant that its older institutions for training priests persisted while it also had the resources to continue starting new institutions. This last point proved particularly important. Unlike Protestants, the Catholic Church established a variety of new universities: in Spain (University of San Pablo CEU, 1933; University of Navarra, 1952; Universidad Cardenal Herrera CEU, 1971), Italy (Pontifical University Antonianum, 1938; LUMSA University, 1939), Portugal (Catholic University of Portugal, 1967), and Germany (Catholic University Eichstatt-Ingolstadt, 1980). Nonetheless, Catholic higher education in Western Europe was no longer the dominant force it once was and existed as a small, specialized sector within the larger state systems of education.

The Contemporary Situation (1981 to the Present)

Within the past three decades, little has changed to alter the secularization of Western European higher education. Currently, throughout the whole of Western Europe I have identified forty-four Christian universities and colleges: eleven Protestant, thirty-two Catholic, and one university that is both Catholic and Anglican. Altogether they enroll around 343,000 students. In only one country (Belgium) does enrollment in Christian institutions comprise more

55. Van Deursen, *The Distinctive Character of the Free University in Amsterdam*, p. 303.
56. Van Deursen, *The Distinctive Character of the Free University in Amsterdam*, p. 386.
57. Van Deursen, *The Distinctive Character of the Free University in Amsterdam*, p. 386.

than 6 percent of the total higher education enrollment (almost 13 percent). The next highest figure is the Netherlands (5.8 percent), followed by Spain (4.3), Italy (2.9), and Portugal (2.9).[58]

With regard to new universities Catholics have started only one new university in Spain (University of Ramón Llull, 1990) and one small pontifical university (Pontifical University of the Holy Cross, 1984). Protestant higher education has been resurrected from its virtual death with six new universities created during this time period, but many of these are rather small or have an unstable Christian identity, as we shall see.

Contemporary Protestant Higher Education in Western Europe

In light of the history of Protestant higher education in Western Europe, the contemporary situation appears particularly dismal. Only eight small Protestant Christian institutions can be found (see Table 1 on p. 149).

Although six of these institutions use "university" in their names and fit the definition of a Christian university used in this volume, all but one of these institutions are closer to slightly enlarged professional schools. For instance, most of these institutions offer only a few majors and do not contain separate faculties or schools. In fact, what is striking about Protestant higher education in Western Europe is that Canterbury Christ Church University is the only Protestant university in Europe with a broad range of liberal arts majors.

In addition to the lack of larger liberal arts institutions, Protestant higher education in contemporary Europe also lacks a larger unified structure or presence on the Continent that could nurture Christian institutions, help them resist secularization pressures, and nurture a conversation about the integration of faith and learning. In other words, no European equivalent to the Council for Christian Colleges and Universities in North America or the Association of Christian Universities and Colleges in Asia has existed. In England, a Council for Church Colleges exists, but most of the member institutions are actually quite secularized and do not even fit our definition.[59] Recently, the development and growth of the International Association for the Promotion

58. These numbers were determined by using the country enrollment figures found at UNESCO, stats.uis.unesco.org/unesco/TableViewer/tableView.aspx?ReportId=168 (accessed March 1, 2011).

59. See Perry L. Glanzer, "Searching for the Soul of English Universities: An Analysis of Christian Higher Education in England," *British Journal of Educational Studies* 56 (June 2008): 163-183.

Table 1: Protestant Institutions in Western Europe

Country	Institution	Confession	Date Achieved Current Status	Students	Funding
Finland	Diaconia University of Applied Sciences	Lutheran	1996	3,000*	Private
Germany	The Protestant University of Berlin (Evangelische Hochschule Berlin)	Lutheran	1972	1,372	Mixed
Germany	The Protestant University of Darmstadt (Evangelische Hochschule Darmstadt)	Lutheran	1971	1,700	Mixed
Germany	Lutheran University of Applied Sciences in Nuernberg (Evangelische Hochschule Nuernberg)	Lutheran	1995	1,300	Mixed
Germany	Evangelical University of Applied Sciences for Social Work, Education, and Care	Lutheran	1991	627	Mixed
Netherlands	Christian University of Applied Sciences	Reformed	1989	4,200	Public
Netherlands	Reformed University of Applied Sciences	Reformed	1987	1,399	Public
Norway	Ansgar College	Lutheran	1913	200	Private
Norway	Diakonhjemmet University College	Lutheran	1980	2,200	Private
UK	Canterbury Christ Church University	Anglican	2005	18,000	Public
UK	Newbold College	Adventist	1901	300	Private

*On seven campuses

of Christian Higher Education (IAPCHE) has begun to fill this gap. Over the past decade it has sponsored a number of conferences in Europe attempting to bring institutions of Christian higher education together for the sharing of ideas (see www.iapche.org).

Catholic Universities

According to our standards for identifying Christian universities there are thirty-two Catholic universities in ten Western European countries and the Vatican (see Table 2 on pp. 150-51).[60]

Table 2: Catholic Higher Education in Western Europe

Country	Institution	Students	Origin	% Publicly Funded
Belgium	Catholic University of Leuven	31,000	1425	85
Belgium	Catholic University of Louvain	21,000	1425	85
France	Catholic Institute of Toulouse	6,300	1877	20-30
France	Catholic University of the West, Angers	12,500	1875	20-30
France	Catholic University of Lyons	7,000	1875	20-30
France	Catholic University of Paris	15,500	1875	20-30
France	Lille Catholic University	15,000	1875	20-30
Germany	The Catholic University of Eichtätt-Ingolstadt	4,900	1980	85
Italy	Catholic University of the Sacred Heart	40,000	1921	23-25
Italy	LUMSA University	6,154	1939	23-25
Italy	Pontifical University of St. Thomas Aquinas	1,200	1577	0

60. These numbers do not include other institutes, seminaries, theology departments in national universities, or colleges within national universities listed on the International Federation of Catholic Universities and the Federation of European Universities websites (see http://www.fiuc.org/cms/index.php?page=amembersENG&id=ICARIN and http://www.fiuc .org/cms/FUCE/fuce.php?page=FUCEmainENG).

Country	Institution	Students	Origin	% Publicly Funded
Italy	Pontifical University of the Holy Cross	1,500	1984	0
Italy	Pontifical Gregorian University	3,500	1556	0
Italy	Pontifical Lateran University	2,500	1773	0
Italy	Pontifical University Antonianum	N/A	1938	0
Italy	Salesian Pontifical University	1,675	1940	0
Netherlands	Radboud University Nijmegen	17,500	1923	70
Netherlands	Tilburg University	12,000	1927	70
Portugal	Catholic University of Portugal	11,000	1968	12
Spain	Comillas Pontifical University	8,726	1904	0
Spain	Pontifical University of Salamanca	8,500	1940	0
Spain	Universidad Cardenal Herrera CEU	10,000	1971	0
Spain	Universidad Católica de Valencia "San Vicente Mártir"	5,500	1969	0
Spain	Universidad San Pablo CEU	19,000	1933	0
Spain	University of Ramón Llull	13,696	1990	0
Spain	University of Deusto	1,300	1886	0
Spain	University of Navarra	10,153	1952	0
Switzerland	Université de Fribourg	10,010	1889	0
UK	Newman University College	2,600	1968	100
UK	St Mary's University College Twickenham	3,800	1850	100
Vatican	Pontificia Università Lateranense	4,000	1556	0
Vatican	Pontificia Università Urbaniana	1,700	1627	0

Similar to the Protestant institutions, a large number of these institutions, the pontifical universities, are more narrowly focused, although in this case the focus concerns the church. In this respect, these universities are actually closer to seminaries, although they do offer degrees outside theology, canon law, sacred music, and the like. These historical pontifical universities have also provided long-lasting examples of historically faithful Catholic institutions, which is a stark contrast to those of Protestants. A striking difference from their Protestant counterparts is that these institutions cooperate through the European Federation of Catholic Universities,[61] which provides for mutual support, conferences, and the sharing of ideas.

An Anglican-Catholic Hybrid

One unique European state institution that has maintained its Christian identity despite, or perhaps because of, the unusual management of the institution by the state is a unique hybrid, Liverpool Hope University in England. In 1972 the British government decided that, based on the shrinking demand for teachers, too many teachers' colleges existed. Consequently, between 1973 and 1982, the state reduced the number of teachers' colleges by one-third. Many church-related teachers' colleges suffered as a result. The Anglican Church had five teachers' colleges closed and eight colleges subsumed in state institutions. Catholic teachers' colleges shrank from fifteen in 1975 to five. All of the Methodist institutions eventually closed or merged.[62] In order to survive, a Catholic and an Anglican teachers' college decided to merge and create a unique institution that later expanded and recently became an official degree-granting English university in 2005. The unique nature of this institution will be explored later in this chapter.

The Global Context and Contemporary Challenges

Part of the reason for the small number of Christian universities in Western Europe is that they have missed out on global trends that have had a positive influence on the growth of Christian higher education in other regions, such as massification and privatization. In addition, they have experienced most

61. See www.fiuc.org/cms/FUCE/fuce.php?page=FUCEmainENG.
62. See Glanzer, "Searching for the Soul of English Universities."

of the negative influence associated with trends related to globalization or centralization that tend to limit growth of Christian higher education.[63] The two exceptions concern the Catholic experience with privatization and the Protestant experience with what can be called professionalization.

Massification and Privatization

Massification refers to the phenomenal growth that occurred after 1980 in the number of students enrolled in higher education around the world.[64] Europe saw the number of students jump from 6,895,000 in 1980 to 14,786,000 in 2006.[65] While Western Europe participated in this growth particularly during the 1980s and 1990s, the growth occurred largely in secular state institutions with few Christian institutions being created to meet this demand.[66] One reason for this failure pertains to the fact that the dominant Protestant traditions (e.g., Anglican, Lutheran, and Reformed) suffered significant institutional decline with regard to overall numbers of adherents, experienced a resultant lack of funding, and virtually stopped creating new institutions since they were content to let the state control higher education and fund theological faculty.

A second reason concerns the lack of privatization in Western Europe. After the fall of communism, a tremendous growth in the privatization of higher education occurred around the world.[67] Western Europe, however, largely missed out on this development.[68] For example, the United Kingdom has only one private institution of higher education in the whole country.

63. For a discussion of these trends see Philip G. Altbach, Liz Reisberg, and Laura E. Rumbley, *Trends in Global Higher Education: Tracking an Academic Revolution* (New York: UNESCO, 2009).

64. Overall, the number of students increased from 51,160,000 tertiary-level students in 1980 to 139,395,000 in 2006. U. Teichler and S. Bürger, "Student Enrollments and Graduation Trends in the OECD Area: What Can We Learn from International Statistics," in *Higher Education to 2030: Demography,* vol. 1 (Paris: OECD, 2008), pp. 151-172.

65. Teichler and Bürger, "Student Enrollments," p. 155.

66. More recently, Western Europe has seen slower growth than other regions. Teichler and Bürger, "Student Enrollments," pp. 151-172.

67. Daniel C. Levy, "An Introductory Global Overview: The Private Fit to Salient Higher Education Tendencies," Program for Research on Private Higher Education Working Paper series, 2006.

68. Program for Research on Private Higher Education, Europe's Private and Public Higher Education Shares (2002-2009), http://www.albany.edu/dept/eaps/prophe/data/international.html (accessed January 26, 2011).

Consequently, strict state regulations make the growth or existence of such institutions extremely difficult. In contrast, as the Eastern European chapter demonstrates, a number of thriving private universities exist in that area.

Protestants have proved too weak within this context to start major institutions. Only in the last three decades have a small number of private, church-sponsored Protestant universities begun to develop once again and most of these are small institutions that focus on a narrow set of fields. The only two institutions with more than 2,200 students are publicly funded. In this respect, outside these few institutions, the future of Protestant higher education currently looks quite bleak.

The Catholic Church, in contrast, has shown the institutional strength and the political capital to overcome these issues. In addition, privatization has made greater inroads in Catholic countries. Portugal, for example, currently has a private university enrollment exceeding 10 percent of the total number of students in universities (27.9 percent).[69] Two other predominately Catholic countries also have a significant private school enrollment (Spain has 9.0 percent and Italy has 6.2 percent) and the majority of this enrollment comes from Catholic institutions. In fact, Catholic universities that obtain full or majority support through private means are now more numerous than those in countries where they receive the majority of funding through public means (twenty-three of thirty-two). Thus, where privatization has occurred to some small degree, Catholic institutions have expanded. The fact that the Catholic Church is finding ways to support universities apart from state support provides evidence for Philip Jenkins's observation that some European Christians have learned "to evolve religious structures far removed from the older assumptions of Christendom."[70]

Based on the above two trends, it would appear that resisting state control and encouraging greater freedom for private religious higher education should remain one of the top priorities of Christian universities in Europe. Still, it should be noted that a number of Catholic institutions and a couple of Protestant institutions have also maintained state funding. In some instances the Vatican negotiates directly with the state governments for special funding and accreditation privileges. Consequently, Protestant and Catholic higher education institutions in the Netherlands and the United Kingdom, as well as Catholic institutions in Belgium and Germany, enjoy significant and in some cases full funding, while Catholic universities in France and Portugal also receive significant state funding. Yet, one of the additional challenges facing state-funded

69. Program for Research on Private Higher Education.
70. Jenkins, *God's Continent*, p. 54.

Christian colleges and universities throughout Europe is centralized attempts to standardize European education, especially through the Bologna process.

Centralization and the Bologna Process

Due to competitive pressures from American universities, European higher education leaders, led by ministers of education, initiated a reform process that was formalized in 1999 when twenty-nine countries signed the Bologna Declaration calling for a unified European higher education area (EHEA) to be completed by 2010. The declaration outlined five major objectives that would create this area, including a common framework of degrees, a system of transferable credits, efforts to eliminate obstacles to mobility, a means of evaluating quality, and the promotion of a European approach to teaching. Later, in 2003 in Berlin, additional countries were added (for a total of forty-two) and a model three-cycle system of degrees is proposed (bachelor's, master's, and doctoral degrees). The whole process has resulted in an increasing centralization of Western European education beyond the realm of nation-states, but it also includes renewed government control of the universities, both of which limit the freedom of religiously affiliated higher education institutions, especially those related to religious minorities.[71] This result is due to the fact that "the Bologna process aims to integrate the national systems (and not the fringe) to the European higher education area" and seeks to keep higher education in the public sphere.[72]

Professionalizaiton

Globally, higher education institutions that focus more on professional skills and majors have also continued to grow. Increasingly, a major concern with this growth is that these institutions place less emphasis on a liberal arts education.[73] There is some room for hope, however, that Christian institutions

71. Jean-Emile Charlier and Sarah Croché, "How European Integration Is Eroding National Control over Education Planning and Policy," *European Education* 37:4 (2005-2006): 7-21; Tamás Kozma, "Political Transformations and Higher Education Reforms," *European Education* 40:2 (2008): 29-45.

72. Kozma, "Political Transformations and Higher Education Reforms," p. 41.

73. Philip G. Altbach, "The Humanities and Social Sciences in Asia: Endangered Species?" *International Higher Education,* no. 52 (Summer 2008); Altbach, "Globalization and Forces for Change in Higher Education," *International Higher Education,* no. 50 (Winter 2008).

may prove different and actually may move in another direction. As mentioned, the small reversal in the number of Protestant institutions was aided by the development of professional schools that expanded into universities due to the increased demand for higher education throughout Europe and the world.[74] For example, the largest church-related Protestant university, Canterbury Christ Church University, began as a teachers' college.[75] Similarly, two new Reformed universities in the Netherlands rose from roots in professional education. The Reformed University of Applied Sciences in the Netherlands originated through the merging of a professional school that offered degrees in social work, nursing, and human resources, another devoted to teacher education, and a theological academy. The Christian University of Applied Sciences in the Netherlands began through a merger between smaller Christian professional schools in social work, journalism, and theology. One small Christian institution in Norway and one in Finland also started with an emphasis on professional vocations.

Whether professional forms of Protestant higher education follow the worldwide trend remains to be seen. At the moment, due to their Christian mission these institutions tend to require additional courses in the humanities, especially theology, Bible, and philosophy, in addition to their professional training. In fact, these changes perhaps indicate a new approach to starting Christian universities in Europe and elsewhere. Whereas throughout the history of higher education, institutes that focused on the development of clergy often evolved into larger universities, now Christian professional schools may become the new seed for such institutions. Even if this happens, Christian higher education will likely continue to exist on the margins in the area where it first flourished.

The Christian Character and Influence of the Protestant and Catholic Universities

Protestant Universities

Since the Protestant universities largely consist of small, church-related institutions, the majority make significant attempts to integrate Christian faith in

74. Evan Schofer and John W. Meyer, "The Worldwide Expansion of Higher Education in the Twentieth Century," *American Sociological Review* 70:6 (December 2005): 898.

75. See Perry Glanzer, "Searching for the Soul of English Universities: An Analysis of Christian Higher Education in England," *British Journal of Educational Studies* 56 (June 2008): 163-183.

a variety of ways. The smaller schools are private (with two exceptions), have closer church ties and governance (e.g., the Reformed University of Applied Sciences requires faculty to be members of the Reformed Church), offer majors related to theology and religious education, or attempt to integrate faith and learning in some curricular manner (e.g., Angsgar College offers a major in psychology with a religious component), encourage the worship life on campus (e.g., Diakonhjemmet University College hosts chapel and has student chaplains), and, unlike many European institutions, require some form of general education that attempts to integrate Christianity.

The major exception to this rule is Canterbury Christ Church University, the one large university that barely meets our definitional standards for a Christian university.[76] While the governing board must still be composed of a majority of Anglicans (nineteen of twenty-five), the university is funded and controlled by the state. As a result, it cannot discriminate among students on the basis of religion when it comes to admissions. Similarly, when it comes to faculty hiring, it cannot discriminate on the basis of religion, unless it can make a case that adherence to certain beliefs constitutes a genuine occupational requirement (GOR). In Canterbury's case, only the chaplain(s) and the chief executive (vice chancellor: principal) qualify. Due to the lack of general education requirements within English higher education generally, there are also no required theology classes and the Christian presence largely exists through a theology department and special institutions such as the National Institute for Christian Education Research and the Anglican Study Centre. While matriculation and graduation are held in the famed cathedral and worship opportunities are available, the general ethos is largely secular, especially when compared to the other smaller Protestant universities.

Catholic Universities

Today secularization pressures continue to weigh heavily on Western European Catholic universities. While many of the Catholic universities begun before the 1900s identify themselves as Catholic and are under the local Catholic bishop's authority, the degree to which the Catholic identity influences the mission, curriculum, and ethos of these universities varies and some would question whether they are really Catholic. For instance, with regard to the mission statements and general public rhetoric James Arthur observes, "many of the Catholic universities in Western Europe say very little about their reli-

76. See Glanzer, "Searching for the Soul of English Universities."

gious mission, other than a general claim on their official websites that they are Catholic or have a Catholic background."[77] He notes that the Catholic universities established in France in the late 1800s, although largely privately funded, still end up playing down distinctly Catholic elements in the curriculum in order to secure teaching and research contracts at the regional or national level. He also points to the fact that the former Catholic University of Nijmegen recently changed its name to Radboud University Nijmegen (St. Radboud was a Catholic bishop and scientist who lived in the tenth century) as a sign of its secularization since it hides its Catholic identity.[78] Other universities such as the Université de Fribourg in Switzerland and Tilburg University in the Netherlands do not even mention their Catholic identity in institutional profiles.[79] In some cases, even when the Catholic identity of the school is mentioned, it is often associated with moral instead of theological matters. A good example comes from the young Catholic university in Germany, the Catholic University of Eichtätt-Ingolstadt, which proclaims:

> The university is committed to academic as well as catholic tradition. In practice, this means on the one hand, that the university is open to students of all confessions, that no study fees are charged, that the exams passed at the KU grant the same rights as those at state colleges and that the freedom of science is guaranteed. On the other hand, the catholic fundament [sic] means for example, that the results of research as well as the everyday way of acting, which the college prepares for, should be critically questioned. For example, company ethics or journalistic ethics are cornerstones of the respective academic programs. Moreover, a special emphasis is placed on the cooperation of disciplines and the open-mindedness, which is also the basis for dialogue with other religions.[80]

Catholic identity in this case is simply associated with generic values such as critical thinking, ethics, the unity of the disciplines, and tolerance.

Nonetheless, there are some significant examples of Catholic universities that emphasize their Catholic identity and make note of larger theological aims.

---

77. Arthur, *Faith and Secularisation*, p. 46.
78. Arthur, *Faith and Secularisation*, p. 49.
79. Université de Fribourg, http://www.unifr.ch/ (accessed March 1, 2011); Profile Tilburg University, http://www.tilburguniversity.edu/about-tilburg-university/profile/ (accessed March 1, 2011).
80. Catholic University of Eichtätt-Ingolstadt at http://www-edit.ku-eichstaett.de/Ueberblick/portraet/kathUni.en (accessed February 28, 2011).

For example, although the University of Navarra in Spain does not actually fall under the authority of the Catholic Church since it is independently run by members of Opus Dei, the institution actually exhibits many characteristics of highly orthodox Catholic universities and its public rhetoric is forthright about its Catholic identity and the role of theology in shaping the university's mission.[81] Other universities under the Church's authority also explicitly acknowledge the theological dimension of the university's mission. The oldest Catholic university, Katholieke Universiteit Leuven, proclaims in its mission statement:

> As a Catholic university, K.U. Leuven is a critical centre of thought within the Catholic community. As such, it is deeply concerned with the relationship between science and faith and with the dialogue between the church and the world. On the basis of its Christian view of humankind and society, K.U. Leuven reflects on the axiological, ethical and religious problems emerging from developments in science and technology and from changes in social and cultural life. . . . Special attention is paid to the personal dignity of human beings, to the protection of the weak and to justice and peace. K.U. Leuven also creates a spiritual climate which fosters the full human and religious development of the members of the university community.

Similar sorts of rhetoric can be found at institutions such as Universidad de Deusto and Universidad Católica de Valencia "San Vicente Mártir."[82] Overall, the Catholic universities exhibit a wide range of attitudes toward their identity in their mission statements and rhetoric.

When it comes to matters of membership, Catholic universities are more consistent in that they do not have requirements for faculty or students except for the positions in the theology and canon law faculties that are directly overseen by the Catholic Church. Consequently, there are few, if any, religious restrictions on the hiring of faculty or admissions standards for students, which has led to some significant changes. For example, the University of Leuven in Belgium has seen its practicing Catholic student body decline from 80 percent in 1974 to 30 percent in 1990 and evidence that it is secularizing is evident.[83]

81. See "Ideario de la Universidad" (Ideals of the University) at http://www.unav.es/servicio/informacion/identidad-mision (accessed February 28, 2011).

82. See Universidad de Deusto, History and Mission, http://www.deusto.es/servlet/Satellite/Page/1102609954978/_cast/%231227879422943%231102609954978/UniversidadDeusto/Page/PaginaCollTemplate (accessed March 1, 2011); Universidad Católica de Valencia "San Vicente Mártir," Mission Statement, http://www3.unicatt.it/pls/unicatt/consultazione.mostra_pagina?id_pagina=15&id_lingua=4.

83. Bart Pattyn, "Is It Wrong to Teach What Is Right and Wrong? The Debate at K.U.

A similar openness can be found in the curriculum. The Western European Catholic universities are different from Catholic universities in North America in that they usually do not have a core curriculum. As a result, only in a few cases (e.g., the Catholic University of Portugal) are courses related to Christianity, theology, or even ethics required of all students. All of the institutions do have robust theology departments that usually address biblical, dogmatic, moral, and pastoral theology, but the extent to which these departments or theological matters influence other disciplines is questionable. A recent study of Radboud University found that "the catholic identity of the university is somewhat lost" and only the theology faculty and students retained any sense of a unique Catholic identity.[84] Students in other faculties appeared to be "in a process of secularization." At many institutions, the Catholic identity appears to be largely nurtured through special institutes (e.g., the Heyendall Institute at Radboud).

The most common way the Catholic identity is fostered comes through the ethos of the university. At almost all these institutions, the liturgy is a central part of the life of these universities, religious orders provide leadership and a strong Catholic presence, student clubs nurture Christian fellowship, and the architectural symbols portray the Catholic atmosphere. Nonetheless, the increasingly secular student body at many of these institutions has resulted in the continued secularization of the ethos as well.

The Unusual Exception

Since Liverpool-Hope University is both an Anglican and Catholic university it does not fit the categories above. It also does not fit in other ways. Liverpool-Hope rightfully boasts of being "one of the most mission-explicit Christian institutions in British higher education" and one could perhaps even say Western Europe.[85] Unlike most Protestant universities, it supports a wide range of faculties (Arts and Humanities, Education, Business and Computing, Sciences and Social Sciences). Unlike most Catholic universities, in the hiring and promotion process they probe candidates' support for the Christian mission of the university and they take efforts to support faculty and staff discussions and

---

Leuben," 2007, at http://www.fondationuniversitaire.be/common_docs/EF6/Pattyn2.pdf (accessed February 22, 2010).

84. Maerten H. Prins, Jacques A. P. J. Janssen, Marinus H. F. van Uden, and Cor P. M. van Halen, "Cultural Diversity in a Catholic University," *International Journal of Education and Religion* 4:2 (2003): 168-185.

85. Prins, Janssen, van Uden, and van Halen, "Cultural Diversity."

development that pertain to the institution's unique mission and values. Most important of all, they have made substantive contributions to scholarship, reflecting on the integration of faith and learning in ways not found among most European institutions.[86] In addition, the university sponsors research centers pertaining to Catholic studies, religion and education, and business ethics. In the curriculum, it offers at least the possibility of dual majors in subjects that might include theology as well as unique undergraduate modules such as educating faith, theology of education, and Christian tradition and modernity.[87] In many respects, Liverpool Hope remains a shining light amidst the secularization of English and Western European education.

Conclusion

Western Europe has largely abandoned Christian higher education. Through a process of nationalization and then secularization, Western European education transformed dramatically. Whereas Christianity and the role of the church was once considered indispensable for the university, today Christian theology is perhaps associated with a department, endowed chair, or residential college within a larger state-funded university. Only in Belgium, Germany, the Netherlands, and the United Kingdom are Christian universities largely publicly funded, but even in these countries the vast majority of their universities are secular. Among the publicly funded Christian schools, only a few schools, such as Liverpool Hope, appear to be shining lights in a rapidly secularizing world.

Christian higher education appears to maintain the greatest strength in systems that encourage decentralization, privatization, and less emphasis on political goals and identities and more emphasis on humanistic goals and identities. In light of the fact that the Western European system is discouraging these trends, the situation for European Christian higher education looks particularly grim. In general, the Christian university movement has largely missed out on the massive growth of higher education in Europe. Today private Christian higher education exists only on the edge of European higher

86. See Jeff Astley, Leslie Francis, John Sullivan, and Andrew Walker, eds., *The Idea of a Christian University* (Milton Keynes: Paternoster, 2004); R. J. Elford, ed., *The Foundation of Hope: Turning Dreams into Reality* (Liverpool: Liverpool University Press, 2003); Marcus Felderhof, Penny Thompson, and David Torevell, eds., *Inspiring Faith in Schools* (Abingdon: Ashgate Publishing, 2007).

87. For additional information, see Glanzer, "Searching for the Soul of English Universities."

education systems that are increasingly centralizing.[88] Moreover, private Christian institutions face tremendous pressures due to their limited funding and centralization pressures that seek to maintain the dominance of the public, national university. Only through small professional universities that meet student demand for credentialing and the occasional flourishing private Catholic university does the European university show future prospects for the growth of Christian institutions. While some scholars ruminate about the dying of the light in American Christian higher education, the light of Christian learning in Western Europe, which was once the brightest in the world, is now perhaps the dimmest.

88. Tamás Kozma, "Political Transformation and Higher Education Reforms," *European Higher Education* 40:2 (2008): 29-45.

CHAPTER 7

Resurrecting Universities with Soul: Christian Higher Education in Post-Communist Europe

Perry L. Glanzer

In the middle of the twentieth century, Christian higher education behind the iron curtain of communist Central and Eastern Europe appeared to be dying. The Communist Party had accelerated a secularization process already taking place in many Eastern European universities by either abolishing theology departments at state universities or separating them from state institutions. They also had removed Christian courses and practices at state universities and replaced them with courses, rituals, and practices aimed at propagating the materialist perspective on human life and history and Marxist-Leninist ideology. Private education was outlawed in almost every country and only one persecuted private Christian university survived, the Catholic University of Lublin. Its rector languished in jail, however, and communist authorities had shut down many of its faculties.[1]

More than a half-century later Christian higher education has been resurrected. Four flourishing Catholic universities in four different countries currently exist that educate more than 35,000 full- and part-time students. Two new Orthodox universities, which could possibly be said to be the first comprehensive Eastern Orthodox universities controlled and directed by a branch of the Orthodox Church, have sprung to life. Five new Protestant institutions, including the first Baptist university in Europe, now educate students in four different post-communist countries. This chapter seeks to set these remarkable developments in

1. John Connelly, *Captive University: The Sovietisation of East German, Czech, and Polish Higher Education, 1945-56* (Chapel Hill: University of North Carolina Press, 2000); Herbert C. Rudman, *The School and the State in the USSR* (New York: Macmillan, 1967).

context, evaluate the Christian nature of these new universities, and then discuss the contributions and challenges these new institutions are facing.

The Historical Context for Christian Higher Education in Post-Communist Europe

Even before the political dominance of the Communist Party, Christian higher education had a much different story in Central and Eastern Europe than in Western Europe for a number of reasons. First, due to various social, political and theological factors, the Eastern Orthodox Church that broke from the Catholic Church in 1054 failed to develop its own universities when universities sprang to life in Europe.[2] Thus, while early Catholic universities did originate in Prague (1347), Krakow (1364), and Vienna (1365), no other universities developed in the East before the Protestant Reformation.[3]

Second, although the Protestant Reformation stimulated the growth of new universities in Western Europe, it had only limited influence in the East. For instance, Protestants only succeeded in creating two universities in Königsberg (present-day Kalingrad) in 1544 and Dorpat (present-day Tartu) in 1632. The Catholics proved the most successful in aiding university formation, with the Jesuits proving particularly creative in Olomouc (1570), Vilnius (1578), Trnava (1635), Lwów (1661), and Breslau (1702) as they sought to counter the influence of the Protestants in the East.

The demise of the Jesuits in the eighteenth century, however, and the rise of powerful empires and nation-states resulted in a third important development. Political entities began playing a much greater role in the creation and governance of universities in Central and Eastern Europe than in the West. For example, in 1773 when Pope Clement XIV made the momentous decision to disband the Jesuit Order, Emperor Joseph II (1780-1790) of the Austro-Hungarian

---

2. For an explanation of these reasons, see Perry Glanzer and Konstantin Petrenko, "Resurrecting the Russian University's Soul: The Emergence of Eastern Orthodox Universities and Their Distinctive Approaches to Keeping Faith with Their Religious Tradition," *Christian Scholar's Review* 36 (2007): 263-284. See also Judith Herrin, "The Byzantine 'University' — A Misnomer," in *The European Research University: An Historical Parenthesis*, ed. Kjell Blückert, Guy Neave, and Thorsten Nybom (New York: Palgrave Macmillan, 2006).

3. Three others developed in Buda, Pecs, and Pozsony, but they did not survive. See Willem Frijhoff, "Patterns," in *A History of the University in Europe*, vol. 2, *Universities in Early Modern Europe (1500-1800)*, ed. Walter Rüegg (series ed.) and Hilde de Ridder-Symoens (vol. ed.) (Cambridge: Cambridge University Press, 1996), pp. 43-110.

Empire was "forced" to step into the void left by the Jesuits.[4] Former Jesuit universities became primarily state-run educational institutions with Catholic affiliations and made changes to reflect this fact. Joseph II opened the universities to Protestants, Orthodox, and Jews (1781) and three years later he outlawed teaching classes in Latin and required all classes to be taught in German (1784). The purpose of these reforms, as Robert Anderson observes, was "to create supra-national loyalty to the dynastic state among peoples of diverse languages and cultures"[5] and "a reformed Catholicism subordinate to the state."[6]

Due to the dominant role of these nation-states, and the Eastern Orthodox Church's traditional subservience to the state, the Eastern church still never established its own universities during this time. Thus, civic rulers in these territories played the primary role in creating universities. In fact, the first four Russian universities started in Moscow (1755), Kazan (1804), Kharkov (1805), and St. Petersburg (1819) began as state enterprises. The Russian Orthodox Church did not found or exert dominant control over any of the emerging Russian universities and did not even have a theology department at the universities.[7] Instead, the training of priests was left to the ecclesiastical academies in Kiev (1632) and Moscow (1687) that were the closest Orthodox institutions to universities.[8] Consequently, "from the beginning, the influence of the church on the Russian universities was very limited."[9] In other Orthodox countries, the Eastern church did play a role in establishing theology departments. For instance, an Orthodox theology faculty opened with the University of Athens in 1837, an Orthodox theology faculty became part of Bucharest University in 1884, and the Bulgarian university started with one.[10] The Or-

---

4. Robert Anderson, *European Universities from the Enlightenment to 1914* (Oxford: Oxford University Press, 2004), p. 26.

5. Anderson, *European Universities*, p. 27.

6. Anderson, *European Universities*, p. 29.

7. Anderson, *European Universities*, p. 26.

8. See Frijhoff, "Patterns," p. 48.

9. Frijhoff, "Patterns," p. 56. It should be noted, however, that Eastern Orthodox teaching and practices still pervaded state universities. For instance, Orthodox Church attendance was required of all university students in Moscow and St. Petersburg. For more, see Konstantin I. Petrenko and Perry L. Glanzer, "The Recent Emergence of Private Christian Colleges and Universities in Russia: Historical Reasons and Contemporary Developments," *Christian Higher Education* 4 (2005): 81-97. Consequently, some scholars have labeled these early Eastern European universities as Orthodox (e.g., Walter Rüegg, "Theology and the Arts," in *A History of the University in Europe*, vol. 3, *Universities in the Nineteenth and Early Twentieth Centuries [1800-1945]*, ed. Walter Rüegg [Cambridge: Cambridge University Press, 2004], p. 405).

10. Christopher Charle, "Patterns," in *A History of the University in Europe*, vol. 3, pp. 42-43.

thodox Christian elements, however, were always subject to the authority and power of the state.

Finally, between 1800 and 1917 Central and Eastern European states and their institutions slowly began secularizing as faith in reason and science increased and nationalistic concerns with technological progress advanced.[11] Communism merely accelerated this trend. Following the 1917 Bolshevik Revolution, communists completely secularized the universities by phasing out any religious teaching and replacing it with disciplines aimed at propagating the materialist perspective on human life and history and Marxist-Leninist ideology. These courses included the history of class struggles in Russia and the West, the history of the Russian Communist Party, foundations of Leninism, and historic materialism. Eventually, universities also began to teach scientific atheism, a course seeking to present to the students the scientific foundations for atheism and to shape in them an atheistic perspective on life.[12]

The major exception to these trends was the only Christian institution that survived communism's forced secularization, and it proved to be a very important one. In 1918 the Polish episcopate established a new Catholic university in order to challenge dechristianization trends in Central and Eastern Europe as a whole and in European higher education in particular. With "For God and Fatherland" as its motto, the University of Lublin, renamed the Catholic University of Lublin in 1928 (Katolicki Uniwersytet Lubelski, or KUL), established as its mission "to conduct scientific research in harmony with reason and faith to educate a new Catholic intelligentsia."[13] One unique characteristic of this university would prove vitally important. KUL sought to challenge European secularization as a privately financed university, a phenomenon that was unique in Europe.[14] It received financial support from the Polish episcopate and churches. Later, in 1922 it also received extensive support from an expatriate group known as Friends of the Catholic University of Lublin.[15] This

---

11. Anderson, *European Universities;* Perry L. Glanzer, "The Role of the State in the Secularization of Christian Higher Education: A Case Study of Eastern Europe," *Journal of Church and State* 53:2 (Spring 2011): 161-182.

12. Glanzer and Petrenko, "Resurrecting the Russian University's Soul."

13. The John Paul II Catholic University of Lublin. Catholic University of Lublin Mission Statement, 2009, available from www.kul.lublin.pl/uk/statement.html; Internet; accessed May 1, 2010.

14. S. Slantcheva and D. C. Levy, *Private Higher Education in Post-Communist Europe: In Search of Legitimacy* (New York: Palgrave Macmillan, 2007).

15. The John Paul II Catholic University of Lublin. History of the University, 2010, http://www.kul.lublin.pl/uk/history/; accessed December 13, 2010.

factor would prove extremely important after the university recovered from almost being destroyed in World War II.

When the university grew from 1,600 to 3,000 students between 1946 and 1951, the Polish Communist Party considered KUL "the most threatening place in higher education."[16] Not surprisingly, the Communist Party sought to weaken KUL, although surprisingly it never outlawed the university completely. The Party likely regretted this fact after one of its ethics professors, Karol Wojtyla, was named Pope John Paul II in 1978. His influence, including a visit to his old university in 1987, helped sustain and guide the institution during the last days of communism and allowed at least one Christian university to survive the attack of communism on Christian higher education.[17]

The Communist and Post-Communist Nature of Eastern European Higher Education

While communists sought to destroy the influence of Christianity in the university, they also sought to tightly control the rest of the university system for their purposes. Thus, they built on some of the key characteristics that already existed in the Eastern European university system as a whole but particularly in Russia: control by an excessively strong state through centralized regulation regarding everything such as access, course content, examination regulations, and the like; the outlawing or restriction of private education; and an emphasis on academic fields that had more instrumental use for the state.[18]

The demise of communism would dent these characteristics in a couple of key ways. First, government funding substantially decreased.[19] For example, in Russia between 1992 and 2000, government expenditures for higher education fell from 1.21 to 0.63 percent of gross domestic product (GDP).[20] Second, as a result of falling state revenues institutions had to look for alternative sources of

---

16. Connelly, *Captive University*, p. 220.

17. George Wiegel, *Witness to Hope: The Biography of John Paul II* (New York: Cliff Street Books, 1999).

18. See, e.g., Andrei Kortunov, "Russian Higher Education," *Social Research* 76:1 (2009): 203-224; Rudman, *The School and the State in the USSR*.

19. Michael David-Fox and György Péteri, eds., *Academia in Upheaval: Origins, Transfers, and Transformations of the Communist Academic Regime in Russia and East Central Europe* (Westport, Conn.: Bergin & Garvey, 2000).

20. Anthony W. Morgan and Nadezhda V. Kulikova, "Reform and Adaptation in Russian Higher Education: An Institutional Perspective," *European Education* 39:3 (2007): 41.

revenue from students and private foundations. Charging students for tuition became possible and countries sought support and later received millions of dollars of aid from Western foundations such as the Open Society Institute, the Ford Foundation, and the MacArthur Foundation. Third, authorities relaxed centralized control and private institutions became legal and quickly grew. In every country, private institutions initially blossomed with more than 1 million students in Russia and more than one-third of all students in Estonia, Poland, and Romania in private institutions at one time.[21] As a result, this massive growth of higher education, or massification as it is often called, resulted in a different type of growth in higher education than in Western Europe, which largely resisted privatization.[22] The vast majority of these private institutions focused on meeting unmet student demand for particular professions that only required part-time professors and limited facilities (e.g., business or technology degrees). As a result, this new sector faced concerns about quality.

In fact, concerns about quality also increased regarding the whole range of higher education institutions due to increasing problems with low professorial pay, academic dishonesty, and lack of physical upkeep.[23] In addition, a demographic crisis began to pose a significant problem for colleges and universities.[24] This crisis was compounded by the fact that due to the centralized state control of higher education under communism, enrollments in higher education had not kept pace with population growth. Consequently, after the demise of communism, enrollment in higher education significantly expanded to reach global norms with private education helping meet this demand. In this respect, Central and Eastern Europe caught up with the massification of higher education occurring around the world.[25] This expansion and the resulting demographic crisis led to a situation where too many institutions existed for a shrinking number of students.

21. Snejana Slantcheva and Daniel C. Levy, "Private Higher Education in Post-Communist Europe: In Search of Legitimacy," in *Private Higher Education in Post-Communist Europe: In Search of Legitimacy,* ed. Snejana Slantcheva and Daniel C. Levy (New York: Palgrave Macmillan, 2007), pp. 1-23. See also Philip G. Altbach and Daniel C. Levy, eds., *Private Higher Education: A Global Revolution* (Rotterdam: Sense Publishers, 2005).

22. Alex Usher, "Ten Years Back and Ten Years Forward: Developments and Trends in Higher Education in Europe Region," paper presented at the UNESCO Forum on Higher Education in the Europe Region: Access, Values, Quality and Competitiveness, May 21-24, 2009.

23. See, e.g., Stephen P. Heyneman, Kathryn H. Anderson, and Nazym Nuraliyeva, "The Cost of Corruption in Higher Education," *Comparative Education Review* 52:1 (2008): 1-25.

24. Anthony W. Morgan and Nadezhda V. Kulikova, "Reform and Adaptation in Russian Higher Education," *European Education* 39:3 (Fall 2007): 39-61.

25. Evan Schofer and John W. Meyer, "The Worldwide Expansion of Higher Education in the Twentieth Century," *American Sociological Review* 70:6 (December 2005): 898-920.

These last two developments, as well as concerns about higher education's relation to political goals, have justified the return of centralized state control in Russia and other post-communist countries.[26] Centralization has also re-emerged in other Central and Eastern European countries due to what is known as the Bologna process.[27] Although there is controversy about what exactly the process means, its aims are usually associated with the Bologna Declaration adopted in 1999 by twenty-nine European countries (with others signing later) that sought to establish a European higher education area. Within this area, common terminology and standards for higher education degrees would be establish by the countries and an American system of degrees (bachelor's, master's. and doctorate) would be adopted. The process has largely been driven by centralized education ministries in various national governments and the organizations they have created in an attempt to integrate European higher education and become competitive with American higher education.

Finally, one other significant development within Eastern European higher education is that Christianity once again plays a role in some state universities. In countries such as Bulgaria, Russia, Romania, Poland, and Ukraine theology departments now exist in some state universities.[28] For instance, Cardinal Stefan Wyszyński University (est. 1999), a university of 18,000 students, is fully funded by the Polish state, but in many respects it is also a Catholic university.[29] One vice rector described the mission of the university as being to teach students "to be fighters for the truth, faith, kindness, and human Christian values."[30] The grand chancellor has been a cardinal and is currently the archbishop of Poland. Three of its faculties, theology, Christian philosophy, and canon law, have a direct relationship with the Vatican. The relationship means that the Vatican plays a role in shaping the curriculum, and decisions about professors in the faculty must have the Vatican's approval. This type of relationship between the church and a state university, however, while consistent with Europe's past, remains an exception rather than the rule.

26. Kortunov, "Russian Higher Education."

27. See Voldemar Tomus, "The Bologna Process and the Enlightenment Project," *European Education* 40:2 (2008): 9-28; Tamás Kozma, "Political Transformations and Higher Education Reforms," *European Education* 40:2 (2008): 29-45.

28. For some history behind these developments in Ukraine and Russia, see Jonathan Sutton, *Traditions in New Freedom: Christianity and Higher Education in Russia and Ukraine Today* (Nottingham: Bramcote Press, 1996).

29. See, e.g., http://www.uksw.edu.pl/en; accessed February 1, 2010.

30. Professor Marek Kowalski, interview by author, May 7, 2008, Lublin, Poland.

PERRY L. GLANZER

The Growth of Christian Higher Education

In the midst of these post-communist trends, new opportunities for Christian higher education throughout the region emerged, particularly for private forms of Christian higher education. More important, unlike the earlier time period, Protestant and Orthodox churches also took part in the significant revival of Christian higher education in post-communist countries. Within the past two decades, five new Protestant, two new Orthodox, and three new Catholic institutions have been created in Eastern Europe and Russia. In fact, the post-communist period has produced the most wide-ranging growth and development of Christian higher education among the three major Christian confessions (see Table 1 below).

Table 1: Christian Higher Education in Central and Eastern Europe

Country	Institution	Confession	Founded	Students	Funding
Hungary	Károli Gáspár University	Reformed	1993	5,000	Public
Hungary	Pázmány Péter Catholic University	Catholic	1992	9,469	Public
Lithuania	LCC International University	Christian (evangelical)	1991	650	Private
Poland	The John Paul II Catholic University of Lublin	Catholic	1918	19,000	Public & Private
Romania	Partium Christian University	Reformed	1998	1,350	Public
Romania	Emmanuel University	Baptist	1990	500	Private
Russia	St. John University	Orthodox	1992	3,000	Private
Russia	St. Tikhon University	Orthodox	2004	2,500	Private
Russia	Zaoksky Adventist University	Adventist	2004	400	Private
Slovakia	The Catholic University of Ružomberok	Catholic	2000	7,700	Public
Ukraine	Ukrainian Catholic University	Catholic	1994	1,200	Private

The three new Catholic universities, as well as the Catholic University of Lublin, now called the John Paul II Catholic University of Lublin, are clearly the strongest among the new Christian institutions in regards to both students and finances. The Catholic University of Ružomberok (CUR) has grown to 7,700 students in the span of a decade[31] and Pázmány Péter Catholic University boasts more than 9,400 students after less than two decades.[32] Three out of the four receive more than half of their financial support from the state. The one that does not receive any state funding, Ukrainian Catholic University (UCU), is perhaps the most unique of the universities. Created to support a part of the Catholic Church that still celebrates the Mass according to the Eastern tradition, it was made possible in December 1, 1989, when Mikhail Gorbachev went to meet with Pope John Paul II. Gorbachev gave a present to the pope by declaring the Greek Catholic Church to be officially legal. Nine years later, when Pope John Paul II visited Lviv, he blessed the cornerstone of what would become "the first Catholic university on the territory of the former Soviet Union."[33] In 2002 the UCU opened its doors.[34]

The Russian Orthodox Church also started what might be considered the first two Orthodox universities in Europe. St. John Orthodox University began in 1992 as a joint initiative sponsored by Father Ioann Ekonomtsev, head of the Department of Religious Education and Catechization of the Moscow patriarchate, and a group of Russian professors. From the start the founders understood St. John's academic mission as combining secular humanities with the historic Orthodox tradition and theological education. Father Ekonomtsev, who is also the rector of the university, told the *New York Times,* "Our purpose was to bring about a synthesis between scholarship and faith, and religion and morality, because scholarship without morality at its core is dangerous."[35] St. John draws on the contemporary model of the "confessional university" similar to Catholic universities in Western Europe and the United States because there are no Orthodox models of broad liberal arts universities.[36] In contrast to St. John, St. Tikhon Orthodox University grew out of underground Bible courses offered during the communist era. Officially supported by the Mos-

31. Dalibor Mikuláš, interview by author, October 17, 2007, Ružomberok, Slovakia.

32. See Pázmány Péter Catholic University, http://www.ppke.hu/index_eng.html; accessed January 11, 2011.

33. Borys Gudziak, "The Ukrainian Catholic University: Achievements, Perspectives and Contributions to Tomorrow's World," 2009, http://www.edukraine.org/inaug.fr.borys.gudziak .html; Internet; accessed May 5, 2010.

34. Father Borys Gudziak, interview by author, May 8, 2008, L'viv, Poland.

35. Marina Lakhman, "Russia's Church-run Campus Has a Secular Goal," *The New York Times,* January 1, 1998, sec. 1, p. 3.

36. Father Ioann Ekonomtsev, interview by author, May 18, 2005, Moscow, Russia.

cow patriarchate, it soon became the most influential theological institution in Russia. It was the first to receive accreditation from the Ministry of Education (1997) and was later called on to develop the national standards for theology that are now used in more than thirty state schools. Within the last half-decade, St. Tikhon has added faculties in history, philology, and pedagogical studies. It now educates two thousand full-time students on its Moscow campus as well as two thousand correspondence students at thirteen satellite campuses around Russia.[37]

Various Protestant groups have also started universities in Hungary, Lithuania, Romania, and Russia. Two universities stem from the tradition of Reformed Christianity that originated in Hungary. Károli Gáspár University (KGU) traces its history to a theological faculty founded in 1855 to train ministers for the Reformed Church of Hungary. In 1900 the Hungarian parliament granted the faculty university status that was later taken away by the Communist Party. After the fall of communism in 1989, the Hungarian parliament gave back the university-level status to the theological faculty. Later in 1993 the General Assembly of the Hungarian Reformed Church approved the establishment of a university with a wide range of faculties, a decision later ratified by the Hungarian parliament. Today, KGU educates more than 5,000 students and remains the largest Protestant university in Europe outside England. The second Reformed university, Partium Christian University, also serves Reformed Hungarian-speaking Christians, but it is located in Romania. Originally a theological faculty in 1990, it added additional majors and eventually separated from the Protestant Theological Institute of Cluj Napoca in 1995 to form a separate university. Today, it is the largest Christian university in Romania.

The two smallest institutions, not surprisingly, are associated with small, minority denominations. Emanuel University (EU) originated from an underground training school for pastors in Romania. After the communist regime fell in December 1989, the new government officially approved the Baptist Biblical Institute located in Oradea as a theological seminary. Later, the Institute expanded its efforts in the mid-1990s to include teacher training, social work, and business, which led it to change its name in 1998 to Emanuel University. In 2000 it received formal accreditation as a private university from the Romanian Ministry of Education. It remains small, with a total student population ranging between four hundred and five hundred.[38] Similar to a number of

37. St. Tikhon's Orthodox University, http://en.pstgu.ru/; accessed December 13, 2010.
38. Paul Negrut, interview by author, October 19, 2007, Oradea, Romania.

the institutions above, Zaoksky Adventist University (ZAU) also originated as a seminary for pastoral training in 1987. In the 1990s it added additional programs. Later, in 2004, the government gave permission for Zaoksky to be an academy that offered non-theological degrees, making it Russia's first faith-based university associated with a specific Protestant tradition. Today, ZAU consists of two separate entities — the Zaoksky Christian Humanities and Economics Institute and the Zaoksky Theological Academy — that educate close to four hundred undergraduate students in the areas of economics, music, religion, social work, and theology.

The final institution, LCC International University in Lithuania, is the only nondenominational institution without official connection to any particular church, although various Mennonite individuals and churches have played a vital role in starting and sustaining the college.[39] It began in 1990, the year Lithuania declared independence from the Soviet Union, through the invitation of Lithuania's young minister of education, Darious Kuolys, to a group of Protestants. When Art DeFehr, one of the original founders, asked why the new Lithuanian government invited Protestants to join such a university, Kuolys told him that "they had studied the west and observed that societies that were more plural and more Protestant tended to be more democratic."[40] Today, LCC grants bachelor's degrees in business administration, English, psychology, and theology (evangelical), as well as a master's degree in teaching English to speakers of other languages (TESOL). Instruction takes place in the English language, so while 60 percent of LCC's 650 students come from Lithuania, the other 40 percent come from twenty-one different countries.[41]

Christianity and the University: What Difference Does It Make?

Overall, the largest number of intentionally Christian higher education institutions that has ever existed in Eastern Europe now exists today. The significant role that Christianity plays in these universities can be ascertained by examining them through the categories Robert Benne suggests can help determine the nature of an institution's Christian commitment: (1) public relevance and rhetoric; (2) membership requirements; (3) theology's role in the curriculum;

---

39. Sarah Klassen, *Lithuania Christian College: A Work in Progress* (Winnipeg, Manitoba: Leona DeFehr, 2001).

40. Klassen, *Lithuania Christian College*, p. 3.

41. LCC International University (2010), http://www.lcc.lt/; accessed June 2, 2010.

(4) worship and ethos; and (5) governance and financial relations with a sponsoring church.[42]

There is a noticeable difference between two sets of institutions that can be explained by the well-known church-sect typology first described by Ernst Troeltsch and later expanded by sociologists.[43] Troeltsch describes the church type as a religious tradition that is usually a majority, seeks to incorporate the masses, and sees itself as part of the dominant social order. In contrast, the sect aspires to purity and direct fellowship among its members. Within this typology, the universities associated with the Catholic, Orthodox, and Reformed traditions represent the church type while the Adventist and Baptist universities represent the sect type. LCC exhibits characteristics of both types, although it largely operates in a more sectarian manner.

The Public Relevance of and Rhetoric Related to the Christian Vision

All of the Christian universities appeal to the Christian tradition as their organizing paradigm in ways that set them apart from secular institutions, and sometimes, all the other institutions in the country. As the UCU rector Rev. Dr. Borys Gudziak noted, "There is no other university in Ukraine that is systematically, consciously, trying to develop a vision of the academic life based on the Eastern Christian tradition."[44] In their mission statements and rhetoric, the church-type universities emphasize the ability of the university to synthesize Christian and secular learning. For instance, KLM's stated mission is: "conducting research in the spirit of harmony between science and faith, along with teaching and educating Catholic intelligentsia as well as co-creating Christian culture."[45] Moreover, these schools expressly proclaim more openness to the larger academic world in their statements. UCU's mission states that it "is an open academic community living the Eastern Christian tradition and forming leaders to serve with professional excellence in Ukraine and internationally — for the glory of God, the common good, and the dignity of the

42. Robert Benne, *Quality with Soul: How Six Premier Colleges and Universities Keep Faith with Their Religious Traditions* (Grand Rapids: Eerdmans, 2001), p. 49.

43. Ernst Troeltsch, *The Social Teachings of the Christian Church,* 2 vols., trans. O. Wyon (New York: Harper and Row, 1960 [1931]); Meredith McGuire, *Religion: The Social Context,* 5th ed. (Long Grove, Ill.: Waveland Press, 2008).

44. Father Borys Gudziak, interview by author, May 8, 2008, L'viv, Ukraine.

45. The John Paul II Catholic University of Lublin, The University, 2009, http://www.kul.lublin.pl/2696.html; accessed May 1, 2009.

human person."[46] Similarly, they clearly want to serve more than the church population. As KGU's present rector put it, "we do not want our university to be in a bad sense sectarian, which means too closed up. We want to be open to new ideas, compatible with academic requirement."[47]

The sectarian schools exhibit a more evangelical attitude. For instance, EU's mission is "to develop the God-given gifts of young men and women by training them in skills with which they can serve their communities, enabling them to live out their Christian faith in their daily lives, and making such a difference in the lives of others that they in turn are drawn to faith and to similar values."[48] This mission is purposely centered on serving the church and not producing intellectuals or professionals for Romanian society. As one administrator shared, "the main goal is to serve the church not to produce intellectuals. Any other university produces intellectuals."[49]

Membership Requirements

When it comes to membership requirements, the church-sect divide is readily apparent. For example, not one of the Catholic universities restricts their students or faculty to Catholics. For instance, KUL faculty members are merely encouraged to "seek the truth diligently,"[50] but they are not required to be members of the Catholic Church. Similarly, neither St. John nor St. Tikhon has strict guidelines for hiring faculty although rectors ask potential faculty questions about their views of Orthodoxy in interviews. The Reformed universities take a similar approach. Theological issues are not always the reason for this policy. At many of these universities interviewees commented that this openness is also due to necessity since a number of Christian institutions have been forced to hire agnostics and atheists to teach courses (e.g., KGU, St. John's University, and UCU). As the former rector of KGU acknowledged, "We cannot fulfill all the faculty positions with devoted Christians."[51] Some exception also exists to this norm regarding faculty hiring. Faculty in the universities that have theology, canon law, or Christian philosophy are expected

46. The Ukrainian Catholic University, n.d., unpublished ms., p. 1.

47. Peter Balla, interview by author, October 15, 2007, Budapest, Hungary.

48. Paul Negrut and Corneliu Simut, Responses to "Christian higher education in post-communist countries questionnaire," 2007.

49. Corneliu Simut, interview by author, October 19, 2007, Oradea, Romania.

50. Professor Slawomir Nowosad, interview by author, May 2, 2008, Lublin, Poland.

51. Ferenc Szûcs, interview by author, October 15, 2007, Budapest, Hungary.

to support each university's Christian mission and must be approved by the church (e.g., the Vatican, the patriarchy).

Students at these church-type universities are also not restricted by faith although in some cases informal barriers apply. In entrance exams the Orthodox universities test students on church history and what the Orthodox call God's Law, focusing on the fundamentals of the Orthodox faith and practice. In addition, prospective students must have a recommendation from a priest or confessor, and the faculty interviews each student. In this respect, students at St. John and St. Tikhon actually have to pass more rigorous "membership" requirements than the faculty. In addition, graduate students in theology and canon law at Catholic universities are asked to produce a baptismal certificate.

Despite the fact that these universities admit students of various religious backgrounds, most exercise a degree of moral authority when it comes to setting forth the university's moral and theological vision. At matriculation in the Catholic universities students sign a vow that they will help and preserve Christian values, and one KUL vice rector shared that students have been dismissed for various offenses such as illegal drug use or hiring prostitutes. Likewise, professors have been disciplined for both theological and moral reasons. Similarly, St. Tikhon manifests its Orthodox commitment through its regulations. If a student comes to the university drunk, he or she will be suspended, and female students are discouraged from wearing pants to theological classes. While St. John did not have such stipulations, some behavior expectations existed. Smoking is strictly prohibited on campus; if a female faculty member is married, it is expected that she wear a covering on her head.[52]

The sectarian institutions usually demonstrated stricter membership requirements.

EU actively seeks to limit both student and faculty membership to "Evangelical born-again" believers and requires both to be active members of a local evangelical church in Romania. Once students are admitted, they have to embrace the university's clear moral and theological guidelines. As President Paul Negrut shared, "The university statement of faith and our ethical standards are not negotiable. . . . We expect students to behave as genuine Christians, while the motto of our university is 'integrity and excellence.'"[53]

At ZAU and LCC all faculty members must be Adventists/Christians, but they do not restrict students outside Adventism/Christianity. One administrator at ZAU, Oleg Lungu, related in an interview, "We would be willing to

---

52. Maria Vladimirova, interview by author, May 16, 2005, Moscow, Russia.
53. Paul Negrut, interview by author, October 19, 2007, Oradea, Romania.

accept as much as 30 percent non-Christians or Christian students from other denominations besides Adventists. We don't have many of them."[54] The low numbers are likely due to the fact that the application requests information about membership in an Adventist congregation, the date of water baptism, information regarding one's involvement in ministry, and even contact information for the student's pastor.

Christianity and the Curriculum

What sets all these universities apart, not surprisingly, is the role of theology in the curriculum. In all of the universities, theology plays a central role and in every case, exerts some influence beyond its disciplinary bounds. For instance, according to one KUL interviewee, the theology faculty of sixty chairs and 150 teaching staff is the largest in the world.[55] This massive department produces 500 master's degrees and forty doctorates each year.[56] In addition, the theology faculty shapes the larger campus life by organizing an "Ecclesiology Week" and a "Spirituality Week" on campus. Similarly, at UCU the largest faculty in the university is the faculty of philosophy and theology (400 students), and the school boasts that the faculty of theology and philosophy "has already become the premier religious institution of higher learning in Ukraine."[57] The influence of two of these faculties also touches every student in that there are general education requirements in theology (while in Europe general education requirements are quite rare). At KUL all first- and second-year students, regardless of specialization, must take courses (or pass examinations) in fundamental ethics (i.e., Christian anthropology), the Bible, and Catholic social teaching. Similarly, at UCU students in the other faculty of humanities and the Catechetical-Pedagogical Institute are also required to take courses in the scriptures, theological ethics, and doctrine from the School of Theology and Philosophy.

At the Orthodox schools, the theology departments remain large (more than 10 percent of students at both institutions) and privileged (e.g., St. Tikhon's president also serves as dean of theology). Required theology courses for non-theological majors vary, although all take some theology. Moreover,

54. Oleg Lungu, interview by author, May 19, 2005, Zaokski, Russia.

55. Oleg Lungu, interview by author, May 19, 2005, Zaokski, Russia.

56. The John Paul II Catholic University of Lublin. Faculty of Theology, 2009, www.kul.lublin.pl/uk/faculties/ft; accessed May 1, 2009.

57. The Ukrainian Catholic University, n.d., unpublished Ms., p. 2.

Orthodoxy influences other parts of the curriculum. For instance, St. Tikhon's dean of history claims the school teaches history "from a Christian worldview"[58] and its pedagogy faculty aims to "return Christian morals to the classroom."[59] St. John offers courses on Orthodox anthropology and theology of language and speech.

Professor Vladimirova in ecology discussed St. John's role in the emerging field in Russia known as ecotheology, "which introduces theological thought about the environment."[60] The dean of the psychology department, who is an Orthodox priest, emphasized that "psychology is taught as a study of the soul in the literal sense."[61]

The sectarian schools demonstrate the greatest commitment to theology.

EU encourages the integration of faith and learning by requiring every liberal arts specialization to have a theological module. As a result, students take courses in New Testament, Old Testament, doctrine, Christian life, missions, evangelism, and Christian ethics. Many of them also take a course in biblical counseling. The reason for such extensive theological requirement is that EU's leadership sees their students as "missionaries: on the market place, in public schools, in social care institutions, on the mission field in another part of the world. No matter where they go, they should be able to embody the Gospel and to articulate the Gospel."[62]

At ZAU integration involved required Bible classes, prayer before classes, faculty encouragement to engage in the integration of Christianity into all disciplines, and a particular view of student development. As one administrator noted, "Adventists have a holistic view of human nature, so we would say that spiritual, intellectual and physical education should be interrelated."[63] An interesting feature of this holistic view is the integration of intellectual pursuits with not only moral and spiritual development but also physical development, an effort that reflects the Adventist perspective on human nature and the importance of physical health. Consequently, one of the first buildings built on campus was a gym.

58. Sergey Vorobyov, interview by author, May 17, 2005, Moscow, Russia.

59. St. Tikhon Orthodox Humanities University, "Pravoslavniy Svyato-Tikhonovsky Gumanitarniy Universitet," 2005, DVD.

60. Maria Vladimirova, interview by author, May 16, 2005, Moscow, Russia.

61. Andrew Lorgus, personal correspondence, May 19, 2005.

62. Paul Negrut, interview by author, October 19, 2007, Oradea, Romania.

63. Oleg Lungu, interview by author, May 19, 2005, Zaokski, Russia.

Worship and Ethos

While European universities usually place less emphasis than North American ones on the co-curricular dimension of higher education, many of these religious institutions, apart from the Orthodox ones, support a robust co-curricular life that seeks to form the whole student. As one KUL professor told me, "Students need formation and not only teaching."[64] At Catholic institutions the ethos of the university revolves around the chapel, which hosts daily Masses. The UCU rector noted that it is his central priority. "I try to be at liturgy at the university every day if it is at all possible."[65] The priority of worship is also reflected in their architecture. At UCU, ZAU, EU, and Pázmány Péter Catholic University the chapels included in the new campus buildings also shape the ethos of the whole institution. At the Catholic institutions, worship is voluntary, but provisions are made to keep it an emphasis. For example, UCU closes the library and other academic offices for its 11:30 Wednesday service. At the sectarian institutions, chapel attendance is required.

A number of universities hold breaks from classes for spiritual retreats, days of recollection, prayer vigils, pilgrimages, and special summer camps. KUL partners with various religious orders, such as the Franciscans, Dominicans, Jesuits, and Carmelites, to foster the spiritual formation of students through pastoral care, sacramental ministry, retreats and spiritual direction, religious instruction serving to deepen religious formation, sponsorship of various religious associations and movements, and psychological and family counseling conducted by university personnel and graduates, and a religious bookstore. Not surprisingly, with all this attention to spiritual formation, 7 percent of students are candidates for a religious order.[66]

Significant resources are also devoted to the spiritual formation of students. At LCC, spiritual growth is fostered by a chaplain and two spiritual formation coordinators. At UCC, each year one priest is responsible for first-, second-, or third-year students, and they have regular meetings and discuss various spiritual topics. At EU every group of students also has a faculty member who serves as a mentor, and the students and mentor meet for Bible study and prayer and have certain events, such as a retreat in the mountains for a weekend. At ZAU students are even required to be involved in an in-depth social ministry six hours per week, such as work in the local hospital and nearby orphanages.

64. Rev. Dr. Hab. Marian Nowak, personal correspondence with author, May 9, 2008.
65. Father Borys Gudziak, interview by author, May 8, 2008, L'viv, Ukraine.
66. Professor Slawomir Nowosad, interview by author, May 2, 2008, Lublin, Poland.

Church Support and Governance

The governance of the various Christian universities varies, although colleges associated with more established leadership structures, such as the Catholic and Eastern Orthodox Churches, are more directly under church leadership. For instance, Cardinal Lubomyr Husar, the head of the Ukrainian Greek-Catholic Church, serves as the Ukrainian Catholic University's grand chancellor, although the ten-member board of trustees that leads the university is not limited to practicing Ukrainian Catholics. One finds a similar mixture among the Orthodox schools. Leaders of both schools are responsible to the ROC hierarchy and directly accountable to it; however, the church does not provide any direct financial support.

The sectarian universities are less connected to a church hierarchy and more guided by theological vision. For instance, LCC is governed by an independent board of directors whose members come from Canada (4), the United States (9), Germany (1), and Lithuania (1). Both the board of directors and the faculty are expected to subscribe to the Apostles' Creed and the Nicene Creed, as well as profess a relationship to Jesus Christ.

Matters are further complicated by the issue of state funding, although here a pattern is much clearer. The sectarian institutions reject state funding to maintain theological purity even though, as in EU's case, such funding is available. Twenty-two percent of its funding comes from student tuition. Twenty-five percent comes from local churches in Romania or Romanians. The school also has an endowment from which it receives 20 percent of the funding. The remaining 33 percent comes from gifts from churches and graduates in the United States, Canada, Great Britain, Germany, Holland, Spain, Italy, and Greece.[67] Similarly, for ZAU, 70 percent of the budget is covered by tuition. Twenty percent is received from the international Seventh-Day Adventist Church and the remaining 10 percent is provided by sponsorships or donations.[68] The bulk of LCC's funding comes from tuition and three different charitable foundations in Canada, Lithuania, and the United States.

In contrast, almost all the Catholic and Reformed institutions receive significant government support. For instance, KGU retains a strong connection with the church, although its funding is largely derived from state-funded student tuition along with some direct government support (19 percent) for

67. Paul Negrut, interview by author, October 19, 2007, Oradea, Romania.
68. Evgenni Dyetev, interview by author, May 19, 2005, Zoekski, Russia.

which they must apply yearly.[69] The Catholic universities in Hungary and Slovakia are fully funded by the state, while KUL receives more than 50 percent of its support from the state.

Creative and Redemptive Influence

One of the hallmarks of Christian universities pertains to their creative and redemptive influence.[70] Although most Christian universities in Eastern Europe are quite young, they have already begun to make significant contributions at many different levels.

The Practices of the University

Perhaps one of the most profound influences of these universities pertains to the countercultural example they demonstrate when it comes to the basic practices of university integrity, particularly in the arena of corruption. For example, the first goal of UCU is to "provide students with a normal academic life, free from concerns of bribery and cheating."[71] Such a goal is tremendously challenging in Ukraine. The rector of a private university in Ukraine actually remarked, "if an American university, with [an] exclusively Nobel prize–winning staff, decided to transfer its base of operations to Ukraine, it would fail to get a license (without a bribe, of course) and could only dream of accreditation."[72] UCU, however, has, to a large degree, successfully achieved this goal. In fact, its efforts received the attention of Ukraine's prime minister, who declared it to be one of only two higher education institutions in the country without corruption.[73] These efforts have also reportedly made it attractive to serious professors. Olena Dzhedzhora, a humanities professor, shared how when the

69. Ferenc Szûcs, interview by author, October 15, 2007, Budapest, Hungary.

70. Perry Glanzer, "Why We Should Discard the Integration of Faith and Learning: Rearticulating the Mission of the Christian Scholar," *Journal of Education and Christian Belief* 12:1 (2008): 41-51.

71. The Ukrainian Catholic University, n.d., unpublished ms., p. 3.

72. Joseph Stetar, Oleksiy Panych, and Bin Cheng, "Confronting Corruption: Ukrainian Private Higher Education," in *Private Higher Education: A Global Revolution,* ed. Philip G. Altbach and Daniel C. Levy (Rotterdam: Sense Publishers, 2005).

73. Comments at 5th Symposium of Central and Eastern European Catholic Universities (CEECU), May 6-8, 2008, L'viv, Ukraine.

university began they had trouble finding Christian humanities professors. As a result, they hired a number of non-Christian professors. Interestingly, when these professors began to be treated with dignity, did not have to deal with bribes, found clean classrooms, and were paid decently, a number progressed on a faith journey since "these values were soon seen as Catholic."[74]

Although small in numbers, scholars at Christian universities have also begun making significant contributions within the scholarly world. UCU professors have produced top-rated scholarship, winning a disproportionate share of prizes for academic books in Ukraine.[75] St. Tikhon professors designed the national theology standards. KUL is particularly noteworthy in this area. It produces world-recognized theology and philosophy scholarship, and administrators claim that their cultural studies, classics, Polish language, and family studies are the best in Poland.[76]

Beyond demonstrating exemplary practices of those commonly associated with a Christian university, many of these institutions make a significant commitment to serving the church. The Catholic, Orthodox, Reformed, and other Protestant universities provide theological training for pastors of their respective churches. The vast majority of Catholic Church leaders in Poland are graduates of KUL, and the new universities promise to provide similar leadership. They also provide scholarship for and about the church. For instance, at UCU one of the first steps to the revival of the theological academy and the creation of the university involved the implementation of an oral history project documenting the underground church. Rector Borys Gudziak remarked, "Kids who are 18 years today, they were born after the church came out of the underground."[77] Thus, all of the students in theology classes undertake an oral interview with a subject, an experience that serves as a unique instrument of faith development for young people. As Gudziak related, "That story of how there were underground seminaries, monasteries, it's an authentically heroic story."[78] As a result of the project, the Institute of Church History currently houses two thousand interviews and more than eight thousand pages of transcriptions from clergy and lay leaders (both men and women) involved with the underground church.

Some of these institutions also attempt to embody the redemptive practices of the church in their social life and ethos. UCU's rector noted that one of the first things he requested involved the establishment of clean toilets (in

74. Comments at 5th Symposium.
75. Father Borys Gudziak, interview by author, May 8, 2008, L'viv, Ukraine.
76. Professor Slawomir Nowosad, interview by author, May 2, 2008, Lublin, Poland.
77. Father Borys Gudziak, interview by author, May 8, 2008, L'viv, Ukraine.
78. Father Borys Gudziak, interview by author, May 8, 2008, L'viv, Ukraine.

recognition of human dignity). The grounds at UCU are meticulous; the symbol of the university is imprinted in the yard's landscaping. When the mayor saw this, he asked if the groundskeeper for the university could do the same thing for the city. Similarly, Zaoksky Adventist University boasts a beautiful campus that stands in stark contrast to its surroundings in the countryside outside Moscow. Of course, the ethos goes beyond looks and extends to the embodiment of a worshiping community. The universities sponsor religious pilgrimages and celebrations, church holidays, special religious services, and mission trips. Even how they perform worship also serves as a witness. UCU has helped give institutional support to the Emmaus Center, the Ukrainian Branch of L'Arche that ministers to people who are mentally disabled, with various students often volunteering. The first Monday of every month they have a liturgy that may involve thirty to forty people who have mental disabilities as well as the same number of parents or supporters. The sermon is conducted in a way that is most conducive to them and one or two of them serve as altar boys. The universities also provide a redemptive community for those scarred by communism. In one case, an interviewee shared how KUL provided a home to a former Communist Party official who had changed his life. According to one interviewee, "This professor is the best pastor in the institute. He tells students — '40 years, it was nothing. Now for 10 years I have found life.'"[79]

Social Transformation

The creative and redemptive influence of these universities extends beyond the campus to the wider social life. KUL graduates have become speakers of both the Polish House and Senate. Before Ukraine's Orange Revolution, in 2001 UCU students were active in protesting corruption, resulting in the Ukrainian secret police visiting Borys Gudziak. As *The Economist* noted, "Shortly afterwards, television news reported that 'rectors who are American nationals are being directly threatened with deportation.' That could only mean Father Gudziak."[80] Other professors were also visited and asked to report. Reportedly, one professor, who was also the founder of Amnesty International in Ukraine, responded, "I've spent ten years in the Gulag and there is nothing you can say to intimidate me."[81] When

---

79. Marian Nowak, conversation at conference, May 8, 2008, L'viv, Ukraine.

80. Pipe dreams, *The Economist,* April 7, 2001, pp. 56-57; http://www.economist.com/node/564095, accessed December 10, 2013.

81. As told by Father Borys Gudziak, interview by author, May 8, 2008, L'viv, Ukraine.

the Orange Revolution took place in Ukraine, the university cancelled classes for three weeks as students traveled to Kiev to protest election fraud. Recently, one of UCU's graduates worked in the Ukrainian presidential administration. The influence of these universities also extends beyond politics in ways that were previously not open to Christians under communist regimes. UCU graduates have started a military chaplaincy, a student chaplaincy, a prison chaplaincy, and orphanages. St. Tikhon serves free lunches to the neighborhood poor. St. John, St. Tikhon, KGU, EU, and UCU train educators for Christian education in public schools as well as churches. UCU started a widely respected religious news service for Ukraine available online (see http://www.risu.org.ua/eng/news/). In fact, UCU stands apart as one of the most innovative, creative and redemptive universities with which this author is familiar.

Challenging Trends for the Future

The State's Regulation of Christian Universities

The major difficulty that all institutions face concerns relationships with the state. In every Eastern European country, universities find themselves subject to a centralized Ministry of Education. These ministries frequently dictate admissions and hiring standards, which courses or majors are to be included in the programs, how many classroom hours are to be allocated for each of them, what content should be covered, and the other specific accreditation procedures the institutions should follow. The influence of the Bologna process also means that state authorities seek to standardize higher education not only within in the country but also with other European institutions and nations. Institutions affiliated with the dominant religion of a country usually do not face as many problems in these areas (the Catholic universities in Hungary, Slovakia, and Poland and the Orthodox universities in Russia), but they still face several limitations.

First, Christian universities confront challenges from the state in being granted the simple freedom to control the membership of both their faculty and students. This challenge exists whether the state provides funds to the university or not. For example, UCU does not receive any government funding, yet it must accept all qualified students who apply no matter their religious identity or beliefs. EU faces the same challenge despite the fact that it receives no state funding. Government accrediting officials recently challenged the university regarding its "discriminatory" theological and moral standards in faculty hiring and student admissions. Rector Paul Negrut explained, "So we had to make a decision that we would rather close down the school than trade our belief or identity. But that's very challenging when you have hundreds of students and they have to live with the prospect that the accreditation agency will not recognize this school."[82] Fortunately, for EU, in this case it was able to remain open. In Russia, the Ministry of Education's response to the demographic crisis resulted in the elimination of the nonprofit status of private universities and the closure of the undergraduate program at the young Russian American Christian University in 2010. State-funded Christian institutions have even less control over their entrance requirements and faculty hiring. Consequently, one professor at KGU estimated that only 20 to 30 percent of students were Christians.[83]

A second state-imposed challenge facing universities concerns the degree of freedom to engage in curricular innovation. A Ministry's guidelines may not provide space for some of the unique ways universities may wish to integrate faith and learning. New developments associated with the Bologna process may exacerbate this situation. One Romanian scholar noted that the recent Bologna process instituted by the European Union also shows potential for creating "new waves of homogenization and secularization" among young European Christian universities since it "is conceptualized by the educational governments as a national reform of higher education" with its primary objective being that of reinforcing national identity.[84] One example of the influence pressures can be seen in the curricular adjustments forced on EU due to this process. Before 2004, the university required all students to receive a double major in theology and another discipline. Theology professor Corneliu Simut describes the advantage of this approach: "In Romania, you could send the guy [the double major] to any remote village, he could pastor, he could teach letters . . . he could get money from the state [as an elementary or secondary teacher]. Now, you have a social work graduate, he goes to that village, but he only has one field in which to specialize."[85] The change Simut describes took place in 2004 due to the Bologna process: "theology was dropped not because we wanted to, but that's the system . . . the law does not allow you to function like that."[86] The most EU can do is require five theology courses of all students. Christian universities in Russia, Hungary, and Slovakia reported similar pressures. For instance, although the Catholic University of Ružomberok has the

82. Paul Negrut, interview by author, October 19, 2007, Oradea, Romania.
83. Peter Balla, interview by author, October 17, 2007, Budapest, Hungary.
84. Szolár, "Church-related Higher Education in Romania."
85. Corneliu Simut, interview by author, October 19, 2007, Oradea, Romania.
86. Corneliu Simut, interview by author, October 19, 2007, Oradea, Romania.

advantage of receiving all its funding from either the Slovak state or the EU, every study program must be approved by the state accreditation board; even the numbers of students in the programs are regulated by the state.[87]

Third, the state also creates pressures regarding financing difficulties. Those universities receiving state funding face the difficulty of being under certain state regulations. For example, one of the challenges facing KUL is that as an institution receiving state funds, it cannot charge full-time students tuition yet it also faces competition for funding from the nine other faculties of theology that exist in other state universities. Consequently, additional funding must come from other sources (e.g., tuition from part-time students, donations from churches). Being state-funded also may not necessarily resolve many other financial limitations since universities around the world are increasingly shifting the cost of public higher education to the individual student.[88]

A final difficulty concerns the fact that most government officials tend to view faith-based education as necessarily a theological education since there are few examples of private professional faith-based higher education institutions. Consequently, those in charge of state accreditation insist that courses of study (e.g., teaching in the social sciences) and expectations for professors, students, and staff follow the pattern of secular state universities. They may also face other difficulties. As Negrut noted, whenever the accrediting agencies came for the first time, they "came with prejudice. They assumed that because we are evangelical Baptist we are stupid, narrow-minded, academically incompetent, and they come with that prejudice."[89] These prior outlooks and prejudices make it difficult for faith-based colleges and universities to win the favor of regional authorities and the federal government agencies as well as acquire or sustain their licenses and accreditation.

Other Trends and Troubles

Beyond issues associated with the state, the universities are confronted by other difficulties. The new private universities face major legitimacy issues.[90] Unlike in the West, most private institutes and universities are still viewed as providing education of a poor quality. Under these conditions, religiously

---

87. Dalibor Mikuláš, interview by author, October 17, 2007, Ružomberok, Slovakia.

88. Philip Altbach, *International Higher Education: Reflections on Policy and Practice* (Chestnut Hill, Mass.: Center for International Higher Education, 2006).

89. Paul Negrut, interview by author, October 19, 2007, Oradea, Romania.

90. Slantcheva and Levy, *Private Higher Education in Post-Communist Europe.*

affiliated institutions of higher education find themselves in a very difficult situation as most people and government officials are unfamiliar with the goals and priorities of faith-based education and tend to misunderstand and disregard this form of higher education.

Since private universities rely heavily on funds coming from tuition, they also have to charge a high enough admissions fee to cover some operating expenses. Most Eastern Europeans are unable to pay high college costs. The rector of St. John University, Father Ekonomtsev, claimed, "Our main difficulties are related to financial support. It is a problem, for instance, to get a facility."[91] This situation makes recruiting a challenge for private higher education institutions. Thus, tuition rarely covers costs. At UCU only 7 to 8 percent of the operating budget is covered by tuition. Most faith-based institutes and universities enjoy some form of support from Western entities that established them or other organizations and individuals that makes it easier for them to offer education at a reasonable price and make it more inclusive. For instance, ZAU receives support from the international Seventh-Day Adventist community; LCC's costs are heavily subsidized by the evangelical Christian community in North America; and KUL and UCU's costs are subsided by Westerners, Western foundations, and Western churches. Such dependence on Western funding, especially in difficult economic times, may prove precarious. It also may lead to an unwanted dependency on the West.[92] Yet, those funded largely within the East are also pressing for more state funding. Administrators at both Orthodox schools claim they have been unsuccessful in obtaining direct monetary state support, although they have received buildings from the state that were originally owned by the Orthodox Church before the Revolution. For St. Tikhon it took a great deal of time and effort to obtain the building; the patriarch even asked Vladimir Putin personally for it.[93]

Another common difficulty concerns the hiring of qualified faculty. Since theological training was difficult to obtain under communism and many Christians were excluded from higher education, many of the current leaders were actually trained as scientists, converted later in life, or are Westerners (e.g., LCC, St. John, St. Tikhon, and UCU). As already mentioned, a number of Christian institutions have been forced to hire agnostics and atheists to teach courses (e.g., KGU, St. John's University, and UCU).

91. Father Ioann Ekonomtsev, interview by author, May 18, 2005, Moscow, Russia.
92. This issue is not unique to Christian higher education. Philip Altbach has addressed this matter in global higher education in general. See *International Higher Education*.
93. Glanzer and Petrenko, "Resurrecting the Russian University's Soul."

An additional challenge involves the lack of living spaces, buildings, or a common campus among these universities. For example, only a few institutions have dormitories (LCU, UCU, and ZAU) and only four exist in one campus area (LCU, KUL, St. Tikhon, and ZAU). Consequently, it remains difficult to build a common ethos through student life programs (largely nonexistent at most campuses) or a common community life.

Finally, the growth of many of these institutions provides its own challenges, especially for those that were originally theological institutions. Throughout the history of Christian higher education, numerous institutions started with the intention of training pastors and other church workers (e.g., Christian missionaries and educators) and then expanded to become liberal arts colleges and universities. In many cases, these institutions secularized.[94] The same difficulty confronts many of the universities in this area (Emmanuel University, KGU, St. Tikhon's University, UCU, and ZAU). As these institutions expand and grow, the challenge will be whether the importance of theology and worship will be reduced.

Future Possibilities

Overall, if these institutions are to fulfill their potential as Christian universities, they will likely have to learn to accomplish some of the following endeavors.

1. Foster creative and redemptive involvement at multiple levels. One of the most impressive young Christian universities in Eastern Europe is Ukrainian Catholic University. What makes the institution unique is that it fosters creative and redemptive activity both in the university world and in the wider social and political world while maintaining a central focus on transformative Christian worship. While not all institutions can attract its caliber of leadership, other universities can certainly learn from the sophisticated nature of its creative and redemptive efforts.
2. Resist the pressures toward accommodating forms of pluralism with regard to both student and faculty membership. These universities face immense pressures to become pluralistic institutions that downplay their unique Christian identity. At their best, these universities find ways to

---

94. George Marsden, *The Soul of the American University: From Protestant Establishment to Established Nonbelief* (New York: Oxford University Press, 1994).

introduce students and faculty to the university's rich Christian tradition in winsome ways. Faculty development and student development retreats in particular, such as those practices at KGU and UCU, have demonstrated tremendous potential for fostering Christian identity and unity.

3. Foster close connections with churches. The strongest institutions are those that have fostered positive relationships with the churches they serve, such as the Orthodox and Catholic institutions, EU and ZAU. Without those relationships, the university ends up serving the public first and the church second. In such a situation, the university can more easily move from fostering Christian forms of humanism to political forms.

4. In a situation of a centralized system of education such as those in post-communist countries, it is crucial for institutions of higher education to be able to build trust relationships with state officials since they have the authority to grant or extend licenses and accreditation as well as to authorize the establishment or the liquidation of any institution of higher education.

5. Be willing to give up state funding and accreditation for religious freedom. The greatest threat to academic freedom in all these universities comes from the state and not the church. The universities must be willing to forgo state funding if they wish to maintain their theological freedom and integrity.

Conclusion

The divide produced by the legacy of communism and the iron curtain Winston Churchill identified may slowly be shrinking in Europe. As the rector of UCU lamented during my visit, "Our students don't even know who Lenin is."[95] Thus, a younger generation may no longer remember how communism almost killed Christian higher education in present-day Eurasia. Fortunately, through the efforts of these new universities, Christian higher education has experienced an exciting resurrection that does not forget the past. Many of these universities hope to keep alive the memory of those who suffered to preserve the faith as well as equip a new generation of Christians for the unique challenges of post-communist life. Yet, they also are engaging in new forms of Christian higher education that did not even exist in the past. In fact, one

95. Father Borys Gudziak, interview by author, May 8, 2008, L'viv, Ukraine.

might argue that Christian higher education in Eastern Europe, although young and still fragile, may be experiencing one of its greatest periods of growth and prosperity.

The recent growth of Christian universities across Eastern Europe also reinforces a point not always understood by the modern media. As Philip Jenkins concludes in his analysis of religion in Europe, "Contrary to expectation . . . Christianity is surviving amid European secularism and often achieving far more than mere survival."[96] The emergence and growing influence of Christian universities in post-communist Eastern Europe confirm this point and demonstrate that the secularization of European higher education is not an inevitable or irreversible outcome of modernity. Instead, the secularization of European universities has occurred within the specific context of the nationalization of higher education, and in the case of Eastern Europe, was accelerated by the antireligious policies of communist regimes. While a close association with the state poses serious challenges for the religious identity of Christian higher education institutions, the examples of these new Christian universities reveal that modern universities can maintain a Christian identity and thrive academically and fiscally by utilizing private funding sources and remaining maximally independent from state control. Moreover, the story of the emergence of Eastern Orthodox universities in Europe demonstrates that religious traditions that had previously been absent from higher education are now becoming more engaged in the academic community. All of these trends counter the assumption of secularization theory that the public role of religion generally and Christianity in particular is waning in the face of modernity, especially in Europe.

96. Philip Jenkins, *God's Continent: Christianity, Islam, and Europe's Religious Crisis* (New York: Oxford University Press, 2007), p. 288.

CHAPTER 8

Christian Higher Education in Mexico

José Ramón Alcántara Mejía

Throughout Latin American history, two powerful forces have shaped higher education. First, the Spanish colonial experience and the attending Catholic Scholastic tradition are a pervasive and enduring conservative social force, with more than five hundred years of history. Since at least the early nineteenth century, however, there has been a second and competing force: Enlightenment liberalism. The historic role of Protestantism in the region is very much tied up with the rise of liberalism. Indeed, Protestantism's very right to exist in many places was protected only with the rise of liberal governments in the nineteenth century. These two historic forces have interacted throughout Latin America, but the Mexican story has some unique features as well, including its role as the pioneer of a third force in Latin America, a radical or revolutionary impulse.

Protestants' historic role in Mexico has been as modernizers and liberalizers, with a powerful influence in education, far beyond their relatively tiny religious presence. Until recently, however, Protestant church groups were not invested in higher education. Now that Protestantism is growing rapidly in Mexico and has shown some potential to develop universities, its educational vision and commitment seem compromised by the more privatized and pietis-

This chapter is developed from a previous work published in Spanish as "Sean transformados mediante la renovación de su mente: el reto cristiano en la encrucijada de la educación cristiana superior en Latinoamérica," in *Presencia cristiana en el mundo académico,* comp. Sidney Roy (Buenos Aires: Kairos, 2001), and in English as "Latin American Higher Education at the Crossroads: The Christian Challenge of Being Transformed Through the Renewal of Understanding," *Christian Higher Education* 1:2-3 (2002): 235-250.

tic values of recent evangelical movements. At the same time, higher education in Mexico has been pressured to "cash in" its Enlightenment-driven humane values in favor of a more economistic and narrowly vocational model, being driven by economic globalization. Can Catholic universities and Protestant ones (as more of them arise) provide an alternative to this powerful technical/commercial model? That should be their mission.

Breaking With the Spanish Colonial Past

The determining factors in higher education in Mexico feature two important phenomena, which are shared with most Latin America countries, especially the two most important features of the region. The first is the Spanish heritage, which is laced with a Roman Catholic, Scholastic, and Counter-Reformation vision. It predominated during the colonial period until the independence struggle that began in 1810 and was consolidated more than ten years later. The second is the irruption of the Enlightenment, with its liberalizing values and vision, which was one of the forces driving Mexico's movement toward independence. The Enlightenment also awakened an interest in the formation of a national culture, including its indigenous roots, under a cosmopolitan and scientific perspective — an interest that was made into an educational program by the new liberal governments.

Latin America's independence era at the beginning of the nineteenth century brought with it a gradual opening for Protestant movements, which entered public affairs through the creation of denominational churches and alternative approaches to education. Protestants gained a place in Latin America, the church historian Pablo Deiros makes clear, because of the end of the Spanish colonial monopoly, under which

> all contact with any country but Spain was prohibited. With independence, these restrictions disappeared and the new republics found themselves exposed to the many currents of modern life. Many of the diplomatic and commercial treaties with Protestant countries included clauses that demanded the freedom of worship and religious tolerance for the citizens of the member countries. In later years, this tolerance (tacit or explicit) would appear in the constitutions of some Latin-American republics.[1]

1. Pablo Alberto Deiros, *Historia del Cristianismo en América Latina* (Buenos Aires: Fraternidad Teológica Latinoamericana, 1992), p. 618.

In Mexico, this reform came about via the proclamation of the constitution of 1857 and the "Leyes de Reforma" by the first indigenous president, Benito Juarez, in 1859-1860, which were later included in the constitution. These documents aimed to strongly limit the role of the Catholic Church in civil affairs, including education, therefore creating a strict separation between church and state but, at the same time, guaranteeing freedom of religion, thus opening the door to other confessions until then excluded by the Catholic colonial regime. Since then and until the second half of the twentieth century, education at all levels was the responsibility of the secular state and therefore could not include religious matters.

After independence, the Roman Catholic Church's formal participation in education was confined to Catholic institutions, which often upheld a very conservative and antagonistic position toward the state. The liberal government, meanwhile, promoted a secular form of higher education that was marked by a nationalistic, Enlightened, and positivistic vision. Public higher education was born to take over the leadership of the university system from the pontifical universities and eventually it did overtake them.

The Protestant Contribution

Protestant participation in education developed as an alternative to Catholic and state education, but it was limited to forming elementary and secondary educational centers. Even so, these schools had a singular effect on Latin American societies, as Jean-Pierre Bastián makes clear:

> School networks were one of the most dynamic Protestant contributions to the Latin-American societies. The pedagogy practiced by the Protestant societies was not reduced to the transmission and elaboration of modern pedagogical methods.... In effect, it was used to affirm a greater acceptance by the liberal sectors of the public and an interested, sometimes enthusiastic, acknowledgement by the government.... This school project also allowed the diffusion of religious and politically democratic values outside of the church buildings and the Protestant community, as well as proposing a moral and religious foundation for the future liberal democracy.[2]

2. Jean-Pierre Bastián, *Protestantismos y modernidad latinoamericana: Historia de unas minorías religiosas activas en América Latina* (Mexico City: Fondo de Cultura Económica, 1994), p. 29.

By the end of the nineteenth century, university education in Mexico reflected some of these liberal trends as well. Its European roots were noticeable, especially in its cultural dimension, which was founded in Renaissance humanism but also had assimilated the Enlightenment and positivism. It was only at the beginning of the twentieth century, under the perceived need for a change that anticipated the Mexican Revolution (1910-1920), that the National University of Mexico was created, on September 22, 1910. It arose in the midst of a discussion between positivism and a more open humanistic philosophy represented by Antonio Caso, who said,

> Let our emerging university never be labeled as a reactionary attempt or as a medieval resurrection. No: in this new institution the same liberal spirit is burgeoning and will live on. . . . Our university — without a theological department — our secular university, a simple scientific and philosophic organization, is the general application of free and positive guidelines. . . . Today's university should be seen as a collection of institutes which, each within its unique boundaries, attempt to construct the greatest possible reciprocity between all the branches of truly independent intellectual activity.[3]

This spirit also permeated Protestant pedagogical thought in Mexico under the shelter of the Mexican Revolution of 1910.[4] Thus in 1917 the book *Historia Patria* (Patriotic History), written by a Methodist, Guillermo Sherwell, was chosen as a universal text for the country, and another Methodist, Andrés Osuna, was director of "the public education of the Revolution between 1916 and 1918."[5] The most prominent of these Mexican Protestant educators, according to Bastián, was

> Moisés Sáenz (1888-1941), director of high schools in Mexico City (1916-1920), sub-director and director of public education (1924-1930). Saenz disseminated the active pedagogy learned from his teacher at Columbia University (New York), John Dewey; and was a pioneer in indigenous edu-

3. Antonio Caso, *Obras completas: I Polémicas* (Mexico City: Universidad Nacional Autónoma de México, 1971), p. xv.

4. The Mexican Revolution opened possibilities, such as free access to higher education, which other Latin American countries began to adopt, particularly after their own revolutionary process, which, we could say, began with the Cuban Revolution in the early 1960s. Furthermore, similar historical foundations gave Latin American secular universities common characteristics such as a strong nationalism with a definitive socialistic and anticlerical orientation.

5. Bastián, *Protestantismos y modernidad*, p. 133.

cation and one of the principal ideologists of the mestizo race. Shortly before his death, in 1940, he founded the Interamerican Indigenous Institute.[6]

Saenz's example is also useful in illustrating the unique characteristics that post-revolutionary education takes on. The recognition that the national culture was of a mestizo character meant the creation of a sense of identity, a project that the state universities took on as their job.[7] Having been formed to "guide the national culture," the leading thinkers of the university, like Caso, Sáenz, and José Vasconcelos, dedicated themselves to the development of an educational curriculum pregnant with a mestizo identity. Vasconcelos summarized this sentiment in what is now the motto of the National Autonomous University of Mexico: "By my people my spirit will speak."

Thus, the Protestant influence on the consolidation of Mexico's post-revolutionary educational system, including higher education, is undeniable. The anti-Catholic attitude of the state since the "Reformation Laws" and through the establishment of the post-revolutionary government welcomed the involvement of the Protestant societies in its liberal agenda, as Bastián has pointed out, not only because it saw in them an ally that would balance the power of the Catholic Church but, more important, because they contributed to a different view about the role of education in the formation of the nation. Such is the case of the Protestant philosopher and educator Alberto Rembao (1895-1962), who in his book *Pneuma: The Theological Foundations of Culture,* articulates what could be considered a Christian worldview for post-revolutionary Mexico, parallel to those (better known) of Caso and Vasconcelos.[8]

Past Becoming Present

A significant change in Mexican higher education began to occur around the middle of the twentieth century, a change signaled by the increasing political

6. Bastián, *Protestantismos y modernidad,* p. 134.

7. "Mestizo" is the term used to designate the Spanish and indigenous origins of Mexicans, as opposed to solely indigenous native ("Indian") or solely descended from native Spanish ("Criollo"). "Mestizo" has an ideological meaning, since it recognized the Indian and Spanish roots, rather than privileging one side in opposition to the other, which was very often the source of discrimination against the Indians.

8. Alberto Rembao, *Pneuma: Los Fundamentos Teológicos de la Cultura,* conferencias presentados con motivo del 40 aniversario de la fundación del Centro Evangélico Unido, de México (Mexico City: Casa Unida de Publicaciones, 1957).

and economic influence of the United States in Mexico, and propelled by the move toward modernization and globalization that acquired force after World War II. While it was in fact a European-dominated model of higher education that drove these changes, Mexican educators saw more immediately some of these changes via American higher education because it was the American universities rather than the European ones that were attracting those students who would become part of the Mexican educational picture of the second half of the century, and thus influencing the direction that the educational process took.

From the 1970s onward, the traditional European model of liberal studies faded away from the curriculum, and was replaced by the new international model, which heavily emphasized the strategic value of science and technology, and secondarily the social sciences and business. Those state universities in Mexico that did not see the magnitude of the changes resulting from a global economy were left behind. This happened to the degree that private universities, including Catholic ones, were sprouting up to fill the need for prepared professionals that could respond to the socioeconomic demands of the end of the century.

This trend was not just a Mexican phenomenon but also a global one, as the Executive Summary of the Report of UNESCO states:

> Much of this report is concerned with the ways in which higher education has responded to the challenge of massification. The "logic" of massification is inevitable and includes greater social mobility for growing segments of the population, new patterns of funding higher education, increasingly diversified higher education systems in most countries, general and overall lowering of academic standards, and other tendencies. (2009, iii)

Thus, as the twentieth century drew to a close, the main concern of the Mexican universities was clearly a reflection of the interests that were also growing in American higher education, that is, the development of narrowly vocational models that were more closely linked to the economic rather than the broader cultural interests of the country. The response of the state in Mexico was the creation of

> a policy headed towards offering working class youth an education of a more technical nature, separate from that which is offered in traditional universities. This policy has pursued the purpose of forming the human resources needed for industrial development through programs designed for those members of the population who would be unable to access traditional

higher education. In other words, the capillarity of higher education has been promoted at the cost of a process of segmentation of the educational institutions, a process that is not functional since it is also correlated with social stratification.[9]

Rollin Kent, reflecting on the higher education policies for Latin America found in documents from CEPAL-UNESCO (1992) and the World Bank, says that these policies are founded on

> a strategy based on four essential elements: a) to stimulate a greater variety of institutions, including the development of private institutions; b) to offer public institutions incentives to diversify their funding sources, including the co-participation of students in cost recovery and linking public funding with performance quality; c) to redefine the role of the government in relationship to higher education; and d) to introduce policies specifically designed to give preference to the goals of quality and equality.[10]

The creating of technical institutes for the training of a "working class," as a form of diversifying higher education and preparing a working force for industrialization, seeking to respond also to the growing demands for postsecondary education, increased the social and, consequently, market value of university education. In other words, the traditional Mexican universities began to be transformed into universities that would respond more to recent trends worldwide. This transformation was marked by the development of graduate programs that aimed to create highly qualified scientific panels that in the last decades of the twentieth century emphasized the development of cutting-edge technologies and social and economic strategies, thus de-prioritizing, in relative if not absolute terms, support for the development of the humanities. This has meant that the social and cultural aspects of higher education have passed into the second place of importance, being increasingly maintained as a merely symbolic rather than an effective presence in curricular decision making.

In other words, the Mexican model has followed blindly what many

9. Carlos Muñoz Izquierdo, "La universidad Latinoamericana ante los nuevos escenarios de la región," in *La universidad Latinoamericana ante los nuevos escenarios de la región,* ed. Bruno Seminario de Marsi and Jorge Fernandez Baca (Mexico City: Universidad Iberoamericana, 1995), p. 17.

10. Rollin Kent, "Puntos para una agenda de políticas de educación superior en América Latina," in *La universidad Latinoamericana ante los nuevos escenarios de la región,* ed. Bruno Seminario de Marsi and Jorge Fernandez Baca (Mexico City: Universidad Iberoamericana, 1995), p. 74.

American educators consider one of the fundamental mistakes in the international system, that of underfunding the humanities and endangering their liberal arts model. Thus in Mexico, while the focus of curricular development strategies responds to the demands of globalization, they do not include a vision of global values, that is, there are not a similar interest and resources to promote critical thinking. Thus, this has led to the adoption of programs that lack a critical vision of reality. The announced objective is to make higher education a viable competitor in the global market, even at the cost of losing those unique social and cultural elements that Mexican universities were originally called upon, by the Revolution, to promote.

Present-day Developments

The brief background given above provides a context for a vision of the role that Christian higher education might play in the current scene. But first, let us look at what has been happening to Mexican higher education in recent decades.

Despite the constitutional restrictions that limited the role of religious institutions in higher education, modernization and globalization have led the state to relax its educational policies. Such relaxation, no doubt under new pressures of the Catholic Church, made possible the creation of several Catholic Christian universities. In 1943 the Jesuit Order founded the Universidad Iberoamericana, one of the first openly Christian universities (although later the definition adopted was "of Christian inspiration"). The lead taken by the Jesuits was soon followed by other Catholic orders or institutions, like the Universidad La Salle, founded in 1962 by the La Salle brotherhood; the Christ's Legionaries, which created the Universidad Anahuac in 1964; and the Universidad Panamericana, which was founded by Opus Dei in 1968.[11]

Since then, all of these universities have consistently been growing and branching out nationally and internationally, becoming a model for private higher education in general. Such universities came to be as a conservative Catholic alternative to the leftist orientation that was perceived in most state universities in the tumultuous 1960s, but they also signaled the growing inter-

---

11. The first private university, the Universidad Autónóma de Guadalajara, was formed in 1935, as a result of an excision from the state university promoted by conservative Catholic groups. Although the religious identity of the UAG has been well known, it does not appear in any of its documents.

est in Christian higher education within the Catholic majority, and in private university education by the growing Mexican middle class.

Mexico has not seen a similar pattern resulting in a Protestant wing of Christian higher education. As far as I know, there are only two fully accredited Protestant universities. The Universidad Montemorelos was formed by the Adventists in 1973 in the state of Nuevo León, and the Universidad Madero was founded by Methodists in 1982 in the city of Puebla. The Universidad Madero is the offspring of that venerable Methodist tradition of the Protestant educational societies of the second half of the nineteenth century, as described above. The Methodists maintained an institute after the Revolution, which became a university in 1982. Thus the Madero Institute took the lead in demonstrating the possibility of a non-Catholic form of Christian higher education. Since then attempts have been made to form other similar institutions by different historic Protestant groups, particularly Presbyterian and Reformed, and by recent evangelical movements, although with limited success in regard to accreditation. This has been, in part, the result of the limited influence that the Protestant church has today in the Mexican government and its Department of Education, but it also seems to be due to a confessional rather than professional approach. In other words, although Catholic institutions are confessional in their history and philosophy, their emphasis tends to be in forming individuals who would become effective participants in society. Contemporary Protestant and evangelical institutions, on the other hand, tend to confine themselves to their denominations' more narrowly religious vocational interests. Thus, besides being under the same pressure of all private institutions, they add to their constraints a "religious" orientation to which only their peers would be sympathetic.

Protestant universities could have followed the model of the Universidad Madero, if they had maintained their liberal democratic philosophies. But Protestantism in Mexico changed dramatically, due to a new evangelistic emphasis that originated mainly from an American missionary wave that hit the country after World War II. The result was a fragmentation within the Protestant movement between those who persevered in the liberal reform movement and others, the more recent ones, who formed an "evangelical" front emphasizing spiritual conversion, personal evangelism, and isolation from the sociopolitical phenomena that surrounded them. In this way, the "evangelical" movement, far from assuming the work historically taken on by Protestantism, confronted it, criticizing it as "liberal" in the theological sense, without recognizing that Mexican "liberal" Protestantism is more the result of a political-historical evolution than a theological one. The emerging evangelical universities, therefore, see their participation in higher education more as a way to maintain denominational isolation and as an evangelistic medium than as a way to participate in the political, social, and cultural life of the country.

The sudden appearance of Catholic and Protestant universities in the second part of the twentieth century also reflects two recent developments: new openings for the creation of private universities due to the insufficiencies of the state model to provide tertiary education to all who are qualified to pursue it, and the ever-increasing introduction of alternative tertiary educational models to those of traditional university degree programs. Subjects and modes of education, which until now had been confined to elementary and secondary education due to the monopoly held by the state over higher education, are now finding their way into tertiary education as well.[12]

Within this realm of private higher education, where private institutions in Mexico now enroll 33 percent of the national total,[13] only a few of them have an openly Christian identity. These are mainly Catholic universities, with only a handful in the evangelical or mainline Protestant traditions.[14] It would be difficult to account for the nature of each one of the Christian institutions, but it is interesting to note a recent trend within non-Christian private universities to include a "values" declaration. This trend is probably because of the influence of the declared Christian "values" which, from the point of view of the educational market, is an asset. Thus, the development of Christian higher education certainly obeys the external global factors driving the rise of private education, but, at least in the Catholic sector, it is also due to the value that its Christian orientation has in society. Is this Christian orientation reflected in the character and thrust of the curriculum? Here the picture is less positive. The fundamental difficulty of private universities, locating funding, has decreed that the most predominant disciplines found in the curriculum are those that respond to the market rather than those based on an educational philosophy. Christian universities tend to reflect private universities' proclivity to offer "commercial" subjects although, in some cases, they make an effort

12. Abraham Ceballos, "Trends in Private Mexican Higher Education and Some Challenges for New Endeavors," unpublished research paper, Calvin College, 2011.

13. ANUIES (in English, National Association of Universities and Higher Education Institutions), statistics for Mexico in 2008-2009, http://www.anuies.mx/servicios/e_educacion/index2.php.

14. The IAPCHE website (http://iapche.org/) lists 1 Protestant and 11 Catholic institutions. In the text above I noted two additional Protestant institutions that are not listed in the IAPCHE database. The Program for the Study of Private Higher Education (PROPHE) website shows that in 2003 there were 785 private tertiary institutions in Mexico. "National Data on Private Higher Education," http://www.albany.edu/dept/eaps/prophe/data/national.html.

to maintain a core curriculum of humanities and even religious subjects.[15] The emerging Protestant universities in Mexico are following the same trend, but, as mentioned above, they seem to be more oriented toward creating a doctrinal space to satisfy denominational needs than toward penetrating the sociocultural environment with a transformational vision.

Present Becoming Future

How can Christian higher education respond to these challenges? Several years ago I had the opportunity to address this issue not only for Mexico but more broadly as well, for Christian higher education is no longer a local issue, but a global one.[16] Thus to answer the question of the future of Christian higher education in Mexico, Latin America, and beyond, we first need to define some of these challenges in more global terms. In particular, we can make good use of the concept that the French philosopher François Lyotard called the "postmodern condition." One of the fundamental characteristics of this outlook that has serious implications for Christian higher education in Mexico and Latin America is its skepticism about grand narratives. It was possibly another French postmodernist, Michel Foucault, who in *The Archaeology of Knowledge*, a work published some forty years ago, was already questioning the commonly accepted historical concepts of tradition, influences, development, evolution, mentality, and spirit, and who called for us to "evict [these] dark forms and forces which are customarily used to link the discourses of humans."[17] Foucault's discourse was reiterated by the French philosopher Jacques Derrida when he suggested that this discipline was no more than "a certain type of literature," that is to say, a way of representing that which until now had been nothing more than a rhetoric of ideas. In the same way, and I believe inspired both by Foucault and

15. Recent educational reforms in Mexico have recognized theological education as a valid discipline for university level studies. This field had been excluded under the more anticlerical regimes of the past.

16. José Ramón Alcántara-Mejía, "Transculturizing the Humanities in Christian Higher Education," in *Christian Higher Education in the Global Context: Implications for Curriculum, Pedagogy, and Administration,* ed. Nick Lantinga (Sioux Center, Iowa: Dordt College Press, 2008), pp. 101-112. See also Perry L. Glanzer, Joel A. Carpenter, and Nick Lantinga, "Looking for God in Higher Education: Examining Trends in Global Christian Higher Education," *Higher Education* 61:6 (2011): 721-755; and Joel A. Carpenter, "New Christian Universities and the Conversion of Cultures," *Evangelical Review of Theology* 36:1 (January 2012): 14-30.

17. Michel Foucault, *La arqueología del saber* (Mexico City: Siglo XXI, 1970), p. 35.

another literary critic, Kenneth Burke, who had already been expounding the same theme in his essay titled "Four Master Figures of Speech," the historian Hayden White questioned the objectivity of historical discourse, concluding that history, in a very wide sense of the word, was simply literature.[18]

The importance of these affirmations is that in some way they seemed to propose, and possibly still do, that the construction of arguments throughout history which have tried to give meaning to the human race and its culture, rests in the notion that there is an established order. Derrida calls this the "metaphysics of presence," which in reality is no more than a verbal construction founded more in rhetorical figures than in reality. In other words, the verbal structures do not refer to reality, they are reality. What we could call "true" reality is something that has been hidden by the grand narratives, and which can only begin to be discovered by "deconstructing" these narratives.

Here is where we are confronted with the two opposite poles of the postmodern condition. On the one hand, the negative side of the denial of the grand narratives is that it has left a vacuum from which only a skeptical if not cynical attitude about reality can arise. This is particularly evident in universities. They seem to have tacitly accepted that their reason for being is not to be centers of knowledge and guides of national culture. Instead, they have embraced a social role promoted by neoliberal economics, which is to serve the global market. It is not surprising, then, that the educational budgets designed by the International Monetary Fund (IMF) and the state are increasingly subjecting schools to an economic project. It comes at the expense of the traditional educational project, which was to form professionals in all disciplines who would respond to the more profound needs of their region.

But on the other, more positive hand, the vacuum created by the postmodern condition is also a criticism against the modernity movement, seen as more rhetoric than reality. This critique has certainly been felt in Mexico and Latin America, where the discussion of identity has generally been more ideological than organic. We see the result in the marginalization experienced by Indian groups and other minorities, which have not decreased but rather are on the rise. Universities, on their part, while proclaiming themselves "guides of national culture," have allowed academic disciplines to separate and specialize, thus creating spheres of technological development without a humanistic vision and spheres of humanistic reflection without regard for the practical

18. Kenneth Burke, *A Grammar of Motives* (Berkeley: University of California Press, 1969), pp. 503-517; Hayden White, *Topics of Discourse: Essays in Cultural Criticism* (Baltimore: Johns Hopkins University Press, 1978).

realities of the country. It is not surprising that these educational models have credibility with native leaders, who in Mexico are proposing indigenous universities as alternatives.

The postmodern vacuum opens other opportunities for reform, possibly led by a Christian model of higher education. But it would need to be more profound than a mere defense of the Scholastic vision, in either Catholic or Protestant versions. I want to propose a model of personal transformation and a major reform of one's political, social, economic, and cultural environment based on a revision of biblical principles to address the challenges of this century. That is to say, we need not only a change in our understanding of reality, a transformation in the way we see and act in the world, but a change in the way we read the scriptures to be informed by our historical reality, so that it will bring about a true renewal of our mind. I see this Christian higher educational model addressing five major challenges.

Five Challenges for Christian Higher Education

1. A crisis of values

One of the fundamental challenges that permeate all spheres of higher education is a crisis of values. What now appears to predominate are the global market values of competition at the expense of social authenticity and personal well-being. It is necessary to respond, not with Scholastic moral ethics, but with a Christian ethic that has as a guiding principle the well-being of our fellow beings, especially those in greatest need (Luke 10:27; 1 John 3:16-17). In this way, we must be transforming an ethic of law into an ethic of grace. Christian higher education should adjust its curriculum to form its graduates to be transformed and transforming people, who see their profession not only as a means toward personal well-being, but above all as a way to serve others. An education that responds to the needs of those who are most marginalized by society over the needs of the market would thus foster a greater participation of all social and economic classes, not just the elites, in the social and cultural development of the nation.

2. Inequality of economic opportunities

Christian higher education should prophetically underline the inequality of economic opportunities that are promoted by current economic models, rather than indiscriminately accepting the ethic of competition. This would mean a vision that transforms social structures into ones in which economic factors are made to serve a social policy that would provide equal opportunities to all people. In this way, one aspect of Christian higher education should be to use their humanities and social science departments to encourage the creation of professionals who can prophesy in the social arena.

3. Cultural homogenization

One of the evident effects of globalization is cultural homogenization: the assimilation of marginalized cultures into a mainstream cultural model that naturally has as its main reference the Western European cultural traditions. We see the effects of this process in Mexico and Latin America in the growing rejection of ethnic diversity and the increased efforts to achieve integration, even at the expense of a loss of identity. From this centralist viewpoint, diversity is a liability that must be eliminated. Christian universities should use their different departments to recover the biblical vision of differentiation. In the face of this homogenized vision of the nation, we must recover the model of the body of Christ, given to us by the apostle Paul. The health and growth of the body and its components depend not on homogeneity but on difference. Against national policies of cultural assimilation, we must rescue the value of diverse cultural identities, not merely for folkloric reasons but because these cultures each embody and contribute to the overall integrity of human culture.

4. Move the issue of marginalization to the center

Homogenization has been possible, not because of the lack of voices from the periphery, but rather because the discourse that was previously located in the periphery has been moved to the center. The social realities out on the margins get ignored in favor of regional policies that obey global interests. This happens in many cases because professionals are not willing to work in the marginalized areas. The neoliberal economic model has changed a field investigator into someone who does her or his work from the office, supported by technology and based on statistical calculations, rather than one who listens to marginalized people. They are left without a powerful voice. Higher Christian education should recover a vision of reality from the margins and the people there by training professionals to follow Jesus' footsteps in walking with the people, and being their advocates before the makers of social and economic policies.

5. Recharge the spiritual and moral vacuum
left by postmodern education

Our schools have been emptied of spaces for personal growth, only to be filled with secular religions, with models of personhood that do not question professional and personal lifestyles that contradict Jesus' walk. Secularism argues the irrelevance of traditional religious models and the lack of credibility of a theological discourse that is not committed to reality. So an integral Christian higher education should include space for reflection on the spiritual dimension of a person, but it should also be pertinent, relevant, and adequate to the reality that the professional will face in the marketplace. It should provide the professional with a spirituality, as Dietrich Bonhoeffer says, for our times. If the graduates of Christian universities are going to face the world with the vision we have described, then they must be equipped, not with a religion, but with a kind of spiritual life that, far from isolating them from the challenges of the world, gives them the resources to face these challenges integrally.

The Future

The professional who has graduated from a Mexican or Latin American Christian higher education institution should be, not merely a professional, but a person transformed through a different way of looking at the world and, in this way, also able to transform his or her surroundings. The religious part of transformation is to be integral, and not merely a doctrinal prerequisite. That is to say, Christian higher education should not emphasize doctrinal conformation as much as experiential transformation.

Returning to the historical beginnings of this chapter, what I am proposing by way of transformation is really the essential spirit of the educational program crafted by Mexican Protestants in the nineteenth century. It offered a true alternative to the dominant colonizing model of education. Protestants influenced the development of new ideas about education that emerged in the liberal and post-revolutionary governments of Mexico in the early twentieth century. Unfortunately, except for the example of Madero University, there has not been a consistent Protestant effort to offer a viable and credible alternative for higher education. Protestants have been preoccupied more recently with denominational or doctrinal concerns, and the new conservative evangelicalism in Mexico has not seen education as a valid form of Christian mission, as some of the Catholic institutions certainly have.

What Mexican Protestants need is a serious reflection on the role of Christian higher education in present-day Mexico. It seems that our times and our commitment to the gospel now call us to retake the vision of the Reformation and adjust it to our historical situation. We need to be not only defending the essential truths of the gospel but above all making them true instruments of understanding and transformation for our youth. They are entering the twenty-first century in the midst of a postmodern environment that is skeptical, materialistic, selfish, cynical, and above all without any authentic hope. Christian higher education in Mexico and Latin America has a great challenge in the midst of this road: to proclaim that true reality, the reality of our Creator and not just of God's creatures. It can only be seen from the cross and through different eyes, with another understanding and another mind: with the eyes and the mind of Christ Jesus.

CHAPTER 9

Christian Higher Education in Brazil and Its Challenges

Alexandre Brasil Fonseca and Cristiane Candido Santos

In order to consider Christianity's role in Brazilian higher education, we need to put it into a Brazilian social context. Brazil is the largest country in Latin America, and in the middle of 2010 its population was estimated at 193 million inhabitants, distributed throughout a territory of 3.3 million square miles. The Brazilian economy is the ninth largest in the world, with a per capita income around $8,000, and the country has amplified its international presence, assuming a prominent position in different international processes and arenas.

Brazil possesses a diversified economy. In addition to leading the field of mass biofuel production, it is the second major exporting country of agricultural products on the planet, and it competes on all the continents in sophisticated markets such as that of airplanes, automobiles, and cell phones, as well as in strategic markets such as iron mining, metallurgy, and petroleum.

Another aspect of Brazil, distinguished in observed indices, is its enormous social inequality, both between geographic regions and within the same city. For several centuries the nation has had a significant concentration of revenue and an established elite. The richest 10 percent retains practically 50 percent of the national wealth, while the poorest 40 percent together do not hold 10 percent of that wealth (World Bank, 2005). This situation has remained relatively constant since this data began to be collected in the middle of the past century and has probably always existed.

Good news in this regard is that a change is occurring in the twenty-first century. There has been a larger investment of public resources in social programs, including a family stipend program called Bolsa Família. According to a recent study, it appears to be "one of the world's largest conditional cash transfer schemes and benefits more than 30 million poor people (i.e. about 16 percent of the national population)."[1] This initiative was introduced in order to address a reality in which close to one-third of the population is poor, living with less than $100 per capita monthly income.

Social inequality also leaves its mark on education. Brazil has a significant inequality of access to higher education, and it is one of the few countries in Latin America that still has not attained a level of higher education for the masses, with at least 15 percent of the youth between ages 18 and 24 having attended an institution of higher learning. In Brazil barely 13 percent of the youth have access to a university, and in some states this percentage remains below 5 percent. In 2007 the average time of study of the Brazilian population was calculated at 7.3 years, one of the lowest in Latin America, and the rate of illiteracy was 10 percent.[2]

Confronted with this picture, we need to ask how Christian higher education addresses Brazil's unique prospects and issues. Therefore, between January and May 2010 we conducted bibliographic and documentary research on Christian higher education in Brazil from its earliest planting to the current moment. First, we briefly review the different historical moments of higher education in Brazil up to the appearance of the first Christian universities, both Catholic and Protestant. We then present quantitative data on the current presence of Christian higher education in Brazil, the evangelical experience as well as the Catholic tradition.

Before we begin, it is important to highlight the religious configuration of the Brazilian people, in whom Christianity has a strong and historic presence, being an important part of their national identity. The majority of the country is affiliated with the Catholic Church (64 percent), which in the last decades has been sharing more and more space with expressions of Pentecostalism (17 percent), as well as denominations identified with historic Protestantism (5 percent). The Assemblies of God (Igreja Evangélica Assembléia de Deus) and the Baptists (Igreja Batista) are the largest evangelical denominations.

There is no doubt that Christian higher education has played an important part in different moments of history in Brazil. The question we think is worth highlighting and reflecting on is how this Christian educational presence can confront inequality and contribute to the construction of a more equal and

1. Kei Otsuki and Alberto Arce, *Brazil: A Desk Review of the National School Feeding Programme* (Wageningen, Netherlands: World Food Programme, 2007), p. 3.
2. Instituto de Pesquisas Econômicas Aplicadas, *PNAD 2007 — Primeiras análises, Comunicado da Presidência*, no. 12 (2008): 2.

just society. The challenges are immense and it falls to Christian higher education to give an answer commensurate with these challenges. It must look for creative and innovative ways to assume its role in constructing a more just and equal society.

Formation and Development of Brazilian Higher Education: Three Moments

There are at least three large historical periods that mark the rise and development of higher education in Brazil. The early Brazilian years (1500-1888) comprise the initial colonial and imperial period. The Portuguese made the early investments in higher education when the Brazil colony actually became the seat of the Portuguese government in 1808.

The following period begins with the proclamation of the republic in 1889, and it ends with the declaration of a a business-military dictatorship in 1964. This period brings together different moments and policies related to education, notably a separation between church and state and the more secular nature of the government. The first Christian universities, all connected to the Catholic Church, date from this period (the 1930s), and the first Protestant universities date from the 1950s. During this second period there was a strong appeal for institutional development, and laws proclaiming the guidelines and bases of Brazilian education were created. This period saw a significant number of Christian universities open.

The third period features the past twenty years, 1990 to 2010, when the federal government offered incentives favoring the opening of private universities as a strategy for making higher education available for the masses (see Figure 1 on p. 210).

Early Brazilian Years (1500-1888)

There is a long initial phase to this story during the colonial era (between 1572 and 1808) when the first initiatives related to higher education gradually emerged. In 1500 Portugal defined Brazil as its colony, unique in an America dominated by the Spanish. With ample lands replete with natural resources, Portuguese policy focused on mines, timber, and plantations and initially led to little cultural development in the colony. While universities were created between the sixteenth and eighteenth centuries in Spanish and English colo-

Figure 1: Christian Universities in Brazil by Year of Creation (1940-2010)

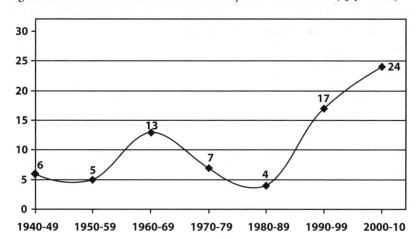

nies,[3] in Brazil this only occurred in the nineteenth century with the creation of the medical schools of Rio de Janeiro and Bahia in 1808. This initial period was described by Anísio Teixeira, an influential Brazilian educator, as a period in which

> The monarchical power, in order to impede any autonomous development of the Brazilian land, closes its frontier, makes Portuguese birth obligatory for functionaries, monopolizes commerce and denies permission in its new lands for manufacture, typography, the printing press and the university, thus placing the Colony in such a narrow dependence on the Metropolis, that it finally, in some sense integrates itself — with its nobility, its clergy and the group of bureaucrats and men of letters all of which were formed in the Metropolis — into small and powerful Portugal. Closed externally to any influence which was not Portuguese, isolated within its immense geography, the Colony was even able to repel invasions by other metropolises which competed with the Portuguese, accomplishing for three centuries, in the solitude of the "sad tropics," a unique social experience marked by the extinction of the aboriginal population, black slavery, the creation of large

3. The first university was founded in Peru, in 1533; Colombia, in 1580; Bolivia, in 1624; Argentina, in 1634; the United States, in 1636; and Chile, in 1738. Renato Stencel, "História da Educação Superior Adventista: Brasil, 1969-1999" (Ph.D. dissertation, Educação Universidade Metodista De Piracicaba, 2007), p. 97.

landed estates *(latifundios)*, and agrarian mercantilism, and by a governmental bureaucracy which was particularly harsh and without imagination but superiorly organized and served by an extraordinary training and educational structure, or indoctrination, proposed as a vigorous and planned cultural transplantation.[4]

The first educational initiatives in the country began with the creation of schools beginning in 1550, principally in Bahia, the seat of the colonial government. The teaching of reading and writing and mid-level instruction were directed toward the children of the elites. Higher education was also offered in "Arts and Theology" in some cases.[5] Education was largely defined by the practices of the Society of Jesus (Jesuits), which began its work in Brazil in 1549. Important emphases of this period were the catechization of the Indians and the training of priests and missionaries. With the union of these two features, the first educational system was formed in Brazil, a system that managed to accomplish the transmission of a homogeneous education that was developed from north to south and that promoted one language, one religion, one vision of the world, and one ideal of the "learned man."[6]

Two schools of medicine, one in Bahia and another in Rio de Janeiro, were created in 1808, and this moment is the effective beginning of higher education in the country. The imperial environment favored the building of grand institutions for cultural diffusion, such as the Royal Museum (Museu Real), the Botanical Garden (Jardim Botânico), the Public Library (Biblioteca Pública), the Regal Press (Imprensa Régia), and later, the Royal Portuguese Reading Chamber (Real Gabinete Português).

These initiatives owe much to the actions of Napoleon throughout Europe, a situation that caused the royal Portuguese family to flee to its distant colony in 1808. In the same year in which this move to Brazil occurred, considered as the moment of the rise of the national state, King João signed a decree creating two institutions of higher education devoted to medicine and instituted courses related to engineering and military careers in the Royal Naval Acad-

---

4. Anísio Teixeira, *Ensino Superior no Brasil. Análise e interpretação de sua evolução até 1969* (Rio de Janeiro: Editora UFRJ, 2005), p. 123.

5. Luiz Antonio Cunha, "Ensino Superior e Universidade no Brasil," in *500 Anos de Educação no Brasil,* ed. Eliane Marta Santos Teixeira Lopes et al. (Belo Horizonte, Brazil: Autêntica, 2003), p. 152.

6. Marcos Marques de Oliveira, "As origens da educação no Brasil: Da hegemonia católica àsprimeiras tentativas de organização do ensino," *Ensaio: aval. pol. públ. Educ. Rio de Janeiro* 12:45 (October-December 2004): 945-958.

emy (Academia Real da Marinha) and the Royal Military Academy (Academia Real Militar).

In 1820 the Royal Academy of Design, Painting, Sculpture, and Civil Architecture (Real Academia de Desenho, Pintura, Escultura e Arquitetura Civil), later called the Academy of the Arts (Academia de Artes), was created, and in 1827 the law schools of São Paulo and Recife were created, especially designed for training the elites of the new Brazilian Empire. The establishment of higher education at the time was strongly pragmatic, confronted with the necessity of the training of administrators for the new nation then taking shape. Isolated courses, poorly integrated and disconnected classes, and technical and professionalizing training mark this period.

At the end of the nineteenth century, the concept of a university became more concrete. Some projects were outlined, but none was executed. Besides encountering resistance from the Catholic clergy, social conservatives, and some positivists opposed to freedom in higher education, the central government did not appear to have the necessary political will to effect this decision.

Protestant groups established an effective and permanent presence in Brazil beginning in the nineteenth century. Several conditions enabled Protestantism to take root:

- a commerce treaty between Portugal and England in 1810 that afforded religious toleration to merchants and settlers
- movements of national liberation that culminated with the political independence of 1822
- concomitant expansion of liberal ideas, advocating removal of church interests from the government
- English leadership of the world capitalist system and emerging influence of the United States with economic interests in Brazil
- streams of migration from these Protestant countries and also from Germany

The Protestant immigrants and Brazilian converts did not build many institutions, however, until the end of the nineteenth century. They coincided with the effervescent and expansive independence movements. The arrival of Protestantism is, therefore, connected to the favorable historic context. Across Latin America, Protestant movements accompanied the rise and spread of other currents of liberal and modernizing thinking and the end of the colonial period. Agents of the Bible societies, missionaries, merchants, English and

American technicians, and industrialists all arrived at once and made their modernizing presence felt during this period.

During his reign, Pedro II wanted to make use of the churches in the social arena. He granted grand facilities to the first Protestant missionaries in appreciation of their knowledge and the practical duties that they could carry out. Moreover, he was hoping for immigration from the Protestant countries. This immigration was indispensable to his governing plan, and it was necessary to guarantee for these colonists the possibility of practicing their religion and educating their children. There was, however, little progress in the first years, for Brazilian nationals began to resist the missionaries, whom they saw as carriers of an ideology that was not suitable to the dominant Brazilian conception of life and ethical values, even though the newcomers possessed a more advanced capitalistic system.

One historic Brazilian event, however, more than any broader context or conditions, made possible the implantation and the expansion of Brazilian Protestantism. That event was the coming of a republican regime. Some of the most important values and cultural elements brought to Brazil by Protestants include the following:

- *Ideas.* In republican Brazil, the growing process of urbanization and the rudiments of the industrialization helped to break traditional customs and make possible the circulation of new ideas. These trends became important factors in the growth and consolidation of Protestantism in Brazil. But the effects of Protestant missionary work can be seen most clearly in the twentieth century, beginning with the democratization of the religious structure, which encouraged the participation of lay church members in important congregational decision making and governance. This experience was completely new in this period and it greatly raised the awareness of a liberal spirit, for it coincided with the modernization of diverse sectors of the Brazilian society.
- *The rise of the laity,* which included social promotion, especially among the most humble strata of the population; their dreams of upward social mobility were being validated.
- *The secularization of the society* through the presentation of an alternative symbolic universe, with the emergence of more than one religion on the national stage. Being Brazilian did not have to mean being Catholic.
- *The spread of a more modern pedagogy* in the schools made them more connected to the modernizing impulses of society.
- *Protestants building liberal alliances,* in many cases, with the positivists,

liberal Catholics, and free thinkers, in the struggle for the laicization of the state, laicization and popularization of education, freedom of speech and worship, and other pursuits tied to the principles of liberal ideology.

One of the most important influences of the Protestants was their salient role in the creation and the development of the Brazilian primary and second-ary schools.[7] Protestant groups used diverse strategies to set up and expand their work in Brazil, but without a doubt, one of their favorite strategies was the establishment of schools. Eventually, they created a vast network of schools in the most important centers of the country. For the Protestants at the time it was simply impossible to compete with the Catholics without the power and influence of education.

The Brazilian Republic (1889-1964)

A second moment, called years of the republic, was the period from 1889 to 1964, and it was then that the national government created the first university in the country. The University of Brazil[8] was founded in Rio de Janeiro in 1920. For generations of leaders who identified education as the central way to de-velop and grow the new nation, it represented the realization of their dreams. At the beginning of the twentieth century, Brazil was betting on its capacity to become a model of the New World and was looking to assume prominence on the international scene.

During this period higher education expanded greatly, still with a strong focus on specialized degree courses and professional studies but with greater velocity and intensity than in the earlier period. The revenues coming from coffee and rubber exports made a larger public investment in education pos-sible, but cycles of expansion and retraction in trade impeded constant and regular financing. Even so, public investment opened university programs of study to many more students. Faced with fewer resources from the state, the Catholic Church had to reinvent itself and establish a new strategy for its permanence in the country. Between 1891 and 1910, when the constitution of the First Republic was in force, ending the exclusive authority of the central government to confer and administer higher education, twenty-seven new

7. Jether Pereira Ramalho, *Prática educativa e sociedade* (Rio de Janeiro: Zahar, 1975).

8. Today it is called the Federal University of Rio de Janeiro (Universidade Federal do Rio de Janeiro).

Catholic institutions of higher learning were created, including some isolated attempts to create universities. All were without success, and they concluded their activities soon after they were created, either by the initiative of state governments or by the institutions themselves.

The first university created by the central government, the University of Brazil (Universidade do Brasil), was the result of the union of the Polytechnic School (Escola Polténica), the School of Medicine (Escola de Medicina), and the School of Law (Escola de Direito). In general the universities created next followed this process of consolidating different institutions, as in the case of the University of Minas Gerais (Universidad de Minas Gerais) (1927). Until this period the influence of French thought in the organization and structure of teaching was strong, but with the creation of universities and the amplification of the educational system, Brazil began to form its own networks of educational thinkers. A "New School" movement had its beginning in this period, and the French influence began to diminish as North American authors and thinkers became more prominent.

In this context the state began to see Protestant education as a potential and important dialogue partner and as a fundamental contributor to its aims to organize a New World south of the equator. Brazil perceived in American economic growth and culture a model that could be incorporated into its own country. Through emulating the educational theory and practice in the United States, such as the ideas of John Dewey, Brazil hoped to erect a new nation that understood education as a science and as a central element for the promotion of equality and the offering of opportunities.[9] Education should be turned "toward life," to useful and practical activities, and for that reason pragmatism was adopted as one of the educational foundations beginning in this period.

Professionals from the Piracicaba School (Colégio Piracicabano) (affiliated with the Methodist Church) and from the American School (Colégio Americano) (Presbyterian Church), later named Mackenzie College (in English no less), acted as advisors in the public educational reform movement that had begun in São Paulo at the end of the nineteenth century. This reform had as its objective the renovation of pedagogical methods. It defended the practice of co-educational classrooms, opposing the Catholic position of organizing separate classrooms for boys and girls. More important, it affirmed as fundamental the freedom of religion, as well as the need to experiment and have laboratories in the schools. This training was to be given in a context in

9. Marcus Vinicius da Cunha, "John Dewey e o pensamento educacional brasileiro: a centralidade da noção de movimento," *Revista Brasileira de Educação*, no. 17 (2001): 86-99.

which student-teacher relations are based in understanding and tenderness and not on the authoritarianism of the principle magister dixit.[10]

This Protestant presence in Brazil was only made possible by the secularization of government begun in 1889. The movement of foreign missionaries, who had begun their activities in Brazil at the beginning of the century, increased with this new definition of the "lay state." There was no interest in the promotion of the "Protestant religion" on the part of Brazilian liberal elites at the time, but there was an interest in what Protestants' education and culture represented and could provide through the education that its missionaries offered.[11]

Protestant initiatives in higher education began in 1891 following changes in legislation that made university studies no longer the exclusive domain of the state. Some of the earliest university-level studies by Protestant institutions include engineering courses offered by the Presbyterian Mackenzie Institute beginning in 1896, and a program in pharmacy and dentistry (1904) and law (1911), offered by the Methodist Granbery Institute in Juiz de Fora, Minas Gerais.[12] These initiatives, however, were isolated courses of study without a greater commitment from church leaders to operate more comprehensive institutions of higher education. The first Christian universities connected to Protestant churches were not created until the middle of the twentieth century, whereas the Catholic Church was establishing new universities in the late 1930s and early 1940s.

The number of students enrolled in higher education near the end of the nineteenth century was around 2,000, a number that rose to 20,000 by 1930.[13] The new constitution of 1934, however, sealed a renewed alignment of the Catholic Church with the Brazilian state, as Brazil witnessed the ascension of an authoritarian state. The Catholic Church was finally regaining intimate access to power after forty years of exclusion from a lay republic with positivist leanings. Three concessions characterized the new church-state union: (1) prohibition of divorce and the recognition of religious marriage by civil law; (2) permission for religious teaching in the public schools; and (3) the ability of the state to finance schools, seminaries, hospitals, or whatever other institution belonging to the church dealt with "collective interest." Della Cava presents the following analysis of these concessions in the constitution:

10. "The master says." Cesar Romero Amaral Vieira, "Contribuição protestante à reforma da educação pública paulista," *Comunicações (Piracicaba)* 9:1 (2002): 256-274.

11. Antonio Gouvêa Mendonça, *O celeste porvir: a inserção do protestantismo no Brasil* (São Paulo: Paulinas, 1984), pp. 155-161.

12. Stencel, "História da Educação Superior Adventista: Brasil, 1969-1999," p. 108.

13. Anisio Teixeira, *A Educação no Brasil* (São Paulo: Cia. Editora Nacional, 1976), p. 87.

The concessions were equivalent to the continual maintenance of Catholicism as a total religious system. They involved, respectively: the ideological definition and the primary cohesion of unity of the society — the family; a permanent mechanism of socialization of new members and a permanent base for the recruitment of new boards — the school system; finally, the guaranteed allocation of scarce national resources for a sector of the Brazilian society which, technically speaking, was economically non-productive.[14]

There was, predictably, a reaction from the modernists of the New School regarding the inclusion of religious instruction. The words of Cecília Meireles, the celebrated Brazilian poet and educator, were harsh, calling this change

> a little provincial decree, to please some priest and attract some sheep. . . .
> It is not believed that any profound religious spirit — no matter what his religious orientation may be — can receive with happiness this decree in which are fermenting the most noxious effects for our homeland and for humanity.[15]

If the support of the Catholic Church interested the state, the church, for its part, did not "hesitate to supply the places that the regime was disposed to concede to it."[16] Before the created vacuum of the end of the Old Republic had ceased, various arenas came to be occupied by a Catholic elite. Their main point of reference was the Centro D. Vital, founded in 1922 by intellectuals of the Catholic Action movement. The Centro's president — Alceu Amoroso Lima — was a major influence in the Ministry of Education.

This movement stressed that Brazilian society found itself in crisis due to the religious ignorance of the people and the divorce between the (Catholic) nation and the government. An alliance was necessary and for this the nation ought to return to religious marriage and Catholic education in the public schools. Brazilian representation in the Holy See and the introduction of military chaplains also arose as solutions.

In this process the Catholic elites who defended the "recatholization of the state" had fundamental importance. In 1932 the Catholic Institute of Higher Studies (Instituto Católico de Estudos Superiores) was created, which later

---

14. Ralph Della Cava, "Igreja e Estado no Brasil do século XX: Sete monografias recentes sobre o Catolicismo Brasileiro," *Estudos CEBRAP,* no. 12 (1975): 15.

15. Valéria Fernandes Lamego, *Farpa na Lira: Cecília Meireles na Revolução de 30* (Rio de Janeiro: Record, 1996), p. 91.

16. Sergio Miceli, *Intelectuais à brasileira* (São Paulo: Companhia das Letras, 2001), p. 219.

gave rise to the Pontifical Catholic University of Rio de Janeiro (Pontifícia Universidad Católica do Rio de Janeiro) in 1940. One year before the University of Santa Ursula (Universidade Santa Ursula), also in Rio de Janeiro, had been created. This period saw the creation of various other Catholic universities (see Table 1 below), which strengthened the strategy of alignment of the church with the state "from above." About this period Vasselai affirms:

> The Vargas Era gave support for the creation of the Catholic University as a private institution. This occurred possibly because an informal pact of collaboration was established between the State and the Church that allowed, on the part of the government, the favoring of Catholic religious instruction in the states and private schools. On the part of the church it acted in such a way that its ideology supported and defended the order that reinforced the doctrine of the New State.[17]

Table 1: Christian Institutions of Higher Education in Brazil (2010)

Institution	Founded	Students	Confession
Universidade Santa Úrsula	1939	5,070	Catholic
Pontifícia Univ. Católica do Rio de Janeiro	1940	2,866	Catholic
Pontifícia Univ. Católica de Campinas	1941	5,710	Catholic
Universidade Católica de Pernambuco	1943	3,240	Catholic
Pontifícia Universidade Católica de São Paulo	1946	7,250	Catholic
Pontifícia Univ. Católica do Rio Grande do Sul	1948	4,758	Catholic
Universidade Presbiteriana Mackenzie	1952	8,192	Presbyterian
Centro Univ. Católico Salesiano Auxilium	1956	3,326	Catholic
Pontifícia Univ. Católica de Minas Gerais	1958	6,165	Catholic
Centro Univ. Nossa Senhora do Patrocínio	1958	6,540	Catholic
Pontifícia Universidade Católica de Goiás	1959	5,395	Catholic
Universidade Católica de Pelotas	1960	1,560	Catholic
Pontifícia Universidade Católica do Paraná	1960	7,000	Catholic
Centro Universitário de Anápolis	1961	3,560	Evangelical
Universidade Católica do Salvador	1961	1,911	Catholic

17. Conrado Vasselai, "As universidades confessionais no ensino superior brasileiro: identidades, contradições e desafios" (Dissertação Mestrado em Educação, Universidade Estadual de Campinas, 2001), p. 61.

Institution	Founded	Students	Confession
Universidade Católica de Petrópolis	1961	1,942	Catholic
Universidade Católica Dom Bosco	1961	2,550	Catholic
Universidade Lutheran do Brasil	1964	10,200	Lutheran
Faculdade Moraes Júnior – Mackenzie Rio	1965	1,280	Presbyterian
Universidade Metodista de Piracicaba	1966	3,960	Methodist
Faculdade de Filosofia Santa Dorotéia	1967	1,270	Catholic
Centro Univ. São Camilo – Espírito Santo	1967	2,425	Catholic
Centro Univ. Católico do Sudoeste do Paraná	1968	3,254	Catholic
Faculdade Evangélica do Paraná	1969	620	Evangelical
Centro Universitário Claretiano	1970	4,500	Catholic
Centro Universitário Metodista Bennett	1971	5,020	Methodist
Universidade Metodista de São Paulo	1971	15,320	Methodist
Centro Univ. Metodista Izabella Hendrix	1972	3,372	Methodist
Universidade Católica de Brasília	1974	1,200	Catholic
Centro Universitário La Salle	1975	4,015	Catholic
Centro Universitário São Camilo	1976	2,885	Catholic
Faculdade Santa Marcelina	1981	1,105	Catholic
Universidade São Francisco	1985	4,005	Catholic
Universidade Católica de Santos	1986	2,110	Catholic
Centro Universitário Luterano de JI - Paraná	1989	951	Lutheran
Faculdade Presbiteriana Gammon	1990	260	Presbyterian
Faculdade São Francisco de Assis	1994	300	Catholic
Faculdade Católica de Anápolis	1995	540	Catholic
Inst. Superior e Centro Educacional Luterano	1996	560	Lutheran
Centro Universitário Luterano de Santarém	1996	820	Lutheran
Centro Universitário Luterano de Manaus	1996	1,160	Lutheran
Centro Universitário Luterano de Palmas	1996	1,762	Lutheran
Faculdade São Camilo	1997	300	Catholic
Faculdade Metodista de Santa Maria	1998	850	Methodist
Faculdade Metodista Granbery	1998	468	Methodist
Faculdade Salesiana de Santa Teresa	1998	260	Catholic
Escola Superior São Francisco de Assis	1998	760	Catholic
Faculdade Batista do Rio de Janeiro	1999	1,170	Baptist

Institution	Founded	Students	Confession
Faculdade Batista Brasileira	1999	700	Baptist
Escola Superior Batista do Amazonas	1999	1,900	Baptist
Inst. Luterano de Ensino Superior de Itumbiara	1999	840	Lutheran
Faculdade 2 de Julho	1999	1,560	Presbyterian
Facul. Católica Rainha da Paz de Araputanga	1999	300	Catholic
Faculdade Adventista Paranaense	2000	290	Adventist
Faculdade Batista de Minas Gerais	2000	650	Baptist
Inst. Luterano de Ensino Sup. de Porto Velho	2001	980	Lutheran
Faculdade Católica de Uberlândia	2001	495	Catholic
Facul. Teol., Filo e Ciências Humanas Gamaliel	2002	750	Assemblies of God
Faculdade São Tomás de Aquino	2002	240	Catholic
Inst. Fil. Teol. N. S. Imaculada Rainha do Sertão	2002	750	Catholic
Instituto Superior de Teologia Aplicada	2003	393	Adventist
Faculdade Anglicana de Erechim	2003	600	Anglican
Faculdade São Camilo	2003	300	Catholic
Faculdade Católica do Ceará	2003	370	Catholic
Faculdade Católica do Tocantins	2003	400	Catholic
Centro Universitário Adventista de São Paulo	2004	2,612	Adventist
Centro Universitário Metodista	2004	4,995	Methodist
Faculdade São Bento do Rio de Janeiro	2004	360	Catholic
Inst. Sup. de Educ. Franciscano N. S. de Fátima	2004	300	Catholic
Faculdade São Bento da Bahia	2004	594	Catholic
Facul. Boas Novas Ciências Teol., Soc. e Biotec.	2005	760	Assemblies of God
Faculdade Evangélica de Brasília	2005	500	Evangelical
Faculdade Católica Stella Maris	2005	600	Catholic
Faculdade Evangélica Cristo Rei	2006	560	Church of Christ
Faculdade Santa Catarina	2006	400	Catholic
Faculdade São Vicente	2006	480	Catholic
Faculdade Adventista da Bahia	2007	600	Adventist

At the end of the 1940s, five universities and 293 institutions of higher education existed in Brazil. At the time a new epoch in the history of Brazil began, one in which direct election and democratic process returned. A significant student movement arose and Brazilian society saw the introduction of the Protestant churches in higher education with the creation of the first Protestant university in the 1950s.

In the 1950s Brazil experienced strong industrialization and rapid economic development, an increase in the occupation of national territory, rural-urban migration, and the expansion and strengthening of the student movement. This was a time of social turmoil and rapid change. The youth, inspired by events like the Cuban revolution, were more and more convinced of their ability to change the world. By 1964, at the end of this period, there were thirty-nine universities in Brazil, with nine controlled by the Catholic Church and one by the Presbyterian Church. All of the others were under control of the federal government. The Law of Directives and Bases of Education (Lei de Diretrizes e Bases da Educação), which more broadly regulated the procedures related to education and was effectively considered the first general order of Brazilian education, was established at this time. The National Students' Union roundly criticized the law, arguing that

> it is not the juridical form but the content itself of the University which ought to be transformed. . . . The concrete measures of reform and democratization of higher education constantly collide with obstacles, those such as professorship for life, entrance exams, the structure for the review of university problems, and many others; these are characteristics of an anachronistic legislation, albeit recent. The fight, essentially, is for the democratization of the University.[18]

In this period there was a great conviction of the necessity of development and investment in areas such as physics and technology rather than merely in an education inspired by the American model. In the context of an ideology of development the Technological Institute of Aeronautics (Instituto Tecnológico da Aeronáutica) was created in 1947, with a strong focus in research. In 1951 the National Council for Scientific Research (Conselho Nacional de Pesquisa Científica, CNPq) was created, which at the beginning had nuclear research as its central focus. At the end of the Vargas era, and with it the close relation-

---

18. Luiz Antonio Cunha, *A universidade crítica: o ensino superior na República Populista* (Rio de Janeiro: Francisco Alves, 1989), p. 143.

ship between the state and the Catholic Church, conditions were ripe within the recently renewed democracy for the creation of Protestant universities. In this context, Mackenzie University (Universidade Mackenzie) was founded in 1952 and recognized. It bore the fruit of the educational experience and work of the Presbyterian Church (Igreja Presbiteriana) that had begun in Brazil already in 1870.

The activities of the Centro Universitário de Anápolis (the University Center of Annapolis), nicknamed UniEvangélica (1961), began at this time, fruit of the collaboration of leaders from different Protestant churches. Soon after, the Lutheran University of Brazil (Universidade Lutheran do Brasil, ULBRA) (1962) was founded. The Methodists, who today have the largest Protestant system of higher education in Brazil, created their first two universities in 1966 and 1971: Universidade Metodista de Piracicaba (Unimep) and Universidade Metodista de São Paulo (Umesp), respectively.

Current Numbers: Christian Higher Education in Brazil and Its Challenges (1964-2010)

The years from 1964 to 2010 represent for most of that period a lamentable time in Brazilian history, first because of marked violence by the state, implemented through a business-military dictatorship that lasted from 1964 until 1989. There were also economic stagnation, high national debt, weakening and almost total extinction of policies promoting social well-being, and an aggravation of inequalities. In 1990 there was finally a full restoration of democracy with direct elections. Later came economic stabilization, the implementation of compensatory public welfare policies, and the orderly electoral change of power among political parties of different ideological hues.

The military government had established a new Law of the Guidelines and Bases of Brazilian Education (1968). It served to whitewash the regime and delimit any possible space for reflection and resistance to it, not to mention the persecutions, prisons, and tortures that had students as one of the principal foci. In the educational field, this period saw the establishment of various accords with the U.S. Agency for International Development (USAID). The military government emphasized industrialization, promoted migration, and enlarged the infrastructure, especially in the communications field. The logic the government pursued was called progress by means of "national modernization," and one of its implications was the expansion of enrollments in higher education, which went from nearly 300,000 students in 1968 to almost 900,000 just five years later in 1973.[19]

After a period of major repression in the 1970s, the decade of the 1980s became known as the "lost decade," having a series of significant steps backward in the field of education. According to figure 1, this was the decade in which the least number of Christian universities were founded since 1940. In 1986 the New Republic began, and it served as a transition between the dictatorial regime and the return to democracy, which happened in 1989 with the election of the first president elected by direct vote since 1962. The period begun in 1990 became known as the "Re-democratization." In it the government was preoccupied with extending higher education to the masses. The government of Fernando Henrique Cardoso (1995-2002, Brazilian Social Democracy Party) attempted to achieve this extension through incentives to private initiatives by means of tax exemptions and programs offering student financing to pursue studies. The evolution of the number of institutions of higher education can be seen in figure 2, below. Even with significant growth in this period, the system of Brazilian higher education still is not large enough to meet the needs of the population.

**Figure 2: Evolution of the Number of Institutions
of Higher Education in Brazil (1980-1999)**

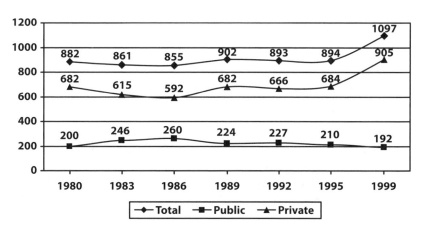

In the twenty-first century the country began to experience a larger phase of growth. Under the presidency of Luis Inácio Lula da Silva (2003-2010,

19. Paulo Nathanael Pereira de Souza, *ABC da Lei de Diretrizes e Bases da Educação* (São Paulo: Edições Loyola, 1993), p. 37.

Workers' Party) an education program was proposed that for the first time harmonized action by the federal government with the needs of the state and municipal governments. It also proposed public education policies that simultaneously considered higher and basic education and acted in favor of strengthening technical instruction. Financing for students to pursue their studies in private universities was increased, and the country experienced an improvement in diverse indices related to education. In these twenty years (1990-2010), 54 percent of the Christian universities were created. Significant growth also occurred among theological schools in this period as a result of the legislation regulating the creation and accreditation of theology courses (figure 3). Previously theological seminaries were understood as independent and they gave out diplomas without regard to the national system of instruction.

Figure 3: Number of Courses of Bachelor in Theology Degree Programs Recognized by Ministry of Education (2000-2008)

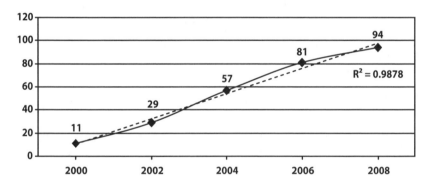

At present, the combination of incentives for student financing and the need to open new courses and meet demand for enrollment has meant that Brazil relies heavily on private institutions along with public universities. Protestant universities established long ago are now opening branch campuses in other cities and states. This is the case especially among the Lutherans. In the Methodist case a teaching network confers identity to new initiatives, and among the Presbyterians, Mackenzie University expanded to Rio de Janeiro through an accord with another institution of higher education.

Other churches have expanded their presence. The Adventist Church possesses an extensive network of elementary education, and in 2000 it adopted a policy directed toward the opening of universities. It is the Protestant denomination that has potentially the greatest possibilities, in the short term, to magnify its presence. The largest evangelical church, the Assemblies of God (Assembléia de Deus), began to participate in higher education with university centers recognized by the government only in 2002. Its presence is connected more to theological education, for which it owns various centers, than to a general university education, for which it has only two centers located in the northern region of Brazil, the area in which the denomination had its beginning (see table 1 above).

Methodists, Lutherans, and Presbyterians represent 81 percent of the enrollment openings offered currently by the evangelical universities. Baptist, Adventist, and interdenominational institutions each represent around 5 percent of the enrollment openings. Of the total number of openings offered by the Christian universities, the three largest evangelical denominations are responsible for 35.1 percent of the total. Those openings are offered by 19 universities in 12 states. The Catholic institutions account for 56.1 percent of these openings, offered by 43 different institutions of higher education distributed in 16 of the 27 federal divisions (see table 1 above).

The Christian universities have played a prominent role in Brazil when we consider that the first institutions already have nearly fifty years of educational experience. These universities have carried out leadership in different areas of knowledge and have contributed to the scientific and educational development of Brazil. Some assumed prominent positions just as much in research as in instruction, and by extension they have developed artistic, academic, and cultural activities of distinction.

A review of the history and relations of these institutions with public power gives rise to some questions about the motivations and the methods used, especially in regard to the role these institutions played in the principal moments of crisis in the country. Education has its basic foundations in the larger project of society. It provides the ideological system that inspires and legitimates national life. Even so, there is a certain autonomy in educational practice, limited only by the degree of threat it poses to the basic foundations of the society. Education is a social practice, carried on in a historical situation, and characterized and ruled by certain basic socioeconomic conditions.

The role to be carried out by Christian higher education requires that it not have as its primary motivation its own maintenance and expansion at whatever cost. The beginning of the Protestant involvement with education in Brazil is marked by a clear understanding of what the missionary task of the church involves. This task includes the formation and establishment of a more rational spirituality with defined moral values, and it is directed toward the progress of the nation.[20]

If at the beginning of the twentieth century a proposal for Protestant education merited attention and prominence in the Brazilian society, why were Protestants unable to maintain that prominence in subsequent years? Among the various possible reasons, we should especially consider the socioeconomic pressures of a country in formation. But it is also worth noting that education had little priority in the principal evangelical denominations that have arisen in recent years. Their failure to focus on education led to their failure to recruit new believers among the Brazilian elite of old. Indeed, the new believers joining the Protestant and Pentecostal churches in recent years are clearly more from a lower-class socioeconomic background.

The recent growth of institutitions of higher education identified in this chapter, however, points to new possibilities for thinking about the relationship between Protestant churches and education. In recent years these churches have built up a significant field of work in mass media, including the acquistion of television and radio channels.[21] And both the historic Protestant and the Pentecostal churches are returning to the field of education as an important field of mission and service. But unlike the Protestant educational movement at the end of the nineteenth century, in which education in and of itself was considered worthy and central, the current movement seems to consider education to be auxiliary rather than a necessary presence, in a different sector of the production of symbolic goods than their main efforts, in mass media.

We do not see any educational proposals from the Protestant and Pentecostal churches that are innovative and outstanding. Nor is there any missionary strategy to make an educational focus a way of serving and attracting elites. We also do not see a focus on higher education for future elites in order to disseminate Protestant faith and worldviews. Part of the absence of this vision in Brazil is attributed by Calvani to the growing influence, beginning in the middle of the twentieth century, of theologies derived from North American fundamentalism.[22]

A look at the mission statements of the institutions formed initially beginning in the 1950s and those of the most recent Protestant institutions of higher education does not lead, however, to the identification of differences between

20. Carlos Eduardo Calvani, "A educação no projeto missionário do protestantismo no Brasil," *Revista Pistis* 1:1 (2009): 53-69.

21. Alexandre Brasil Fonseca, *Evangélicos e mídia no Brasil* (Bragança Paulista: Edusf, 2003).

22. Calvani, "A educação no projeto missionário," p. 67.

them. In general, the mission statements all affirm the institutions' foundation on Christian principles, and in some cases they affirm the centrality of ethical values as well. And in general these statements all propose an education that will contribute to society. Two important themes, however, are absent from the mission statements of these Protestant universities, new and old. None of them defend higher education as an encouragement for students to participate in the struggle to overcome the social and regional inequalities in Brazil. The other absent item is any affirmation that education ought to prepare the student to reflect critically on the society in which he or she lives. So we see declarations of a mission to be Christian, but that is identified more with support for society than with social critique or reform.

The first Christian universities in Brazil, Catholic and Protestant, came to occupy an important space of higher education, beyond what was offered by the state. Both have distinguished themselves in relation to the larger mass of secular private institutions with regards to better quality, serving as educational leaders in some regions and in some areas of knowledge. Some of these universities still have as their profile attending to the Brazilian elite, offering an education of superior level with elevated prices. In general these institutions have occupied an important social role, positioning themselves as an alternative to the large and deficient state universities (escolões, "big schools") on the one hand, and to the lower-quality, consumer-driven private schools, where two maxims are found: "he or she paid — he or she passed"; "he or she pretends that he or she teaches — I pretend that I learn."

The recent growth of Protestant initiatives in higher education seems to be more a combination of structural factors, such as increased government incentives to private institutions and the regularization of courses of study in theology, than a consolidated vision and Christian proposal for higher education. With the opening of these new institutions of Christian higher education, however, new spaces and opportunities are also being opened for the exercise of a Christian faith that can effectively contribute to the development and improvement of life in the Brazilian society. Yet it is critically important for these new universities to be more concerted and strategic in their Christian vision. Many of these new universities are found near big cities, so they can make an important contribution to the growth of enrollment opportunities in Brazilian higher education. Participating in the effort to ensure higher education for the masses in Brazil is a necessary contribution that Christians can make today. We hope that this offer will bring in its wake some appropriate pedagogical reflection, and that it will make an effective contribution to the formation of university graduates. We need them to see a a collective, public purpose for their education and to bring new perspectives to the social, economic, and environmental development of their country. Christian institutions of higher education must avoid the uncritical reproduction of educational models and systems that are merely commercial and end up having as their only objective the private desires and plans of their owners and controllers.

Christian universities' addressing of these issues can be deepened when there is greater interaction between these institutions and the formation of networks that facilitate faculty and curricular development. Christian academics can then design and offer alternative courses of study that are defined by the real and deeper national needs and not simply by the demands of a market that at times ignores the greater common good. To act as organizations directed toward public welfare: this is the challenge facing organizations of Christian education. It is a great opportunity as well, due to their scope and scale. They seem to possess the critical mass to contribute significantly to higher education, with an outlook and approach that responds effectively to the different demands present in society. In the Brazilian case an interesting example for the Christian universities to consider is the community universities, which, based on their structures and organization, have been able to respond locally to the needs for democratization in higher education in an innovative fashion and acting in network.[23]

Another opportunity for Christian universities to do something fresh and influential is to reconsider their social engagement. They could promote their pursuit of excellence and prominence in university extension activities within neighboring communities. They could feature an education that stays in constant dialogue with practice, and that promotes the engagement of its students in service placements. This "service-learning" emphasis, subsidized by the adoption of active teaching methodologies, could represent a significant differential of these institutions. They could broaden and deepen initiatives such as "Mackenzie Volunteer," for example, with a more interactive pedagogy. This initiative of Mackenzie University has broad reach, but that boils down to an isolated action confined to one month per year.[24] It has only limited dialogue with the institutional courses of study.

The principles that guide Christian higher education, if in fact they are

23. Consórcio das Universidades Comunitárias Gaúchas (COMUNG) e Associação Catarinense das Fundações Educacionais (ACAFE). "Universidades comunitárias: Pioneiras na democratização do acesso à educação superior com compromisso social, inovação e qualidade," para a elaboração do *Documento Referência do Fórum Nacional de Educação Superior* (2008), government document found at http://portal.mec.gov.br/dmdocuments/comung_acafe.pdf.
24. http://www.mackenzie.br/mackenzievoluntario.html.

used responsibly and effectively to impose an educational agenda, represent enormous possibilities for contributing to the consolidation and construction of Brazilian democracy. Higher education in Brazil must turn its attention to questions related to inequality by promoting inclusion and ways to support the success of students coming from the lowest classes. Christian higher education in Brazil needs to conscientiously opt for the formation of the largest possible number of critically minded citizens, and reject the comfortable role of merely reproducing traditional elites.

The transformation so hoped for in Brazil and already underway since the end of the 1990s needs to find its support and foundations both from a public and free university system that serves a large number of students with a quality education and from the Christian institutions. They can contribute to the training of an elite sensitive to social reality. The transformation must also have as its foundation both processes that favor the entrance of more and more people to higher education, thus serving as a vehicle through extension and research as well as instruction that is accessible to a larger portion of the population. In different moments of Brazilian history Christian education brought important contributions and values. We hope that now it is being challenged effectively to be "salt and light" in the educational field and in contemporary Brazilian society.

CHAPTER 10

Quest for Identity and Place:
Christian University Education in Canada

Harry Fernhout

Overview

During the past half-century, secularization has dominated the story of religion in Canadian society, and it has been a prevalent pattern in Canadian higher education as well. In English Canada, Protestant vision and values were still woven into the fabric of society in the first part of the twentieth century, and they were present on both denominational and nondenominational university campuses. In both French and English Canada, Catholic institutions were closely aligned with the intellectual traditions and social vision of the Roman Catholic Church. By the end of the 1960s, however, a profound shift had taken place. In English Canada the cultural influence of Protestantism was greatly diminished, and universities became places "whose public voice was predominantly secular."[1] Secularization also had a profound impact on both French and English Catholic institutions. That is not the end of the story of Christian university education in Canada, however. Over the past fifty years a number of Protestant, primarily evangelical, colleges and universities have emerged, and they are making a concerted effort to establish their credibility and carve out a niche in Canadian higher education. A significant number of Catholic institutions, meanwhile, are addressing issues of institutional identity and mission in response to Pope John Paul II's Apostolic Constitution on Catholic Universities, *Ex Corde Ecclesiae* (1990). These developments signal

1. Catherine Gidney, *A Long Eclipse: The Liberal Protestant Establishment and the Canadian University, 1920-1970* (Montreal: McGill-Queen's University Press, 2004), p. xxv.

230

a hopeful new era for Christian higher education in Canada, and suggest a potentially fruitful convergence of interests among Protestant and Catholic Christians in their common desire to make a constructive contribution to Canadian society.

Secularization in Canadian Higher Education

The development of higher education in Canada was significantly shaped by the nation's French (Roman Catholic) and British (primarily Protestant) colonial past. From the time of British settlement, English Canada maintained strong historical and cultural ties with Britain, and the early development of universities in English Canada followed British models. A few of Canada's oldest Protestant institutions came into existence prior to the Canadian Confederation in 1867 by means of charters granted by the British crown. After 1867 new colleges and universities were established, particularly as new provinces joined the Confederation. Some of these, such as McMaster University in Ontario, were denominational entities; others, such as the University of Toronto and the University of British Columbia, were established by provincial governments as non-sectarian institutions. The Catholic Church played a dominant role in the development of higher education in Quebec both before and after Confederation, while Catholic dioceses and religious orders also established a significant number of institutions of higher learning in English Canada.

In key respects the development of higher education in Canada followed a different path than in the United States. In his chapter on the United States in this volume, George Marsden describes a "free-market religious economy" in the post–American Revolution period that facilitated the founding of many private Protestant colleges by enterprising religious leaders. In Canada this free enterprise, frontier spirit in education did not occur. Although Canada never had an officially established church, unofficial Protestant and Catholic establishments existed in English Canada and Quebec respectively, resulting in the close involvement of both government and dominant churches in higher education. Canada did not develop a large number of private or independent colleges and universities alongside a system of provincial (state) institutions. Consequently, when the process of secularization pervaded Canadian universities in the latter half of the twentieth century, there were virtually no Christian institutions other than Bible colleges and seminaries to provide an alternative to the dominant paradigm.

While there are divergent opinions regarding the causes and dynamics of secularization in universities, the process is generally seen to involve the breakdown of a shared vision of the unity of knowledge and truth, the loss of a sense of moral community, and the privatization of religious commitment. Factors such as the proliferation of disciplines and specializations, an increased emphasis on research and graduate programs (rather than on teaching and the formation of undergraduates), and the rapid expansion of universities in both size and number also play into the process. In short, secularization in Western society and in the universities involves the decline of a broadly shared Christian frame of reference. Scholars have suggested that the secularization process in Canada followed the "British pattern" of "institutional erosion" whereby the informal religious establishments that persisted within major social institutions well into the twentieth century broke down and the worldview of leaders in key societal institutions, including universities, shifted.[2] According to Mark Noll, this pattern stands in contrast to secularization in the United States, where the more fragmented, populist, and non-established structures of Christianity (including the large number of private Christian colleges) were less susceptible to the forces of secularization in the cultural mainstream.[3]

The rapid secularization process in Canada was epitomized by the "Quiet Revolution" in Quebec, where the influence of the Catholic Church in various social spheres waned rapidly in the 1960s. Existing Catholic universities were secularized, leaving a Catholic influence only in some faculties of theology. Similar but less dramatic transitions took place in English Canada. Existing universities with denominational roots expanded rapidly with provincial support to meet broad public enrollment and program demands, and became "nonsectarian" in the process. Meanwhile, new public universities were established on a secular footing. Some Protestant and Catholic institutions became constituent components of larger universities, offering courses or programs in traditional areas of strength. While some of these institutions maintained a clear sense of their religious identity and mission, others retained only a few vestiges of Christian identity, such as chaplaincies. Broadly speaking, "public" and "secular" became interchangeable concepts in discourse about postsecondary education.

Despite the powerful impetus of secularization, a significant number of denominational theological colleges survived (and have, in some cases, thrived) within secular university contexts in English Canada. These colleges

---

2. David Martin, *A General Theory of Secularization* (Oxford: Basil Blackwell, 1978), p. 7.
3. Mark Noll, *A History of Christianity in the United States and Canada* (Grand Rapids: Eerdmans, 1992), p. 549.

are typically related to older mainline Protestant denominations (Anglican, Presbyterian, and United Churches), or to the Catholic Church. For example, the Toronto School of Theology is a consortium of seven publicly funded Protestant and Catholic theological colleges affiliated with the University of Toronto.[4] The existence of denominational theological colleges within secular universities represents an accommodation of the old informal religious establishment within the dominant secular paradigm. Denominational institutions are afforded space to engage in theological work while the main work of the university occurs in a secular space. Since mainline Protestants in Canada typically equate Christian higher education with theological education and equate university education with secular education, this arrangement is broadly regarded as normal and satisfactory. Within mainline Protestant denominations, and to a large extent in the Catholic Church, few perceive a need to develop alternative, faith-shaped institutions in response to the secularization of university education.

The Emergence of Protestant Evangelical Higher Education

Beginning in the late nineteenth century and continuing in the first half of the twentieth, evangelical Christians outside Canada's mainline denominations founded a significant number of Bible colleges or institutes, particularly in western Canada.[5] These institutions were characterized by "concern for correct doctrine, a Bible-centered curriculum, and practical training — especially in evangelism."[6] Some of these institutions encouraged university or seminary training of faculty and the accreditation of programs while others regarded such standards as less important than the personal spiritual experience of instructors (and students). During the first half of the twentieth century, Canadian evangelicals' vision of Christian postsecondary education was largely limited to equipping people for church ministry or for missionary service at home or abroad. While evangelicals regarded universities as potentially risky

4. See its website, www.tst.edu. Theological colleges and seminaries associated with non-mainline denominations are typically independent (or associated with independent colleges or universities) and do not receive public funding.

5. For an overview of the Bible college movement in Canada, see Al Hiebert, *Character with Competence Education* (Steinbach, Manitoba: Association of Canadian Bible Colleges, 2005).

6. John Stackhouse, *Canadian Evangelicalism in the Twentieth Century: An Introduction to Its Character* (Toronto: University of Toronto Press, 1993), p. 75.

environments for young people's personal faith, they nonetheless viewed secular university education as both viable and acceptable for students seeking "secular" vocations.

This situation changed significantly during the 1960s and subsequent decades. John Stackhouse identifies three significant changes in Canadian evangelicalism in this period that led to new ventures in higher education. First, evangelical Christians generally became more interested in higher education (particularly for pastors and missionaries). Second, they became more self-conscious of their identity in distinction from mainline denominations and began building alternative structures and institutions, such as the Evangelical Fellowship of Canada. Third, evangelical Christians expanded their understanding of Christian vocation, increasingly recognizing that all vocations are in service to God.[7]

According to Stackhouse, these trends are clearly visible in the development of Trinity Western College (later Trinity Western University) in British Columbia. Trinity Western began as a two-year junior college of the Evangelical Free Church, with active support from the American branch of the church and its Trinity College in Deerfield, Illinois. Stackhouse suggests that the American leaders understood "the role of presuppositions" in thought and culture and the need to work out their implications in each area of human learning.[8] Trinity Western was initially promoted to the Canadian churches in ways that linked to their Bible college tradition: as a place where students could get a solid footing for eventual seminary studies or for training for domestic and overseas missions. As Canadian evangelicals increasingly recognized that most university students are not called to church ministry or mission work, and that other vocations are valid paths for Christian service, Trinity Western was repositioned as a place to prepare young men and women to be effective Christian contributors to Canadian society. As the institution expanded its four-year degree programs in the 1970s, it was increasingly portrayed as an alternative to secular universities, a place where students could be affirmed and strengthened in faith rather than running the risk of having their faith undermined.

Even so, Stackhouse suggests, Trinity Western typically did not publicly portray its educational program in terms of a "whole world-and-life view" that permeated all the curricular offerings. Rather, Stackhouse argues, Trinity Western's public positioning in the 1980s communicated that it was a place

---

7. Stackhouse, *Canadian Evangelicalism*, p. 145.
8. Stackhouse, *Canadian Evangelicalism*, p. 148.

where the arts and sciences "are taught neutrally, once purged of un-Christian . . . perspectives and conclusions, and this takes place within the context of the distinctively evangelical qualities of doctrinal orthodoxy and 'pietistic' behavioral standards."[9] The impetus for a more holistic and integral understanding of the mission of Christian higher education eventually came from within Trinity Western, from its faculty and academic leaders. In the past two decades Trinity Western has increasingly emphasized the integration of faith into all areas of the curriculum.

Trinity Western's story illustrates the increasing interest in and appetite for Christian higher education in Canadian evangelical communities. Fueled by this appetite, since the 1990s six former Bible colleges have developed new programs and succeeded in securing the designation of "university" or "university college."[10] Each has experienced shifts in positioning and outlook similar to that of Trinity Western.

A quite different dynamic led to the development of three institutions associated with the Christian Reformed Church in Canada. During the 1950s a large number of Dutch immigrants of Reformed persuasion came to Canada and founded, along with their churches, a network of Christian elementary and secondary schools. In the 1950s and 1960s a significant number of students from these immigrant communities made their way to Calvin College in Grand Rapids, Michigan, or to Trinity Christian College in Palos Heights, Illinois, or Dordt College in Iowa. Many Dutch Canadian immigrants brought with them the theological and social vision of the Dutch theologian and statesman Abraham Kuyper and the early leaders of the Free University that Kuyper founded in 1880 in Amsterdam. Kuyper understood the Christian faith as a "world-and-life view" that stood in opposition to the secular Enlightenment worldview of his day. Kuyper and his followers emphasized that Christ, as the one in whom all things were created and redeemed, lays claim to every square inch of created reality, including every domain of knowledge. Consequently, Christ-followers should be engaged in every area of culture, including higher education.[11]

---

9. Stackhouse, *Canadian Evangelicalism,* p. 151.

10. The "university college" designation is used in some provinces to distinguish institutions offering undergraduate degree programs from large universities with postgraduate programs. Some university colleges are free-standing while others are federated with large universities. In the province of Alberta the designation applies only to faith-based institutions.

11. Kuyper presents this vision in his inaugural speech at the opening of the Free University in 1880: "Sphere Sovereignty," in *Abraham Kuyper: A Centennial Reader,* ed. James D. Bratt (Grand Rapids: Eerdmans, 1998), pp. 461-490.

Dutch immigrants to Canada took up this challenge with considerable passion, despite limited resources. Interestingly, a significant number of these new Canadians were persuaded that the place to begin in higher education was at the graduate school level. They wanted to train young professors to develop a Christian perspective in their discipline rather than the outlooks and ideologies they would inevitably absorb at secular graduate schools. The vision was that a graduate school would, in time, foster the development of distinctively Christian undergraduate programs. It led in 1967 to the founding of the Institute for Christian Studies (ICS) in Toronto as a graduate school of philosophy and the philosophy of various disciplines. However, ICS did not grow beyond a small, philosophically focused institution and the grand vision remained unfulfilled. Consequently the impetus grew to build undergraduate institutions to provide education that would equip students with a Christian worldview and enable them to contribute to Canadian culture as Christians in their chosen vocations. Another high priority was the preparation of a new generation of teachers for Christian elementary and secondary schools. Inspired to large degree by this Reformed vision, The King's College (later The King's University College) in Edmonton, Alberta, opened its doors in 1979. In 1982 Redeemer College (later Redeemer University College) was launched in Hamilton, Ontario. Both institutions have grown significantly and today welcome students and faculty from a wide variety of denominational backgrounds. While ICS, King's, and Redeemer have no formal ties to the Christian Reformed Church, they receive significant financial support from Christian Reformed members and congregations.

Today there are fourteen Protestant/evangelical institutions that fit the profile of a "Christian university" that is used in this book.[12] These institutions are spread from coast to coast in six of Canada's ten provinces. The highest concentration (five institutions) is found in the province of Alberta.

Six of the fourteen institutions were designed from their inception to offer university-type programs in the arts/humanities, sciences, social sciences, and/or some professional areas. Five are primarily undergraduate institutions, and one is a graduate school. They are:

12. There are a number of significant theological colleges and other types of institutions in Canada that do not fit this profile. Regent College in Vancouver and McMaster Divinity College in Hamilton are influential theological colleges in Canadian evangelical circles. Conrad Grebel University College, a Mennonite institution affiliated with the University of Waterloo, is an example of a different model of Christian higher education. It offers undergraduate and graduate courses in various fields (such as arts, music, peace and conflict studies, and theological studies) leading to a University of Waterloo degree.

- Canadian University College, Lacombe, Alberta; founded by Seventh-Day Adventists in 1919
- Institute for Christian Studies, Toronto, Ontario; founded by Christian Reformed members in 1967
- Redeemer University College, Hamilton, Ontario; founded by Christian Reformed members in 1982
- St. Stephen's University, St. Stephen, New Brunswick; founded by "trans-denominational" evangelicals in 1975
- The King's University College, Edmonton, Alberta; founded by Christian Reformed members in 1979
- Trinity Western University, Langley, British Columbia; founded by the Evangelical Free Church in 1962

The other eight institutions were founded as Bible or theological colleges, typically in the first half of the twentieth century. In most cases the transition to university-type programs was initiated within the past twenty years. Given their institutional background, the curricular programs at these institutions tend to be stronger in the humanities and/or social sciences and less developed in the natural sciences. Seven of these institutions are permitted to use the word "university" in their name; the other (Briercrest College) is working toward this goal. These eight institutions are:

- Ambrose University College, Calgary, Alberta; created in 2007 through the merger of Alliance University College and Canadian Nazarene University College. Predecessors: Canadian Bible College, founded in 1941, and Canadian Nazarene College, founded in 1940
- Booth University College, Winnipeg, Manitoba; founded in 1982 as a theological school and seminary of the Salvation Army; designated as a university college in 2010
- Briercrest College, Caronport, Saskatchewan; founded in 1935 as Briercrest Bible Institute, by nondenominational evangelicals; changed to Briercrest Bible College in 1982
- Canadian Mennonite University, Winnipeg, Manitoba; founded in 1998 through the amalgamation of three Mennonite colleges: Mennonite Brethren Bible College/Concord College (est. 1944); Canadian Mennonite Bible College (est. 1947); and Menno Simons College (est. 1989)
- Concordia University College, Edmonton, Alberta; founded in 1921 as Concordia College by the Lutheran Church in Canada; renamed in 1995

- Crandall University, Moncton, New Brunswick; formerly Atlantic Baptist University; founded in 1949 as the United Baptist Bible Training School
- Providence University College, Otterburne, Manitoba; founded in 1925 as Winnipeg Bible Training School by nondenominational evangelicals; designated as a university college in 2011
- Tyndale University College, Toronto, Ontario; founded in 1894 as Toronto Bible College, by nondenominational evangelicals; renamed Ontario Bible College in 1968; became Tyndale University College in 1998

These fourteen institutions enroll a total of about ten thousand students. Although the number of institutions has expanded in recent years as former Bible colleges transition to university-type programs, total enrollment has not increased dramatically. With two exceptions (Trinity Western University and Concordia University College), enrollment at each institution is less than one thousand students. Two institutions (Institute for Christian Studies and St. Stephen's University) are small by design. For most of Canada's Protestant evangelical colleges and universities, increasing student enrollment to enhance institutional sustainability is a crucial challenge.

In a national context that regards postsecondary education as a "public" and secular domain, these fourteen institutions are typically viewed as "private" and, by some, as "sectarian." Although individual institutions have made important gains in terms of profile and reputation, these small Protestant institutions play a minor role on the broad stage of postsecondary education. Canada's geographical vastness and varying regional education policies make it difficult for these institutions to develop a common profile and critical mass. Given the dominance of the secular university paradigm, and given their relatively small size and limited resources, Protestant evangelical universities and colleges face many challenges as they seek to find a niche in postsecondary education, establish credibility, and make a significant contribution to Canadian higher education.

Government Relations: The Challenges of Accreditation, Degree-Granting, and Funding

One of the first critical challenges for any emerging university or college is to establish its credibility through a quality assessment process or accreditation. There is no national system of program assessment or institutional accreditation in Canada. While the Association of Universities and Colleges of Canada

(AUCC) conducts thorough organizational and academic reviews before admitting institutions to membership, it is a service agency, not an accrediting body. Education is a provincial jurisdiction under the Canadian Constitution; provincial governments have the power to charter general or specific degree-granting authority, and policies vary considerably from province to province. Some provinces have formal agencies and processes to deal with new degree program proposals; others do not. This means that the Protestant evangelical universities and colleges, spread as they are over six Canadian provinces, operate in differing regulatory environments with regard to degree accreditation and quality assurance. In most provinces (with Alberta as a notable exception) these institutions have faced a very significant struggle simply to establish their legitimacy, to secure appropriate degree-granting authority, and to secure a place at the postsecondary education table.

The experience of Christian institutions in the province of Ontario illustrates this challenge. In the 1960s Ontario adopted a policy that restricted standard (or, in government parlance, "secular") degree-granting authority to the secular, publicly funded universities. The underlying assumption was that programs offered by Christian institutions were by definition theological in nature and consequently should lead to theological (or "qualified") degrees. When this policy became law in the early 1980s, the Institute for Christian Studies (ICS) found itself under pressure to accept a theological designation for its philosophy program. After a persistent lobby, ICS was authorized to grant a master of philosophical foundations degree — a designation that satisfied the provincial government because it was not a standard degree (i.e., master of arts) and which partially satisfied ICS because the designation was consistent with the nature of its program. Redeemer University College faced similar challenges. The provincial government determined that Redeemer, as a Christian institution, should be restricted to offering a bachelor of Christian studies degree instead of bachelor of arts, and a bachelor of Christian education instead of a bachelor of education. Redeemer coped with these restrictions for more than fifteen years while it built a strong academic reputation through its faculty and graduates. During this period Redeemer also secured full membership in the AUCC. These successes, combined with an intense political effort, led in 1998 to the passage of special legislation empowering Redeemer to grant bachelor of arts and bachelor of science degrees. In 2003 Redeemer's bachelor of Christian education was replaced by the standard bachelor of education designation.

During the 1990s the Ontario provincial government faced pressure from several out-of-province institutions and non-Canadian universities to authorize their degree programs in the province. As it transitioned from Bible college to university programs, Tyndale University College also pursued new degree-granting status. In 2000 Ontario responded by enacting legislation that enabled "private" institutions to apply for standard degree-granting authority upon a favorable review by a newly created Postsecondary Education Quality Assessment Board (PEQAB). Under these new provisions Tyndale University College gained the right to grant bachelor's degrees in several fields and ICS secured provincial approval to grant M.A. (Philosophy) and Ph.D. (Philosophy) degrees. This access to a quality assessment process and standard degree-granting authority represented a major advance over the previous regime. The Protestant evangelical institutions in Ontario remain outside the postsecondary mainstream, however; PEQAB has no jurisdiction over degree programs at Ontario's public universities, and the Ontario University Quality Assurance Council, created in 2010, excludes "private" Christian degree-granting institutions.

In the 1990s Trinity Western University encountered particular challenges in securing accreditation for its teacher education program, a process that required the approval of the British Columbia College of Teachers (BCCT), the provincial body governing the teaching profession. Despite a positive recommendation from its own assessment committee, the BCCT refused to accredit Trinity Western's program because of the university's requirement that students sign a statement of community standards, including a commitment to refrain from premarital sex, adultery, and homosexual behavior. The BCCT concluded that these prohibitions indicated that Trinity Western graduates, when they became teachers, would inevitably have a prejudicial attitude toward students who might be struggling with issues of sexual identity and orientation. Thus the BCCT concluded that Trinity Western's program followed discriminatory practices that were contrary to the public interest and public policy. Trinity Western took the matter to court and won a ruling ordering the BCCT to accept its review committee's recommendation to approve the program. The case eventually went to the Supreme Court of Canada, which ruled in Trinity Western's favor in 2001. At all levels, the courts found that there was no evidence that Trinity Western graduates would discriminate against gay or lesbian students. These court rulings are recognized as landmark decisions for interpreting and balancing religious freedom and individual rights to nondiscrimination on the basis of sexual orientation.[13]

Policies in Alberta followed a trajectory quite different from that in other

---

13. *Trinity Western University v. College of Teachers*, 1 S.C.R. 772, 2001 SCC 3. http://scc .lexum.org/en/2001/2001scc31/2001scc31.pdf.

provinces. The Christian influence in Alberta's relatively small population remained significant throughout the 1950s and 1960s. In fact, in the late 1960s Alberta became the first jurisdiction in North America to provide modest operational funding for Christian elementary and secondary schools. By the early 1980s Alberta was home to four Christian postsecondary institutions. Although small, these institutions could muster a significant government lobby among various constituencies in the province. Responding to this reality, Alberta created a Private Colleges Accreditation Board (PCAB) with a mandate to make recommendations to the government concerning new degree programs proposed by these institutions. From its inception this board included at least one person familiar with the Christian institutions. In 2003 PCAB was transformed into the Campus Alberta Quality Council (CAQC) with a broad mandate to review new degree programs, including those proposed by the major universities. The standards developed for the "private" institutions were, in effect, refined and applied to all postsecondary institutions. CAQC has since emerged as a leader in a movement to develop pan-Canadian degree standards.

Policies with regard to public funding for Protestant evangelical colleges and universities also vary significantly from province to province. Ontario, British Columbia, New Brunswick, and Saskatchewan provide no operational funding for "private" institutions. Manitoba provides significant operating grants to Canadian Mennonite University (because it is designated as a "provincial university") and a much lower level of funding for Providence University College and Booth University College. On the other end of the spectrum, Alberta offers significant financial support to the five (four Protestant and one Catholic) Christian university colleges offering provincially approved degree programs. In 1989 Alberta agreed to provide operating grants pro-rated at 75 percent of those given to the public universities for similar programs (on a per student basis). Although funding formulas have fluctuated over time, the grants remain very significant, representing between 25 and 30 percent of the total operating budgets of Alberta's Christian university colleges.

Despite enjoying a measure of acceptance reflected in public funding, Alberta's Christian university colleges were, until recently, not included in province-wide administrative structures for government relations. Often policy changes were applied to these institutions as an afterthought. However, for the past several years the province has advanced a "Campus Alberta" concept, with an emphasis on coordinating and streamlining postsecondary education of all types. The five Christian university colleges are considered to be part of Campus Alberta, and representatives of this sector are increasingly included in province-wide deliberations. While this model provides an opening for Christian institutions to participate as partners in the system, it also brings significant challenges. Government priorities tend to focus on economic growth and the need for highly skilled labor in Alberta's resource-based economy. Research priorities focus on technological innovations and commercialization. These priorities are not well-suited to Christian institutions oriented to the humanities, sciences and social sciences, embodying a distinctive worldview, and educating for faithful Christian living in the contemporary society, which often calls for a critical assessment of dominant cultural values and priorities. The Christian institutions inevitably experience pressures to conform to prevailing educational models and priorities. As a relatively small component of the system, their unique contribution and potential can easily be overlooked in province-wide planning. Nevertheless, the Alberta context provides a unique opportunity in Canada for formal participation and cultural witness in postsecondary education.

The issues of program accreditation, degree-granting authority, and funding illustrate the varying ways in which provincial governments and their agencies have responded with policies, or lack thereof, when confronted with governmentally unplanned and independently organized universities and colleges.[14] In most Canadian jurisdictions governments dealt with these matters slowly and begrudgingly. Independent Christian institutions have gained considerable ground with provincial governments in the past two decades, however, winning at least the necessary breathing room to function as university-level degree-granting institutions.[15]

The Challenges of the Guild: The AUCC, the CAUT, and Academic Freedom

While the Protestant evangelical universities and colleges struggled with the challenge of establishing their right to exist and grant degrees in their re-

14. This unplanned, "surprise" factor of growth in nongovernmental higher education, and governments' scramble to respond, is a worldwide pattern. See especially Daniel Levy, "The Unanticipated Explosion: Private Higher Education's Global Surge," *Comparative Education Review* 50:2 (2006): 217-240.

15. In the province of Saskatchewan the granting of "standard" degrees is still limited to the two existing public universities. In August 2011 a government-commissioned study recommended that the province create an agency to assess degree program proposals from other institutions. If this recommendation is adopted, the door may be opened for Briercrest College to seek normal degree-granting status.

spective provinces, some of them encountered equally difficult challenges in finding acceptance in the national associations that represent mainstream universities and their faculties.

The Association of Universities and Colleges of Canada (AUCC), founded in 1911, consists of ninety-five public and private not-for-profit universities and university degree–level colleges. The AUCC interacts with the federal government on issues such as research funding and international programs, and fosters communication among universities and governments, industry, and the public. Member institutions must meet various criteria, including academic programs characterized by breadth and depth in the liberal arts and/or sciences, and clearly articulated policies on academic freedom and intellectual integrity. The presidents of the member institutions constitute the voting body of the AUCC. While it does not constitute accreditation, membership in the AUCC functions as a de facto standard of academic reputability and enhances eligibility for research grants and other government programs. While a significant number of Catholic institutions were already members of the AUCC, it was vital for some of the new Protestant evangelical institutions emerging in the 1980s and 1990s to gain AUCC membership to help establish their academic credibility.

In 1984 Trinity Western University succeeded in securing membership in the AUCC. Redeemer University College was admitted soon after, and The King's University College was granted provisional membership in 1987. However, when King's sought full membership, some members of the AUCC became nervous about the inclusion of new, relatively small Christian institutions that required faculty members to commit to a statement of faith as a condition of employment. The AUCC board declared a moratorium on new memberships, and launched a review of the implications of the faith requirement for the practice of academic freedom at the new institutions. The review resulted in the adoption of an additional membership criterion: an institution requiring adherence to a statement of faith and/or code of conduct that might be perceived to constrain academic freedom must make those conditions of employment clear before the time of hiring, and must have adequate provisions for due process and fairness in any dispute related to these requirements.

The AUCC's ambiguous embrace of its new Christian members was palpable in this criterion. Although there are many conceivable threats to academic freedom that are not necessarily connected to religion — such as internal institutional politics, ideological conflicts, or funding pressures — the statement of faith issue was singled out as a key concern by the predominantly secular AUCC membership. AUCC leaders clearly had reservations about a Christian institution's capacity to foster genuine academic freedom. Symbolic of this ambiguity was the AUCC's decision to place an asterisk in the Association's membership directory beside the names of institutions requiring adherence to a statement of faith.

Over time, as the new Christian institutional members matured and participated in AUCC activities and programs, their acceptance in the AUCC seemed to become less ambiguous. In 2005 the AUCC adopted a revised academic freedom statement and removed the clause regarding statements of faith from the membership criteria, instead making it the responsibility of committees conducting institutional reviews of prospective members to ensure that requirements such as a faith statement were clearly stated prior to employment, to ensure that procedures to deal fairly with conflicts over such issues were in place. The asterisks were removed from the membership directory. Since then Canadian Mennonite University has been admitted to membership without controversy. In recent AUCC planning sessions the diversity of the membership (including the independent faith-based institutions) has been identified as a valued organizational characteristic. A new statement on academic freedom, adopted in 2011, recognizes that the responsibility of an institution to organize its academic mission is part of the legitimate context of academic freedom. But some AUCC leaders remain uneasy with regard to the newer Protestant evangelical institutions. In 2010 the AUCC rejected an application for membership from Crandall University because of concerns over the institution's code of conduct. The AUCC is currently reviewing its membership criteria once more, and several Christian institutions are preparing to apply for admission. It remains to be seen whether the AUCC will continue to make room for new faith-based members or whether the predominant values and outlooks of secular universities will make it difficult for Christian institutions to participate.

Another important organization is the Canadian Association of University Teachers (CAUT), which consists of 65,000 university academic staff. CAUT portrays itself as the staunch defender of academic freedom, which it defines as "the right to teach, learn, study and publish free of orthodoxy or threat of reprisal and discrimination."[16] The CAUT normally investigates academic freedom issues only in response to specific complaints. In 2008, however, the CAUT undertook its own investigation of Trinity Western University (TWU) to determine whether the institution employs a "faith test" in faculty hiring and whether TWU faculty members enjoy a full measure of academic free-

16. "Academic Freedom," Canadian Association of University Teachers, accessed November 25, 2011. http://www.caut.ca/pages.asp?page=140.

dom. Not surprisingly, the investigating committee found ample evidence that TWU's hiring criteria include a faith requirement. The committee took note of TWU's statement in its Academic Calendar that it is "committed to academic freedom in teaching and investigation from a stated perspective, i.e., with parameters consistent with the confessional basis of the constituency to which the University is responsible, but practiced in an environment of free inquiry and discussion and of encouragement of integrity in research."[17] The committee concluded that TWU's policies represent unwarranted and unacceptable constraints on academic freedom, and recommended that the institution be placed on a list of institutions found to have "imposed a requirement of a commitment to a particular ideology or statement as a condition of employment."[18] The CAUT initiated similar investigations of Canadian Mennonite University in Manitoba and Crandall University in New Brunswick, and drew similar conclusions. While "blacklisting" by CAUT has no immediate implications for Christian institutions in terms of their membership in the AUCC or for their relationships with provincial governments, this development has the potential to create an aura of doubt in public perceptions of the academic reputation of Christian institutions.

In the fall of 2010 Redeemer University College was informed that it was next in line for a CAUT investigation. Redeemer announced publicly that it would not cooperate since the outcome of the investigation was a foregone conclusion. At the same time the CAUT's investigations drew national media attention, with some commentators calling CAUT's effort a "witch hunt." A group of professors at mainstream universities, themselves members of CAUT, launched a petition calling on the CAUT to desist, noting that the concept of academic freedom came into being in the Christian intellectual tradition. In late 2010 the CAUT responded to these pressures by announcing that while it would remain vigilant in monitoring violations of academic freedom, it would not launch new investigations of Christian institutions.

There is an important difference between the AUCC's and the CAUT's approaches to academic freedom. The AUCC, as an organization of universities, recognizes a legitimate place for institutional autonomy in setting the context for defining and applying principles of academic freedom. Individual academic freedom functions within this context, undergirded and protected by principles

17. "Report of an Inquiry regarding Trinity Western University," Canadian Association of University Teachers, October 2009, p. 4, accessed November 25, 2011. http://www.caut.ca/uploads/TWU_Report.pdf.

18. "Report of an Inquiry," CAUT, October 2009, p. 11, accessed November 25, 2011. http://www.caut.ca/uploads/TWU_Report.pdf.

and procedures for due process when differences or conflicts occur. While this approach is articulated in secular terms, it provides an opening for institutional pluralism. The CAUT's approach, on the other hand, is hegemonic. It focuses solely on the autonomy of the individual scholar. According to the CAUT, any contextual framework constitutes a constraint of doctrine or orthodoxy that must be rejected.[19] This approach cannot conceive of Christian institutions as voluntary academic communities working with a shared understanding of what is true and how the world works. But such voluntary communities of scholars practice a genuine species of academic freedom — the freedom to form "schools of thought" according to commonly held beliefs. Canada's Protestant Christian colleges and universities face the challenge of advocating for a pluralist rather than a hegemonic understanding of academic freedom. To that end these institutions need to build alliances with others who understand these dynamics, particularly Catholic colleagues and sympathetic leaders in the AUCC.

The Challenge of Generating a Public Profile

Besides the challenges of establishing the right to operate in provincial contexts and carving out a niche in the wider academic arena, Protestant evangelical institutions confront an urgent need to raise their individual and collective profile among the general public and, more important, among the Christian public. This was clearly demonstrated in 2007, when Christian Higher Education Canada (CHEC)[20] in partnership with the Evangelical Fellowship of Canada commissioned Ipsos Reid (a global opinion-research firm) to conduct an extensive national survey of perceptions of Christian higher education and to assess the market potential for CHEC member institutions.[21] Twelve percent of the respondents to the survey identified themselves as evangelical Christians. Of the respondents who did not already have some direct connection

19. I am indebted to Justin Cooper, president emeritus of Redeemer University College, for the distinction between secular pluralist and secular hegemonic views of academic freedom.

20. Christian Higher Education Canada is an independent organization that aims to foster institutional cooperation and to raise public awareness of Christian postsecondary education in Canada. CHEC consists of 32 member institutions offering a wide range of Bible college, seminary, university, and graduate programs. Collectively CHEC institutions serve more than 17,000 students.

21. For a detailed discussion, see Al Hiebert, "Only in Canada: A Study of National Market Potential for Christian Higher Education Canada (CHEC) Institutions," *Christian Higher Education* 10:5 (2011): 397-421.

with CHEC member institutions, 75 percent did not know what the expression "Christian higher education" meant, and could not name a single institution offering this type of education. Though most respondents favored the idea of studying in a community of people who share the same values and beliefs, others opposed such education because of a perceived "single perspective bias." This concern was evident to some degree even among evangelical respondents, indicating a perception that secular universities are somehow more "objective" than Christian institutions. Still, 65 percent of evangelical respondents indicated that they would consider Christian higher education (for themselves or their children). Those who were favorably inclined identified faith integration, small class sizes, and the quality of teaching relationships as desirable features of Christian institutions.

The results of this market study can be summarized as a "bad news/good news" scenario for Protestant evangelical colleges and universities. The bad news is that institutions of Christian higher education are relatively unknown in Canada, except among a particular segment of the population. Even among evangelical Christians these institutions do not attract their "market share."[22] The good news aspect of this situation is that these institutions have a fresh story to tell, particularly among segments of the population with some predisposition to consider Christian higher education.

In recent years several Christian universities have succeeded in raising their profile by participating in national student satisfaction surveys. For almost twenty years *Maclean's*, Canada's leading weekly news magazine, has published an annual ranking of more than sixty Canadian universities using a complex set of criteria. *Maclean's* has consistently excluded Christian institutions, but in 2002 the *Globe and Mail*, Canada's leading national daily newspaper, launched an annual report based on an extensive survey of students at all AUCC-member institutions. For the past four years the eligible Protestant evangelical universities have typically ranked at or near the top of their size category on important academic measures such as quality of teaching, student-faculty interaction, class size, and overall student satisfaction. In fact, these institutions have garnered some of the best ratings in the nation, regardless of institutional size. In recent years *Maclean's* has also published student satisfaction data based on results of the National Survey of Student Engagement

22. Total university enrollment in Canada (excluding community colleges and technical institutes) stands at about 900,000 students. Total enrollment in CHEC institutions of all types represents only 1.9 percent of this number, while evangelical Christians constitute roughly 12 percent of the general population.

(NSSE) and the Canadian Undergraduate Survey Consortium (CUSC). The Christian institutions that participate typically appear at or near the top of the national rankings. These excellent results have begun to draw attention among Christians and the general public, and have boosted confidence among faculty, students, and supporters. Participation in these national contexts has helped to address the critical need to raise the profile of Christian higher education in Canada, particularly among Christians.

The Challenge of Identity: The Role of Faith in Learning

An unanticipated benefit of struggling at the margins to find a unique and legitimate niche in Canadian higher education is the inherent need to become articulate regarding institutional identity and the role of faith in shaping the academic experience. Considering the relative youth of their movement, Canadian Protestant evangelical institutions have generated a rich engagement with these issues. Examples from the publications of three institutions (Trinity Western University, Redeemer University College, and The King's University College) illustrate the development and future promise of such engagement.

Trinity Western University's strategic direction statement, *Envision the Century*, favorably quotes Pope John Paul II's statement that "faith and reason are like two wings on which the human spirit rises to the contemplation of truth,"[23] and goes on to say that the university seeks to "unite faith and reason through mature scholarship and research in undergraduate and graduate studies."[24] These formulations might suggest that faith and learning are here conceptualized as two complementary domains (as in the wings metaphor) or as two domains that must be united (or integrated) through the application of Christian presuppositions about the nature and purpose of life and the world. Redeemer University College's *The Cross and Our Calling*, by contrast, does not begin with two spheres but situates the entire academic enterprise within the (cosmic) biblical story of redemption, in interaction with the story of Western culture. The University College's calling to witness to the good news of God's coming kingdom in the contemporary context calls for an approach that

> works from the scriptural story to an elaboration of a Christian worldview, thence to a philosophical articulation . . . and on to the formulations of

23. *Envision the Century*, Trinity Western University, 2008, p. 12.
24. *Envision the Century*, p. 10.

various disciplines. . . . There must be an inner connection between the Gospel and scholarship. That is, since faith will always shape scholarship, we strive to bring Scripture's teaching to bear in a formative way on theoretical work.[25]

In this approach faith is the inner dynamic of all scholarship; the challenge is not to accomplish the "integration of faith and learning," but rather to understand the inherent "role of faith *in* learning."[26]

While it clearly articulates an integral understanding of faith's role in scholarly activity, *The Cross and Our Calling* is not as expansive in elaborating what this starting point means for Redeemer's approach to teaching, or to the social and spiritual formation of the academic community. Trinity Western's *Envision the Century,* on the other hand, devotes considerable attention to the latter. It states that the university's commitment to transformation fosters a commitment to "grow in community as a people of grace, maturity and wisdom, who possess deep and abiding appreciation for the created order and the Creator God."[27] Jonathan Raymond, Trinity Western's president, stresses the importance of understanding the university as a dynamic social-spiritual ecology. "While all universities seek to be intellectual hotbeds . . . not all look to develop the whole person, including the social-spiritual nature of each student."[28] The Christian university is "by design and by its essence or core nature" an intellectual, social-spiritual ecology. Understanding this is essential to the university's commitment to personal and community transformation. To that end, the university community's ecology must be one that models the very outcomes it aspires to promote in its graduates.[29]

It appears that Redeemer and Trinity Western each emphasize an integrally Christian understanding of key aspects of the academic enterprise, reflecting their institutional traditions; in Redeemer's case the emphasis falls on the integral role of faith in scholarship, while in Trinity Western's case it falls on the integrality of the university as a community of faith. These respective

25. *The Cross and Our Calling,* Redeemer University College, 2007, p. 15.

26. For a helpful discussion of differing approaches to interpreting the role of faith learning, see Robert Sweetman, "Christian Scholarship: Two Reformed Strategies," *Perspectives* 16:6 (2001): 15.

27. *Envision the Century,* p. 12. This emphasis on spiritual formation reflects an important dimension of vision of Trinity Western's founders who, as noted previously, came from a tradition of Bible college education with an emphasis on the development of Christian character.

28. Jonathan Raymond, *Called to a Higher Purpose* (Langley, British Columbia: Trinity Western University, 2009), p. 31.

29. Raymond, *Called to a Higher Purpose,* p. 50.

emphases have significant potential to strengthen and reinforce each other in the common quest for a holistic approach in Christian higher education.[30]

Raymond explicitly links his notion of the university's social-spiritual ecology to Nicholas Wolterstorff's elaboration of a biblical understanding of shalom as human (or creaturely) flourishing. Reflecting on some of the pitfalls of understandings of higher education in his neo-Calvinist tradition, Wolterstorff proposes "educating for shalom" as a "more comprehensive, a more holistic model." He calls for an approach "that incorporates the arts, the sciences, the professions, and yes, the worship and piety of humanity, along with humanity's wounds, and brings them together into one coherent whole."[31] For Wolterstorff, the biblical idea of shalom has two important dimensions. On the one hand, shalom is a vision of a world in which every creature lives in harmony in right relationships with God and other creatures to realize the joy and well-being of all to the glory of God (as in Isaiah 65). On the other hand, shalom is an ethical imperative in a world filled with pain, suffering, and woundedness; it is a call for us to respond as ambassadors of reconciliation to the absence of shalom wherever it occurs because "we see the tears of God behind the wounds of the world."[32] In short, a passion for human flourishing and the reconciliation of all things in Christ should characterize the university's ecology and its orientation in the world.

The King's University College has built on the theme of "educating for shalom" in its efforts to articulate its identity and strategic direction:

> Shalom . . . provides the central animating idea of our mission: to provide university education that inspires and equips learners to bring renewal and reconciliation to every walk of life as followers of Jesus Christ the Servant King. Our desire is that this vision and call be reflected in all our programs

---

30. A possible way forward in connecting these emphases may be found in James K. A. Smith's challenge to envision higher education as "not primarily about the absorption of ideas and information, but about the *formation* of hearts and desires." Christian institutions have often focused on shaping a Christian mind through the (worldview-shaped) curriculum, leaving the formation of "hearts and desires" to co-curricular programs. Smith's challenge to re-vision the Christian university education as fundamentally a heart-formative rather than a mind-formative process can be understood as a call to apply Raymond's ecology metaphor to the entire academic enterprise, including the formal curriculum and scholarship as well as the "social-spiritual" context. See James K. A. Smith, *Desiring the Kingdom: Worship, Worldview and Cultural Formation* (Grand Rapids: Baker Academic, 2009).

31. Nicholas Wolterstorff, *Educating for Shalom*, ed. Clarence Joldersma and Gloria Goris Stronks (Grand Rapids: Eerdmans, 2004), p. 24.

32. Wolterstorff, *Educating for Shalom*, p. xiii.

and practices as a university. The King's University College aspires to . . . [be] an educational community that shapes the hearts and minds of its members and equips people, particularly a younger generation, for full participation in culture — developing gifts, exploring knowledge, and shaping life in the direction of restoration and renewal.[33]

This convergence of themes in these three institutions' efforts to articulate the role of faith in learning suggests an opportunity for creative and fruitful discussion across the various Christian traditions they represent. Fostering ongoing engagement with these issues should help keep Canada's relatively young Protestant Christian higher education movement conceptually sharp and strategically mindful of its distinctive mission and place in the Canadian postsecondary landscape.

Recent Developments in Canadian Catholic Higher Education

The secularization process in Canadian higher education dealt a severe blow to Catholic colleges and universities.[34] Prior to the Quiet Revolution in Quebec in the 1960s, there were three Catholic universities and forty classical colleges in the province.[35] Today the Association of Catholic Colleges and Universities of Canada has no institutional members in Quebec. Across English Canada, the erosion was serious as well. Of the thirty-two Catholic colleges, universities, and seminaries existing in English Canada in 1971, twelve no longer exist or are no longer recognizable as Catholic institutions. In 1967 Canadian Catholic university leaders joined colleagues from several other countries at a consultation in Wisconsin calling for "true autonomy and academic freedom in the face of authority of whatever kind, lay or clerical, external to the academic community itself."[36] Motivated by this spirit, many Catholic institutions weakened or severed their ties with the Catholic Church, transitioned

---

33. *Strategic Direction 2010-2015,* The King's University College, 2010, p. 7.

34. I am indebted to John Stapleton of the University of Manitoba for sharing his analysis of trends and issues confronting Catholic higher education. Stapleton is conducting research for a monograph on this subject.

35. Terence J. Fay, *A History of Canadian Catholics: Gallicanism, Romanism, and Canadianism* (Montreal: McGill-Queen's University Press, 2002), p. 279.

36. "Land O'Lakes Statement on the Nature of the Contemporary Catholic University" (position paper adopted by seminar participants, Land O'Lakes, Wisconsin, July 20-22, 1967), accessed November 25, 2011. http://consortium.villanova.edu/excorde/landlake.htm.

to lay leadership, and hired faculty without reference to a Catholic sense of mission. In some cases Catholic institutions federated with large universities experienced pressure to conform to secular priorities to maintain access to funding. In other Catholic institutions collective bargaining and labor militancy among faculty and staff undermined institutional Catholic identity. With a weakened identity, Catholic institutions lost their special appeal to Catholic students. While once it was generally assumed that Catholic students would study at Catholic universities, today the vast majority of Catholic students attend secular universities.

In Canada, as in other nations, there has been a renewed focus on the identity and mission of Catholic higher education in the last twenty-five years, sparked by the spiritual and intellectual leadership of Pope John Paul II. John Paul II addressed the mission of Catholic education in several publications, culminating in his influential Apostolic Constitution on Catholic Universities, *Ex Corde Ecclesiae* (1990). This document identified four essential characteristics of an authentically Catholic university:

- a Christian inspiration not only of individuals but of the university community as such
- a continuing reflection in the light of the Catholic faith on the growing treasury of human knowledge, to which it seeks to contribute its own research
- fidelity to the Christian message as it comes to us through the church
- institutional commitment to the service of the people of God and the human family in their pilgrimage to the transcendent goal that gives meaning to life[37]

Ex Corde Ecclesiae connected the mission of the university directly to the church's work of evangelization; the Catholic university, in its functions of research, teaching, and dialogue with culture, "is a living *institutional* witness to Christ and his message, so vitally important in cultures marked by secularism, or where Christ and his message are still virtually unknown."[38] Pope Benedict XVI carried this emphasis forward, calling for a "new evangelization," a recovery of the spiritual vitality of the early church, to address the ongoing

---

37. John Paul II, Apostolic Constitution on Catholic Universities, *Ex Corde Ecclesia* (Rome, 2009), paragraph 13, accessed November 25, 2011. http://www.vatican.va/holy_father/john_paul _ii/apost_constitutions/documents/hf_jp-ii_apc_15081990_ex-corde-ecclesiae_en.html.

38. John Paul II, *Ex Corde Ecclesia*, paragraph 49.

secularization of church and society.[39] For Benedict XVI, as for John Paul II, Catholic universities have an important role in this global mission.

In 1985 the Vatican's Congregation for Catholic Education issued a Schema on Higher Education and invited responses from the Catholic universities and bishops around the globe. In Canada this sparked a dialogue that led to the formation of the Association of Catholic Colleges and Universities of Canada (ACCUC). The ACCUC currently has twenty member institutions in seven provinces. The membership consists of:

- two free-standing (or autonomous) universities (St. Francis Xavier University in Nova Scotia and St. Thomas University in New Brunswick)
- one independent university college (St. Mary's University College in Alberta)
- ten liberal arts colleges federated or affiliated with secular universities (University of St. Michael's College at the University of Toronto, King's and Brescia University Colleges at the University of Western Ontario, Sudbury College at Laurentian University, St. Jerome's University at the University of Waterloo, St. Paul's College at the University of Manitoba, St. Thomas More College and St. Peter's College at the University of Saskatchewan, Campion College at the University of Regina, and St. Joseph's College at the University of Alberta)
- six schools of theology (Assumption College in Windsor, Ontario, Dominican University College in Ottawa, Newman Theological College in Edmonton, Regis College in Toronto, St. Mark's College in Vancouver, and St. Paul's University in Ottawa)
- one two-year liberal arts college (Corpus Christi in Vancouver)

Eleven of these institutions are members of the Association of Universities and Colleges of Canada. Two of the ACCUC member institutions (St. Mary's University College and Corpus Christi College) were founded in the past twenty-five years, inspired in part by the focus on Catholic identity and mission embodied in *Ex Corde Ecclesiae*. Two additional new small Catholic colleges have not sought membership in the ACCUC but have, interestingly, forged relationships with Protestant evangelical institutions. Redeemer Pacific is located at Trinity Western University, and Our Lady Seat of Wisdom Academy in Ontario has an affiliation agreement with Redeemer University

---

39. In 2010 Pope Benedict XVI established the Pontifical Council for the Promotion of the New Evangelization.

College. While these two institutions exist on the margins of Catholic higher education, their affiliations may point to the possibility of new forms of ecumenical collaboration in Christian higher education.

The fact that fully half of the ACCUC's members are federated or affiliated with secular universities reflects an important strategic difference between Catholic institutions and Protestant evangelical universities and colleges. The federated or affiliated Catholic institutions typically do not strive to offer full university programs. Their programs draw on areas of strength in Catholic thinking (theology, philosophy, ethics) and Catholic perspectives on social engagement (education, social work, social justice, etc.). As Michael Higgins notes,

> Federated and affiliated institutions are expected to bring a unique and valued tone, character and complementary dimension to the larger constituent sector or reality. In other words, the constituent universities . . . expect their Catholic federates or affiliates to be distinctive in mission, complementary in their educational philosophy, and not engaged in needless replication or assimilation.[40]

These institutions seek to provide a Catholic voice within the larger university, and a Catholic intellectual and social environment for university students.

The Protestant evangelical institutions, meanwhile, are less enamored with a complementarist approach, seeking instead to bring a Christian outlook and philosophy of education to bear on the entire university curriculum. Since they strive to provide an alternative to secular university education, there is little incentive to seek affiliation with another institution (and, vice versa, little incentive for a secular university to link with an institution that wants to do much of what the university itself is doing). From a Catholic "complementarist" perspective this Protestant strategy may appear to involve (in Higgins's words) "needless replication" and isolation; from a Protestant perspective the Catholic strategy may appear to cede large tracts of university education to secular thinking and to run the risk of assimilation by dominant worldviews or ideologies. This basic difference in strategy will require respectful and thoughtful consideration if Catholic and Protestant institutions venture to explore areas of collaboration in future years.

While the emergence of the ACCUC marks a renaissance in Catholic higher education, the association represents only a very small segment of Ca-

---

40. Michael Higgins, "Catholic Higher Education in Canada," in *Sciat ut Serviat,* ed. Guy Real Thivierge and Michele Jarton (Paris: Federatio Internationalis Universatatum Catholicarum, 2009), p. 236.

nadian university education as a whole. Of the twenty ACCUC members, only St. Francis Xavier University has more than four thousand students. While Catholic colleges and universities are committed to research, all of the liberal arts–type ACCUC member institutions are primarily undergraduate institutions. It is also significant that three members of the ACCUC, including both St. Francis Xavier University and St. Thomas University, have not been in a position to meet the Catholic Church's requirement to "append, adopt or integrate the Canadian Ordinances of *Ex Corde Ecclesiae*."[41] In other words, at the remaining full-fledged Catholic universities Catholic identity is the subject of considerable debate or unease as a result of previous secularizing tendencies. If the outcome of this debate is a decision not to affirm *Ex Corde Ecclesiae*, the ACCUC will lose some of its most established and nationally influential members. Without these members the ACCUC would increasingly resemble the Protestant evangelical sector in terms of the number of institutions.

Because of their long histories and/or relationships with existing universities, most ACCUC member institutions share few of the challenges faced by Protestant evangelical institutions with regard to establishing legitimacy and academic credibility. Most of the Catholic institutions receive public funding, either directly or through the host university. The federated or affiliated institutions participate actively in decision making at the host university, while the free-standing institutions are respected participants in the wider academic community. As the preceding overview indicates, however, Canadian Catholic institutions face significant challenges of their own. Prominent among these is the challenge to maintain (or rebuild) a vibrant sense of identity and mission, and to gain the support of important constituencies (e.g., faculty or government) for movement in the direction of a greater sense of Catholic identity. In the Catholic context the relationship of universities to the church presents a particular challenge; the concept of university autonomy is deeply ingrained in the academic culture, and consequently Catholic institutions that seek to forge stronger relationships with the church should anticipate turbulence.

Looking Forward: Shared Challenges in Canadian Christian Higher Education

Protestant evangelical and Catholic institutions also share important challenges. These include the absence, in both sectors, of well-developed graduate

41. Higgins, "Catholic Higher Education in Canada," p. 236.

schools to conduct advanced research that reflects their institutional missions, and to prepare a new generation of faculty members who deeply understand and are committed to those missions. This also applies to institutional leadership. Protestant evangelical and Catholic institutions, like mainstream universities, experience rapid turnover in leadership. The preparation of new presidents and deans who have vision for and are attuned to institutional mission is a task that cannot be left untended. Protestant evangelical and Catholic institutions also share the challenge of finding ways to draw a greater number of secondary school graduates to their institutions; the vast majority of Protestant evangelical and Catholic students pursue their university studies in secular environments. Even a subtle shift in these enrollment patterns would greatly enhance the viability of institutions in both sectors.

In the final analysis Protestant evangelical and Catholic universities share the task eloquently expressed by Pope John Paul II: "to be a living *institutional* witness to Christ and his message, so vitally important in cultures marked by secularism, or where Christ and his message are still virtually unknown."[42] This vision for Christian higher education transcends all denominational boundaries. Protestants and Catholics alike can gather around it in Canada and collaborate for the benefit of the gospel in the coming decades.

---

42. John Paul II, *Ex Corde Ecclesia,* paragraph 49.

CHAPTER 11

A Renaissance of Christian
Higher Education in the United States

George Marsden

For most of the twentieth century the dominant paradigm for understanding the role of religion in modern Western culture was some variation of the secularization thesis. As modern science, technology, industrialization, urbanization, cultural mobility, education, tolerance, and mass culture advanced, traditional religious faiths would recede. Modernization theory projected such trends onto the rest of the world: as Western-style modernity advanced, traditional religious faiths could be expected to give way to more cosmopolitan and secular outlooks.

In higher education, this secularization paradigm has been, if anything, even stronger and more certain. Formative studies in the 1950s on the rise of American academic freedom and of modern university discourse voiced a growing expectation in higher education that religious dimensions were not only regressive but regressing as well. By the 1960s, this assumption reigned supreme. Religious colleges and universities persisted, but they were thought to be atavistic survivors with an uncertain future.[1]

Today such seemingly commonsensical paradigms are in a state of crisis in general social theory, if not yet in higher education. While secularization theories indeed predicted a dramatic decline of the churches in most of Western Europe and Great Britain, the pattern has not followed either in the most

---

1. Richard Hostadter and Walter P. Metzger, *The Development of Academic Freedom in the United States* (New York: Columbia University Press, 1955); David Riesman, *Constraint and Variety in American Education* (Garden City, N.Y.: Doubleday, 1958); and Laurence R. Veysey, *The Emergence of the American University* (Chicago: University of Chicago Press, 1965).

highly industrialized of modern nations, the United States, or in most of the rest of the world as it has been rapidly modernizing. Both Christianity and Islam have been growing at remarkable rates and the rising prominence of Islam has made it apparent that religion remains a potent force in international politics. In the case of the growth of Christianity the shift of its center of gravity to outside the West does fit secularization/modernization theory in one respect since the rise of Christianity entails the decline of traditional local religions. Yet at the same time the types of Christianity that have been growing the fastest in the non-Western world have been distinctly traditional and supernaturalist in much of their theologies, even if often innovative in their practices. Theologically traditionalist but practically innovative Christianity, then, seems to be a sort of traditional religion that can be well adapted to modernization.[2] And indeed, as the recent International Association for the Promotion of Christian Higher Education (IAPCHE) study shows, Christian movements and traditions outside Europe and the United States have been busy founding new universities, nearly two hundred of them over the past quarter-century.[3]

Mark Noll, in *The New Shape of World Christianity*, argues that understanding the history of American Christianity is important for understanding world Christianity. He summarizes his argument as follows:

> The main point of this book is that American Christianity is important for the world primarily because the world is coming more and more to look like America. Therefore, the way that Christianity is developed in the American environment helps to explain the way Christianity is developing in many parts of the world. But the correlation is not causation: the fact that globalization and other factors have created societies that resemble in many ways what Americans experienced in the frontier period of their history does not mean that Americans are dictating to the world.[4]

2. The adaptability of Christianity is not confined to practically innovative sorts, as the growth of Roman Catholicism throughout many eras and in many circumstances, ancient and modern, including its growth in the non-Western world today, testifies. Nonetheless, the growth of the practical innovative sorts of Christianity both in the United States and in the non-Western world today is the most striking and most relevant development for the present purposes.

3. Perry L. Glanzer, Joel A. Carpenter, and Nick Lantinga, "Looking for God in the University: Examining Trends in Christian Higher Education," *Higher Education* 61:6 (2011): 721-755.

4. Mark A. Noll, *The New Shape of World Christianity: How American Experience Reflects Global Faith* (Downers Grove, Ill.: IVP Academic, 2009), p. 189.

Noll does not provide analysis of how his thesis might apply to Christian higher education, but it is worth reflecting on the extent to which it may apply. The most striking development in Christian higher education in the United States is, as we shall consider below, that there seems to be something of a renaissance in recent decades, especially in, but certainly not limited to the evangelical Protestant sector. Such a renaissance is especially notable in the way in which it counters the old secularization theory. One of the cardinal assumptions of that theory was that as higher education advanced, traditional religion would diminish. In the mid-twentieth century, at the time of the heyday of the theory, it had to be observed that in the United States traditional religion survived and even flourished. But the prevailing explanation was that it did so in cultural backwaters. Wide access to higher education, based largely on scientific models, was supposed to be one of the things that would bring such people "into the twentieth century." In fact, however, much of the growth of evangelical Christianity in the past half-century has been in suburban and high-tech areas where higher education is increasingly widespread.[5] As more and more evangelicals have become educated they have helped support and develop a network of colleges and small universities that are academically sophisticated and up to date, yet are distinctly Christian in mission. Not only have these institutions contradicted all predictions of higher education's progressive secularization, they have participated in, and perhaps in some ways helped to precipitate, a growing conversation among scholars in mainline Protestant- and Catholic-founded institutions about the role of Christian faith in higher education.[6] The presence of such academically strong Protestant colleges and universities, together with some Roman Catholic counterparts, raises the question of the extent to which these schools might, as Noll's general thesis would suggest, be setting precedents for the many Christian colleges and universities throughout the world. In this case it would not be just the experi-

---

5. Christian Smith, *American Evangelicalism: Embattled and Thriving* (Chicago: University of Chicago Press, 1998).

6. See, e.g., Andrea Sterk, ed., *Religion, Scholarship and Higher Education: Perspectives, Models and Future Prospects: Essays from the Lilly Seminar on Religion and Higher Education* (Notre Dame, Ind.: University of Notre Dame Press, 2002); Paul Dovre, ed., *The Future of Religious Colleges,* Proceedings of the Harvard Conference on the Future of Religious Colleges, October 6-7, 2000 (Grand Rapids: Eerdmans, 2002); Thomas Albert Howard, ed., *The Future of Christian Learning: An Evangelical and Catholic Dialogue* (Grand Rapids: Baker Academic, 2008); and Richard T. Hughes and William B. Adrian, *Models for Christian Higher Education: Strategies for Success in the Twenty-First Century* (Grand Rapids: Eerdmans, 1997). A very large share of this conversation has been sponsored by the Lilly Endowment.

ence of Americans in the frontier era (meaning the first half of the nineteenth century),[7] but also more recent American experience, in which evangelical Christian movements and Roman Catholic traditions have made their way as minorities in a religiously plural society, which provides a precedent. In some cases, such as the rise of Daystar University in Kenya, American involvement and influence are obvious. In many other instances, however, the case is not so clear. Nevertheless, the more recent developments of Christian higher education in the United States are themselves dependent on some precedents set in the frontier era. They also are dependent on some antecedents in American Christian higher education that suggest what to avoid. We can best understand the features of current American Christian higher education by first stepping back and looking at the larger history of the enterprise, first the Protestant side, and then the Roman Catholic experience.[8]

The most evident reason why American Protestant higher education has been so resilient in recent decades is the same as the reason why American evangelicalism in general has been so resilient: it is adapted to the American atmosphere of free enterprise in religion. This pattern took shape during the first half of the nineteenth century, or what Noll calls the frontier era. Disestablishment of the churches meant that religion was placed on a voluntary principle from early in the nation's history. Already the extended Great Awakening of the colonial era had proved that the voluntary principle was a source of religious vitality. In the half-century or so following the American Revolution America developed a thriving, diverse, competitive free-market religious economy marked by extensive popular revivals that have become collectively known as the "Second Great Awakening."

Disestablishment and the diverse (even if mostly Protestant) free-market economy had important and lasting effects on the structure of American higher education. Diversity made it no longer feasible for the state to sponsor only one sort of denominational education as had been true in Great Britain and some of the American colonies. Yet American higher education in its early years still had both public and religious functions. In the middle of the nineteenth century the overwhelming majority of college presidents were clergymen, even at state universities. This mix of Protestant religion and pub-

---

7. Joel Carpenter points to historic echoes from that era. See his essay, "The Christian Scholar in an Age of World Christianity," in *Christianity and the Soul of the University*, ed. Douglas V. Henry and Michael D. Beaty (Grand Rapids: Baker Academic, 2006), pp. 73-74.

8. Documentation for the summary that follows can be found in George M. Marsden, *The Soul of the American University: From Established Protestantism to Established Nonbelief* (New York: Oxford University Press, 1994).

lic service in higher education meant that enterprising religious leaders who wished to found a Protestant college could often expect to gain support, including government support, from the local community. The sheer size of the expanding American frontier helped foster this highly decentralized system of higher education. Anyone with enough energy and support could found a college. At first the leadership came largely from Congregationalists and Presbyterians who had a strong educational tradition and a sense of mission to bring Protestant civilization to the expanding West. Before long, however, these were joined by more populist religious groups, such as the Methodists, Disciples of Christ, and Baptists, which as they became more middle class wished to establish their own colleges.[9] Meanwhile Roman Catholics, whose numbers were swelled by immigration after 1840, were establishing their own network of colleges as alternatives to the dominant Protestant education.[10] So the precedents were established: American higher education would be immensely decentralized and diverse and religious groups were free to establish and maintain schools of their own liking almost wherever and whenever they wanted. We may contrast that with the Canadian model in which higher education fell more under the guidance of the provinces and the major denominations and there was much less proliferation of sectarian institutions. In the United States, many of the nineteenth-century Protestant colleges had a quasi-public function (and state schools had religious functions), but any sectarian or churchly group not satisfied with the available alternatives was free to establish its own institutions as well.

The dual public/religious character of most colleges and universities in the United States, as attractive as that was in the era before the American Civil War when Protestantism was the dominant religion, had significant unforeseen consequences during the eras that followed. Since a Protestant ethos could be taken for granted in most of the country in the era before the Civil War, these colleges made little effort to engage in what today is called the "integration of faith and learning." They did typically have one capstone course on "moral philosophy" taught by the clergyman-president, but other than that they largely relied on the good influences of required chapel and took for granted that the

9. This story is well told in its institutional dimensions by William C. Ringenberg, *The Christian College: A History of Protestant Higher Education in America,* 2nd ed. (Grand Rapids: Baker Academic, 2006). Timothy L. Smith, *Uncommon Schools: Christian Colleges and Social Idealism in Midwestern America, 1820-1950* (Bloomington: Indiana Historical Society, 1978), is especially good on the visions and values that drove this movement.

10. The must-read here is Philip Gleason's magisterial history: *Contending with Modernity: Catholic Higher Education in the Twentieth Century* (New York: Oxford University Press, 1995).

natural sciences and the classical arts could be assumed to be in harmony with Christian teachings.

With the rise of research universities in the era following the Civil War into the first half of the twentieth century the place of religion in America's leading schools changed dramatically. The era was marked by industrial growth, technological expansion, urbanization, and rapidly increasing ethnic and religious diversity. The new universities were increasingly shaped by scientific and technological interests and their missions were to serve the whole nation rather than parochial interests. The research ideal emphasized free inquiry, meaning free from ideological biases, and was based largely on the natural scientific model of considering only natural factors in one's inquiries. Most universities still had a Protestant heritage and so were in principle sympathetic to religious concerns. Since universities were now seen as essentially public non-sectarian institutions, however, if religion touched the curriculum it was typically reduced to moral principles[11] (as it often was in Protestant modernism), and seen as serving a function of promoting shared public moral values. The literature and art of Western civilization were often presented as a bearer of this shared moral heritage.[12] It was fine if some students and faculty might hold more traditional and sectarian religious views, but these were regarded as essentially personal and private matters that normally would have no overt bearing in the public domain of mainstream academia.

The secularization of the mainstream universities was thus part of a larger process of the privatization of traditional and exclusivist religious beliefs in twentieth-century American culture. Not all of the culture was secularizing, but the public culture was, excepting in some formal and symbolic ways. The highest education was defined as part of the public domain, so that sectarian religious views were regarded as out of place in classrooms or research. But religion of any sort was still free to flourish in the private domain.

During the first two-thirds of the twentieth century, when this privatization was secularizing formerly Protestant universities, mainstream Protestant denominations retained hundreds of their own colleges that had been founded during the nineteenth century. These colleges were still sufficiently "private" to be able to offer the particulars of their denominational heritage, especially in religion courses, and to retain chapel and support for personal religious belief.

---

11. See Julie A. Reuben, *The Making of the Modern University: Intellectual Transformation and the Marginalization of Morality* (Chicago: University of Chicago Press, 1996).

12. See James Turner's discussion of the humanities in Jon H. Roberts and James Turner, *The Sacred and the Secular University* (Princeton, N.J.: Princeton University Press, 2000).

At the same time, true to their nineteenth-century heritage, they typically saw themselves as public to the degree of being open to diverse student bodies and offering more intimate versions of the university curriculum. After the cultural upheaval of the 1960s, which among other things brought attacks on Protestant privilege, most of these schools gravitated toward the public part of their missions. In most cases the particulars of the denominational heritage became vestigial and religious concerns centered on public morality and tolerance. Faculty hiring involved no religious tests, so faculties became nearly as diverse as at state schools, and the curricula remained based on university models reflecting almost exclusively public concerns.[13]

Meanwhile American Roman Catholic schools were on a different trajectory. Like Protestants, Catholics founded hundreds of colleges and universities. Even though since the mid-nineteenth century Catholicism had been the largest single denomination in the United States, it was a minority group among Protestants who were not only collectively more numerous but had a longstanding grip on most political and cultural power. The Roman Catholic Church in America had therefore to act somewhat like a sectarian group, despite its announced aspirations to cultural dominance. Catholic higher education in America accordingly was marked by a strongly defensive posture. To be Catholic was to be set apart and through the first two-thirds of the twentieth century Catholics marked such differences visibly by displaying religious symbols or engaging in distinctive practices such as eating fish on Fridays. Such cultural separatism was also embodied in an entire network of separate institutions, from parochial schools to hospitals. In that era no one could mistake a Catholic campus, both because of its statuary and the presence of many priests or nuns on the faculties wearing their distinctive garb. Such distinctiveness was reinforced by the militantly defensive stance of international Catholicism against modern secular thought. In response to secularism the church revived the philosophy of Thomas Aquinas and this neo-Thomism provided an all-encompassing philosophical framework for a distinctly Catholic view of things. By the 1950s, leading Catholic intellectuals were complaining that the ready-made intellectual formulae of neo-Thomism invited anti-intellectualism and cultural isolation and helped account for Catholics' relative lack of attainment in American intellectual life.

In the 1960s the combination of the wider acceptance of Catholicism as symbolized by the election of John F. Kennedy, the migration of many Cath-

---

13. Douglas Sloan, *Faith and Knowledge: Mainline Protestantism and American Higher Education* (Louisville, Ky.: Westminster John Knox, 1994), traces mainline Protestant efforts to reassert a religious purpose for higher education in the 1950s and its rapid demise in the 1960s.

olics from ethnic neighborhoods to suburbs, the emerging cultural upheavals of the era, and the new openness in the Catholic Church sparked by Vatican II brought the neo-Thomist synthesis crashing down and launched Catholic higher education on a new course. The main direction of this course was toward acceptance in the American intellectual and cultural mainstream. In that respect they were following the direction charted by formerly Protestant schools. Faculty hiring was increasingly opened to persons of all viewpoints, thus diminishing Catholic presence that was already diminished by a sharp decline in religious vocations and numbers of priests and nuns on faculties. But unlike most mainline Protestant schools, American Catholic schools of the later twentieth century were only decades away from an era (the 1950s) when they had a very strong baseline of conspicuous religious identity. Some were shaped substantially by impulses to escape that strong Catholic identity. At the same time most Catholic schools retained some Catholic presence by still having some members of religious orders on their faculties. They also offered opportunities for formal Catholic worship, a not incidental factor in a tradition in which practice is the pre-eminent mark of being faithful. Furthermore, religious orders still retained, though in varying degrees, some governing influence at Catholic schools, so that those concerned to preserve "Catholic identity" might have administrative support that would counter the inevitable erosion of identity that would result from purely open hiring practices.[14]

The result of all these factors is that by the early twenty-first century, although there are some 250 schools listed as members of the Association of Catholic Colleges and Universities, these cover a wide spectrum with respect to Catholic identity. At one end of the spectrum are Catholic schools in which the Catholic identity has become largely vestigial so that they "resemble once and formally Protestant institutions that have become functionally secular."[15] At such schools the word "Catholic" will not be apparent or in any easily accessible place on the school's website.[16] At the other end of the spectrum are mostly smaller schools, such as Ave Maria University, Christendom College, and Franciscan University of Steubenville,[17] which in recent decades have been founded or reshaped by a dedication to recovering the strongly traditionalist

---

14. Gleason, *Contending with Modernity*, is the definitive account here.

15. Mark Noll, "Reconsidering Christendom?" in Mark A. Noll and James Turner, *The Future of Christian Learning: An Evangelical and Catholic Dialogue* (Grand Rapids: Brazos Press, 2008), p. 53.

16. "Least Catholic Catholic Schools," *First Things* 207 (November 2010): 21.

17. These are the top three listed by *First Things* 207 as "Most Catholic Catholic Schools," p. 20.

Catholicism faithful to papal teachings. These colleges hire only Catholic faculty and shape everything around cultivating a distinct and (in the American context) sectarian religious identity.[18] In the middle are those, of whom the University of Notre Dame is the best known, which have tried to steer a middle course. On the one hand, they have made efforts to become fully accepted in the academic and intellectual mainstream and have been open to hiring faculty of other faiths or who profess no faith. On the other hand, they have made strenuous efforts to retain a substantial Catholic identity. In the case of Notre Dame those efforts have included a policy that at least half of the faculty should be committed Catholics.[19]

In the meantime another type of Protestant college and university has risen to prominence in American church-related higher education. These are the evangelical or "Christian" colleges most easily identified as the more than one hundred members of the Council for Christian Colleges and Universities (CCCU). The origins of almost all these schools are in denominations or religious movements outside the mainline Protestantism that long dominated American higher education. Most have origins in smaller Protestant groups, such as Holiness, Pentecostal, or fundamentalist churches that during the twentieth century were shaped by sharp dissent against the inclusivism of mainline Protestantism and against secular trends in the culture. Quite a few originated as Bible colleges. Others, such as Mennonite or Christian Reformed, represented ethno-religious enclaves that defined themselves in part by their stances in respect to the mainstream culture and its Protestant denominations. Southern Baptists also often had a comparably conservative regional-religious character. A few have mainline Protestant origins, mostly Presbyterian, and represent conservative movements within the mainstream.

A half-century ago this segment of American higher education appeared marginal and beleaguered. Christopher Jencks and David Riesman in their classic study *The Academic Revolution,* published in 1968, described them as "holdouts" whose futures looked "bleak" and whose survival depended on social conditions that would continue to allow them to define themselves by their protests against mainstream cultural trends.[20] Jencks and Riesman were

18. Noll, "Reconsidering Christendom," p. 53. I am following his typology.

19. See *The Challenge and Promise of a Catholic University,* ed. Theodore M. Hesburgh, C.S.S. (Notre Dame, Ind.: University of Notre Dame Press, 1994), for reflections on Notre Dame's ongoing efforts. See also James Turner's contributions to *The Future of Christian Learning.*

20. Christopher Jencks and David Riesman, *The Academic Revolution* (New York: Doubleday, 1968), pp. 328 and 333.

looking at these schools through the lens of the secularization thesis in which modernization was an inexorable secularizing cultural force and the survival of holdouts had to be explained. Ironically, many of these colleges were defined by their own version of a secularization thesis. While most did not oppose modernization as such (they had no trouble adopting the latest technology, for instance) they did believe that the mainstream culture was steadily sliding in an alarming secular direction and that it was their duty to defend the faith by standing against these trends. Unlike most mainstream Protestant colleges that in the earlier twentieth century had been comfortable being both Christian in their interests and yet part of the cultural mainstream, most of these evangelical schools were marked by a distinctly sectarian DNA.

What Jencks and Riesman could not have anticipated in the 1960s was a small renaissance in evangelical higher education beginning in the latter decades of the twentieth century. The overarching reason for this resurgence was the resilience of evangelicalism itself. In 1967 William McLoughlin, a leading historian of American religion, published an influential article in *Daedalus,* "Is There a Third Force in Christendom?" His answer was that the many evangelical groups, including burgeoning Pentecostals, were essentially conservative and reactionary rather than the leading edge of the wave of the future.[21] We can now see that that was wrong both regarding the United States and world Christianity. Evangelicalism in its countless varieties has become the most prominent segment of American Christianity. Evangelicalism's strength has been accompanied by rising affluence among many of its constituents and hence rising levels of academic attainment. As more evangelicals have become college-educated more have become interested in building their own educational institutions that can compete with secular universities, at least on the undergraduate level. Furthermore, increasing numbers of evangelical college graduates meant that more evangelicals were going on to graduate schools in pursuit of academic vocations. That in turn meant that, in the perpetually tight academic marketplace of recent decades, aspiring evangelical colleges could assemble excellent faculties that were both committed to evangelical faith and could compete with the academic mainstream.[22]

21. William G. McLoughlin, "Is There a Third Force in Christendom?" *Daedalus* 96:1 (Winter 1967): 43-68.

22. Christian Smith, *American Evangelicalism: Embattled and Thriving* (Chicago: University of Chicago Press, 1998), traces the upward social and educational mobility of American evangelicals; for trends among evangelicals in higher education, see Paul Dovre, ed., *The Future of Religious Colleges,* Proceedings of the Harvard Conference on the Future of Religious Colleges, October 6-7, 2000 (Grand Rapids: Eerdmans, 2002), e.g., R. Judson Carlberg, "The

These changes that were driven in part by socioeconomic factors were accompanied by an intellectual renaissance. As recently as 1994 Mark Noll could publish *The Scandal of the Evangelical Mind,* which famously begins with the remark that "The scandal of the evangelical mind is that there is not much of an evangelical mind."[23] Noll lamented a long-standing anti-intellectualism that was characteristic of most of American evangelicalism. That anti-intellectualism was related to the populist and market-driven characteristics of the movement. Simple dichotomies and simplistic formulas preached better than did complexities and helped promote evangelical numerical growth. The fundamentalist controversies of the twentieth century reinforced these tendencies by accentuating defensive stances and simple dichotomies between secularists or liberals on the one hand and true Christians on the others. Often these dichotomies helped foster deep distrust of mainstream higher education and all contemporary intellectual trends. Twentieth-century evangelical higher education was often marked by a Bible school mentality of cultivating only those intellectual pursuits directly useful for promoting the faith and by a defensiveness regarding contemporary intellectual and cultural life.[24]

Even by the time Noll published his lament, there were many signs that the situation was changing, if not in evangelicalism as a whole, at least in some significant parts. Universities and colleges of the CCCU, the increasingly strong faculties they were assembling, and evangelicals scattered throughout other church-related and mainstream academia were affirming "the integration of faith and learning." That project involved engaging the latest intellectual and cultural trends not solely from a defensive point of view but also with a view toward appropriating the best from contemporary intellectual and cultural

---

Evangelical Vision: From Fundamentalist Isolation to Respected Voice," pp. 224-245. See also Robert Benne, *Quality with Soul: How Six Premier Colleges and Universities Keep Faith with Their Religious Traditions* (Grand Rapids: Eerdmans, 2001), which compares evangelical Protestant Wheaton and Calvin with Catholic Notre Dame, Lutheran Valparaiso and St. Olaf, and Baptist Baylor.

23. Mark A. Noll, *The Scandal of the Evangelical Mind* (Grand Rapids: Eerdmans, 1994), p. 3.

24. Virginia Lieson Brereton, *Training God's Army: The American Bible School, 1880-1940* (Bloomington: Indiana University Press, 1990), reveals both the practical success and the cultural and intellectual shortcomings of evangelical Bible colleges. More traditional liberal arts colleges run by evangelicals in the first half of the twentieth century did not fare much better. See Michael Hamilton, "The Fundamentalist Harvard: Wheaton College and the Enduring Vitality of American Evangelicalism, 1919-1965" (Ph.D. dissertation, University of Notre Dame, 1994).

life as means of strengthening and deepening evangelical understandings of all aspects of God's creation.

The project of "integrating faith and learning" was derived not so much from the heritage of American evangelicalism as from the Reformed heritage of Abraham Kuyper. Kuyper's views, formulated in the late nineteenth century in the Netherlands, were among other things better adapted to modern pluralism than were most American evangelical outlooks. The early-nineteenth-century American evangelical experience had been shaped in the context of cultural dominance. The prevailing assumption had been that, even though it was important that individuals convert to Christianity, the principles of Christianity and the principles of mainstream American democratic culture could be largely co-extensive. Natural science and scientific thinking in general were considered to be objective and in harmony with Christianity if rightly understood. When, after Darwin, natural science and most other modern thought turned against traditional Christianity, biblicist evangelicals were left on the defensive. They retreated into Bible institutes and fundamentalist colleges, even while occasionally making forays into the cultural mainstream, most notably in crusades against the teaching of biological evolution in America's public schools, as though they were going to "take back" their control of the mainstream culture. What was lacking in twentieth-century fundamentalistic evangelism was any adequate theory about the proper relationship between Christianity and pluralistic culture. Evangelicals alternated between closed defensive postures and rhetoric about "winning" America.

In the meantime the Kuyperian outlook had developed in a Dutch setting in which Kuyper recognized that various sorts of Protestantism (especially liberal and traditional), Roman Catholicism, and various secular viewpoints all had legitimate claims to participate in the cultural mainstream. Furthermore, their differences were not going to be resolved by some sort of objective adjudication that all right-thinking people would agree on. Rather, as Kuyper famously put it, since there are "two kinds of people," regenerate and unregenerate, there are "two kinds of science."[25] Hence Christians could be fully engaged with the modern sciences and with modern intellect and culture without illusions that everyone would be persuaded by their views. Furthermore, Christians operated with the recognition that every square inch of reality was

25. Kuyper explains his view in *Principles of Sacred Theology*, trans. J. Hendrik De Vries (Grand Rapids: Baker Book House, 1980 [1898]), pp. 150-159. For a fuller exposition of the difference of this position from that of American traditions, see George Marsden, "The Evangelical Love Affair with Enlightenment Science," in Marsden, *Understanding Fundamentalism and Evangelicalism* (Grand Rapids: Eerdmans, 1991), pp. 222-252.

God's creation and they ought to be engaged with understanding it all and using it for its right purposes. Hence Kuyperianism provided a way of understanding in a pluralistic setting how Christians ought to be "in the world but not of the world." They were to be fully engaged with the culture, yet always with a sense of difference — a Christian perspective. Moreover, Kuyperianism emphasized that these principles needed institutional embodiment. It would not do simply to rely on public institutions and hope that Christian principles would prevail or at least somehow survive. Rather it was part of the Christian mission to the world to build educational institutions that were shaped by distinctive perspectives.

Such outlooks proved well suited to the American evangelical environment of the late twentieth and early twenty-first centuries. Kuyperianism was not, of course, the only factor shaping the outlook of the CCCU colleges; each had its own heritage and some, such as the Mennonite colleges, offered substantial alternative approaches to higher education. Yet the Kuyperian ideals — of "integration of faith and learning" and developing "Christian perspectives" within communities shaped by committed Christian faculties that can offer holistic education — have become pervasive among evangelical colleges. These commitments undergird their aim to prepare graduates who fully engage a complex, high-tech, pluralistic world.[26]

If we are evaluating Mark Noll's thesis in *The New Shape of World Christianity* that the American evangelical models developed in the frontier era, or the nineteenth century, provide important precedents for more recent world Christianity, the argument should be modified regarding at least one aspect of higher education. The nineteenth-century American model of religious free enterprise, including the founding of educational institutions, is indeed relevant. But the characteristic of the nineteenth-century American precedents that does not fit global Christianity today is that the United States had been a predominantly Protestant culture. Hence much of American Protestant higher education was built on the premise that firm lines of demarcation did not have to be developed between the interests of Christianity and the interests of a modernizing culture. In the twentieth century that led much of mainstream Protestant higher education to let down its guard, as it opened its hiring to faculty who had no Christian commitments and perspectives. Inevitably that

26. Joel A. Carpenter, "The Perils of Prosperity: Neo-Calvinism and the Future of Religious Colleges," in *The Future of Religious Colleges,* Proceedings of the Harvard Conference on the Future of Religious Colleges, October 6-7, 2000, ed. Paul Dovre (Grand Rapids: Eerdmans, 2002), pp. 185-207, shows that these views eventually pervaded the broader evangelical college network.

GEORGE MARSDEN

change led to the disappearance of Christian outlooks on those campuses. In most places around the world today, the experience of American evangelicals in the later twentieth century, which recognized the realities of an irretrievably pluralistic culture and intellectual outlook, seems more relevant. It points to the advantages of building institutions that are both not only deeply involved with studying modern culture, but also fully committed to distinctly Christian perspectives. Christian institutions of higher learning need to be fully engaged with modern culture, but they need also to cultivate some sectarian sense that to be Christian involves being frankly set apart from the cultural mainstream.

Striking that balance between cultural engagement and maintaining distinct Christian identity is one of the great challenges for Christian higher education in modernized societies. As we have seen, earlier denominational American colleges that defined themselves primarily as "public" institutions in the sense of serving the wider culture eventually came simply to adopt the standards of the culture and hence lost their distinctive Christian perspectives. Fundamentalistic schools, by way of contrast, defined themselves as so strictly set apart from the cultural mainstream that they became dedicated to more thoroughly "private" concerns of developing Christian character, individual skills, and tools for evangelism and missions. The balance is to be found in some version of the formula of being "in the world and not of the world." Among the essential tasks to which Christian communities are called is that of engaging and serving the larger communities of which they are a part. To do that they must remain distinctly Christian communities, keeping some standards that set them apart. But at the same time one of the most important functions of Christian *educational* communities is to point the way toward constructive engagement with the rest of the world both through service and explicit witness.[27]

The CCCU represents, of course, only one small segment of American Christian higher education. It has been, however, the fastest growing. From 1990 to 2004, all public four-year campuses in the United States grew by about 13 percent, and all independent four-year campuses (including many schools with broad religious or denominational connections) grew by about 28 percent. But schools associated with the CCCU grew by nearly 71 percent.[28] According to statistics from 2010, there are a total of 900 self-reported religiously affiliated

27. For a helpful exposition of the varying strategies by which today's Protestant and Catholic institutions balance Christian identity and cultural engagement, see Benne, *Quality with Soul.*

28. From Council of Christian Colleges and Universities website, January 2009.

270

institutions in the United States. They make up about 22 percent of the total number of American colleges and universities, and they enroll approximately 1.7 million students, or about 9 percent of the nation's 19 million post-secondary students. Of the 900, 255 are Roman Catholic, 150 are seminaries, and 200 are Bible colleges. According to the CCCU website, which has compiled these statistics, about 100 others are "fairly intentional about integrating faith and mission," and about another 100 "essentially have neglected their faith mission." Apparently, the schools in the "fairly intentional" group must vary widely in degree of commitment. For instance, Bob Jones University and Liberty University would be in this grouping since they are not among the 111 CCCU schools. They would be very strongly intentional in relating faith to learning and would be close to the Bible colleges in degree of commitment. At the other end of this spectrum would be schools that still have a denominational affiliation but no commitment to integrating faith and mission beyond some offerings in religion courses and voluntary chapel. A significant group in the middle would be those ninety-four schools affiliated with the Lilly National Network of Church-Related Colleges and Universities, which promotes a collaborative effort to "explore and discuss the relationship of Christianity to the academic vocation, and strengthen the religious nature of church-related institutions through a variety of activities and publications." Centered at Valparaiso University, the Lilly Network (with ninety-four members in 2011) includes some CCCU schools, but many more that are not, including a sizeable number of Lutheran schools, other mainline Protestant schools, and Roman Catholic schools. One notable difference between the CCCU and the Lilly Network is that the CCCU requires that schools hire only Christians for full-time faculty and administrative positions while the Lilly Network does not.

The vitality of each of these groups is part of the larger renaissance of developing Christian perspectives in a pluralistic world. Christian higher education in the United States is not confined to specifically Christian institutions. The same forces that have brought excellent faculties to Christian colleges and universities have also brought increasing, even if relatively small, numbers of committed Christian faculty into the academic mainstream of essentially secular institutions.[29]

29. Two recent sociological studies trace the rise of evangelical intellectuals within secular academe and beyond. See John Schmalzbauer, *People of Faith: Religious Conviction in American Journalism and Higher Education* (Ithaca, N.Y.: Cornell University Press, 2003), and D. Michael Lindsey, *Faith in the Halls of Power: How Evangelicals Joined the American Elite* (New York: Oxford University Press, 2007). Lindsey surveys the state of evangelical intellectual life generally, pp. 75-113.

Despite these evidences of the burgeoning of distinctly Christian institutions and scholarship in recent decades, one needs to step back and get a realistic view of its relationship to American higher education as a whole. As noted above, all of the 900 religiously affiliated institutions combined enroll only approximately 1.7 million (or less than 10 percent) of a total of the approximately 19 million students enrolled at degree-granting institutions of higher learning in the United States. That 1.7 million is about one-third of the enrollment at all private colleges and universities. So the reality is that more than two-thirds of American students attend government institutions at which it is difficult, though not impossible, to relate Christianity to scholarship in any substantial way. That difficulty is compounded by the fact that during the twentieth century the federal government invested huge amounts in higher education for technical research, so that most of higher education is oriented toward technical areas. Furthermore, something like two-thirds of all students take degrees in career-oriented fields rather than in the traditional arts and sciences.[30] The percentage of those majoring in the humanities (where Christian perspectives have traditionally made the most conspicuous difference) has been in single digits.[31]

These statistics point to another of the great challenges to Christian higher education in modernizing societies. Contemporary societies are increasingly defined by technological concerns and interests. "Technological" in this sense means (as Jacques Ellul long ago suggested) not only learning the skills to engage technology, but also whole realms of endeavor. One of the largest and most prevalent of these is everyday commerce, which is increasingly driven by the demands of developing the most rational and efficient techniques for maximizing profits. Massive resources and energies are also poured into understanding and controlling the natural world as in the areas of natural science, engineering, and medicine. Even sports and leisure are often dominated by research-driven efforts to perfect winning techniques and equipment. In these technological frameworks that shape so much of contemporary culture, higher education comes to be viewed increasingly as an economic exchange. Educational consumers invest in obtaining technical skills that will later have

30. "Trends in Undergraduate Career Education," National Center for Educational Statistics, Issue Brief, March 2005, pp. 1-3. At the baccalaureate level the career fields figure in 2000-2001 was 60 percent, and 71 percent at the sub-baccalaureate. These figures had actually dropped from 66 percent and 78 percent respectively in 1984-1985.

31. The humanities figure is 8 to 9 percent, about half of that of the late 1960s. *Inside Higher Education*, website, October 1, 2010, "Liberal Arts I: They Keep Chugging Along," by W. Robert Connor and Cheryl Ching.

practical payoffs, most easily measured in economic terms. Clearly, the more higher education is defined in such technological-economic terms, the more difficult it becomes for Christian perspectives to play a substantial role. Most particularly, if exposure to the humanities and even the more critically attuned social sciences disappears from most students' higher education, then it is unlikely that those students will have substantial opportunities to gain broadly humane, not to mention Christian, perspectives from their collegiate experience.

On the positive side, however, these trends point toward some focused opportunities for Christian higher education today. In the United States, even though Christian higher education represents only a small segment of all higher education, it trains at least a more considerable portion of the one-third of students whose degrees are in the traditional arts and sciences. Furthermore, even in the traditional arts and sciences, much of secular undergraduate education today suffers from an incoherence that is perhaps inevitable in a highly pluralistic environment. True to the technological nature of the contemporary world, professors are trained in the narrow specialties of their sub-disciplines and are rewarded for specialized publications more than for excellence in undergraduate education. Not only are the arts and sciences of huge state universities shaped by such trends, but even some of the best of private secular undergraduate institutions suffer from them as well. One striking example is provided by Harry Lewis, the former academic dean of Harvard College, who questions whether even Harvard undergraduates get a coherent education. In his recent book, *Excellence without a Soul,* Lewis reflects on what he sees as a lamentable decline in Harvard undergraduate education since the time when he was an undergraduate in the early 1960s. Lewis says that both faculty and students measure higher education largely in terms of advancing their own careers and that, as a result, the college does very little toward contributing to what used to be a major goal of undergraduate education, that is, to "transform teenagers . . . into adults with the learning and wisdom to take responsibility for their own lives."[32] In such a context, Christian higher education provides an attractive alternative for that part of the population that has traditional views of what collegiate education ought to involve, that is, if they are looking for an undergraduate experience that offers community and intellectual coherence,

32. Harry Lewis, *Excellence without a Soul: How a Great University Forgot Education* (New York: Public Affairs, 2006), p. xiv. Also see Anthony T. Kronman, *Education's End: Why Our Colleges and Universities Have Given Up on the Meaning of Life* (New Haven, Conn.: Yale University Press, 2007).

and helps to broadly prepare young people for lives of service and accomplishment. In other words, at its best, it can offer excellence with soul.

Finally, American Christian colleges and universities provide some suggestive examples of pluralistic higher education in a pluralistic world. Because American higher education has been so decentralized, and because so much of it had religious roots, it has been relatively successful to date in resisting standardization that would be prejudicial to religiously defined institutions. Ever since the early twentieth century, pressures for such standardization have been considerable, coming in the name of science, academic freedom, and separation of church and state, and in the interests of promoting diversity itself. Considerable voices in academia proclaim that religiously-defined higher education is by definition inferior to secular higher education. Phi Beta Kappa, for instance, has a policy of denying chapters of that prestigious honor society to schools that have religious requirements for the hiring of faculty. During the twentieth century the American Association of University Professors, the chief agency promoting academic freedom, sometimes regarded schools with religious restrictions in hiring as thereby being second-class academic institutions. Nonetheless, despite such pressures, the prevailing view has come to be that so long as schools have made their religious restrictions clear, they are free to operate within such self-imposed bounds.[33] Accrediting agencies recognize this same principle of mission-driven variety and pluralism. Government agencies likewise have generally acknowledged the right of schools to use religious criteria for hiring, despite some strong pressures to declare that religiously based restrictions should be banned on the grounds that they violate nondiscrimination laws.[34] Especially strong are efforts to deny such nondiscrimination exemptions to religious institutions that would refuse to hire openly practicing gays and lesbians for faculty and administrative positions. Nonetheless, to date, most courts and legislatures have recognized the right for "conscience exemptions" on such issues, not only due to long-standing

33. Indeed, in recent years the AAUP has sponsored several conferences to entertain fresh perspectives on religion's role in higher education. There appears to be some growing appreciation for religious institutions in these circles. Mary Burgan, the retired general secretary of the AAUP, cited Calvin College as an example of how faculty can exercise intellectual, moral, and institutional authority in an era when faculty authority has been deeply eroded. She finds Calvin's case to be doubly remarkable, in that it comes from a seriously religious college. Burgan, *Whatever Happened to the Faculty? Drift and Decision in Higher Education* (Baltimore: Johns Hopkins University Press, 2006), pp. 205-206.

34. I have discussed these issues in greater detail in *The Soul of the American University* and in *The Outrageous Idea of Christian Scholarship* (New York: Oxford University Press, 1997).

American regard for freedom of conscience but also probably in no small part due to deference to the size and strength of Roman Catholic institutions.[35]

Ironically, arguments to restrict distinctive religious views and practices are often made in the name of diversity. Those who make such arguments believe that every institution in American society should be open to the same sorts of diversity as is public life. But the irony is that such well-meant objectives amount to a latter-day version of the melting-pot ideal. In effect, the ideal is that distinctively religious institutions ought to be assimilated into mainstream American life and become essentially alike, except that they might have some added religious options on the side. In higher education such ideals would mean that religious criteria could not be used in hiring faculty or administrators. If such a pursuit of "diversity" were followed to its conclusion, faculties would all reflect the ideological profile of the American professoriate in general. Schools that formerly had been defined by distinctly religious stances would become internally more diverse than they are now, but their ideological outlooks would become virtually indistinguishable from each other and from those of state-run schools.

A far more constructive way of promoting diversity and multiculturalism is to foster diversity among institutions. Part of the genius of the American experiment has grown out of the fact that from the beginning the nation was remarkably diverse, both ethnically and religiously. Even though at first most of the religious groups were Protestant, the many divisions within Protestantism had the beneficial societal effect of forcing recognition that the state ought to encourage "free exercise" and freedom of conscience in the shaping of religious institutions. In the United States this principle has meant that although the state has interests in regulating practices that might endanger the health and safety of its citizens, so far as is possible it should try to let religious communities live by their own standards. That has meant, among other things, that religious communities should be free to build educational institutions that would be defined by their distinctive religious beliefs and practices. Such educational institutions have performed important functions of helping to preserve distinct ethno-religious communities (as well as religious communities that are ethnically multicultural) over the course of generations. Without such communities, the nation would be culturally less diverse.

The American model, which indeed took its shape in the frontier era of the

---

35. Catholic universities, such as Notre Dame, may be open to hiring gays and lesbians for some, but not all positions. They have been allowed to resist including "sexual orientation" in their nondiscrimination statements in job advertisements.

early nineteenth century, can provide a precedent for maintaining diversity in the contemporary world in which almost every nation includes a multiplicity of ethnic and religious groups. Encouraging such diversity can be good both for the religious groups and for the nation. In the American case, religious groups have benefited from being free to develop their own distinctive religious institutions, and these are instrumental in passing belief from generation to generation. Such religious communities have been among the major contributors to the moral capital that is necessary to cultivating a law-abiding citizenry who will play by the rules in a democratic society.

Religiously based educational institutions, furthermore, can also be important contributors toward helping their supporting religious communities grow beyond narrowly sectarian, inward-looking, and partisan interests. In the United States, for instance, one of the problems with market-driven religion is that it is susceptible to simplistic populist either/or formulas that are not only anti-intellectual, but also which cultivate simplistic "us" and "them" mentalities. If, however, such communities are encouraged to develop their own distinctive higher education, that education can have moderating influences. Especially once that education matures and, for instance, embraces broader traditions of the liberal arts, it will be training more people in religious communities to be considering how they can serve the wider public good in ways that go beyond their efforts to make converts. The growth of the schools of the CCCU and similar religiously based colleges and universities in the United States provides examples of how such maturity can be achieved without sacrificing the essentials of particular faiths. Public officials and even secularists who may be distrustful of strongly religious communities ought to consider the ways it serves the public interest to permit and even to promote religiously based institutional diversity in higher education.

Evaluating the Health of Christian Higher Education around the Globe

Perry L. Glanzer and Joel Carpenter

Christian universities occupy a dynamic niche, both in higher education and in Christian institutional life. They seem to follow some of the same general trends that mark the growth and location of Christian churches around the world.[1] If Christian higher education continues to expand, both in enrollments and in number of universities, its main growth, like that of the churches, will lie outside Western Europe and North America. Over the past two decades institutional growth in Christian higher education has slowed to a trickle in the West, but in places such as Eastern Europe, Asia, and Africa, it has taken off. In Africa alone, more Christian universities have been organized over the past decade than have commenced in all of the rest of the world. In other cases, the type of growth is changing. Latin America is seeing the growth of more Protestant universities than ever before, as rising Protestant movements there mature and take on more institutional tasks. There are now more Lutheran and Presbyterian universities in Latin America than in Europe.[2] And

---

1. For scholarship about the growth patterns of global Christianity, see Lamin Sanneh, *Whose Religion Is Christianity? The Gospel beyond the West* (Grand Rapids: Eerdmans, 2003); Philip Jenkins, *The Next Christendom: The Coming of Global Christianity*, rev. ed. (New York: Oxford University Press, 2007); Mark A. Noll, *The New Shape of World Christianity: How American Experience Reflects Global Faith* (Downers Grove, Ill.: IVP Academic, 2009); and Douglas Jacobsen, *The World's Christians: Who They Are, Where They Are, and How They Got There* (Malden, Mass.: Wiley Blackwell, 2011).

2. Perry L. Glanzer, Joel A. Carpenter, and Nick Lantinga, "Looking for God in the University: Examining Trends in Global Christian Higher Education," *Higher Education* 61:6 (2011): 721-755.

just as the Anglican churches across Africa now vastly outnumber those in the United Kingdom, so too there are now more overtly Anglican universities in Africa than in the United Kingdom. The remarkable vigor and growth of Christianity in the global South and East is an obvious driver behind the rise of new Christian universities. And beyond these tales of growth in a variety of contexts, our chapter authors also reveal some common themes regarding the trends, challenges, and opportunities facing Christian higher education around the globe.

Common Themes in the Global History of CHE

First we note some common themes in the history of this movement. There is no global history of Christian higher education available, but a review of the history of Christian higher education in the nations and regions covered in these chapters reveals some important shared patterns, which we think could make for a common narrative.

The Creative Work of Christian Missionaries

While scholars often criticize the imperial nature of older Western mission work, it simply must be recognized that many of the earliest and most prestigious universities in countries around the world would not exist except for the creative energy and pioneering work of Christian missionaries who sought to serve the educational needs of the local population.[3] It is widely known that the earliest and most well-known American universities started as Christian colleges, but this book's chapters on Brazil, China, India, Kenya, and South Korea also reveal that missionaries played a vital role in starting the small religious educational institutions in these areas that eventually grew into universities. Moreover, these missionaries frequently overcame the opposition of colonial political powers, local governments, and even other missionaries to accomplish this important creative work.[4] Ironically, their work was actually

3. Robert D. Woodberry, "The Missionary Roots of Liberal Democracy," *American Political Science Review* 106:2 (2012): 244-274, argues even more broadly that missionaries' educational, humanitarian, and economic work has undergirded the development of democracy and national well-being worldwide.

4. See, e.g., Dana Robert, "The Methodist Struggle over Higher Education in Fuzhou, China, 1877-1883," *Methodist History* 34 (April 1996): 173-189,and Ben C. Hobgood, "History of

aided in some cases by what is sometimes seen as a negative historical development for Christianity in higher education — secularization. The political secularization of a nation-state, meaning the abandonment of an official religion, sometimes opened up a nation for Christian higher education, as it did in Japan; or for the educational work of a minority Christian confession, as it did for Protestants in a number of Latin American nations.

Nationalization and Secularization

Even so, secularization, and another process that I will call nationalization, have most often worked against Christian purpose and mission within universities. The story of the secularization of American Christian universities focuses on the secularization of intellectual and academic assumptions and foundations, but in the global context, we have found that the nation-state is a far more pervasive and powerful secularizing force. As Hans Kohn, the well-known scholar of nationalism, observed, "Nationalism is a state of mind in which the supreme loyalty of the individual is felt to be due the nation-state."[5] This "state of mind" could also apply to the mission and culture of an institution. The nationalization of a university or university system simply means the process whereby leaders change the governance, purposes, curriculum, and culture of a university or of an entire university system to uphold the interests and ideology of the state.

While nationalization often contributes to secularization, it does not necessarily entail secularization. By secularization I mean the removal of Christianity from a privileged position in a university or college's mission, governance, public rhetoric, membership requirements, curriculum, and ethos (e.g., worship).[6] The reason that nationalization does not entail secularization

---

Protestant Higher Education in the Democratic Republic of the Congo," *Lexington Theological Quarterly* 33 (Spring 1998): 23-38.

5. Hans Kohn, *Nationalism: Its Meaning and History* (Princeton, N.J.: D. Van Nostrand, 1955), p. 9.

6. C. John Sommerville provides an insightful overview of the five understandings of secularization employed by scholars. When discussing secularization scholars may refer to the secularization of society, institutions, activities, populations, or mentalities or some combination of these five. My definition would encompass all these types of secularization within a university setting. In other words, secularization occurs when a particular college or university separates itself from church governance and financial support (secularization of institutions), drops religious requirements for entrance, and no longer requires Bible or theology courses (activities), the faculty and students are not held to any religious requirements (populations),

in higher education is that nation-states may choose to support a variety of religious forms of education. Consequently, Christianity is still supported at some nationalized universities that continue to sponsor theology departments, as in the case of South Africa. In a nationalized university system such as South Korea's, Christian universities may receive partial public support. Even so, the nationalization of universities generally has led to their secularization.

Both the nationalization and secularization of higher education, moreover, are political processes. They come as the result of organized efforts to promote change. In other words, secularization has not been a natural and inevitable historical process, but instead it became a social movement among intellectuals, setting out to accomplish something akin to a political revolution.[7] Accordingly, Christian higher education declined or died in various places not because it followed some sort of natural or inevitable sociological pattern, but through the concerted actions of political and intellectual agents and agencies. We have found, accordingly, that universities that are exceptions to the secularization pattern are not mere evolutionary "outliers" or denizens of the academic backwaters that time has passed by. They are actively cultivated academic countercultures.

Two basic types of political secularization have occurred, our studies show. The first type was the product of political revolution, and it resulted in the abrupt demise of Christian universities, such as occurred in France after its revolution[8] and in Eastern Europe[9] and China[10] after communist revolutions. In these cases, Christian higher education was forcefully nationalized and secularized within a short period of time. The second type of political

and scholars abandon the use of Christianity to make sense of the world and their work (mentalities). C. John Sommerville, "Secular Society/Religious Population: Our Tacit Rules for Using the Term 'Secularization,'" *Journal for the Scientific Study of Religion* 37 (June 1998): 249-253.

7. Christian Smith, "Rethinking the Secularization of American Public Life," in *The Secular Revolution: Power, Interests and Conflict in the Secularization of American Public Life*, ed. Christian Smith (Berkeley: University of California Press, 2003), pp. 1-96.

8. Robert Anderson, *European Universities from the Enlightenment to 1914* (New York: Oxford University Press, 2004), pp. 39-50.

9. See my chapter on Eastern Europe in this volume as well as Perry Glanzer, "The Role of the State in the Secularization of Christian Higher Education: A Case Study of Eastern Europe," *Journal of Church and State* 53:2 (2011): 161-182.

10. Although, as Peter Ng's chapter indicates, nationalization and secularization were occurring in more gradual ways in China before the communist revolution. See also Jessie Gregory Lutz, *China and the Christian Colleges, 1850-1950* (Ithaca, N.Y.: Cornell University Press, 1971), and Daniel H. Bays and Ellen Widmer, eds., *China's Christian Colleges: Cross-Cultural Connections, 1900-1950* (Palo Alto, Calif.: Stanford University Press, 2009).

secularization involved a two-part process. First came the gradual national-ization of the universities, during which time the universities were considered to be both Christian and national institutions, but over time national purposes took precedence. One British parliamentary critic of the Christian nature of Oxford University in the 1800s expressed a typical attitude: "Oxford ought to be a national institution but is bound hand and feet by the clergy of one sect."[11] Thus, national leaders increasingly required their older, more prestigious uni-versities to fulfill a nationalist agenda. The secularizing intellectual revolution stimulated by the Enlightenment helped to undergird this national vision, but state power made the changes happen.

These developments happened worldwide, albeit at different times. They occurred in Western Europe and Latin America in the late nineteenth and early twentieth centuries[12] and in Africa[13] and parts of Asia in the twentieth century. In Africa, Asia, and Latin America, we see a common pattern. Chris-tian groups, particularly religious orders or mission societies, come to or arise in a territory and start a school for basic education and theological training. The institution grows and adds fields of study. After the institution blossoms into a university or a specialized professional or technical institute, the state, for a variety of reasons, nationalizes it. The particular religious sponsor, in the eyes of political leaders, increasingly seems divisive, sectarian, or oppressive since the universities now have a broad mission to serve the whole nation. Enlightenment-inspired secular rationalism seems like a neutral common ba-sis that avoids sectarian rivalries in a national institution. Therefore, leaders insist that the Christian identity must be discarded or moved to the margins. This argument was often bolstered by secular-minded intellectuals who sought liberation from religious identities, communities, and ideas.

This secular revolution, while tremendously powerful, was not always inevitable or thoroughgoing, and its effects have varied by the nature of the predominant Christian tradition involved. Older Catholic universities that proclaim a Christian identity have survived in many places, such as Belgium, Colombia, Italy, the Philippines and Venezuela, largely because of the inde-

11. V. H. H. Green, *Religion at Oxford and Cambridge* (London: SCM Press, 1964), p. 153.

12. See, in this book, my chapter on Western Europe and the chapter on Mexico by José Ramón Alcántara Mejía. See also Robert Anderson, *European Universities from the Enlighten-ment to 1914* (New York: Oxford University Press, 2004), and Daniel C. Levy, *Higher Education and the State in Latin America: Private Challenges to Public Dominance* (Chicago: University of Chicago Press, 1986), pp. 26-65.

13. Y. G.-M. Lulat, *A History of African Higher Education from Antiquity to the Present: A Critical Synthesis* (New York: Praeger, 2005).

pendent strength and cultural authority of the Roman Catholic Church. Furthermore, as the chapters on Brazil and Eastern Europe indicate, a period of social and political "recatholization," after an earlier period of secularization, encouraged the creation of newer Catholic universities as well.

In contrast to the Catholic universities, Protestant universities appear to be much more susceptible to nationalization and secularization. Protestants' decentralized organization and unstable communal solidarity make them less able to withstand pressures to conform their institutions to nationalizing norms. Not one Protestant-founded university anywhere in the world that was started before 1817 still proclaims a Christian identity, and many have become secular in much shorter order. Reformed or Presbyterian institutions are good examples of this worldwide trend. Presbyterian or Reformed universities on virtually every continent have been nationalized and many others, even if remaining independent, have become secular universities. Prominent examples include MacKenzie University in Brazil, Yonsei University in South Korea, the Free University of Amsterdam in the Netherlands, Potchefstroom and Stellenbosch Universities in South Africa, and Princeton and Rutgers Universities in the United States. Forman Christian College in present-day Pakistan provides a fairly recent example. Started by a Presbyterian missionary in 1864, the college grew to become one of the most prestigious private colleges and it educated many Pakistani national leaders. In 1972, however, the college was nationalized by the Pakistani government.[14] Still, even for Protestant institutions, secularization comes in various shades and degrees, which vary by region. The oldest Protestant college that still claims its Christian identity is not in Europe or North America; it is CMS College in India (f. 1817). India's approach to religious pluralism within a modern secular state has evidently been more accommodating than that of many nations in the West.[15]

The Eastern Orthodox Church proves to be an odd case in that it has never overseen a university that secularized. This is true, however, mainly because the church founded no universities until the twentieth century. Universities considered "Orthodox" by some historians, such as the early Russian universities, were always controlled by the government and not the Orthodox

---

14. Forman Christian College, "Heritage," www.fccollege.edu.pk/about/heritage (accessed January 2, 2013). Interestingly, in 2003 the government returned the college to the Presbyterian Church of the USA. Even so, the university has remained fairly secular.

15. Besides CMS College (1817), three other Christian colleges that still profess a Christian identity started before 1837: Bishop's College (1820), Scottish Church College (1830), and Madras Christian College (1837).

Church.[16] The oldest Eastern Orthodox collegiate institution actually started in India. Eastern Orthodox universities did not exist in Europe before the midtwentieth century, and only after the Soviet Union fell did two Eastern Orthodox universities emerge in the traditional Orthodox territory of Russia.[17]

Liberal Democracy and Privatization

Another huge theme that runs through our reconnaissance of Christian higher education worldwide is "privatization." In spite of the state's domination of the higher education scene worldwide, there has been a persistent and now in many places a rapidly growing presence of higher education that is organized independently of the state. In order to understand privatization, however, it is important to see how "public" and "private" categories came to be. Christian universities started before the development of the private-public dichotomy that emerged in America.[18] While today we call Harvard, Yale, and Princeton private universities, they started as "public" colleges, charged with responsibility for the whole society, in the same way that the established church was a public institution.[19] Since the modern university grew out of the European context, this European model of church-state-university partnership was initially followed in most areas colonized by the Europeans. For example, the original Latin American universities were creations of such partnerships.[20]

The rise of pluralistic liberal democracies that protected the rights of religious minorities would change this context in two ways. First, as mentioned above, as many nation-states cast off old religious establishments and became religiously neutral or hostile to religion, they also increased their control over universities. In these contexts, universities that had been partnerships between the state and the church were either forcefully secularized (as in France,

16. For an explanation of these reasons, see Perry Glanzer and Konstantin Petrenko, "Resurrecting the Russian University's Soul: The Emergence of Eastern Orthodox Universities and Their Distinctive Approaches to Keeping Faith with Their Religious Tradition," *Christian Scholar's Review* 36 (2007): 263-284. See also Judith Herrin, "The Byzantine 'University' — A Misnomer," in *The European Research University: An Historical Parenthesis*, ed. Kjell Blückert, Guy Neave, and Thorsten Nybom (New York: Palgrave Macmillan, 2006).

17. Glanzer and Petrenko, "Resurrecting the Russian University's Soul."

18. See, e.g., the *International Handbook of Universities, 2010.*

19. George Marsden, *The Soul of the American University* (New York: Oxford University Press, 1994), p. 39.

20. Daniel C. Levy, *Higher Education and the State in Latin America* (Chicago: University of Chicago Press, 1987), pp. 28-29.

Eastern Europe, and China) or gradually secularized (as in Canada, much of Western Europe, and Latin America). Under liberal democratic regimes, new colleges or universities were formed as secular state institutions, reflecting the pervasive assumption, across great stretches of the globe, that the development of new universities and national university systems was deemed to be the domain of the state.

In most of these contexts, churches and Christian educational groups came to see that if they valued Christian modes and outlooks for learning, they would need to build their own privately funded schools and universities. Churches and Christian intellectuals came to this conclusion at widely varying rates, however. In the United States, this pattern persisted from the early republic onward, and it has resulted in the most robust networks of Christian higher education in the world. In Latin America, however, intellectuals and national leaders joined together in the nineteenth century to secularize the universities and expel the Catholic Church. According to Daniel Levy's landmark study of this scene, "Clerics were often purged from the professoriate; faculties of theology were closed. . . . The national universities generally became the State's higher education arm."[21] As we see in our chapters on Brazil and Mexico, Latin American Protestant intellectuals heartily endorsed and participated in the secularization of education. In the late nineteenth and twentieth centuries the Catholic Church responded by creating private universities across the region (e.g., Catholic University of Chile, 1888; Catholic University of Peru, 1917; Pontifical Bolivian University, 1936; Catholic University of Ecuador, 1946; and the six Catholic universities created in Brazil from 1939 to 1948). Protestants, who as oppressed minorities tended to side with the new secular regimes, came very late to the field of Christian higher education in Latin America.

A rather different pattern of nationalization and religious response occurred in Canada, as Harry Fernhout's chapter reveals. The older, mainline Protestant denominations founded several universities in the nineteenth century, but then they largely supported the state's taking them over in the mid-twentieth century and they saw no need for Christian educational alternatives. Meanwhile, Catholics operated their schools and universities under special dispensations from the state. Only recently, at the initiative of some of the smaller Protestant groups, have a few new Christian universities arisen in Canada.

In many European colonial outposts of Africa and Asia, the state did not initially fund educational institutions, so the church began numerous schools,

21. *Higher Education and the State*, p. 31.

colleges, and universities as part of its mission efforts. In these cases, a church or a particular mission group helped start some of the very first colleges or universities, while the government gave permission or perhaps land but did not found or fund the institutions. The development of Christian higher education in India came about in just this way, as our chapter on India notes. Until 1815, the English East India Company banned all private enterprise in the Company's territories. After that ban was lifted in 1815, Christian missionaries helped start CMS College (1817), Bishop's College (1820), Scottish Church College (1830), and Madras Christian College (1837), institutions that have kept their Christian identity to this day.[22]

In sum, while we expected to learn quite a bit in this study about church and university relations, we have found that the state has been dominant as the universities' significant other. Today the state continues to be a powerful shaping force affecting Christian higher education. The nationalization of most higher education systems means that a central ministry of education or some other government entity controls the funding and the authorization of degree-granting in higher education and determines the legal frames for private higher education. Liberal democracy, the political system that created "public" and "private" spheres and tended to exclude religion from public life, is, ironically, a major enabler of Christian universities. Few Christian universities exist in countries that do not have a liberal polity, such as in mainland China or on the Arabian Peninsula. Furthermore, when democracy was taken away in certain countries, such as during military dictatorships in Brazil and Nigeria, or under communism in Eastern Europe, the growth of Christian universities slowed, reversed, or was not even possible. So as our chapter authors make clear, Christian higher education relies on government policies that allow diverse forms of religious universities, and these policies are almost always the creation of liberal democracies.

As we have seen, however, "privatization" has come to mean more than absence of state ownership or liberalization of state control. It also connotes the essentially "private" or "personal" (or pecuniary) reasons for gaining a university education, over against the broader traditional aims of serving God and the public good. In our day, the aims and purposes of higher education have become ever more contested, and Christian universities cannot ignore these issues.

22. *The Christian College in India: The Report of the Commission on Christian Higher Education in India* (London: Oxford University Press, 1931), pp. 63-64. The oldest Christian college in America that still identifies itself explicitly as Christian is a women's college: Judson College, founded in Alabama in 1838.

The Present: Christian Higher Education in Light of Current Trends in Higher Education

Massification

In spite of the historic patterns of nationalization and secularization in higher education throughout the world, we have seen recent patterns of growth for Christian universities in Africa, Asia, post-communist Europe, and Latin America. And as George Marsden shows in the United States, its more mature, built-out systems of Catholic and Protestant higher education are enjoying something of a renaissance, bringing the whole idea of higher education's inevitable secularization into question. Much of this growth, however, is part of the whole university sector's response to the tremendous increase in the number of students graduating from secondary schools and demanding higher education, a worldwide phenomenon scholars call massification.[23] Christian higher education is growing, but it is in fact a small part of the rapidly expanding tertiary education sector. Table 1 below indicates the percentage of students that Christian higher education institutions educate in each country.

Table 1: Number and Percentage of Students in Christian Higher Education by Region

	Total Student Enrollment*	Christian University Student Enrollment†	Percentage
AFRICA			
Angola	66,251	7,000	0.11
Cameroon	220,331	1,970	0.01
Democratic Republic of the Congo	377,867	11,832	0.03
Ghana	203,376	19,685	0.1
Ivory Coast	156,772	600	0.01
Kenya	167,983	17,392	0.1
Liberia	52,251	2,100	0.04
Malawi	10,296	627	0.06
Mozambique	28,298	3,270	0.12

23. Philip Altbach et al., *Trends in Global Higher Education* (Paris: UNESCO, 2009), pp. vi and 5-7.

	Total Student Enrollment*	Christian University Student Enrollment†	Percentage
Nigeria	1,391,527	30,759	0.02
Rwanda	62,734	1,718	0.03
South Africa	740,000	579	<0.01
Tanzania	85,113	12,651	0.15
Uganda	123,887	14,670	0.12
Zimbabwe	94,611	5,700	0.06
ASIA — MIDDLE EAST			
Lebanon	202,345	25,749	0.13
ASIA — NORTHEAST			
China–Hong Kong	254,273	11,193	0.04
Japan	3,836,314	160,454	0.04
South Korea	3,269,509	256,701	0.08
Taiwan	1,270,194	132,833	0.1
ASIA — SOUTH			
India	18,648,923	**269,584	0.01
ASIA — SOUTHEAST			
Indonesia	5,001,048	**93,041	0.02
Philippines	2,651,466	**276,402	0.1
Thailand	2,497,323	27,800	0.01
EUROPE			
Austria	308,150	200	<0.01
Belgium	425,219	52,000	0.12
Finland	296,691	3,000	0.01
France	2,172,855	37,500	0.02
Germany	2,131,907	4,900	<0.01
Hungary	397,679	13,065	0.03
Italy	2,011,713	60,000	0.03
Lithuania	210,744	620	<0.01
Netherlands	618,502	35,000	0.06
Norway	219,282	2,300	0.01
Poland	2,149,998	17,364	0.01
Portugal	373,002	11,000	0.03
Romania	1,098,188	2,000	<0.01

	Total Student Enrollment*	Christian University Student Enrollment†	Percentage
Russia	9,330,115	5,800	<0.01
Slovakia	234,997	7,700	0.03
Spain	1,800,834	77,000	0.04
Switzerland	233,488	10,000	0.04
UK	2,415,222	15,286	0.01
Ukraine	2,635,004	780	<0.01
LATIN AMERICA			
Argentina	2,387,049	126,341	0.05
Bolivia	352,545	16,840	0.05
Brazil	6,115,138	**452,687	0.07
Chile	876,243	88,871	0.1
Colombia	1,674,420	**103,822	0.07
Costa Rica	110,717	2,000	0.02
Dominican Republic	293,565	29,962	0.1
Ecuador	534,522	**24,614	0.05
El Salvador	150,012	9,633	0.06
Honduras	147,740	10,000	0.07
Jamaica	71,352	5,300	0.07
Mexico	2,705,190	**44,385	0.02
Nicaragua	103,577	**25,298	0.24
Panama	135,209	4,500	0.03
Paraguay	236,194	**1,420	0.01
Peru	957,437	42,706	0.04
Puerto Rico	249,372	18,174	0.08
Trinidad & Tobago	16,920	500	0.03
Uruguay	161,459	7,580	0.05
Venezuela	2,123,041	31,938	0.02

	Total Student Enrollment*	Christian University Student Enrollment†	Percentage
OCEANIA			
Australia	1,199,845	26,050	0.02
Papua New Guinea	9,943	3859	0.39

*The total student enrollment numbers are taken from the most recent enrollment statistics provided by UNESCO. See stats.uis.unesco.org/unesco/TableViewer/tableView.aspx?Report Id=168 (accessed 27 April 2012).

†The enrollment statistics for universities were in almost all cases taken either from the web sites of the institutions or the *International Handbook of Universities,* vols. 1-3, 21st ed. (New York: Palgrave Macmillan, 2010). Numbers marked with ** are incomplete.

In only three countries are 15 percent or more of students educated in Christian institutions (Papua New Guinea, 39 percent; Tanzania, 15 percent; Nicaragua, 24 percent). Thus, the reality is that while Christian higher education used to dominate higher education in Europe, North and South America, and China, in almost every country in which it currently exists today, it is only a small minority in a system dominated by secular institutions.

Of course, in many countries this small minority market is still significant. In eleven other countries Christian universities enroll between 10 and 14 percent of the student population (Angola, 11 percent; Belgium, 12 percent; Chile, 10 percent; Colombia, 10 percent; Dominican Republic, 10 percent; Ghana, 10 percent; Kenya, 10 percent; Lebanon, 13 percent; Mozambique, 12 percent; Philippines, 10 percent; and Uganda, 12 percent). The tremendous growth of Christian higher education in Africa is demonstrated by the fact that almost half of the countries in this category are from Africa. All the other countries benefit from the presence of large Catholic universities.

The data reveal, therefore, that despite the growth of Christian higher education in various parts of the world, much of this growth merely filled the niche in the Christian university market that had been absent. For instance, while a number of new institutions have come into being in Eastern Europe within the past two decades, Christian institutions still do not educate more than 4 percent of students in any of these countries. Moreover, the legacy of communist oppression of religion still can be seen institutionally. While many Eastern European countries are now more religious in popular outlook and behavior than Western European ones,[24] and the chapters on European Chris-

24. Philip Jenkins, *God's Continent: Christianity, Islam, and Europe's Religious Crisis* (New York: Oxford University Press, 2007).

tian higher education reveal a similar growth in Christian higher education, Western Europe still exceeds Eastern Europe in the percentage of students attending Christian colleges or universities. Similarly, while the chapters on South Korea and Nigeria reveal the tremendous growth in these countries, Christian institutions still only educate 8 percent of the country's students in South Korea and only 2 percent of students in Nigeria. Thus, while Christian higher education continues to grow in these areas, it educates only a small percentage of the overall college population. Christian higher education is surging, but the larger context is still public dominance.[25]

Privatization and Access

Today, because of the seemingly unquenchable popular demand for higher education, many governments — even those that had no nongovernmental universities — have begun to charter them. Around the world, perhaps 30 percent of all tertiary enrollments are now in privately chartered institutions, and it is clear that Christian higher education is riding this privatizing wave. According to our database, only 7 percent of Christian universities receive the majority of their funding from the state (see table 2 on p. 291). These institutions are in England, Hungary, India, the Netherlands, Poland, and Slovakia. Furthermore, only 15 percent receive any direct funding from the state, and the majority of these institutions are in India. In contrast, the vast majority of Christian institutions around the world are now largely privately funded and will likely remain so in the near future. In places where Christian universities are growing the most, it is largely due to new freedom for privately funded universities more generally. So Christian universities prosper in countries that allow a large degree of privatization, as in Brazil, Indonesia, Japan, Korea, India, and Nigeria, while they are virtually nonexistent in countries with very little by way of a private sector in higher education, such as Austria, New Zealand, and the United Kingdom.[26] The result is that the fortunes of Christian higher education will largely rise and fall with the freedom and prosperity of private higher education in countries around the globe. Of the sixty-eight Christian universities started since 1995 (forty-four of which began in Africa) only four received some sort of government funding. Even in countries such as India,

25. Mahlubi Mabizela, "Private Surge and Public Dominance in Higher Education: The African Perspective," *Journal of Higher Education in Africa* 5:2-3 (2007): 15-38.

26. Altbach et al., *Trends in Global Higher Education*, p. xiv.

Table 2: Funding Patterns of Christian Universities by Region

Region	Majority of Budget State Funded	Less than Half of Budget State Funded	Privately Funded (state funding indirect)	Could not Determine
Africa			76/76 (100%)	
Asia-Middle East			8/8 (100%)	
Asia-Northeast			72/72 (100%)	
Asia-Southeast			68/68 (100%)	
Asia-South	21/165 (13%)	69/165 (42%)	14/165 (8.5%)	61/165 (36.5%)
Europe	14/59 (24%)	15/59 (25%)	30/59 (51%)	
Latin America	4/139 (2.5%)	3/139 (2%)	133/139 (95.5%)	
Oceania		3/8 (33%)	5/8 (66%)	
Total	39/595 (7%)	90/595 (15%)	404/595 (68%)	61/595 (10%)

where Christian colleges receive government support, an increasing number of the new institutions are privately funded institutions.[27]

In many regions this reality poses a distinct disadvantage to Christian institutions when it comes to academic achievement and prestige. Students, by and large, prefer to enroll in well-funded public institutions with low or no tuition charges and which tend to be selective in admissions. Private institutions, including private Christian institutions, are in such contexts the students' "fallback" options. What should be noted, especially for American readers, is that while older private Christian universities around the globe may be more selective and prestigious, most private Christian institutions around the world are relatively new institutions that serve a wider audience and are not prestigious. The exceptions to this generalization are South Korea and some of the older institutions in India.

This reality also means that global Christian higher education will always struggle to address another global trend in higher education — inequalities in access. Despite the rise in the number of students enrolled in higher education, the privileged classes have maintained an advantage when it comes to access to higher education.[28] Private Christian institutions, which by necessity require

27. J. Dinakarlal, "Christian Higher Education in India: The Road We Tread," chapter 5 of this book.
28. Altbach et al., *Trends in Global Higher Education,* pp. vii-viii, 37-50.

more tuition than state-funded institutions, will always have difficulty addressing this problem. The few that make extraordinary efforts to admit low-income students, such as Christian institutions in India that make outreach to lower classes part of their central mission, will be able to do so due to aid from the state. But aid from the state, as our chapter on Canada illustrates, usually has increased regulation attached to it.

Privatization is not only an enabler of Christian higher education, but it poses a problem as well, in three ways. First, the general reputation of secular private universities, which are often for-profit entities that focus on a few cheaper and more profitable lines of job training and struggle to maintain quality, may adversely affect the reputation of Christian universities. This latter development could spur the second threat — an overly regulatory government that may place extensive compliance burdens on private education or even make efforts to shut it down. For instance, due to the declining student population in Russia, the Russian government has instituted protectionist policies that favor its public universities and prevent a number of new Christian institutions from being chartered as universities. Furthermore, as a number of chapters indicated, even in liberal democracies increased government regulations that seek to standardize higher education have created new barriers to Christian higher education in regard to courses they may offer, campus rules or practices they may institute, faculty they may hire, or even how they state their mission and purpose. In reaction, some Christian universities have isolated themselves from the larger society, even to the point of forgoing accreditation, to the point where, as our chapter on Mexico points out, they become so sectarian that they do not serve any but their sponsoring constituencies.

So Christian universities have a deeply ambivalent relationship with privatization. They benefit from government's liberalization of university chartering. They do not fully share the institutional profiles of many secular private institutions, but they often are tagged with the private sector's overall reputation. And ultimately, the very idea of "private" is ill-suited to Christian people and their agencies. They do not accept the modern notion that religion is for one's private life only; they continue to insist that the truth and peace they have found is meant to benefit everyone. So they persist in aiming to serve the common good, even while preserving some ideas, values, and life-patterns that are not favored by the majority of their fellow citizens. It is a difficult dance to maintain: being in the world, for the world, but not fully of the world. But this much is clear: uncritically accepting a "private sphere" designation is not a great option for Christian universities.

Globalization

Globalization is another important trend influencing higher education around the world. Philip Altbach and his associates define globalization in its higher educational context as "the reality shaped by an increasingly integrated world economy, new information and communications technology (ICT), the emergence of international knowledge network, the role of the English language, and other forces beyond the control of the academic institutions."[29] Three things about globalization, our authors have found, are of particular importance for Christian higher education institutions.

First, global networks have suddenly made it possible to be aware of the numerous Christian institutions due to their presence on the World Wide Web and their leaders' international networking. These days, if an institution does not exist on the Web, then for all practical purposes it does not exist. Institutions are becoming defined by their virtual presence and representation.

Second, global communication networks also create mutual awareness and make regional and even global alliances among Christian universities more possible than ever. Whereas partnerships formed on the basis of denominational affiliation are still important,[30] other forms of regional and global alliances are arising. In the United States and Canada, the Council for Christian Colleges and Universities enlists 118 member institutions (and fifty-three international affiliates). Elsewhere in the world are the All India Association of Christian Higher Education (http://aiache.net/index.html), the Association of Christian Colleges and Universities in Asia, and the International Association for the Promotion of Christian Higher Education (IAPCHE) (http://www.iapche.org).

Finally, the English language has taken on a central role in fostering this global dialogue. As table 3 on page 294 reveals, almost half of the Christian colleges and universities *outside North America* have English as the instructional language (the vast majority of these being in India and the Philippines) and another 11 percent of them give some instruction in English. Moreover, more than three-fourths (76 percent) of Christian institutions outside North and South America give instruction in English. The importance of English for

29. Altbach et al., *Trends in Global Higher Education,* p. iv.

30. See, e.g., the Colleges and Universities of the Anglican Communion (http://www.cuac.org/53810_53925_ENG_HTM.htm?menupage=61263) and the International Federation of Catholic Universities (http://www.fiuc.org/cms/index.php?page=homeENG).

Table 3: Language of Instruction by Region

Region	Instruction Mainly in English	Instruction Partly in English	Instruction in Other Language
Africa	59/76	4/76	13/76 (10 French, 3 Portuguese)
Asia-Middle East	4/8	2/8	2/8 (2 French)
Asia-Northeast		33/72	39/72 (Chinese, Japanese and Korean)
Asia-Southeast	46/68	8/68	14/68 (Indonesian)
Asia-South	161/165	4/165	
Europe	7/59	12/59	40/59 (multiple)
Latin America	4/139	4/139	131/139 (Spanish and Portuguese)
Oceania	8/8		
Total	289/595 (49%)	67/595 (11%)	239/595 (40%)

new institutions in Africa is particularly noteworthy since Africa has shown the greatest growth in the number of Christian institutions over the past two decades. In this respect, Christian institutions reflect Altbach's point that "The rise of English as the dominant language of scientific communication is unprecedented since Latin dominated the academy in medieval Europe."[31] Of course, this trend also could lead to a detrimental form of cultural homogenization of which our chapter author on Mexico, José Ramón Alcántara Mejía, warns. The domination of English in international meetings and projects also has the potential to isolate institutions from Latin America, East Asia, and Francophone Africa.

Instrumentalization

Another global trend influencing education concerns what may be labeled instrumentalization, or a narrowing of the aims and purposes of the university. Altbach and his co-authors observe that "the mission of most countries today is to teach less of the basic disciplines and offer more in the way of professional programs to a far wider range of students than in the past."[32] While

31. Altbach et al., *Trends in Global Higher Education*, p. iv.
32. Altbach et al., *Trends in Global Higher Education*, p. x.

the state plays some role in this trend, private schools in particular are often linked to commercial or soft technical fields (e.g., accounting and IT rather than math and engineering) that are cheap to teach and promise immediate salaried jobs. Consequently, they reduce investment in libraries, labs, cultural offerings, community service, general education, and research.[33] Most of the chapters in this book drew some attention to this worldwide trend.

To what degree is CHE, especially since the vast majority of it is now privately funded, participating in the reduction of general education and the liberal arts and focusing on professional education? Part of the answer to this question can be discerned from examining the nature of the new universities being started. There is clearly a new addition to the old pattern of how many Christian institutions were formed. In the past, a large percentage of Christian universities would often start as seminaries, Bible colleges, or theological institutions. They would then expand to offer other majors. Since these institutions were birthed in aspects of the liberal arts (e.g., studying languages, history, and philosophy as well as theology), they continued to emphasize them. While this old pattern still occurs, a new pattern has also become more pronounced, particularly in Europe. New Christian institutions are starting by offering technical and professional majors because of the specific needs in these fields and the financial benefit of focusing on high-demand lines of work. One finds this trend not only in the countries in Western Europe (e.g., the Netherlands and the United Kingdom) but also in Africa and Asia.

Yet, an overview of the majors of institutions found in the database of global Christian higher education reveals that around the globe a significant majority of these new institutions, while clearly emphasizing practical professions that can help the local population (e.g., many of the new institutions have business, economics, or technology majors), also provide liberal arts majors and service-oriented professional majors. In other words, they may have a major interest in commercial/technical fields, but a significant majority also offer majors in theology, philosophy, and languages that serve the church or teaching, social work, nursing, and economic development that focus on serving the common good of the community.

Consider the sixty-eight Christian universities started since 1995. As mentioned earlier, forty-four of these institutions originated in Africa. All but five

33. Daniel C. Levy, "The Unanticipated Explosion: Private Higher Education's Global Surge," *Comparative Education Review* 50:2 (2006): 217-240; Daniel C. Levy, "An Introductory Global Overview: The Private Fit to Salient Higher Education Tendencies," Program for Research in Private Higher Education (PROPHE), Albany, State University of New York, PROPHE Working Paper no. 7, 2006.

of these institutions provide a major in business, management, or commerce. More than half (twenty-five) also provide majors in some kind of information technology or computer science. Still, many of these institutions focus on the helping professions. Twelve offer education degrees, ten offer degrees in the health sciences or nursing, ten more offer degrees in agriculture, and nine offer law degrees. Thus, while the kind of practical vocational focus that characterizes the new-wave secular private institutions also exists in Christian university networks, these Christian institutions also offer majors that are more service-oriented, in fields often called the "helping professions." Twenty-one of these new institutions also provide majors in theology, twenty-three have some sort of science major, and seventeen have arts or humanities majors beyond theology.

The other new Christian universities outside Africa evidence a similar pattern. Sixteen of the twenty-four offer business majors and ten offer some form of computer degree. Helping professions are scattered throughout (five offer nursing, three offer social work, and five offer education degrees). Interestingly, only seven offer theology degrees, but sixteen offer some major in the arts. In sum, even without the state financing, these new Christian universities show significant commitments to offer higher education in the so-called service professions and the liberal arts and sciences. They give every appearance of still pursuing the broad cultural mission of the church in their educational priorities.

Christian universities' persistence in these old, broad, and noble educational aims and purposes signals a willingness to swim against the current tides of globalization in higher education. Around the world, educational aims and priorities are being subjected to economistic evaluations of the relative worth of various major concentrations and degree programs. In a number of universities in the United Kingdom, humanities and arts majors now must pay higher tuitions than business, science, and technology majors. Across Europe, the Bologna process enforces a three-year bachelor's degree in most subjects, which all but eliminates any provision for general education or many electives. All across Asia, says Philip Altbach, the social sciences and humanities are in such rapid decline in enrollments that they seem to be in a death spiral.[34] Even in the United States, where general education requirements are a pervasive part of a standard undergraduate education, this common standard is under fire, as are traditional humanities and social sciences degrees.

---

34. Philip G. Altbach, "Globalization and Forces for Change in Higher Education," *International Higher Education*, no. 50 (Winter 2008). *International Higher Education* is published online at http://www.bc.edu/bc_org/avp/soe/cihe/

We would like to say that Christian educational leaders worldwide have developed a sturdy and independent perspective on these trends, but all too often, their first impulse is to respond in kind. Not a few of them are earnestly promising that their institutions will equip students to meet the global demands for commercial and technical workers. "Our society has impatiently demanded . . . professional workers," says Dr. Sung Kee Ho, president of SungKyul University in Korea. "We are recognizing today's problem and making the well-fitted and capable people prepared for tomorrow in our global community. It is the mission of our University to educate and train the faithful, competent, professional and creative leaders."[35]

We need to recognize that in the emerging global economy, access to technology and skills has become a matter of fundamental justice to the poor, who have been cut off from them. Acquiring relevant skills is a form of ownership, no less important than land or money. People need the means to make their work more knowledge-laden, and thus more valuable. A new assault on poverty cannot be simply the redistribution of wealth or the fencing out of foreign capitalists. Yet Christian educators need to reason these matters through more than they do now; they need to develop a critical appreciation of the globalizing demands they face. And certainly they will want to lead their students to develop a fully orbed Christian perspective on globalization and other current realities. Yet it is difficult to see how educators and students can cultivate a fully orbed Christian perspective within the narrowly focused curricular tracks that universities are developing worldwide. Unless students take courses that address the social, economic, theological, cultural, and ethical issues that form the world in which their professions operate, they will have few resources for understanding and applying the Bible's call to work for justice and to love mercy.

The Future

We do not want to leave the impression that these great global forces spell doom for Christian higher education. To the contrary, the main thrust of this book is to point to the surprising recovery or fresh creations of Christian higher education. The massive growth of higher education to meet mass demand, and the increasing space created for private education by nations that

35. "Message from the President," www.sungkyul.ac.kr/english/information (accessed January 2005).

are liberalizing control and ownership of the field, have established remarkable opportunities for the growth of Christian higher education worldwide. In many lands, Christian colleges and universities have taken advantage of these historic forces in ways that serve the church and the common good. Nonetheless, we should be sober about the realities facing Christian higher education around the globe. Christian higher education is and will likely remain a minor segment of higher education in almost every country and within a global higher education system that is largely governed, funded, and directed and controlled by an educational administrative apparatus associated with secular nation-states, professional societies, and elites. The agendas of this establishment will frequently contest the central mission and values of Christian higher education.

So what can the leaders of global Christian universities do to strengthen their institutions in light of this context? They need to continue to focus, first, on building a positive vision instead of taking a defensive posture toward the culture. The best defense, football strategists are wont to say, is a good offense. Even so, they will need to think creatively and redemptively about how to deal with the particular threats of a fallen world. The following pages explore some possibilities.

1. Unique Missions and Not Unique Forms

North American Christians have sometimes tended to see the liberal arts college as the ideal institution for Christian higher education. As a result, there are very few Christian research universities and hardly any Christian community or technical colleges in the region. When considering the global context, however, Christians need to think more creatively about the various forms their institutions can take. What does need to be retained, however, is the view that Christian universities set themselves apart when they conceive of their mission in light of the overarching Christian story. Therefore, they must focus on developing humans made in God's image for Christ and Christ's kingdom and not merely citizens for this world or professionals for jobs. This focus requires asking the question of how they can participate in God's creative and redemptive work in the multiple types of universities and multiple levels of the university.

2. *Creatively Incarnating Christian Distinctives*

The rush to meet the needs produced by massification or the restrictions posed by state partnerships will continue to prove a challenge to creating programs that focus on the holistic development of students. Christian education has proven and must continue to prove itself different in this area. While the findings mentioned earlier indicate that Christian universities have continued to develop majors in other fields beyond professional vocations, it should also seek the holistic education of students in professional programs.

General Education

In most cases, global universities outside North America offer no such thing as general education. Christian universities that seek to educate students to love God holistically provide a vibrant countercultural witness when they require a general education or core curriculum that focuses on educating students to be fully human.[36] For instance, this would mean that the moral education provided in such courses would focus not only on providing technical knowledge of ethical theory or even certain basic moral competencies in ethical reasoning. Instead, it would set forth and seek to incarnate a holistic vision of human flourishing grounded in Christ and the vision of the kingdom of God.

The Range of Majors

New Christian universities usually offer majors that meet particular needs in society. North American Christians often belittle a jobs-oriented focus of higher education in favor of a liberal arts model, but they forget that a liberal arts education was historically designed for the person of means with the time and money to engage in this form of well-rounded education. As these chapters reveal, in many places in the world, the Christian community must focus on providing education that can lead to a job. The key for Christian institutions in this situation is to provide a wider range of vocational options — not merely focusing on business and computing but also on teacher education and the full range of helping or service professions beyond teaching.

---

36. For an example of what this might look like, see Perry L. Glanzer and Todd C. Ream, *Christianity and Moral Identity in Higher Education* (New York: Palgrave Macmillan, 2009).

Majors or Professional Degree Programs That Incorporate Broader (Including Faith) Perspectives

In light of the professional-technical emphasis of most global universities, Christian universities will stand apart by offering additional courses, as well as instruction within the basic courses in the field, which address larger theological, philosophical, and ethical issues. In other words, they need to incorporate the liberal arts into more professionally focused forms of education. Most science and social science majors never study the historical, philosophical, sociological, or ethical dynamics that shape their disciplines. In this respect, the Christian professional societies, such as the Christian Engineering Society,[37] which have developed in North America need to be fostered in other global contexts because these societies have focused on curricular and worldview-driven issues within the contexts of professional education. Such societies can encourage an educational conversation that widens the scope of typical professional education to include theological context, holistic ethical concerns, and how one's professional life fits into a larger vision for human flourishing.

University administrators need to reinforce these conversations by making room for general education units within professional degree programs. Even while the Bologna process seems to be pushing the world toward ever-narrower specialization within three-year degree programs, there are some interesting counter-moves afoot. We think, for example, of the universities in Hong Kong expanding to a four-year bachelor's degree calendar in order to add general education requirements.[38] Christian universities should applaud — and emulate — such moves.

Student Life

Global universities tend to neglect the holistic needs of students by offering very little when it comes to student life programming and oversight. We have to admit that there is very little discussion of the co-curricular dimension of global Christian universities in our chapters. Yet, we know from research done in the United States that much of the consolidation of students' undergraduate learning happens outside the classroom and in students' co-curricular experi-

37. http://www.calvin.edu/academic/engineering/ces/.
38. Janel Marie Curry, "Cultural Challenges in Hong Kong to the Implementation of Effective General Education," *Teaching in Higher Education* 18:2 (2012): 223-230; David Jaffee, "The General Education Initiative in Hong Kong: Organized Contradictions and Emerging Tensions," *Higher Education* 64:2 (August 2012): 193-206.

ences.[39] On the global scene, where so many universities are strictly commuter institutions that give little attention to how students put living and learning together, global Christian universities could benefit greatly and provide a stark countercultural witness by investing time, creativity and resources into the student life side of education.

Broader Christian Partnerships

While various Christian denominations have sustained supportive partnerships with universities for a long time, other forms of partnerships have only recently developed and these too need more support. Many of these new Christian universities need wisdom as they think through how to integrate faith and learning. There are some global partnerships that have emerged, such as the International Association for the Promotion of Christian Higher Education (IAPCHE), which is linking Christian universities and educators worldwide and providing programs and resources for institutional and faculty development. These kinds of partnership can help universities think about issues of faith and learning at multiple levels. For instance, the two Latin American chapter authors cite the lack of redemptive social engagement among the new evangelical and Pentecostal movements and their universities. One wonders if broader partnerships with Christian universities such as those in India, which are more fundamentally engaged in economic development and social reform, could help foster redemptive ideas in Latin America about how to engage problem issues creatively.

Christian universities also need to develop or to support existing regional fellowships of Christian universities such as the Council for Christian Colleges and Universities and the Lilly Fellows Network of Church-related Colleges and Universities in North America, the Asian Christian Universities and Colleges group in East and Southeast Asia, and the All India Association of Christian Higher Education. In addition, IAPCHE is developing regional partnerships in areas currently lacking structures such as Europe, Africa, and Latin America. These kinds of partnerships will prove particularly important to sharing global ideas regarding the integration of faith and learning that can stimulate out-of-the-box, creative thinking.

Finally, there is a greater need for "bilateral" global partnerships between

---

39. Alexander W. Astin, "Student Involvement: A Developmental Theory for Higher Education," *Journal of College Student Development* 40:5 (1999): 518-529.

older and more settled Christian universities and newly founded ones in dynamic settings of need. The University of Notre Dame provides a positive example. The formation of the University of Notre Dame Australia (f. 1989) marked the beginning of the first Christian university in Australia, and this university would not have been possible without the help of the University of Notre Dame in the United States. As one chronicler of the history wrote, "Indeed, the early NDUS commitment and involvement was the perhaps most important single factor in causing this project to proceed beyond the feasibility study stage."[40] Notre Dame has participated in similar global partnerships with young Eastern European Catholic universities. Protestants have not been nearly as successful in this endeavor.

Addressing the Threats

The Domineering State

One of the major threats to Christian universities around the world, as almost every chapter attests, is increasing centralized government control of education. As our data and the recent global history of Christian higher education reveal, Christian universities appear to flourish best when a pluralistic system of higher education is fostered. In recent years, centralized state systems have responded to the great demand for higher education by awarding university charters to non-state institutions. But even where this new pluralism has emerged, state systems are reasserting their power. And in some nations, state command and control impulses are still very strong. Christian universities will need to form partnerships with other nongovernmental institutions to protect their freedom as they seek to create and sustain a robust civil society. Christian university leaders should remain wary of government funding since it is linked to government control, and they should continue to take full advantage of laws allowing for the creation of private universities. While public funding is not always detrimental to the survival and integrity of Christian universities, such funding usually comes with particular limitations on programs or hiring. Protestants have been notoriously susceptible to losing their institutions to these powers and dominions, and there is a reason the vast majority of vibrant Protestant Christian universities are largely privately funded.

40. Peter Tannock, "The Founding of the University of Notre Dame Australia," broome .nd.edu.au/university/history.shtml (accessed May 2, 2012).

The Market

The expanding market for higher education has fed the global growth of Christian higher education, but the current higher education boom will not go on indefinitely, particularly in areas such as Russia and Europe, where the population declines and demand for higher education slackens. Market pressures may pose tremendous threats to the unique vision and mission of Christian universities. For instance, extra general education classes in theology, Bible, and ethics or required chapel classes may add to the cost or time of obtaining a degree in some contexts, and thus prove a hindrance to the expansion of one's enrollment. Furthermore, market pressures may induce some institutions to expand revenue-producing majors such as business and technology at the expense of offering courses in theology, Bible, philosophy, or ethics. In addition, hiring full-time staff that supports the Christian mission of the institution may be seen as financially burdensome, especially in contexts where the competitors work mainly with cheaper part-time instruction. In these cases, Christian leaders will sometimes be faced with the choice between being faithful to what is best for their Christian educational mission and fostering the survival of the institution at the expense of either the Christian mission or academic integrity (see, for example, the chapters on India, Nigeria, South Korea, and the United States). Christian leaders must remember that institutions are not people. The death of an institution can lead to the rebirth and resurrection of something quite different and more lasting.

Christian Unfaithfulness

Fundamentally, the above two threats only prove effective when Christians succumb to their lures. The most fundamental threat facing the Christian university is when Christians lose their way and substitute other loves such as academic prestige, love for knowledge or humanity, or even institutional survival for their first love: for God, God's truth, and God's reign. If history teaches us anything about sustaining academic institutions designed to further the love of God with our minds, desires, and actions, it proves how incredibly difficult it is to maintain these priorities over the decades. Like unfaithfulness in marriage, academic unfaithfulness becomes pervasive and ultimately fatal. Only by God's pervading and prevailing grace can Christian institutions ultimately resist this threat. They need communities of the faithful to uphold them in prayer, support them with students and funds, and hold them accountable to their original aims and purposes.

Redemptive Engagement

Sustaining the redemptive work of Christian universities requires a vibrant connection to Christian communities. Yet, one of the striking things about the chapters in this volume is the limited attention our authors have given to the role of church, except with regard to the Catholic Church in several nations and the Protestant churches mainly in the South Korean context. Is the global church abandoning support for the university? We think not. In Africa, Asia, and Latin America, we see denominations eagerly encouraging the startup of new Christian universities. And the Roman Catholic and Adventist communities of faith have built extensive global networks of colleges and universities by emphasizing first and foremost their service to Christ and the church, and most notably by preparing graduates for vocations, whether the priesthood in the Catholic context or healthcare and teaching amongst the Adventists. These vocations as a matter of course serve the common good, but only as they "seek first the kingdom of God." By contrast, Protestant colleges and universities have demonstrated a continual tendency to be captured by what for Christians must be more contingent and secondary academic goals, such as academic excellence or national service. It also appears that while specific Christian traditions continue to encourage the startup of universities, the amount of support and attention given to universities by denominations may be diminishing. In this respect, we may also need new creative ways of thinking. What appears to be growing is the role of mega-churches and mega-pastors in starting universities as illustrated by the growth of Oral Roberts, Liberty, and Regent universities in the United States, Central University College in Ghana, and Hansei University in South Korea. Perhaps mega-churches may become natural partners for Christian universities in their vicinities.

While global partnerships will help with the sharing of ideas, Christian universities need to think about the generation of ideas as well. To be healthy and sustainable, they cannot continue to rely only on the borrowing and perhaps retrofitting of ideas issuing out of secular intellectual frames and factories. Ideally, there should be at least one or two Christian universities in a region that are devoted to producing postgraduate studies and students. They can become centers for producing discoveries, ideas, and cultural products that are animated by Christian vision and intelligence. It would be much easier for graduates from a Christian university in Lithuania to attend a Christian research university in Hungary to study how to produce creative and redemptive forms of scholarship with relevance for that region than either to refit what they have learned at a nearby secular university or at a Western European

Christian university. Similarly, a Christian research university located in West Africa would be much better equipped than a North American one to supply the surrounding region with creative and redemptive scholarly ideas relevant to the local context. We need to have some of the Christian universities develop into successful research universities and take leadership in fields of scholarship. Christian universities currently cover the imparting of knowledge with growing competency, but they need to have some sister institutions that become adept at producing knowledge as well. Without them, the ecosystem of Christian higher education is incomplete and perhaps not sustainable.

Conclusion

Christian scholars are first and foremost followers of Christ and servants of God's reign. They are secondarily and contingently servants to their professions, nations, or some other masters. But in order to sustain those priorities, we must begin to think globally about education and our professions, in the light of the Christian church's story, and how our realm of work has grown with it. We must learn and tell the story of Christian higher education from around the globe, something we have not yet done. We need, more concretely, to learn and tell the stories of educational saints and pioneers who began small Bible schools that have grown into institutions that serve the church and humanity in tremendous ways. We must also tell the tragic stories of dead-ends and failures along the way, and how some of our best academic creations have been distorted and rerouted by competing visions and desires. North American institutions and their people in particular need to come as learners into this larger global enterprise. They have been blessed with abundant opportunities and material resources for Christian higher education, but they have much to learn about being good learners and partners and guests. They have much to share, but even more, we believe, to gain. Signs of God's reign are breaking through, with the agency of some remarkable disciples. There is so much to see, so much to learn, about God's grace and goodness, in so many places.

Select Bibliography

The published sources that our authors consulted make quite a rich collection, one that represents the lively and growing attention that scholars are paying to international higher education. We offer this selection of titles from our authors' notes, plus a few more, as a way of helping someone who wants to follow particular lines of interest, or find out more about higher education in a particular part of the world, in comparative terms, or in some of its recent transnational trends. Some of our chapters' sources came from fairly volatile bases, such as news media and nongovernmental organizations' websites, which frequently change and rearrange content. So we limited the citations below to publications that are not exclusively available online, and thus can be expected to be more broadly and assuredly accessible. That being said, there are two online sites in particular that proved to be valuable to our authors and to the compiling of this bibliography. They are worth many visits:

1. The Center for International Higher Education (CIHE), accessed (on January 28, 2013) at http://www.bc.edu/research/cihe/. CIHE is located at Boston College, and is directed by Philip Altbach, a prolific and world-renowned scholar of international higher education. This site conveys a great deal of information about the study of international higher education, and it is the home of a very informative online journal, *International Higher Education.*

2. The Program for Research on Private Higher Education (PROPHE), accessed (on January 28, 2013) at http://www.albany.edu/dept/eaps/prophe/publications.html. PROPHE is located at the Albany campus of the State

University of New York, and is directed by Daniel C. Levy, one of the leading scholars of private higher education worldwide. This site offers working papers, edited volumes, links to special journal issues that focus on private higher education, dissertations in this field, news reports, and a bibliography.

GLOBAL HIGHER EDUCATION

Altbach, Philip. *International Higher Education: Reflections on Policy and Practice.* Chestnut Hill, Mass.: Center for International Higher Education, 2006.

Altbach, Philip G., and Daniel C. Levy, eds. *Private Higher Education: A Global Revolution.* Rotterdam: Sense Publishers, 2005.

Altbach, Philip G., Liz Reisenberg, and Laura E. Rumbley. *Trends in Global Higher Education: Tracking an Academic Revolution.* A Report Prepared for the UNESCO 2009 World Conference on Higher Education. Paris: UNESCO, 2009.

Levy, Daniel. "The Unanticipated Explosion: Private Higher Education's Global Surge." *Comparative Education Review* 50:2 (2006): 217-240.

Schofer, Evan, and John W. Meyer. "The Worldwide Expansion of Higher Education in the Twentieth Century." *American Sociological Review* 70:6 (December 2005): 898-920.

GLOBAL CHRISTIAN HIGHER EDUCATION

Arthur, James. *Faith and Secularisation in Religious Colleges and Universities.* New York: Routledge, 2006.

Carpenter, Joel A. "New Christian Universities and the Conversion of Cultures." *Evangelical Review of Theology* 36:1 (January 2012): 14-30.

————. "New Evangelical Universities: Cogs in a World System or Players in a New Game?" In *Interpreting Contemporary Christianity: Global Process and Local Identities,* edited by Ogbu U. Kalu, pp. 151-186. Grand Rapids: Eerdmans, 2008.

Glanzer, Perry L., Joel A. Carpenter, and Nick Lantinga. "Looking for God in Higher Education: Examining Trends in Global Christian Higher Education." *Higher Education* 61:6 (2011): 721-755.

Lantinga, Nicholas, ed. *Christian Higher Education in the Global Context: Implications for Curriculum, Pedagogy, and Administration.* Sioux Center, Iowa: Dordt College Press, 2008.

Higher Education — Regions

Africa

Ajayi, J. F. Ade, Lameck K. H. Goma, and G. Ampah Johnson. *The African Experience of Higher Education.* Athens: Ohio University Press, 1996.

Altbach, Philip G., and Damtew Teferra, eds. *African Higher Education: An International Reference Handbook.* Indianapolis: Indiana University Press, 2003.

Banya, Kingsley, and Juliet Elu. "The World Bank and Financing Higher Education in Sub-Saharan Africa." *Higher Education* 42:1 (January 2001): 1-34.

Karram, Grace. "The International Connections of Religious Higher Education in Sub-Saharan Africa: Rationales and Implications." *Journal of Studies in International Education* 15:5 (2011): 487-499.

Lulat, Y. G.-M. *A History of African Higher Education from Antiquity to the Present: A Critical Synthesis.* Westport, Conn.: Praeger Publishers, 2005.

Mabizela, Mahlubi, Daniel C. Levy, and Wycliffe Otieno, eds. "Private Surge amid Public Dominance: Dynamics of the Private Provision of Higher Education in Africa." *Journal of Higher Education in Africa/Revue de l'Enseignement Supérieur en Afrique* 5:2-3 (special issue 2007).

Mulatu, Semeon. "Transitioning from a Theological College to a Christian University in East African Context: A Multi-Case Study." Ph.D. dissertation, Southern Baptist Theological Seminary, 2012.

Nguru, Faith. "What Can Christian Higher Education Do to Promote Educational Well-Being in Africa?" In *Christian Higher Education in the Global Context,* edited by Nicholas Lantinga, pp. 135-150. Sioux Center, Iowa: Dordt College Press, 2006.

Rinsum, Henk J. van. " 'Wipe the Blackboard Clean': Academization and Christianization — Siblings in Africa." *African Studies Review* 45:2 (2002): 27-48.

Sawyerr, Akilagpa. "Challenges Facing African Universities: Selected Issues." *African Studies Review* 47:1 (April 2004): 1-59.

Teferra, Damtew, and Philip G. Altbach. "African Higher Education: Challenges for the 21st Century." *Higher Education* 47:1 (January 2004): 21-50.

Thayer, Bev. "Private Higher Education in Africa: Six Country Case Studies." In *African Higher Education: An International Reference Handbook,* edited by Damtew Teferra and Philip G. Altbach, pp. 53-60. Bloomington: Indiana University Press, 2003.

Varghese, N. V. *Private Higher Education in Africa.* Paris: International Institute for Educational Planning, 2004.

Africa — Nigeria

Babalola, D. O. *The Compass: The Success Story of Babcock University, One of the First Three Private Universities in Nigeria.* Ikenne-Remo, Nigeria: G. Olarotayo, 2002.

Muzeli, Jibril. "Nigeria." In *International Handbook of Higher Education*, Part One: *Global Themes and Contemporary Challenges*, edited by James J. F. Forest and Philip G. Altbach, pp. 919-934. Dordrecht, Netherlands: Springer, 2006.

Osagie, Anthony U., ed. *Change and Choice: The Development of Private Universities in Nigeria*. Benin City: Rawel Fortune Resources, 2009.

State of Private Universities in Nigeria. Report of the 2003 Annual Monitoring and Quality Assurance of Private Universities in Nigeria. Abuja: National Universities Commission, 2003.

Africa — Kenya

Abagi, Okwach, Juliana Nzomo, and Wycliffe Otieno. *Private Higher Education in Kenya: New Trends in Higher Education*. Paris: International Institute for Educational Planning, 2005.

Mutula, Stephen M. "University Education in Kenya: Current Developments and Future Outlook." *International Journal of Educational Management* 16:3 (2002): 109-119.

Ngome, C. "Kenya." In *African Higher Education: An International Reference Handbook*, edited by Philip G. Altbach and Damtew Teferra, pp. 359-371. Bloomington: Indiana University Press, 2003.

Osongo, Jane. "The Growth of Private Universities in Kenya: Implications for Gender Equity in Higher Education." *Journal of Higher Education in Africa* 5:2-3 (2007): 111-133.

Otieno, Wycliffe. "Private Provision and Its Changing Interface with Public Higher Education: The Case of Kenya." *Journal of Higher Education in Africa* 5:2-3 (2007): 173-196.

———, and Daniel Levy. "Public Disorder, Private Boons? Inter-sectoral Dynamics Illustrated in the Kenyan Case." PROPHE Working Paper no. 9, July 2007. Program for Research on Private Higher Education (PROPHE), Albany, State University of New York.

Asia

Altbach, Philip G., and V. Selvaratnam, eds. *From Dependence to Autonomy: The Development of Asian Universities*. Dordrecht, Netherlands: Kluwer Academic Publishers, 2002.

Dinakarlal, J., ed. *Christian Higher Education and Globalization in Asia/Oceania: Realities and Challenges*. Sioux City, Iowa: Dordt College Press, 2010.

Elwood, Douglas J., ed., *The Humanities in Christian Higher Education in Asia: Ethical and Religious Perspective*. Quezon City: New Day Publishers, 1978.

Fenn, William Purviance. *Ever New Horizons: The Story of the United Board for Christian Higher Education in Asia, 1922-1975*. North Newton, Kans.: Mennonite Press, 1980.

Asia — China

Bays, Daniel H., and Ellen Widmer. *China's Christian Colleges: Cross-Cultural Connections, 1900-1950*. Palo Alto, Calif.: Stanford University Press, 2009.
Corbett, Charles H. *Lingnan University*. New York: Trustees of Lingnan University, 1963.
Feiya, Tao, and Peter Tze Ming Ng. *Jidujiao daxue yu Guoxue yanjiu* (Chinese Studies Research and Christian Colleges in China). Fujian: Fujian Educational Press, 1998.
Gernet, Jacques. *China and the Christian Impact*. Cambridge: Cambridge University Press, 1985.
Jia-feng, Liu, and Liu Tianlu. *Christian Universities During the Sino-Japanese War Time*. Fuzhou: Fujian Educational Press, 2003.
Lutz, Jessie. *China and Christian Colleges, 1850-1950*. Ithaca, N.Y.: Cornell University Press, 1971.
Ng, Peter Tze Ming. *Changing Paradigms of Christian Higher Education in China, 1888-1950*. Lewiston: Edwin Mellen Press, 2002.
———. "From Theological Education to Religious Studies — An Enquiry into the Development of Religious Education at Yenching University, China." *Journal of the History of Christianity in Modern China* 2 (October 1999): 45-62 (in Chinese).
———. "Secularization or Modernization: Teaching Christianity in China since the 1920s." *Studies in World Christianity* 5:1 (January 1999): 1-17.
Zhang Kaiyuan, and Arthur Waldron, eds. *Zhongxi wenhua yu Jiaohui Daxue* (Christian Universities and Chinese-Western Cultures). Wuhan: Hubei Educational Press, 1991.

Asia — South Korea

Association for University History. *What Are Universities in the Transition Period?* Seoul: Hangilsa Publishing, 2000 (in Korean).
Christian Institute of Social Studies/Korea Institute for Christian Cultural Studies, Soongsil University. *Asia in the 21st Century and the Christian University*. Seoul: Yulrinmunwha, 1988.
Eun, Jun-Kyuan. "The Identity Crisis of the Christian University and the Future." *Contemporary Theology* 10 (1985): 156 (in Korean).
Fisher, James E. *Democracy and Education in Korea*. Seoul: Yonsei University Press, 1970.
Han, Kyu-Won. *A Study of Nationalistic Education in Korean Christian Schools*. Seoul: Gukhakjaryowon, 2003 (in Korean).
Kang, Hee-Chun. "The Future of the Christian University." *Yonsei Journal of Theology* 7 (2002): 213.

Kang, Yung-Sun. "Mission Through Christian Liberal Arts Education." *University and Mission* 1 (1999): 31-48 (in Korean).

Kim, Jong-Chul. *A Study of Korean Higher Education*. Seoul: Pakyoungsa, 1979 (in Korean).

Kim, Se-Yeul. "Asian Prospect and the Christian University in Korea: Focusing on the Case of Hannam University." In *Asia in the 21st Century and the Christian University*, edited by CISS/KICCS, pp. 29-48.

Kim, Yung Han. "Soongsil's 1st Century and 2nd Century." In *Asia in the 21st Century and the Christian University*, edited by CISS/KICCS, pp. 232-274.

Lee, Jeong-Kyu. *Historic Factors Influencing Korean Higher Education*. Somerset, N.J.: Jimoondang International, 2000.

————. *Korean Higher Education: A Confucian Perspective*. Edison, N.J.: Jimoondang International, 2002.

————. "Religious Factors Historically Affecting Premodern Korean Elite/Higher Education." *The SNU Journal of Education Research* 8 (1998): 31-63.

————. "The Role of Religion in Korean Higher Education." *Religion & Education* 29:1 (2002): 49-65.

————. "A Study of the Development of Contemporary Korean Higher Education." Unpublished Ph.D. dissertation, University of Texas at Austin, 1997.

Lee, Kyae-Jun. "The Identity of the Christian University and Its Future Task." *University and Mission* 2 (2000): 7-34 (in Korean).

Lee, Suk-Jong. *The Christian University and Education: The Identity of the Christian University and Its Search for a New Way*. Seoul: Yaeyung Communication, 2007 (in Korean).

Min, Kyung-Bae. "The History of Campus Mission in Korean University." In *The Christian University and Campus Mission*, edited by Kyae Jun Lee, pp. 41-71. Seoul: Junmangsa, 1997 (in Korean).

Paik, George I. *The History of Protestant Mission in Korea 1882-1910*. Pyongyang: Union Christian College Press, 1929.

Park, Joon Surh. "The Task and Future of the Korean Christian University Graduate School Education." In *Asia in the 21st Century and the Christian University*, edited by CISS/KICCS, pp. 275-300.

Son, Bong-Ho. "Academic Achievement and the Christian Faith: Christian Higher Education in East Asia." *Christian Higher Education* 1:2-3 (2002): 165-187.

————. "Christian Higher Education in Korea: Problems and Prospects." *Proceedings of the International Symposium on Christian Higher Education*. Pusan: Kosin University Press, 1996.

Underwood, Horace H. *Modern Education in Korea*. New York: International Press, 1926.

Wood, C. W. "The Realities of Public Higher Education in Korea." *The Journal of Higher Education* 32:7 (1961): 377-386.

Yoo, Yong-Ryul. "The First Modern College: Soongsil College." In *What Are Univer-*

sities in the Transition Period? edited by the Association for University History. Seoul: Hangilsa Publishing, 2000 (in Korean).

Asia — India

Abrol, Dinesh. "Commercialisation of Higher Education: Implications of the GATS 2000 Negotiations." *Social Scientist* 33:9/10 (September-October 2005): 75-89.

Commission on Christian Higher Education in India. *The Christian College in India: The Report of the Commission on Higher Education in India.* London: Oxford University Press, 1931.

Dickinson, Richard, and S. P. Appasamy. *The Christian College and National Development.* Madras: Christian Literature Society, 1967.

——. *The Christian College in Developing India: A Sociological Inquiry.* London: Oxford University Press, 1971.

Dinakarlal, Premalatha. "Religious Diversity and Christian Higher Education in India: Prospects and Problems." In *Christian Higher Education and Globalization in Asia/Oceania: Realities and Challenges,* edited by J. Dinakarlal. Sioux City, Iowa: Dordt College Press, 2010.

Gnanadason, Joy. *A Forgotten History.* Chennai: Gurukul Lutheran Theological College and Research Institute, 1994.

Gnanakan, Ken. "Response to Bong Ho Son." In *Christian Higher Education and Globalization in Asia/Oceania: Realities and Challenges,* edited by J. Dinakarlal, pp. 15-20. Sioux City, Iowa: Dordt College Press, 2010.

Gupta, Asha. "International Trends and Private Higher Education in India." *International Journal of Educational Management* 22:6 (2008): 565-594.

Gupta, Asha, Daniel C. Levy, and Krishnapratap Bhagwantrao Powar, eds. *Private Higher Education: Global Trends and Indian Perspectives.* New Delhi: Shipra Publications, 2008.

Jacob, Mani, ed. *Directory of Church-related Colleges in India.* New Delhi: All India Association for the Promotion of Christian Higher Education, 1995.

Jacob, Reny, and Carolyne John, eds. *Directory of Church-related Colleges in India.* New Delhi: All India Association for the Promotion of Christian Higher Education, 2001.

Tilak, Jandhyala B. G. "Fees, Autonomy and Equity." *Economic and Political Weekly,* February 28-March 5, 2004, pp. 870-873.

——. "Transition from Higher Education as a Public Good to Higher Education as a Private Good: The Saga of Indian Experience." *Journal of Asian Public Policy* 1:2 (2008): 220-234.

Europe

Anderson, Robert. *European Universities from the Enlightenment to 1914.* Oxford: Oxford University Press, 2004.

Blückert, Kjell, Guy Neave, and Thorsten Nybom, eds. *The European Research University: An Historical Parenthesis.* New York: Palgrave Macmillan, 2006.

Kozma, Tamás. "Political Transformations and Higher Education Reforms." *European Education* 40:2 (2008): 29-45.

Ridder Symoens, Hilde de, ed. *A History of the University in Europe.* Vol. 1, *Universities in the Middle Ages.* Cambridge: Cambridge University Press, 1992.

————. *A History of the University in Europe.* Vol. 2, *Universities in Early Modern Europe (1500-1800).* Cambridge: Cambridge University Press, 1996.

Rüegg, Walter, ed. *A History of the University in Europe.* Vol. 3, *Universities in the Nineteenth and Early Twentieth Centuries (1800-1945).* Cambridge: Cambridge University Press, 2004.

Tomus, Voldemar. "The Bologna Process and the Enlightenment Project." *European Education* 40:2 (2008): 9-28.

Europe — Western

Astley, Jeff, L. Francis, J. Sullivan, and A. Walker, eds. *The Idea of a Christian University.* Milton Keynes: Paternoster, 2004.

Bebbington, David. "The Secularization of British Universities since the Mid-Nineteenth Century." In *The Secularization of the Academy,* edited by George Marsden and Bradley J. Longfield, pp. 259-277. New York: Oxford University Press, 1992.

Elford, R. J., ed. *The Foundation of Hope: Turning Dreams into Reality.* Liverpool: Liverpool University Press, 2003.

Glanzer, Perry L. "Searching for the Soul of English Universities: An Analysis of Christian Higher Education in England." *British Journal of Educational Studies* 56 (2008): 163-183.

Green, V. H. H. *Religion at Oxford and Cambridge.* London: SCM Press, 1964.

Van Deursen, A. T. *The Distinctive Character of the Free University in Amsterdam, 1880-2005: A Commemorative History.* Translated by H. D. Morton. Grand Rapids: Eerdmans, 2005.

Europe — Eastern

Connelly, John. *Captive University: The Sovietisation of East German, Czech, and Polish Higher Education, 1945-56.* Chapel Hill: University of North Carolina Press, 2000.

David-Fox, Michael, and György Péteri, eds. *Academia in Upheaval: Origins, Trans-*

fers, and Transformations of the Communist Academic Regime in Russia and East Central Europe. Westport, Conn.: Bergin & Garvey, 2000.

Glanzer, Perry. "The First Ukrainian Christian University: The Rewards and Challenges of Being an Eastern Anomaly." *Christian Higher Education* 11:5 (2012): 320-330.

————. "The Role of the State in the Secularization of Christian Higher Education: A Case Study of Eastern Europe." *Journal of Church and State* 53:2 (Spring 2011): 161-182.

Glanzer, Perry, and Claudiu Cimpean. "The First Baptist University in Europe: An Explanation and Case Study." *Christian Higher Education* 8:5 (2009): 1-11.

Glanzer, Perry, and Konstantin Petrenko. "Resurrecting the Russian University's Soul: The Emergence of Eastern Orthodox Universities and Their Distinctive Approaches to Keeping Faith with Their Religious Tradition." *Christian Scholar's Review* 36 (2007): 263-284.

Klassen, Sarah. *Lithuania Christian College: A Work in Progress.* Winnipeg, Manitoba: Leona DeFehr, 2001.

Kortunov, Andrei. "Russian Higher Education." *Social Research* 76:1 (2009): 203-224.

Morgan, Anthony W., and Nadezhda V. Kulikova. "Reform and Adaptation in Russian Higher Education: An Institutional Perspective." *European Education* 39:3 (2007): 39-61.

Rudman, Herbert C. *The School and the State in the USSR.* New York: Macmillan, 1967.

Slantcheva, S., and D. C. Levy. *Private Higher Education in Post-Communist Europe: In Search of Legitimacy.* New York: Palgrave Macmillan, 2007.

Sutton, Jonathan. *Traditions in New Freedom: Christianity and Higher Education in Russia and Ukraine Today.* Nottingham: Bramcote Press, 1996.

Latin America

Alcántara Mejía, José Ramón. "Latin American Higher Education at the Crossroads: The Christian Challenge of Being Transformed Through the Renewal of Understanding." *Christian Higher Education* 1:2-3 (2002): 235-250.

————. "Sean transformados mediante la renovación de su mente: el reto cristiano en la encrucijada de la educación cristiana superior en Latinoamérica." In *Presencia cristiana en el Mundo Academic,* edited by Sidney Roy. Buenos Aires: Kairos, 2001.

Bastian, Jean Pierre. *Protestantes, Liberales y Francomasones: Sociedades de Ideas y Modernidad en América Latina, Siglo XIX.* Mexico City: Fondo de Cultura Económica, 1993.

————. *Protestantismos y Modernidad Latinoamericana: Historia de Unas Minorías Religiosas Activas en América Latina.* Mexico City: Fondo de Cultura Económica, 1994.

Latin America — Mexico

Acosta Silva, Adrián. *La Educación Superior Privada en México.* IESALC Report. www.iesalc.unesco.org. 2005.

Alcántara Mejía, José Ramón. "Latin American Higher Education at the Crossroads: The Christian Challenge of Being Transformed through the Renewal of Understanding." *Christian Higher Education* 1:2-3 (2002): 235-250.

————. "Transculturizing the Humanities in Christian Higher Education." *Journal of Latin American Theology* 3:1 (2008): 26-43.

Bastian, Jean Pierre. *Los Disidentes: Sociedades Protestantes y Revolución en México, 1872-1911.* Mexico City: Fondo de Cultura Económica, 1993.

————. *Protestantismo y sociedad en México.* Mexico City: Casa Unida de Publicaciones, 1983.

Caso, Antonio. *Obras Completas: I Polémicas.* Mexico City: Universidad Nacional Autónoma de México, 1971.

Kent, Rollin, ed. *Las Políticas de Educación Superior en México Durante la Modernización.* Mexico City: ANUIES, 2009.

————. "Puntos para una agenda de políticas de educación superior en América Latina." In *La universidad Latinoamericana ante los nuevos escenarios de la región,* 71-82. Mexico City: Universidad Iberoamericana, 1995.

Vasconcelos, José. *La raza cósmica.* Mexico City: Austral, 1948.

Latin America — Brazil

Calvani, Carlos Eduardo. "A educação no projeto missionário do protestantismo no Brasil." *Revista Pistis* 1:1 (2009): 53-69.

Cunha, L. A. "Ensino Superior e Universidade no Brasil." In *500 Anos de Educação no Brasil,* edited by E. M. T. Lopes. Belo Horizonte: Autêntica, 2003.

————. *A Universidade Crítica: O Ensino Superior na República Populista.* Rio de Janeiro: Francisco Alves, 1989.

Cunha, M. V. "John Dewey e o pensamento educacional brasileiro: a centralidade da noção de movimento." *Revista Brasileira de Educação* 17 (2001): 86-99.

Della Cava, R. "Igreja e Estado no Brasil do Século XX: Sete Monografias Recentes sobre o Catolicismo Brasileiro." *Estudos CEBRAP* 12 (1975): 5-52.

IPEA. Instituto de Pesquisas Econômicas Aplicadas. *PNAD 2007 — Primeiras análises.* Comunicado da Presidência, no. 12, 2008.

Lamego, V. *Farpa na Lira: Cecília Meireles na Revolução de 30.* Rio de Janeiro: Record, 1996.

Lima, A. A. *Memórias Improvisadas: Diálogos com Medeiros Lima.* 2nd ed. Rio de Janeiro: Vozes & Educam, 2000.

Mendonça, A. G. *O Celeste Porvir: A Inserção do Protestantismo no Brasil.* São Paulo: Paulinas, 1984.

Miceli, S. *Intelectuais à brasileira.* São Paulo: Companhia das Letras, 2001.

Oliveira, M. M. "As origens da educação no Brasil: Da hegemonia católica às primeiras tentativas de organização do ensino." *Ensaio: aval. pol. públ. Educ* 12:45 (2004): 945-958.

Ramalho, J. P. *Prática Educativa e Sociedade.* Rio de Janeiro: Zahar, 1975.

Stencel, R. *História da Educação Superior Adventista: Brasil, 1969-1999.* Tese Doutorado em Educação, UNIMEP, 2007.

Teixeira, A. *Educação no Brasil.* São Paulo: Cia. Editora Nacional, 1976.

―――. *Ensino Superior no Brasil. Análise e Interpretação de Sua Evolução até 1969.* Rio de Janeiro: Editora UFRJ, 2005.

Vargas, G. *Diário 1930-1936.* Rio de Janeiro: Siciliano & FGV, 1995.

Vasselai, C. *As Universidades Confessionais no Ensino Superior Brasileiro: Identidades, Contradições e Desafios.* Dissertação Mestrado em Educação, Unicamp, 2001.

Vieira, C. R. A. Contribuição protestante à reforma da educação pública paulista. *Comunicações (Piracicaba)* 9:1 (2002): 256-274.

North America — Canada

Fay, Terence J. *A History of Canadian Catholics: Gallicanism, Romanism, and Canadianism.* Montreal: McGill-Queen's University Press, 2002.

Gidney, Catherine. *A Long Eclipse: The Liberal Protestant Establishment and the Canadian University, 1920-1970.* Montreal: McGill-Queen's University Press, 2004.

Hiebert, Al. *Character with Competence Education.* Steinbach, Manitoba: Association of Canadian Bible Colleges, 2005.

―――. "Only in Canada: A Study of National Market Potential for Christian Higher Education Canada (CHEC) Institutions." *Christian Higher Education* 10:5 (2011): 397-421.

Higgins, Michael. "Catholic Higher Education in Canada." In *Sciat ut Serviat*, edited by Guy Real Thivierge and Michele Jarton. Paris: Federatio Internationalis Universatatum Catholicarum, 2009.

Raymond, Jonathan. *Called to a Higher Purpose.* Langley, British Columbia: Trinity Western University, 2009.

North America — United States

Benne, Robert, *Quality with Soul: How Six Premier Colleges and Universities Keep Faith with Their Religious Traditions.* Grand Rapids: Eerdmans, 2001.

Burtchaell, James Tunstead, *The Dying of the Light: The Disengagement of Colleges and Universities from Their Christian Churches.* Grand Rapids: Eerdmans, 1998.

Dovre, Paul J., ed. *The Future of Religious Colleges.* Grand Rapids: Eerdmans, 2002.

Gleason, Philip. *Contending with Modernity: Catholic Higher Education in the Twentieth Century.* New York: Oxford University Press, 1995.

Hughes, Richard T., and William B. Adrian, eds. *Models for Christian Higher Educa-*

tion: *Strategies for Success in the Twenty-first Century*. Grand Rapids: Eerdmans, 1997.

Marsden, George M. *The Outrageous Idea of Christian Scholarship*. New York: Oxford University Press, 1997.

―――. *The Soul of the American University: From Protestant Establishment to Established Nonbelief*. New York: Oxford University Press, 1994.

Noll, Mark, and James Turner, *The Future of Christian Learning: An Evangelical and Catholic Dialogue*. Grand Rapids: Brazos Press, 2008.

Piderit, John. *Catholic Higher Education: A Culture in Crisis*. New York: Oxford University Press, 2010.

Reuben, Julie A. *The Making of the Modern University: Intellectual Transformation and the Marginalization of Morality*. Chicago: University of Chicago Press, 1996.

Ringenberg, William. *The Christian College: A History of Protestant Higher Education in America*. 2nd ed. Grand Rapids: Baker Academic, 2006.

Roberts, Jon H., and James Turner. *The Sacred and the Secular University*. Princeton, N.J.: Princeton University Press, 2000.

Schuman, Samuel. *Seeing the Light: Religious Colleges in Twenty-first Century America*. Baltimore: Johns Hopkins University Press, 2009.

Sloan, Douglas. *Faith and Knowledge: Mainline Protestantism and American Higher Education*. Louisville, Ky.: Westminster John Knox Press, 1994.

Tewksbury, D. G. *The Founding of American Colleges and Universities before the Civil War*. Mansfield Centre, Conn.: Martino Publishing, 2011 (original work published 1932).

Veysey, Lawrence. *The Emergence of the American University*. Chicago: University of Chicago Press, 1965.

Wolterstorff, Nicholas. *Educating for Shalom*. Edited by Clarence Joldersma and Gloria Goris Stronks. Grand Rapids: Eerdmans, 2004.

Oceania

Dinakarlal, J., ed. *Christian Higher Education and Globalization in Asia/Oceania: Realities and Challenges*. Sioux City, Iowa: Dordt College Press, 2010.

Gillan, Michael, Bill Damachis, and John McGuire. "Australia in India: Commodification and Internationalisation of Higher Education." *Economic and Political Weekly*, April 5-11, 2003, pp. 1395-1403.

Sands, Edward Wilfird, and Willem Berends. "Tertiary Education in Australia: Part I." *Christian Higher Education* 11:5 (2012): 293-302.

―――. "Tertiary Education in Australia: Part II." *Christian Higher Education* 11:5 (2012): 303-309.

Contributors

JOEL CARPENTER is professor of history and director of the Nagel Institute for the Study of World Christianity at Calvin College. For many years his scholarship focused on American religious history, and his best-known work is *Revive Us Again: The Reawakening of American Fundamentalism* (Oxford, 1997). In recent years he has been thinking and writing about Christian higher education and world Christianity. His latest book is *Walking Together: Christian Thinking and Public Life in South Africa* (ACU Press, 2012).

J. DINAKARLAL serves as IAPCHE's Asia/Oceania director. He taught English for thirty-four years at Scott Christian College (auton.) in Nagercoil, India. He has been a leader in the All-India Association for Christian Higher Education and the Student Christian Movement of India. In addition to numerous publications, he has been honored with a national award for innovative teaching and has served on many peer review teams to assess and accredit colleges in India.

HARRY FERNHOUT is president emeritus of The King's University College in Edmonton, Canada, where he served from 2005. From 1990 to 2005 he served as president of the Institute for Christian Studies in Toronto. He has held many important leadership and advisory posts in Canadian and international Christian educational networks, and has published several essays on the nature of Christian higher education. He is particularly interested in "educating for shalom" as the central animating metaphor for Christian engagement in higher education.

ALEXANDRE BRASIL FONSECA serves as an advisor to the presidency of the Republic of Brazil. Before that, he was an associate professor of sociology at the

Federal University of Rio de Janeiro. From 2010 to 2012 he was the director of that university's Center of Educational Technology for Health. He has conducted re-search and has published in a broad array of topics in sociology, including religion, media, food and culture, and health education. One of his notable publications is in English: "Religion and Democracy in Brazil: A Study of the Leading Evangelical Politicians," in *Evangelical Christianity and Democracy in Latin America,* ed. Paul Freston (Oxford, 2008).

Musa A. B. Gaiya is a professor of church history at the University of Jos, Nigeria. He is also an ordained minister with the ECWA (Evangelical Church Winning All) denomination. He has published several books and articles, most notably *Christi-anity in Africa* (University of Jos Press, 2002), and is the co-editor of *Churches in Fellowship: A Story of TEKAN* (Africa Christian Textbooks, 2005). Currently he is involved in a research program on global Pentecostalism.

Perry L. Glanzer is professor of educational foundations in the Department of Educational Administration and Resident Scholar in the Baylor Institute for Studies of Religion at Baylor University. He is the co-author with Todd Ream of *The Idea of a Christian College: A Reexamination for Today's University* (Cascade, 2013), *Christianity and Moral Identity in Higher Education* (Palgrave-Macmillan, 2009), and *Christianity and Scholarship in Higher Education* (Jossey-Bass, 2007). In addition, he has published more than fifty journal articles and book chapters on topics related to Christian higher education, religion and education, and moral education.

Nicholas Lantinga is professor of international relations at Handong Global University. For nine years he served as director of the International Association for the Promotion of Christian Higher Education (IAPCHE) and built up its world-wide membership and programs. Most notable among his publications is *Christian Higher Education in the Global Context* (Dordt College Press, 2008).

George Marsden is the Francis A. McAnaney Professor of History emeritus at the University of Notre Dame. He has also held positions at Calvin College and at the Duke University Divinity School. Among his many publications in American religious and cultural history are two books on higher education: *The Soul of the American University* (Oxford, 1994) and *The Outrageous Idea of Christian Scholar-ship* (Oxford, 1997). He is currently working on a book about C. S. Lewis's classic work, *Mere Christianity.*

José Ramón Alcántara Mejía is professor of humanities at the Iberoameri-can University in Mexico City, a well-known drama critic, an ordained Lutheran pastor, and an influential participant in student Christian, social justice, and environmental movements. He is the former chairman of the board of IAPCHE. His best-known scholarly publication is *The Hidden Path: Poetics and Hermeneutics in the Castellan Works of Fray Luis De León* (in Spanish, Iberoamerican University, 2003).

PETER TZE MING NG served as professor of religious education for twenty-three years at the Chinese University of Hong Kong. He has held many guest appointments in mainland China and has established networks worldwide in the fields of education studies and the history of Christianity. His most recent books include two co-edited with Jan A. B. Jongeneel et al.: *Christian Mission and Education in Modern China, Japan and Korea* (Peter Lang, 2009), and *Christian Presence and Progress in North-East Asia: Historical and Comparative Studies* (Peter Lang, 2011). More recently he wrote *Chinese Christianity: An Interplay between Global and Local Perspectives* (Brill, 2012).

FAITH W. NGURU is the deputy vice chancellor of Riara University, Kenya. Her scholarly expertise is in mass communications. From 1989 to 2012, she taught at Daystar University, Kenya, and served in various leadership positions. She maintains research interests in media studies, Christian ministries, and education. She is also involved in Christian primary and secondary schooling and holds regular workshops for educators on developing a Christian worldview.

CRISTIANE CANDIDO SANTOS is a bachelor and licentiate in social sciences at the Federal University of Rio de Janeiro, Brazil. She earned a master's degree in sociology with concentration in anthropology at the same institution. Currently she teaches sociology in private high school institutions. Her research themes are set around religious practices and forms, more specifically on neo-Pentecostal practices in urban areas of Rio de Janeiro.

KUK-WON SHIN has taught philosophy and culture since 1994 at Chongshin University in Seoul, South Korea, and he has been a leader in the Christian ethics movement in Korea. He has authored, co-authored, or edited thirteen books, and has translated five books from English into Korean. He is best known in Korea for his Christian worldview book, *Spectacles of Nicodemus: Kindly Explained Christian Worldview* (IVP Korea, 2005). He also has published academic and popular articles on Christian worldview, hermeneutics, media ethics, and culture.

Index

Aberdeen University, 138
Academic Revolution, The (Jencks and Riesman), 265
Academic Staff of Nigerian Universities Union (ASUU), 28
Academy of the Arts (Academia de Artes), 212
Achievers University, 34
Adeboye, Enoch, 31
Adrian, William B., 36
Africa, 8, 9, 16, 20, 277, 278, 281, 303; educational tradition in from the pre-colonial period, 44-47; Francophone Africa, 294; information and communication technology (ICT) education in, 64-65; nongovernmental higher education in, 13; teaching issues in African private universities, 62-64; "Western"-style universities in, 45-46. *See also* Africa, Christian higher education (CHE) in; East Africa; *specifically listed individual African nations;* Sub-Saharan Africa
Africa, Christian higher education (CHE) in: Christian universities, 21, 22-23, 43-44, 65-67, 293, 295-296; financing of Christian universities, 60-62; governance of Christian universities, 59-60; identity issues of CHE, 58-59
Africa International University (AIU), 56, 57
African Nazarene University, 53
African University, 35
Al-Azhar, 45
Alcántara, José, 2
Alexandria Museum and Library, 44-45
All India Association for the Promotion of Christian Higher Education (AIAPCHE), 112, 113, 293, 301
Allen, Young J., 69
Altbach, Philip, 6, 27, 293, 294, 296
Ambrose University College, 237
American College (India), 129
American School (Brazil), 215
Amoroso, Alceu, 217
Anderson, Robert, 141, 165
Anglican Church, 152; role of in the formation of English universities, 143
Anglican University, 100
Anglo-Chinese College, 68n1
Angola, 289
Angsgar College, 157
Anyang University, 99
Apostolic Constitution on Catholic Uni-

versities (*Ex Corde Ecclesiae* [1990]), 230, 252, 253, 255
Aquinas, Thomas, 263
Archaeology of Knowledge, The (Foucault), 201
Arthur, James, 7, 157
Asia, 9, 17, 20, 277, 281, 303. *See also* East Asia
Asian Christian Universities and Colleges, 301
Assemblies of God, 208
Association of Catholic Colleges and Universities, 264
Association of Catholic Colleges and Universities in Asia, 293
Association of Catholic Colleges and Universities of Canada, decline in the membership of, 251-252
Association of Christian Schools International (ACSI), 67
Association of Christian Universities and Colleges in Asia (ACUCA), 79, 79n32
Association of Universities and Colleges of Canada (AUCC), 238-239, 254-255; approach of to academic freedom, 245-246; and CHE, 242-246; founding of, 243; membership of, 243, 253; revised academic freedom statement of, 244
Assumption University, 253
Australia, 17, 301
Austria, 146n52, 290
Ave Maria University, 264
Avison, Oliver R., 91n3
Awe, Muyiwa, 28

Babcock University, 33, 38; budget of, 40-41; emergence of from the Adventist Seminary, 35-36; funding of, 39
Bacon, Francis, 120
Baekseok University, 5, 93, 99, 104
Bahia, 210, 211
Banya, Kingsley, 29
Baptist Biblical Institute, 172
Baptists, 208, 261; Southern Baptists, 265

Bastián, Jean-Pierre, 193, 194
Bates, Miner S., 82
Belgium, 145, 147-148, 161, 281, 289
Benedict XVI (pope), 252-253, 253n39
Benne, Robert, 5, 173
Benson Idahosa University, 33; evolution of from the Church of God Bible School, 35
Bible, the, 67
Bishop's College, 282n15, 285
Bologna Declaration (1999), 155, 169
Bologna process, 155, 169, 184, 185, 296, 300
Bolsa Família, 207
Bong Ho Son, 120
Booth University College, 237, 241
Bose, Subash Chandra, 130
Bowen University, 17, 33
Brazil, Christian higher education (CHE) in, 207-209, 278, 285, 290; concessions leading to church-state union in Brazil, 216-217; and the development of Brazilian higher education, 209; during the Brazilian Republic (1889-1964), 214-222; during the "lost decade" (1980s), 223; early history of (1500-1888), 209-214; influence of the Adventist Church in Brazil, 224-225; influence of the Assemblies of God, 225; and "national modernization," 222-223; recent growth of Protestant initiatives in higher education, 227-228; the role/task of CHE in Brazil, 225-226; specific Christian institutions of higher education in Brazil, 218-220; specific statistics and challenges concerning CHE in Brazil (1964-2010), 222-229; and the Vargas Era, 218, 221-222
Brescia University College, 253
Breslau, 164
Briercrest College, 237
British Columbia College of Teachers (BCCT), 240
Bucharest University, 165
Buddhism, 74, 95, 95n15

Bulgaria, 169
Burke, Kenneth, 202
Byzantium, 134n1, 136

Calvani, Carlos Eduardo, 226
Calvin College, 104, 235
Cambridge University, 138, 140, 146, 146n53
Campion College, 253
Campus Alberta Quality Control (CAQC), 241
Canada, 22, 284, 291, 293; and the "Quiet Revolution" in Quebec, 232; secularization of higher education in, 231-233, 251; secularization of society in, 230-231; total university enrollment in, 247n22; "university college" designation in, 235, 235n10. *See also* Canada, Christian higher education (CHE) in
Canada, Christian higher education (CHE) in, 22, 284; in Alberta, 240-242; and the challenge of generating a public profile, 246-248; and the challenge of institutional identity, 248-251; challenges faced by CHE with the AUCC and the CAUT, 242-246; and the Christian Reformed Church, 235-236; emergence of Protestant evangelical higher education, 233-238; government relations with Christian higher education institutions, 238-242; and the problem of degree-granting authority in Canada, 239-240, 242, 242n15; recent developments in Canadian Catholic higher education, 251-255; shared challenges of CHE, 255-256
Canadian Association of University Teachers (CAUT), 244-246; approach of to higher education, 245-246
Canadian Mennonite University, 237, 241, 244, 245
Canadian Undergraduate Survey Consortium (CUSC), 248
Canadian University College, 237
Canterbury Christ Church University, 156, 157

Cardinal Stefan Wyszyński University, 169
Cardoso, Fernando Henrique, 223
Carey, William, 111, 117
Carnegie Foundation, 60
Carpenter, Joel, 24, 30, 36, 123-124; on the dangers of Christian universities pursuing wealth alone, 37
Caso, Antonio, 194
Catholic Institute of Higher Studies, 217-218
Catholic universities (general): in Canada, 231, 232-233; in China, 78; in Eastern Europe, 2; in Latin America, 2, 21; in Mexico, 198, 200; and the privatization of higher education, 153-154; in the United States, 263-265
Catholic University of America, 13
Catholic University of Chile, 284
Catholic University of Eastern Africa, 21, 43
Catholic University of Ecuador, 284
Catholic University of Eichtätt-Ingolstadt, 158
Catholic University of Lublin (Katolicki Uniwersytet Lubelski [KUL]), 166-167, 170, 175, 176, 177, 179, 181, 182, 183, 186, 187, 188
Catholic University of Lyons, 145
Catholic University of Mons, 145
Catholic University of Nijmegen, 158
Catholic University of Peru, 284
Catholic University of Portugal, 160
Catholic University of Ružomberok (CUR), 171, 185
Catholic University of the West, 145
Catholicism/the Catholic Church/Catholics, 193, 198, 209, 214-215, 260, 261, 268, 271, 303; Catholic elites and the "recatholization of the state" in Brazil, 217-218, 282; growth of, 258n2; power of in Brazil, 216-217
Cava, Della, 216-217
Central China University, 69, 73, 84
Central University College, 304
Centralization, 152, 154-155, 161, 169

Centre for Historical Research on China Christian Colleges, 85-86
Centre for the Promotion of Christian Higher Education in Africa (CPCHEA), 41
Centre for the Study of Religion and Chinese Society, 85-86
Centro D. Vital, 217
Centro Universitário de Anápolis, 222
CEPAL-UNESCO, 197
"Challenges for Emerging Christian Universities" (conference), 57
Chaucer, Geoffrey, 125
Cheeloo University, 73
Chile, 21, 210n3, 289
China, 14, 280, 284, 285; "Christianity fever" *(jidujiaore)* in, 81; "culture fever" *(wenhuare)* in, 81; May Fourth Movement in, 70-71; missionaries in, 68-69, 77-78n26; resurgence of Christian studies in mainland China, 81-87. *See also* China, Christian higher education (CHE) in; China, and the end of missionary schools in the twentieth century
China, and the end of missionary schools in the twentieth century, 70-72; and the broader conception of religious education, 74-75; and the emphasis on the study of national culture, 73-74; and patriotism in Christian colleges, 75-78
China, Christian higher education (CHE) in, 68-70, 87-89; and the "process of modernization," 72. *See also* Catholic universities: in China
China Christian Colleges Catalogues, 85
Chinese Academy of Social Sciences (CASS), 83
Chinese Civil War (1947-1950), 77
Chinese Communist Party, 77
Chinese Nationalist Party (Kuomingtang), 77
Chinese studies research centers *(Guoxue yanjiu suo)*, 73
Chinese University of Hong Kong, 80

Chongshin University, 35, 98, 104
Christ Church College (India), 118
Christendom College, 264
Christian Bilingual University of Congo, 20
Christian College Consortium in America, 36
Christian higher education (CHE), 1-3, 43-44, 161, 250n30, 305; contexts of, 7-8, 203-205; current trends in, 286-297; expansion of, 16-17; lack of scholarly literature concerning, 5-6; as providing education to Christians by Christians, 54; reasons for the rise of new Christian universities, 18-20. *See also* Christian higher education (CHE), future of; Christian higher education (CHE), global health of; Christian higher education (CHE), specific challenges faced by; *specifically listed individual countries, Christian higher education (CHE) in*
Christian higher education (CHE), future of, 297-298; and addressing future threats to CHE, 302-303; and broader Christian partnerships, 301-302; and creatively incarnating Christian distinctives, 298-300; unique missions, 298
Christian higher education (CHE), global health of, 277-278; and the creative work of Christian missionaries, 278-279; and globalization, 292-293; and instrumentalization, 294-297; and liberal democracy and privatization, 283-285; and massification, 286-290; and nationalization and secularization, 279-283; and privatization and access, 290-292
Christian higher education (CHE), specific challenges faced by, 3; the crisis of values, 203; cultural homogenization, 204; inequality of economic opportunities, 203-204; the marginalization issue, 204-205; recharging of the spiritual and moral vacuum left by postmodern education, 205

Christian Higher Education Canada (CHEC), 246-247; total enrollment in, 247n22

Christian Higher Education Faculty Development Network (CHEFDN), 63

Christian hospitals, 52

Christian Medical College, 126

"Christian university": definition of, 3: definition of "Christian," 4-8; definition of "university," 4; distinction between a Christian university and a non-Christian university, 52; the university as a "Christian" invention, 134-135; what is the meaning of a Christian university? 51-52, 56

Christian University of Applied Sciences, 156

Christian Worldview Studies Association of Korea, 107-108

Christianity, 4, 18-19, 56, 70, 73, 87, 94, 140, 167, 190, 266, 268; adaptability of, 258n2; and the birth of higher education, 136-138; and Chinese culture, 79, 81; divisions of, 35; and Korean religious culture, 95n15; social implications, 146-147; world/global Christianity, 258, 269. *See also* Marginalization, of Christianity in state universities

Christians, and modern science, 268-269

Christ's Legionaries, 198

Chung Chi College, 78-79, 79-80, 80n35, 85-86, 88, 89

Chung Chi Divinity School, 80

Chung Yuan University, 78n27, 79

Church Missionary Society (CMS [Anglican]), 55, 111, 117

Church of South India, 111

CMS College, 111, 117, 282, 285

Colish, Marcia, 136

Colombia, 281, 289

Colonialism, 93

Commission for Higher Education (Kenya), 47-48, 57

Concordia University College, 237, 238

Confucianism, 74, 95, 95n15

Corpus Christi College, 253

Council for Advancement and Support of Education (CASE), 27n11, 39

Council of Christian Colleges and Universities (CCCU), 67, 265, 267, 269; growth of, 270-271, 276, 293

Council for Church Colleges (England), 148

Covenant University, 33, 34-35, 41; market-driven nature of, 36-37; success of, 37-38

Crandall University, 238, 244, 245

Czechoslovakia, 146n52

Daystar Communications, 51

Daystar Publications, 51

Daystar University, 21, 35, 43, 53-54, 62, 260; "membership" policy of, 53; and the problem of "false testimony," 54

DeFehr, Art, 173

Deiros, Pablo, 192

Democratic Republic of Congo, private universities in, 30

Deng Xiaoping, 81

Derrida, Jacques, 201, 202

Desai, Morarji, 130

Dewey, John, 215

Diakonhjemmet University College, 157

Dinakarlal, J., 4

Dinakarlal, Premalatha, 112, 114

Directory of Church Related Colleges in India (AIAPCHE), 112, 114, 116, 131

Disciples of Christ, 261

Dixiaoren yu Situ leideng zai hua jiaoyu huodong (The Educational Activities of Calvin Mateer and John Leighton Stuart in China [Shi Jinghuan]), 82

Dominican Republic, 289

Dominican University College, 253

Dordt College, 235

Dorpat, 164

Durham University, 143

Dzhedzhora, Olena, 181-182

East Africa: Christian higher education (CHE) in, 43-44, 51, 62; higher education in, 6; state-sponsored university system in, 46

East Asia, 3, 294

East India Company, 285

Eastern Europe, 277, 280, 282, 284, 285, 289

Eastern Orthodox Church, 180, 282-283

Eastern Orthodox universities, 163, 164, 165, 165n9

Economic and Financial Crimes Commission (EFCC), 32

Education: reductionism in, 95; in technology and business, 23, 23n43

Egypt, 45; monasteries in, 45; Ptolemaic, 45

Ekonomtsev, Ioann, 171, 187

Elu, Juliet, 29

Emanuel University (EU), 172, 175, 176, 178, 179, 184-185, 186, 188, 189

Emmaus Center, 183

Enlightenment, the (Mexican), 192, 193

Ethiopia, 45

Europe, 16-17, 22, 277, 295; medieval, 293. *See also* Eastern Europe; Postcommunist Europe, Christian higher education (CHE) in; Western Europe, Christian higher education (CHE) in

European higher education area (EHEA), 155

European Union (EU), 185, 186

Evangelicalism, 259-260, 266, 269-270; anti-intellectual tradition of, 267; evangelical Bible colleges, 267n24

Ewha Hakdang, 91

Excellence without a Soul (Lewis), 273

Ferguson, John, 73

Fernhout, Harry, 284

Finland, 146n52

First International Symposium on the History of Pre-1949 Christian Universities, 82

Fonseca, Alexandre, 2

Ford Foundation, 60, 168

Foucault, Michel, 201-202

"Four Master Figures of Speech" (Burke), 202

Fourah Bay College, 45

France, 141, 145, 154, 158, 280

Franciscan Missionaries of Mary Society, 126

Franciscan University of Steubenville, 264

Free University of Amsterdam, 144, 146-147, 282

French Revolution, the, 141; Protestant universities that survived the French Revolution, 143

Friends of the Catholic University of Lublin, 166

Frost, Robert, 131-132

Fryer, John, 69

Fu Jen Catholic University, 78

Fudan University, 86

Fujian Normal University, 86

Fukien Christian University, 70, 84

Gaiya, Musa, 17

Galgalo, Joseph, 56

Geng Rong, 73

German Academic Exchange Service (Deutscher Akademischer Austausch Dienst [DAAD]), 60

Germany, 141, 143, 147, 161

Ghana, 13, 25, 39, 289, 304; private Christian universities in, 37

Ginling Women's College, 69, 84

Gitari, David, 55

Glanzer, Perry, 2, 21

Glasgow University, 138

Global Christian Higher Education, 16

Global Christian Higher Education Project, 43, 44, 44n3

Globalization, 103, 293-294, 296; effect of on higher education in India, 119-120

Globe and Mail (Toronto), student satisfaction survey of, 247

Gnanadason, Joy, 115

Gnanakan, Ken, 120, 122

Goethe, Johann Wolfgang von, 66

Gorbachev, Mikhail, 171

Great Britain, 145, 257, 260
Gudziak, Borys, 174, 182, 183
Gutzlaff, K. F. A., 91n4
Gwanghyewon (Widespread Relief
    House), 91, 91n3

Handong Global University, 1-2, 99-100,
    104, 107
Hangchow University, 69, 84
Hangzhou University, 84
Hansae University, 99, 107
Hansei University, 304
Hansin University, 99, 100
Hapdong Presbyterian Church, 99
Hapsburg Empire, 140
Harvard University, 13, 74n15, 283
He Guang Fu, 83-84
He Xiaoxia, 83
Higgins, Michael, 254
Higham, John, 19
Higher education, 134n1, 250n30; chang-
    ing understanding of the purpose of,
    10-11; Christianity and the birth of,
    136-138; "crisis" of, 8; and the public
    good, 11-12; religion's role in, 274n34;
    secular privatization of, 18; the univer-
    sity as a "Christian" invention, 134-135;
    vision of in medieval Europe, 10.
    See also Christian higher education
    (CHE); Higher education, growth of;
    Private higher education
Higher education, growth of, 8; and
    massification (expansion to meet de-
    mand), 8-9, 27, 152-154; and privatiza-
    tion, 10-12, 152-154, 161; systemic strain
    due to increased demand, 9-10
Historia Patria (Sherwell), 194
Historical discourse, 202
HIV/AIDS, 18, 56
Ho, Sung Kee, 297
Hong Kong Baptist College, 79
Hong Kong Baptist University, 79, 80-81
Hong Kong Lingnan University,
    79-80n34
Hu Shih, 77
Huazhong Normal University, 84, 86

Hungary, 172, 185, 290
Hus, John, 138
Husar, Lubomyr, 180

Igbinedion, G. O., 40
Igbinedion University, 33; budget of, 40
Imo Technical University, 30
Imperialism, 71, 73, 81
Income generation activities (IGAs),
    61, 62
India, 4, 8, 22, 290, 303; education of
    women in, 115-116; educational loans
    in, 122-123; effect of globalization on
    higher education in, 119-120; ex-
    pansion and privatization of higher
    education in, 118-123; illiteracy in, 132;
    number of private educational institu-
    tions in, 118; profit-driven atmosphere
    of private colleges in, 120-122. *See also*
    India, Christian higher education
    (CHE) in
India, Christian higher education (CHE)
    in, 111-112, 131-133, 278; autonomy,
    university status, and Christian higher
    education, 124-126; beginnings of, 112-
    114; breakdown of student and faculty
    religious affiliations in, 131; challenges
    to early Christian institutions in India,
    114-117; contributions of, to India, 130-
    131; early Christian colleges in India,
    117-118; number of Christian colleges
    and universities in India, 113-114; pri-
    vatization and, 123-124; quality of, 126;
    role of missionaries in the creation of,
    111-113, 114-115, 116-117. *See also* India,
    Christian higher education (CHE) in,
    three major challenges faced by
India, Christian higher education (CHE)
    in, three major challenges faced by:
    the anti-conversion bills in India, 127-
    128; interference of the government
    with the internal affairs of Christian
    colleges, 129-130; lack of respect
    shown to minority rights, 128
India Today, survey of the quality of
    higher education in India, 126

Indonesia, 17, 290
Information and communication technology (ICT), 64-65, 292
Institute of Christian Studies (ICS), 236, 237, 238, 239, 240
Institute of Church History, 182
International Association for the Promotion of Christian Higher Education (IAPCHE), 2, 7, 41, 63, 67, 148-149, 200n14, 258, 293, 301
International Leadership University, 56
International Monetary Fund (IMF), 18, 60, 202
"Is There a Third Force in Christendom?" (McLoughlin), 266
Islam, 34, 74, 134n1, 136, 258
Italy, 147, 148, 153, 281

Jacob, Mani, 114
Janeiro, 210
Japan, 32, 77, 91, 279, 290
Japanese International Co-operation Agency (JICA), 60
Jencks, Christopher, 265-266
Jenkins, Philip, 135
Jesuits, 118, 126, 139, 198, 211; disbanding of the order by Pope Clement XIV, 140, 164-165
Jesus Christ, 67, 88, 89, 180
Jiaohui xuexiao yu zhongguo jiaoyu jindaihua (Church Schools and the Modernization of Chinese Education [He Xiaoxia and Shi Kinghuan]), 83
Jiqing Lin, 73
John Paul II (pope), 167, 171, 230, 248, 252
Joint Admission and Matriculation Board (JAMB), 26
Joint Admission and Matriculation Board Examinations (JAMBE), 26, 39
Joseph II (emperor), reform of European universities by, 164-165
Juarez, Benito, 193

Kabarak University, 49
Kalam, A. P. J. Abdul, 130
Kalu, Ogbu, 35

Károli Gáspár University (KGU), 172, 175
Kasali, Musiande, 1, 20
Katholieke Universiteit Leuven, 144, 159
Kazan, 165
Kearns, James Fleming, 115
Keimyung University, 96
Kennedy, John F., 263
Kent, Rollin, 197
Kenya, 13, 18, 21, 23, 43-44, 278, 289; CHE institutions in, 47-58, 65-67; Christianity in, 44n2; development of private universities in, 30; and the "identity crisis" issue, 55; integration of Christian faith and scholarship in, 55; number of Christian universities in, 49-50; number of universities in, 46; university enrollment in, 46-47
Kenya Education Network (KENET), 64
Kharkov, 165
Khartoum University College, 25
Kiev, 165
Kim, Young Gil, 1
King's University College, The, 236, 237; membership of in the AUCC, 243; and the strategy of "educating for shalom," 250-251
Kingsbury, Charles, 63
Kohn, Hans, 139
Konigsberg, 164
Korea, history of Christian higher education (CHE) in, 91-95; "graduate colleges" in, 94-95n13; influence of the military on education, 93n11; mission schools, 91-93; and mixtures of different religions, 95n15; and the Yi Dynasty, 92, 95n15. See also South Korea, Christian higher education (CHE) in
Korea Christian Academy of Management, 108
Korean Christian Philosophy Society, 108
Korean Students in All Nations conferences, 109
Korean War (1950-1953), 93
Kosin University, 98, 104

Krakow, 164
Kuolys, Darious, 173
Kuyper, Abraham, 144, 235, 268-269
Kwame Nkrumah University of Science
and Technology (KNUST), 37

Lagos Business School, 39
Larbi, Kingsley, 37
Latin America, 9, 17, 22, 202, 204,
281, 284, 294, 303; first universities
founded in, 210n3; Presbyterian uni-
versities in, 277
Laurentian University, 253
Lawacih (Flashes of Light [al-Rahman
Jami]), 34
Lawyer's School (later Seoul Junior Col-
lege of Law), 91
LCC International University, 173, 174,
176, 179, 187; Board of Directors of,
180
Lebanon, 289
Legge, James, 73
Leipzig University, 138
Levy, Daniel, 284
Lewis, Harry, 273
"Leyes de Reforma," 193
Liberalism, theological, 143; "liberal
Protestantism," 199-200
Liberty University, 304
Lille Catholic University, 145
Lilly Fellows Network of Church-related
Colleges and Universities, 301
Lingnan College, 79
Lingnan University, 70, 73, 76n21, 79,
80-81, 84
Lithuania, 172, 173
Liu, James T. C., 82, 82n39
Liverpool Hope University, 152, 161
Living Faith Church, 34
London Missionary Society, 68
Lovedale Missionary Institute for Afri-
cans, 58-59
Loyola College (India), 126
Loyola-Chicago University, 13
Lungu, Oleg, 176-177
Luther, Martin, 138

Lutheran University of Brazil, 222
Lwów, 164
Lyotard, François, 201

MacArthur Foundation, 168
Mackenzie College, 215, 228
MacKenzie University, 282
Maclean's, student satisfaction survey of,
247-248
Madero Institute, 199
Madonna University, 31-32, 33, 34
Madras Christian College, 118, 129,
282n15, 285
Makerere University College, 25, 46, 62
Makhado, Samson, 66
Mambo, Esther, 56
Manekshaw, Sam, 130
Mao Zedong, 77
Marginalization, of Christianity in state
universities, 135, 140, 143, 204-205
Marsden, George M., 95n14, 231, 286
Marshman, Joshua, 111, 117
Martin, W. A., 69
Marxism, 81, 94
Massification, 8-9, 27, 153-155, 286-289
Mateer, Calvin, 69
McLoughlin, William, 266
McMaster University, 231
*Meiguo chuanjiaoshi yu wanqing zhong-
guo jindaihua* (American Missionaries
and the Modernization of China in
the Late Qing Period [Wang Lixin]),
83
Meireles, Cecília, 217
Mejía, José Alcántara, 294
Mennonites, 265
Messiah College, 51
Mestizo, 195, 195n7
Methodist Granbery Institute, 216
Methodists, 19, 152, 199, 222, 261
Mexican Revolution (1910-1920), 194,
194n4
Mexico, Christian higher education
(CHE) in, 191-192, 294; and the break
with the colonial past, 192-193; and
changes in the Mexican higher educa-

tion system, 195-198; and educational reform, 201n15; future of, 201-203, 205-206; present-day developments, 198-201; the Protestant contribution to, 193-195
Michigan, narrowing of the vision of higher education in, 11n17
Mishra, Alya, 131
Modernism/modernity, 144, 190
Moi, Daniel Arap, 49
Monasteries (Christian), 45
Moscow, 165
Mozambique, 28
Muge, Alexander, 55
Multiculturalism, 103

Nairobi Evangelical Graduate School of Theology (NEGST), 56, 57
Nairobi International School of Theology (NIST), 56, 57
Nanjing Normal University, 84
Nanjing University, 84, 86
Narayanan, K. R., 130
National Autonomous University of Mexico, 195
National Council for Scientific Research (Brazil), 221
National Council of Churches (Kenya), 55
National Students' Union (Brazil), 221
National Survey of Student Engagement (NSSE), 247-248
National Universities Commission (NUC), 32, 41
National University of Mexico, 194
Nationalism, 139, 143
Nationalization, 279-283; of Western European universities, 139-142, 161
Natural science, 268
Negrut, Paul, 184-185, 186
Neo-Marxism, 81
Neo-Thomism, 263, 264
Netherlands, the, 143-144, 148, 154, 161, 290
New School (Brazil), 217

New Shape of World Christianity, The (Noll), 258, 269
New Zealand, 290
Newman Theological College, 253
Ng, Peter, 12
Nguru, Faith, 13, 21, 23
Nicaragua, 289
Niebuhr, H. Richard, 96, 98
Nigeria, 17, 18, 285, 290, 303; colonial colleges (the "Asquith" colleges) founded in, 25; "cults" on campuses in, 28; development/emergence of private universities in, 24-25, 31-33; disruption of public universities by staff strikes, student riots, and corruption, 28; government policy toward private universities, 32-33; growth of higher education in, 27-28; Islamic private universities in, 34; mismanagement of public universities in, 28-29; problems facing higher education in, 26-29; Roman Catholicism in, 31; "second-generation" universities in, 25-26; theological base of universities in, 35-36; total number of universities in, 32; university education in, 25-30. See also Nigeria, Christian higher education (CHE) in
Nigeria, Christian higher education (CHE) in: challenges faced by Christian universities in, 39-41; Christian primary and secondary schools in, 38; Christian universities in (2009), 42; emergence of Christian universities, 33-39; problems with staff development in Christian universities, 40, 40n63
Nigerian Baptist Convention, 30
Nigerian Defence Academy, 25
Njoya, Timothy, 55
Noble College, 118
Noll, Mark, 232, 258-259, 267, 269
Normal University, 84

Obasi, Isaac N., 33, 38
Okogie, Anthony Olubunmi, 31

Okpako, John, 40
Okullu, Henry, 55
Olomouc, 164
Omoregie, Edoba B., 38
Onnuri Church, 107
Ontario University Quality Assurance
   Council, 240
Open Society Institute, 168
Opus Dei, 159
Oral Roberts University, 5, 304
Osagie, Anthony A. U., 39
Osuna, Andrés, 194
Our Lady Seat of Wisdom Academy, 253
Oxford University, 138, 140, 146, 146n53,
   281
Oyedepo, David O., 36

Pan Africa Christian College, 56
Pan African University, 33, 39-40
Papua New Guinea, 289
Partium Christian University, 172
Paul (the Apostle), 204
Pázmány Péter Catholic University, 171,
   179
Peking University, 80, 86
Peking University (Beida), 84; Depart-
   ment of Religion of, 85
Pentecostal Assemblies of Canada
   (POAC), 56
Pentecostalism, 208; Pentecostal
   churches in Brazil, 226
People's University of China, 84, 86
Pepperdine University, 13
Pheko, S. E. Mutsoko, 51
Philip (the Apostle), 88
Philippines, the, 281, 289
Piracicaba School, 215
Pluralism, 274-275, 283-284
*Pneuma: Los Fundamentos Teológicos de
   la Cultura* (Rembao), 195
Poland, 169, 182, 290
Polytechnic School, 215
Pontifical Bolivian University, 284
Pontifical Catholic University of Rio de
   Janeiro, 218
Portugal, 146n52, 147, 148, 153, 209, 210

Post-communist Europe, Christian higher education (CHE) in,
   163-164, 189-190; communist and
   post-communist nature of Eastern
   European higher education, 167-169;
   and the creative/redemptive influence
   of social transformation, 183-184; and
   the creative/redemptive influence of
   university practices, 181-183; future
   possibilities for, 188-189; growth of
   CHE in, 170-173; historical context of,
   164-167; problems facing Christian
   universities, 186-188; and state regulation of Christian universities, 184-186.
   See also Post-communist Europe,
   determining the nature of Christian
   higher education (CHE) in
Post-communist Europe, determining the nature of Christian higher
   education (CHE) in, 173-174; through
   church support and governance, 180-
   181; through the curriculum, 177-178;
   through membership requirements,
   175-177; through public relevance and
   rhetoric related to Christian vision,
   174-175; through worship and ethos,
   179
Postmodernism, 81
Postsecondary Education Quality Assessment Board (PEQAB), 240
Potchefstroom University, 282
Prague, 164
Presbyterians/Presbyterian Church, 221,
   222
Princeton University, 13, 282, 283
Private Colleges Accreditation Board
   (PCAB), 241
Private higher education, 6, 6n10, 10-12,
   12n20, 152-154; differences and simi-
   larities between private and Christian
   education, 20-23. *See also* Private
   higher education, characteristics
   of; Private higher education, global
   growth of
Private higher education, characteristics of: addressing the access needs

of students, 14; corporate leadership, 15-16; focus of on practical education suitable for immediate job placement, 15; lack of emphasis on cultural and social service programs, 15; lack of research and postgraduate programs, 14-15, 15n27; narrow educational mission, 16; spontaneity and localization, 14; use of part-time professors, 15

Private higher education, global growth of, 12; new nongovernmental examples of private education, 12-13; and the rise of for-profit universities, 13-14

Privatization, 18, 118, 123-124, 153-155, 262-263; and access, 290-292; and liberal democracy, 283-285. *See also* Higher education: secular privatization of

Program of Research on Private Higher Education (PROPHE), findings of concerning private universities, 14-16

Protestant Reformation, 138-139, 164

Protestant Theological Institute of Cluj Napoca, 172

Protestants/Protestantism, 199, 208, 265, 268; in Brazil, 212-213, 226; cultural elements brought to Brazil by Protestants, 213-214; "liberal Protestantism," 199-200; Mexican Protestants, 205-206; universities of, 199, 200-201, 209

Providence University College, 238, 241

Prussia, 145

Putin, Vladimir, 187

Pyongtaek University, 99

Pyrate Confraternity, 28

Qinghua University, 86

Racial segregation, 59

Radboud University, 158, 160; Heyendall Institute of, 160

Radhakrishnan, S., 130

Rahman Jami, Abd al-, 34

Rationalism, 96n16

Raymond, Jonathan, 249

Redeemer Pacific College, 253

Redeemer University College, 236, 237, 239, 245, 253-254; membership of in the AUCC, 243; strategic direction statement of *(The Cross and Our Calling)*, 248-249

Redeemer's University, 39

Reductionism: in education, 95; theological, 103

Reformed Church of Hungary, 172

Reformed Free University of Amsterdam. *See* Free University of Amsterdam

Reformed University of Applied Sciences, 156, 157

Regent University, 304

Regis College, 253

Religion and Education: St. John's University as an Evangelizing Agency (Xu Yihua), 83

Religious fundamentalism, 132

Rembao, Alberto, 195

Renaissance University, 34

Research Centre for the Study of Christianity in the Institute of World Religions, 83-84n47

Restore Educational Rights Campaign (China), 71

Richard, Timothy, 69

Riesman, David, 265-266

Rockefeller Foundation, 60

Roman Catholicism. *See* Catholicism/the Catholic Church/Catholics

Romania, 169, 172-173, 185

Ross, John, 91n4

Rousseau, Jean-Jacques, 139

Royal Academy of Design, Painting, Sculpture, and Civil Architecture, 212

Royal Military Academy (Academia Real Militar), 212

Royal Naval Academy (Academia Real da Marinha), 211-212

Rüegg, Walter, 137

Russia, 169, 172, 185, 292

Russian American Christian University, 185

Russian Orthodox Church, 171

Rutgers University, 282

Sáenz, Moisés, 194-195
Sarah Tucker College, 116
Sawyerr, Akilagpa, 29, 37
Scandal of the Evangelical Mind, The
  (Noll), 267
Scandinavia, 143
Schleiermacher, Friedrich, 143
Scotland, 146n52
Scott Christian University, 57
Scott Theological College, 57
Scottish Church College, 118, 282n15, 285
Second Great Awakening, 19
Secularization, 3, 96, 102, 135, 141, 159,
  161, 185, 259; and communism, 166; in
  Eastern Europe, 163; in Europe and
  Great Britain, 257-258; global reach
  of, 279-283; of government in Brazil,
  216; of mainstream universities in the
  United States, 262-263; of mentalities,
  142; political secularization, 280-281;
  of religion and education in Canadian
  society, 230-233; scholarly under-
  standings of, 279-280n6; of Western
  European universities from 1981 to the
  present, 147-148; of Western European
  universities from World War I to 1980,
  146-147
Seoul Imperial University, 92
Seoul Woman's University, 96, 101n26
Serampore College, 111, 117
Seventh-Day Adventists, 35, 36, 39, 180,
  199, 303
Severance Union Medical College, 91
Shalom: concept of, 250; "educating for,"
  250-251
Shamanism, 95n15
Shandong University, 84
Shanghai University, 86
Shangtung Christian University, 69
Sherwell, Guillermo, 194
Shi Jinghuan, 82, 83
Shin, Kuk-won, 20
Sichuan University, 84, 86
Silva, Luis Inácio Lula da, 223-224

Simut, Corneliu, 185
Sino-Japanese War, 77
Slovakia, 185, 290
Smith, Donald, 51
Smith, Faye K., 51
Smith, James K. A., 250n30
Smith, Timothy L., 19
Society of Jesus. *See* Jesuits
Sommerville, C. John, 142; on secular-
  ization, 279-280n6
Song Mei Ling (Madam Chiang), 76
Soochow University, 69, 78
Soong Jun University, 96
Soongsil Hakdang, 91, 92
South Africa, 23n43
South African College, 46, 58
South China Women's University, 70
South Korea, Christian higher education
  (CHE) in, 8-9, 17, 90, 90n1, 92-95,
  109-110, 278, 290, 303; Christian institutions' support (including financial)
  for CHE, 106-110; Christian student
  groups, 108-109; current issues and
  challenges facing CHE, 95-100; declining enrollment in Christian colleges,
  105-106; diversity of denominations,
  106-107; educational societies, 108;
  expansion of Christian colleges into
  large universities, 99; government
  regulations and, 96-97; and the
  growth of Christianity, 19; and Korean
  missionaries working in other parts of
  the world, 109, 109n37; and *Minjung*
  (people's) theology, 94, 100; and the
  struggle for democratization, 93-94;
  the task and vision of, 100-106; and
  "theological colleges," 98-99
Southeast Asia School of Theology,
  80n35
Soyinka, Wole, 28
Spain, 141, 145, 147, 148, 153
Spalding, Dean, 66
St. Aloysius College, 118
St. Andrew's University, 138
St. Francis Xavier University, 253, 255
St. Jerome's University, 253

St. John Orthodox University, 171, 176, 184, 187
St. John's College (Agra, India), 118
St. John's College (Palayamkottai, India), 118
St. John's Medical College (Bangalore), 126
St. John's University (Shanghai), 69
St. Joseph's College (Alberta, Canada), 253
St. Joseph's College (Bangalore, India), 118
St. Joseph's College (Tiruchirappalli, India), 118
St. Mark's College, 253
St. Mary's University College, 253
St. Paul's United Theological College, 55
St. Paul's University (Kenya), 55; degrees offered by, 55; total enrollment of, 55-56
St. Paul's University (Nigeria), 35
St. Paul's University (Ottawa, Canada), 253
St. Peter's College, 253
St. Petersburg, 165
St. Stephen's College (New Delhi), 118, 126; legal battles of, 129
St. Stephen's University (New Brunswick), 237
St. Thomas More College, 253
St. Thomas University, 253, 255
St. Tikhon Orthodox University, 171-172, 176, 178, 184, 187, 188
St. Xavier's College (Kolkatta, India), 118, 126
St. Xavier's College (Mumbai, India), 118, 126
Stackhouse, John, 234
Stanford University, 13
Stella Maris College, 126
Stellenbosch Gymnasium, 58
Stellenbosch University, 58, 282
Stuart, John Leighton, 72, 73
Sub-Saharan Africa, 9, 17; number of private universities in, 48
Sudbury College, 253

Sungkyul University, 99, 297
Switzerland, 143, 145, 157

Taehak (Great School), 91
Taiwan, 17; Christian colleges in, 78n28
Tansian University, 39
Tanzania, 289; development of private universities in, 30
Taoism, 74
Technological Institute of Aeronautics, 221
Teferra, Philip, 27
Teixeira, Anísio, 210
Thailand, 17
Thoburn, Isabella, 116
Tilak, Jandhyala, 122-123
Tilburg University, 158
Timbuktu, 45, 45n5
Tonghap Presbyterian Church, 99
Toronto School of Theology, 233
Treaty of Nanking (1842), 68
Trinity College, 234, 235
Trinity Western University (TWU), 234-235, 237, 238, 253; "faith test" of, 244-245; and the issue of academic freedom in, 245; membership of in the AUCC, 243; problems of with the British Columbia College of Teachers (BCCT), 240; strategic direction statement of (Envision the Century), 248, 249n27
Trnava, 164
Troeltsch, Ernst, 174
Tübingen University, 138
Tung Hai University, 78n27
Tyndale University College, 238, 240

Uganda, 289; private universities in, 30
Uganda Christian University, 62
Ukeagbu, Nnanna, 30
Ukraine, 169, 174, 181; the Orange Revolution in, 183-184
Ukrainian Catholic University (UCU), 171, 174, 175, 177, 179, 181-182, 183-184, 187, 188, 189
Ukrainian Greek-Catholic Church, 180

"Ultra-Ganges Mission Plan," 68
Union Christian College, 91
United Kingdom, 154, 161, 278, 290
United States, 9, 196, 210n3, 293, 303;
Christian universities in, 13; rise
of research universities in after the
Civil War, 262; secularization of
mainstream universities in, 262-263;
tradition of independently founded
colleges and universities in, 12. *See
also* United States, Christian higher
education (CHE) in
United States, Christian higher education (CHE) in, 257-276, 263n13;
challenges of, 270, 272-273; and
the dual public/religious character
of colleges and universities in the
United States, 261-262; and economic
diversity, 260-261; and ethno-religious
congregations, 265-266; and evangelicalism, 259-260, 268-270; influence of
Kuyper on, 268-269; and the "integration of faith and learning," 267-268,
269; opportunities for, 273-274; and
pluralism, 274-275; and privatization,
262-263; and the promotion of diversity and multiculturalism, 275-276;
renaissance of, 259-260, 271; resiliency
of, 260
Universidad Anahuac, 198
Universidad Católica de Valencia, 159
Universidad de Deusto, 159
Universidad La Salle, 198
Universidad Madero, 199
Universidad Montemorelos, 199
Universidad Panamericana, 198
Universidade Metodista de Piracicaba,
222
Universidade Metodista de São Paulo,
222
Université Catholique de Louvain, 144
Université de Fribourg, 145, 158
University College at Achimota, 25
University College Ibadan, 25
University Grants Commission, 123, 126
University of Alberta, 253

University of Athens, 165
University of Berlin, 143
University of Bologna, 136
University of Brazil, 215
University of British Columbia, 231
University of Cape Town, 46, 58
University of Dar-es-Salaam, 46
University of Delhi, 129
University of East Africa, 46
University of Eastern Africa Baraton
(Adventist), 53
University of Fribourg, 145, 158
University of Hong Kong, 79
University of Liberia, 45
University of Lublin (later the Catholic
University of Lublin), 166-167; and the
Polish Communist Party, 167
University of Manitoba, 253
University of Minas Gerais, 215
University of Mkar, 38
University of Nairobi, 46, 62
University of Navarra, 159
University of Nanjing, 84
University of Nanking, 69, 73
University of Notre Dame, 13, 265,
275n35, 301-302
University of Notre Dame Australia, 301
University of Paris, 136
University of Phoenix, 13, 15n27
University of Regina, 253
University of Santa Ursula, 218
University of Saskatchewan, 253
University of Shanghai, 69
University of Sierra Leone, 45
University of St. Michael's College, 253
University of Toronto, 231, 233, 253
University of Waterloo, 253
University of Western Ontario, 253
U.S. Agency for International Develop-
ment (USAID), 222

Van Rinsum, Henk J., 25
Varghese, N. V., 62
Vasconcelos, José, 195
Vasselai, Conrado, 218
Vatican, the, 144, 149, 169, 253

Venezuela, 281
Venkataraman, R., 130
Verheul, H., 147
Veritas University, 35
Vienna, 164
Vilnius, 164
Vladimirova, Maria, 178

Wales, 146n52
Wang Lixin, 83
Ward, William, 111, 117
West China Union University, 70, 73, 84
Western Europe, Christian higher education (CHE) in, 134-135, 142n37, 161, 281, 284; birth of higher education in Western Europe, 136-138; Catholic universities, 144-145, 147, 149-152; Christian values expressed in the first European universities, 137; contemporary situation in Western Europe (1981 to the present), 147-149; contributions of the Protestant Reformation to CHE in Europe, 138-139; from the 1790s to the 1930s, 145-146; hybrid Anglican-Catholic university in England, 152, 160; nationalization of Western European universities, 139-142; Protestant universities, 143-144, 148-149; role of the Catholic Church in, 137-138, 139, 147. See also Western Europe, Christian higher education (CHE) in, challenges faced by
Western Europe, Christian higher education (CHE) in, challenges faced by, 153-154; centralization and the

Bologna process, 155; the Christian character of Protestant and Catholic universities, 156-161; massification and privatization, 153-155; professionalization, 155-156
Wheaton College, 51
Wilson College, 118
Wittenberg University, 138
Wolterstorff, Nicholas, 250
World Bank, 18, 47, 60, 197; policy of on education in developing countries, 29-30
Wycliffe, John, 138

Xu Yihua, 82-83

Yale University, 13, 76n29, 283
Yanjing Daxue (Mao Zedong), 77
Yenching University, 69, 72, 77, 84; courses offered by, 74-75
Yoido Full Gospel Church, 107
Yonsei University, 282
Yuguang Chen, 73

Zaoksky Adventist University (ZAU), 173, 176, 178, 179, 180, 183, 187, 188, 189
Zaoksky Christian Humanities and Economics Institute, 173
Zaoksky Theological Academy, 173
Zeleza, Paul, 44, 45, 58
Zhang Kai Yuan, 81-82, 82n39
Zhao Zi-chen (T. C. Chao), 85
Zhejiang University, 86
Zhongshan University, 84, 86
Zhuo Xinping, 83